Israel's Path to Europe

T0362069

Relations between the new state of Israel and the European Union in the first twenty years of the Community's existence were a major policy issue given the background of the Holocaust and the way the new nation was established. This book focuses on Israel-European Community relations from 1957 to 1970—from the signing of the Treaty of Rome (1957), which officially established the Common Market, to the conclusion of Israel's Free Trade Agreement with the Community. It reveals a new and key facet of Israeli diplomacy during the country's infancy, joining the many studies concerning Israel's relations with the United States, France, Germany and Britain.

Gadi Heimann is Professor in the Department of International Relations at the Hebrew University of Jerusalem. He is the author of *Franco-Israeli Relations, 1958–1967* (Routledge 2017).

Lior Herman is Assistant Professor in the Department of International Relations at the Hebrew University of Jerusalem.

Routledge Studies in Modern European History

Italy Before Italy
Institutions, Conflicts and Political Hopes in the Italian States, 1815–1860
Marco Soresina

Ethnic Cleansing during the Cold War
The Forgotten 1989 Expulsion of Bulgaria's Turks
Tomasz Kamusella

The Peace Discourses in Europe, 1900–1945
Alberto Castelli

Israel's Path to Europe
The Negotiations for a Preferential Agreement, 1957–1970
Gadi Heimann and Lior Herman

Liberalism in Pre-revolutionary Russia
State, Nation, Empire
Susanna Rabow-Edling

Bringing Cold War Democracy to West Berlin
A Shared German-American Project, 1940–1972
Scott H. Krause

Greeks without Greece
Homelands, Belonging, and Memory amongst the Expatriated Greeks of Turkey
Huw Halstead

The Mediterranean Double-Cross System, 1941–1945
Brett E. Lintott

For more information about this series, please visit: www.routledge.com/history/series/SE0246

Israel's Path to Europe

The Negotiations for a Preferential
Agreement, 1957–1970

Gadi Heimann and Lior Herman

LONDON AND NEW YORK

First published 2019
by Routledge
2 Park Square, Milton Park, Abingdon, Oxon OX14 4RN

and by Routledge
52 Vanderbilt Avenue, New York, NY 10017

First issued in paperback 2020

Routledge is an imprint of the Taylor & Francis Group, an informa business

British Library Cataloguing-in-Publication Data
A catalogue record for this book is available from the British Library

Library of Congress Cataloging-in-Publication Data
A catalog record has been requested for this book

ISBN 13: 978-0-36-758741-3 (pbk)
ISBN 13: 978-0-8153-6697-3 (hbk)

Typeset in Goudy
by Swales & Wills Ltd, Exeter Devon, UK

Contents

Acknowledgments

We would like to thank the many people who have helped us in the course of writing this book. We are grateful to Eilat Aviv, Michael Della Rocca, Batsheva Haas and Netta Lehan for their research assistance and support. We would also like to thank Ambassador Sergio (Yitzhak) Minerbi for his thoughtful and useful insights. Dr. Rebecca Wolpe provided excellent translation and editing and we are indebted to her services. There are also several people to thank at Routledge. Robert Langham, Michael Bourne and Julie Fitzsimons provided help, guidance and useful advice. We also thank two anonymous reviewers for their helpful suggestions. We wish to express our sincere gratitude to the Levi Eshkol Institute at the Hebrew University of Jerusalem and the Leonard Davis Institute for International Relations at the Hebrew University of Jerusalem for generously supporting this research. Last but not least, it would not have been possible to complete this project without the constant support and love of our partners, Ganit and Einav.

Chapter 4 partially draws on Heimann, G. (2015) "The Need to be Part of Europe: Israel's Struggle for an Association Agreement with the EEC, 1957–1961," *Israel Studies* 20(1): 86–109. Permission was obtained from Indiana University Press.

Illustrations

Figure

Tables

Introduction

This book is a tale of trade negotiations. Such an admission would not seem to be an especially promising tactic to attract the interest of potential readers. For good reasons, trade history is one of the least popular fields among historians of diplomacy and scholars of international politics. However, trade relations are almost certainly the most common form of interaction in international relations. Indeed, diplomatic activity to improve the terms of trade constitutes part of the daily, routine interactions between nations. Wars, economic crises, natural disasters and political revolutions all attract the attention of diplomatic historians, as is clear from a perusal of the history shelves in any university and even more so from the rows of reference literature books in public libraries. Yet these events are exceptional; they do not reflect the daily activities of the diplomatic world. Just as we cannot understand the physiological world solely through a study of pathological phenomena—diseases, mutations, damage from environmental factors—so too it is impossible to gain a complete picture of diplomacy by concentrating only on crises and wars. Understanding twentieth-century international relations (and this is no less true, perhaps even more so, in the twenty-first century) requires an examination of the "bread and butter" of diplomatic activity: ongoing relations and negotiations to improve the terms of trade conditions in global markets.

However, this fact alone is unlikely to convince a busy person to devote time and effort to reading this book. Yet there is another, more persuasive, reason, at least for anyone interested in the short history of the State of Israel. The reader may be surprised to discover that decision makers in Jerusalem viewed the trade agreement negotiations with the EEC as one of Israeli diplomacy's most significant tasks in the 1960s. Dozens of experts from a range of fields—law, economics, industry, agriculture, entrepreneurship, marketing, negotiations—were recruited either on a permanent or ad hoc basis to join the offensive which the Israelis launched on the fortified walls of the EEC. Prime Ministers, Ministers, Knesset Members, officials at the various financial and economic ministries, heads of state-owned companies and a range of business people undertook hundreds of journeys to the capitals of the EEC's six member states to garner support for Israel. For representatives at Israel's embassies in Western European countries, the negotiations with the Community were a constant concern; in some embassies, a special official was appointed to handle the issue. In addition to the manpower allocated to the campaign, substantial financial resources were also invested in it, as was explicitly recognized by Israeli politicians and officials involved in the efforts. In one of his reports to the Knesset Foreign Affairs and Defense Committee in the summer of 1963, the Executive Director of the Ministry of Foreign Affairs, Aryeh Levavi, admitted explicitly that: "I do not think a greater effort has been invested in any Israeli foreign policy campaign in recent years, and even more than that, in the entire field known as diplomacy."[1] When appointed as Finance Minister, Pinchas Sapir, who diligently applied himself to the negotiations with the Community in his role as Minister for Trade and Industry, commented on the importance of this issue, noting the extent of activity: "Had you seen the files of memoranda, telegraphs and correspondence—there is so much, that a truck would need to transport it."[2] Foreign Minister Golda Meir described the arrangement with the EEC as a vital interest for Israel, second only to security concerns,[3] while Prime Minister Ben-Gurion stated that it was decisive for the country's future.[4] When Levi Eshkol replaced Ben-Gurion as Israeli premier, following a lengthy term as Finance Minister, he clarified that:

> My change of office has not altered the importance I attach to the matter [a comprehensive agreement with the EEC]. This is one of the most important things for the State of Israel, for Israel's economy. I do not want to say that it is 'a decisive factor', because we hope that nothing can be decisive for our fate, but it is serious, important and, for good reason, we have toiled over it for so many years.[5]

These words demonstrate the great importance which the Israelis attributed to the matter, a significance which was not confined to the economic arena alone. Rather the Israelis perceived the relationship with the EEC as of political and even security importance. Therefore, it is no exaggeration to compare this episode of trade negotiations to other events at the top of Israel's agenda in the same period which, by contrast, have received academic attention: border incidents and acts of retribution, the development of relations with the US government, the ties with France and the aid policy in Africa.

Yet despite the importance of the topic, the reader may well ask whether the history of trade negotiations can also be interesting. Indeed, it can. The story of the negotiations between Israel and the EEC in the years 1958–1970 is the tale of an Odyssey, a long, exhausting and often despondent journey to a point seemingly within reach; yet every time it appears on the horizon, it slips further away. Similarly to Odysseus in Homer's famous epic, the Israeli diplomacy vessel embarked on its journey full of confidence that it would reach its destination quickly. However, the journey was beset by hardships and Israeli negotiators required a great degree of resourcefulness, cunning, inventiveness and patience. At an early stage researching this book, we concluded that this is the essence of the story and therefore decided to write it as a saga, a chronological story depicting the adventures of the "protagonists": in this case, the Israeli politicians, diplomats and economic experts who participated in the exhausting negotiations. The structure and style of this book are intended to convey to the reader something of the thoughts, feelings and emotions experienced by the characters involved in the tale: it is the story of the prolonged, exhausting journey along a path which often led to dead ends or, even worse, brought the adventurer once again back to the very beginning.

The kernel of the story is as follows: after a long and exhausting campaign lasting more than a decade, following many years of treading water, Israeli diplomats were able to reap an impressive achievement. The signing of an agreement between Israel and the EEC in 1970 satisfied many Israeli ambitions and went far beyond what they should have achieved according to a simple analysis of the bargaining chips at the disposal of the two negotiating parties. From the very outset, statesmen and diplomats from The Six (i.e. EEC member states) viewed acquiescing to Israel's requests as a political burden, an economic danger and a source of legal complication. However, they were unwilling to dismiss the Israelis empty handed due to the special sensitivity which characterized relations between Europe and Israel, a product of the murky historical legacy, pro-Israeli public opinion in European countries and, occasionally, their strong strategic ties with Israel. The Europeans mistakenly believed that they would be able to satisfy the Israelis with meager trade gestures and likewise erroneously assumed that they would be able to rely on objective, technical and legal excuses to reject Israel's requests. Indeed, they failed to consider two factors: firstly, the skill and resourcefulness of the Israeli diplomats in searching for a solution to every European reservation and obstacle; and secondly, the pragmatism of the Israelis, who would remain at the negotiating table at any price, avoiding offering the Europeans an easy way out of the problem.

Alongside its main argument, this study includes two further, central claims. The first regards the great importance, perhaps we should even dare to say existential importance, which the Israelis attributed to achieving an arrangement or agreement with the EEC. They viewed this not only as an economic necessity, but also a political asset. At an early stage, they became convinced that an association agreement was the only way to satisfy their needs and therefore clung to this aim in the face of repeated failures. Eventually they reached a pivotal juncture and were forced to decide whether they should insist on this negotiation channel at any price or to adopt a more flexible line. Some supported the first option; however, eventually the second line was accepted—a fateful decision which was responsible for the Israeli success. The second claim concerns the role of the European Commission in the negotiations with Israel. Throughout the negotiations, the Commission was more supportive of Israel than any other state, apart from the Netherlands. The Commission planted in the hearts of the Israelis the hope that an association agreement was realistic and, even after retreating from this alternative, continued to endorse an arrangement with Israel. It was the Commission which eventually recommended a preferential trade agreement with Israel. The explanation for the Commission's positive approach is anchored in the importance which this institution attributed to conducting the negotiations—and reaching an arrangement—with Israel in the efforts to advance its own ideological and political interests.

Scholars have paid little attention to the history of Israel's relations with the EEC in its first years. Although a number of studies discuss Israel-EEC relations in general, they principally focus on periods later than that under discussion in this book.[6] The first decade of Israeli-EEC relations rarely receives any attention; when it does, this is usually by way of background information or introduction. No less evident is the perspective from which existing scholarly literature examines the relations between Israel and the EEC: most concentrate on the economic or legal dimensions of these links.[7]

However, three studies concentrate specifically on the relations between Israel and the EEC in its first years. Ilan Greilsammer's study (in French) concerns the development of relations between the two parties from the signing of the Treaty of Rome until the beginning of the 1980s, describing the milestones in the history of their relations. As well as the fact that his study is pioneer and revealing, he also expertly depicts and explains the outlooks of the different parties throughout the negotiations. Yet despite this, the section of Greilsammer's work concerning the period at the heart of the present study is limited. Likewise, for the most part, Greilsammer relies on press reports, in addition to oral interviews which he conducted. The lack of access to archival sources prevented him from relating the stories which played out behind the scenes—how the two sides consolidated their negotiating strategies, the formal and informal meetings between diplomats and experts, confidential understandings between Israeli politicians and diplomats on the one hand and their counterparts among the Six and the EEC on the other, and more. The second study is Michael Rom's *On the Path of Israel's International Commercial Policy* (in Hebrew), which examines the relations between Israel and the EEC from a practitioner's perspective. Indeed, as a senior official in the Israeli Ministry of Trade and Industry, the author was involved in formulating the Israeli negotiating strategy. His book provides important insights into the Israeli perspective. However, it tends to focus on economic and technical legal aspects and likewise provides no discussion and analysis of the European viewpoint.

The third study concerning the history of Israel-EEC relations is Sharon Pardo's illuminating article on the secret conversations between Shimon Peres, then Director General of the Ministry of Foreign Affairs and Jean Monnet, one of the architects of European integration. Based on extensive archival material, Pardo portrays the ambition of Israeli decision makers and senior politicians such as Ben-Gurion and Peres to achieve full membership of the then consolidating community.[8] However, this article concentrates on a very narrow time frame (1957) and does not cover the negotiations which Israel conducted with the EEC over the course of a decade. In addition to these items, other scholarly works concerning Israel's relations with one of The Six or Europe in general mention the negotiations with the EEC. Howard Sachar's enlightening study surveys Israel's relations with the European countries (including the USSR) over four decades.[9] Yet he dedicates no more than a few paragraphs to the story of these negotiations, even though it was of great importance to Israel and accounted for a significant volume of Israeli diplomacy with The Six in the relevant period. The book

Uneasy Neighbors by Sharon Pardo and Joel Peters, complements Sachar's work, focusing on Israel's relations with the European Union.[10] Yet only one chapter describes the development of the relationship in the first three decades and this issue does not play a central role in the book.

The present work draws on a wide range of historical documents collated from archives in Israel and Europe, among them principally the Israel State Archives (Foreign Ministry Files, Prime Minister's Office, Ministry of Trade and Industry, Finance Ministry, Agriculture Ministry, the Knesset) and the EU Archive in Brussels (Council of Ministers' Files, Commission). In addition, relevant materials were amassed from the Foreign Ministries of the member states (France, Germany, Italy, the Netherlands, and Belgium, with the exclusion of Luxembourg) as well as private archives, such as that of Ben-Gurion in Sde Boker and the Hammel Archive in Brussels. Likewise, in an effort to complete gaps in the puzzle, we examined the memoirs of figures involved in the events. In addition to these archival sources, we utilized collections of diplomatic documents from Israel, France (DDF) and the USA (FRUS), alongside hundreds of articles published in the daily press in Israel and abroad. The collection of documents published by Sharon Pardo and Joel Peters concerning relations between Israel and the EU was also useful.[11] Finally, we explored a wide range of studies regarding various related topics. For example, the *Israel Economy Quarterly* served as an inexhaustible source of raw data concerning the Israeli economy, concurrently providing important analytical interprÉtation. The extremely rich scholarship concerning European integration also constituted an important source of information.

The first two chapters of the book provide important background concerning the EEC and Israel necessary for understanding this saga and how it unfolded. Chapter 1 outlines the establishment of the EEC, its features and the characteristics of its member states. It opens by describing European integration, from the establishment of the Organization for European Economic Cooperation (OEEC, 1949), to the founding of the European Coal and Steel Community (1951) and the signing of the Treaty of Rome (1957) and surveys the range of economic and political motivations which led the six founding member states to pursue this specific path.[12] Likewise, it analyzes the main articles of the Treaty of Rome relevant to the topic of this study: the establishment of the customs union, the Common Agricultural Policy, conditions for accession (article 237) or association (article 238) to the EEC, and articles relating to trade relations (articles 111–14). It then outlines the various relevant institutions within the EEC, discussing their structure, authority and agendas. Particular focus is placed on the European Commission and its leadership, because this body played a central role in shaping European-Israeli relations. Finally, it discusses the economies of the six member states, evaluating how the establishment of the EEC affected their economic development.

Chapter 2 provides a portrait of the Israeli economy in the 1950s, thus enabling the reader to understand why the Israelis attributed such weight to association with the EEC. It begins by outlining the difficulties that the leaders of the young state faced in the years immediately following its establishment—these included mass immigration, unemployment, capital shortage and an increasing trade balance deficit. It then describes the impressive growth of the Israeli economy in the first decade of the state's existence and the reasons for this, detailing the new policy initiated by Minister of Trade and Industry Pinchas Sapir to accelerate industrialization and transform Israel from a largely agrarian-based economy into an export-led industrial country, with the textile industry spearheading this process. However, agriculture remained the most important sector of the country's economy and continued to account for the majority of its exports: in this respect, the citrus industry played an especially prominent role. Western Europe was the principal consumer of Jaffa products and therefore the Israelis viewed an arrangement (association) with the EEC as of vast importance. In addition, Israel's industrial exports were especially tailored to the tastes of developed economies, while transportation costs made Western Europe the only market in which these products could be sold at competitive prices. This combination of factors led Israeli decision makers to determine that association with the Community constituted an essential national interest. The chapter concludes with a discussion and explanation of the Israeli leadership's optimistic outlook vis-à-vis achieving this ambitious aim.

Chapter 3 depicts how Israeli leaders reacted to the challenge of the EEC's establishment, including the special inter-ministerial committee tasked with determining the country's response. The chapter surveys the variety of opinions on the matter, ranging from the enthusiasm for some kind of connection with Europe in the Ministry of Foreign Affairs to the Finance Ministry's more reserved position, motivated by concerns that this would have a detrimental effect on the developing Israeli economy. As a first step, Israeli decision makers pursued what appeared to be the most promising path: association with the OEEC. However, they soon realized that this aim would be far more difficult to achieve than they had at first believed. Simultaneously, the Israelis tried to discover in which direction the wind was blowing: they dispatched a letter to the EEC requesting consideration of Israel's export needs and permission to establish a diplomatic representation in Brussels. The discussions of this Israeli request within Community institutions are indicative of a trend which characterized the interactions over the coming years: the ministers were extremely dubious of any step which could be interpreted as according Israel preferential treatment, while the European Commission adopted a much more positive stance, determining that the Israeli approach served its own interests. The chapter includes a comprehensive discussion of the motivations behind these different attitudes.

The surprising Israeli decision to seek an association agreement with the EEC according to article 238 of the Treaty of Rome, and the driving forces behind this development, are discussed in Chapter 4. At first the Israeli Ministry of Foreign Affairs decided to progress gradually, satisfying itself with talks regarding a trade agreement to ensure the future of the country's citrus exports to the Community. However, senior Commission officials began to signal that an Israeli attempt to attain association, similar to Greece's, would be welcome, hinting that the Commission would support such a request. A visit by an Israeli representative in Brussels, during which he spoke with the President of the Commission and the Commissioner responsible for Foreign Affairs, convinced the Israelis that this was an opportune time to seek association. Thus they launched an intensive diplomatic campaign in the capitals of The Six to garner support for their goal, involving the highest echelon of Israeli leadership: Prime Minister Ben-Gurion and Foreign Minister Golda Meir. However, their conversations with European statesmen revealed strong opposition to the idea of Israeli association—for a range of reasons—across the Community. No Community member state, apart from the Netherlands, promised to endorse the Israeli request. Yet despite this situation, the Israelis decided to try their luck—the result, of course, was complete failure.

Chapter 5 discusses the Israeli fixation upon association, despite the European states' evident lack of enthusiasm. Likewise, it describes the eventual decision to relinquish this goal, once the Israeli leadership understood that by clinging to it they were likely to torpedo any chances for an arrangement with the EEC. The Israelis did not despair following their first failures to achieve association. Rather, they intensified the pressure in Paris, Bonn and The Hague, where they enjoyed significant influence. Israel's supporters found themselves in an uncomfortable position, leading them to suggest that the Israelis settle for a trade agreement based on articles 111–14 of the Treaty of Rome, instead of association. This was a pivotal moment in the relations between Israel and the Community, although it was not adequately understood at the time. By agreeing to consider negotiations regarding a trade agreement, the Europeans accepted Israel's controversial claim that the country deserved special consideration. From this point onwards, the Community could not dismiss the Israelis empty-handed, even though technically Israel had no special rights over and above those of other countries. The Israelis at first did not accept the "compromise" proposed by the Europeans, and in July 1961 submitted a formal request to the Council of Ministers to begin negotiations regarding an association agreement; once again they received a negative response. This led to Jerusalem's re-assessment of the situation: the Finance and Foreign Ministers argued in favor of accepting the European compromise, feeling certain that this was the optimal outcome at the present time; they believed that in the future it would be possible to improve the relationship further. With a view to advancing an arrangement with the EEC, the Finance Minister initiated a wave of economic reforms, the most important of which was the abolition of the multiple exchange rates system and a sharp depreciation in the value of the Israeli pound. In so doing, he hoped to signal to the Europeans that the Israeli economy was sufficiently mature and reliable to be tied with Europe. The chapter investigates why the Israelis regarded association as such an attractive option, concluding that alongside economic considerations, the Israelis hoped to reap political benefits.

Chapter 6 concerns the European attempts to obstruct and delay the decision to initiate negotiations and the Israeli success in ensuring that the resolution to begin talks was finally passed in September 1962. Not everybody in the Community was pleased with the "deal" which offered Israel a trade agreement to protect the country's main export products, in return for Israel relinquishing its association dream. There were a variety of reasons for this. Firstly, Italy, the main opponent of the negotiations, was motivated principally by economic considerations, because its exports competed with Israeli products. Secondly, the member states' Foreign Ministries were concerned that a positive decision regarding Israel could have detrimental effects on The Six's relations with Arab states. And thirdly, Community officials, mainly in the Council, feared that the Israeli precedent would encourage other countries to submit similar requests. They were also aware of the legal problems involved in granting trade benefits to third countries due to conflicts with the GATT agreement. The opponents' main tactic was to postpone the decision, demanding "further examination" of the technical problems involved. In response, the Israelis established a team of experts from all the relevant government ministries (Finance, Trade and Industry, Agriculture), tasked with supplying detailed reports which would refute any claims of "ambiguity." Concurrently, in the summer of 1962, Israel embarked on its most massive diplomatic campaign to date. The focus of the campaign was Paris, where Israel enjoyed a significant degree of influence. The Israelis succeeded in persuading more than a hundred members of the French legislature to write letters to Foreign Minister Couve de Murville demanding that he accede to Israel's request. Great pressure was placed on the President's office via a number of his close associates who were friends of Israel. These efforts eventually bore fruit and France's agreement to endorse the Israeli request paved the way for a positive decision by the Council of Ministers in September 1962. One of the main reasons for Europe's response was the feeling that following four years' worth of approaches, the Israelis could not be dismissed empty handed. Yet no less important was the belief that the negotiations could be brought to a stalemate, thus preventing any agreement.

The nadir in relations between Israel and the EEC is the focus of Chapters 7 and 8. The Israeli leaders soon understood that the EEC's willingness to open negotiations did not signify any willingness to grant significant trade benefits. In fact, because the member states believed that the Israelis were motivated principally by political considerations, they were sure that the gesture of beginning official negotiations would satisfy Israel. When the talks began, the Europeans were shocked to discover that the Israelis expected a comprehensive arrangement which would in reality grant their country a special status vis-à-vis the EEC. At this stage, the opponents of the agreement began to employ a new tactic: minimizing the proposed trade benefits to such an extent that the Israelis, for reasons of national pride, would not be able to accept them. Thus Israel was offered trade benefits limited to only four products and amounting to $72,000 per year—a sum which did not even cover the costs of the Israeli delegation in Brussels. Indeed, many among the Israeli public and the decision-making echelon believed that the negotiations should be terminated immediately. In contrast, others understood that this would play into the hands of the agreement's opponents and therefore argued that Israel must stay at the negotiation table at any price, even if this meant being satisfied in the first stage with a paltry and humiliating agreement. They understood that the agreement granted Israel institutional privileges which would make it easier to widen the arrangement's scope in the future. Following a long and bitter internal Israeli debate, this opinion was finally victorious. In June 1964, Israel and the EEC signed a non-preferential trade agreement. It was clear to both sides that the agreement was almost entirely without content.

Chapters 9 and 10 discuss the period between the signing of the first agreement and the conclusion of the preferential agreement six years later. The latter was far more significant than its predecessor, granting Israel special privileges in its trade with the EEC. In fact, Israel was the first non-European state which was not a former European colony to receive such preferential treatment. These chapters attempt to explain how the Israelis managed to conclude such an agreement, when the Community had no real interest in such a step and was concerned by the possible negative ramifications. It demonstrates that the Israelis effectively used argumentation, making it difficult for opponents of the agreement to refuse their requests. The Commission had its own reasons for supporting the Israelis, and its Fall 1966 report wholeheartedly recommended a comprehensive arrangement with Israel, either in the form of association or a preferential agreement. Had the Six Day War not broken out, the sides would have reached a comprehensive agreement in 1967. However, the conflict initiated a complete change in the attitude of France, which consequently became the most stubborn opponent of an arrangement with Israel. As a result, the French began to cast doubt on Israel's right to special treatment from the EEC. However, it was too late to employ such reasoning: following a decade of intense contacts, the Community's obligation to Israel was already established. West Germany and the Netherlands acted as Israel's patrons, finally forcing France to withdraw its opposition. In 1970, Israel and the EEC signed a preferential agreement.

Notes

1 Aryeh Levavi to the Foreign Affairs and Defense Committee, ISA, Knesset, file 8160/1, July 16, 1963.
2 Pinchas Sapir to the Foreign Affairs and Defense Committee, ISA, Knesset, file 8160/1, July 16, 1963.
3 ISA, FM, file 948/17, December 29, 1961.
4 State of Israel, ed. *State of Israel's Foreign Policy Documents* (Jerusalem: National Archives, 1981). Vol. 14, Doc. 307, 12/01/1960.
5 Eshkol to a press conference held on July 10, 1963, ISA, FM, file 1960/5, July 12, 1963.
6 Guy Harpaz, "The European Neighborhood Policy and Its Impact on the Israel-European Union-United States Triangle," *San Diego International Law Journal* 6 (2004); Sharon Pardo and Joel Peters, *Uneasy Neighbors: Israel and the European Union* (Lanham: Lexington Books, 2009); Richard W. T. Pomfret and Benjamin Toren, *Israel and the European Common Market: An Appraisal of the 1975 Free Trade Agreement*, vol. 161 (Tubingen: Mohr, 1980).
7 Efrayim Aḥiram and Alfred Tovias, *Whither EU-Israeli Relations? Common and Divergent Interests* (Frankfurt am Main: Peter Lang, 1995); Ilan Greilsammer and Joseph. Weiler, eds., *Europe and Israel: Troubled Neighbours*, vol. 9 (Berlin: Walter de Gruyter, 1988); Pierre Emmanuel Uri, *Israel and the Common Market* (Jerusalem: Weidenfeld & Nicolson, 1971); Moshe Hirsch, Eyal Inbar and Tal Sadeh, *The Future*

Relations between Israel and the European Communities: Some Alternatives (Tel Aviv: Bursi, 1996); Michael. Rom, *In the Path of Israel's International Commercial Policy: The Preferences and the European Common Market* (Tel Aviv: Tel Aviv University Press [Hebrew], 1998); Philippe Velilla, "Les Relations Entre l'Union Européenne Et Israël, Droit Communautaire et Droit Des Échanges Internationaux: Le Cas Du Commerce Agricole" (Paris 1, 1999).

8 Sharon Pardo, "The Year That Israel Considered Joining the European Economic Community," *JCMS: Journal of Common Market Studies* 51, no. 5 (2013): 901–15.

9 Howard M. Sachar, *Israel and Europe: An Appraisal in History* (New York: First Vintage Books, 2000).

10 Sharon Pardo and Joel Peters, *Uneasy Neighbors: Israel and the European Union* (Lanham: Lexington Books, 2009).

11 Sharon Pardo and Joel Peters, *Israel and the European Union: A Documentary History* (Lanham: Lexington Books, 2012).

12 At the beginning of 2018, the European Union included 28 member states.

References

Aḥiram, Efrayim, and Alfred Tovias. *Whither EU-Israeli Relations? Common and Divergent Interests*. Frankfurt am Main: Peter Lang, 1995.

Greilsammer, Ilan, and Joseph Weiler, eds. *Europe and Israel: Troubled Neighbours* Vol. 9. Berlin: Walter de Gruyter, 1988.

Harpaz, Guy. "The European Neighborhood Policy and Its Impact on the Israel-European Union-United States Triangle." *San Diego International Law Journal* 6 (2004): 295.

Hirsch, Moshe, Eyal Inbar and Tal Sadeh. *The Future Relations between Israel and the European Communities: Some Alternatives*. Tel Aviv: Bursi, 1996.

Pardo, Sharon. "The Year That Israel Considered Joining the European Economic Community." *JCMS: Journal of Common Market Studies* 51, no. 5 (2013): 901–15.

Pardo, Sharon, and Joel Peters. *Israel and the European Union: A Documentary History*. Lanham: Lexington Books, 2012.

Pardo, Sharon, and Joel Peters. *Uneasy Neighbors: Israel and the European Union*. Lanham: Lexington Books, 2009.

Pomfret, Richard W. T., and Benjamin Toren. *Israel and the European Common Market: An Appraisal of the 1975 Free Trade Agreement*. Vol. 161, Tubingen: Mohr, 1980.

Rom, Michael. *In the Path of Israel's International Commercial Policy: The Preferences and the European Common Market*. Tel Aviv: Tel Aviv University Press [Hebrew], 1998.

Sachar, Howard M. *Israel and Europe: An Appraisal in History*. New York: First Vintage Books, 2000.

State of Israel, ed. *State of Israel's Foreign Policy Documents*. Jerusalem: National Archives, 1981.

Uri, Pierre Emmanuel. *Israel and the Common Market*. Jerusalem: Weidenfeld & Nicolson, 1971.

Velilla, Philippe. "Les Relations Entre l'Union Européenne Et Israël, Droit Communautaire et Droit Des Échanges Internationaux: Le Cas Du Commerce Agricole." *Paris 1*, 1999.

1   The path to economic integration

This chapter discusses the path to European economic integration. It outlines the context, interests, capacities and institutional settings and constraints which are essential in understanding the negotiations between the EEC and Israel.

Historical background: the establishment of the European Economic Community

In March 1957, at a momentous event, Six West European countries—France, West Germany,[1] Italy and the three Benelux nations—gathered in Rome to sign the Treaty establishing the EEC, the essence of which was the creation of a *common market*. A common market is one of the most ambitious and far-reaching possibilities for international economic integration,[2] far beyond a *customs union*. Whereas countries in a *free trade area* eliminate mutual tariffs and cancel trade quotas, membership of a customs union requires in addition the implementation of a common tariff policy vis-à-vis third parties. A common market supplements the customs union with deeper and extensive arrangements: free movement of goods, services, capital and labor. Finally, a common market also involves generating and coordinating common policies in a range of fields, including foreign trade, agriculture, welfare, labor, consumer protection, health and safety and more.[3] Thus, the members of a common market relinquish and share a substantial portion of their economic sovereignty and are precluded from reaching autonomous decisions with regard to considerable policy areas. The high level of integration characteristic of a common market also has far-reaching political significance. In some cases, a political union develops following economic integration: both the American and German Federations began as customs unions. Sometimes economic integration is motivated by political, no less than economic, considerations: the establishment of the common market in Europe is a clear example of such a case.[4] This enterprise was rooted in fears of another war in Europe following Germany's economic recovery. In addition, a number of West European statesmen simultaneously recognized that the future of their nations—in terms of security, welfare and prestige—required that Europe would become "more than a geographical term," using Metternich's language. For hundreds of years, the nations of Europe had constituted the center of the world. However, in the wake of the Second World War, two peripheral giants—the USA and USSR—had emerged as superpowers, swiftly relegating the proud European states to a secondary status. Nations which until only recently had ruled the world found themselves pushed aside and confronted by a series of new challenges—security, economic and political—without the tools necessary to confront the new reality effectively. Indeed, following the Second World War, West Germany's steel production was greater than it had been on the eve of the First World War—18.7 million tons in 1952 as opposed to 17 million in 1913. Yet while in 1913 this figure represented 20% of global production, by 1952 West Germany's share of the international steel market had declined to 8.7%. France's steel production (10.9 million tons) totaled a third of the amount produced by the USSR, while Italy's (3.5 million) constituted less than a tenth of this.[5] The European countries understood that the solution to this current crisis was to overcome their traditional rivalry, historical enmity and the fresh wounds left by the war in order to join hands and consolidate their power. The only way for the French, Germans, Italians, or Dutch to attain a central role in the international arena was as "Europeans."[6] Indeed, the conditions for such a step were ripe. The trauma of the two recent world wars had clarified beyond any doubt that the powers of divisiveness—national chauvinism, historical residue, together with religious, linguistic and ethnic divides—were responsible for the great disasters that had beset the continent and caused its present humiliation. It was thus essential to find a way to overcome these divides. Concurrently, many believed that the European nations possessed a sufficiently wide and strong common basis to enable close cooperation and even future unification. Many French, Germans and Italians felt that they shared a history and tradition which had been molded, it should be noted, by centuries of bitter struggles and bloodshed. Two of these visionaries, Jean Monnet and Robert Schuman, translated these new yearnings into action. Others, less idealistic and more practical, desired integration mainly for economic reasons; the latter did not view European integration as a tool designed to disintegrate the nation state, but rather as a way to strengthen it, following two world wars which had brought their countries to the brink of collapse.[7]

The first buds of European integration in the economic field appeared as early as the customs union agreement signed by the exiled governments of Belgium, the Netherlands and Luxembourg in London in 1944 and later implemented in 1948. This became the kernel of future economic integration on the continent and the model which guided it. Furthermore, in 1947 France and Italy signed an agreement concerning the establishment of a parallel customs union, although this entailed greater difficulties than those facing the relatively integrated economies of the Benelux countries and was never implemented. The process of European integration was accelerated by US economic aid to the Western European countries in the framework of the Marshall Plan (1947) and the establishment of the Organization for European Economic Cooperation (OEEC) in 1949. This body, intended to coordinate between the countries receiving aid, served as an initial foundation for economic cooperation between nations that had recently slaughtered one another on the battlefield. The visionaries dreaming of a Federal Europe—such as the Frenchmen Robert Schuman and Jean Monnet, the German Walter Hallstein, the Italian Alcide de Gasperi, or the Belgian Henri Spaak—desired much more and viewed the OEEC only as an initial basis for a continually deepening process of integration.[8] However, the hopes of the European Federalists, which were shared by the US, that the organization would develop into a free trade area or a customs union proved unrealistic, largely due to the negative attitude of the UK and other nations, including the Scandinavian countries. The alternative was to relinquish the idea of a wide framework involving all Western European countries and focus on those which in principle viewed the integration process positively. However, the supporters of European integration were realistic and pragmatic; aware of the problems and obstacles they faced, they preferred to consolidate a strategy of gradual, stage-by-stage progress. Indeed, they discerned that first stage in such a process must necessarily center upon the limited sectors wherein the nations felt that cooperation was desirable:[9] for this reason, it was decided in this first stage to focus on the coal and steel sectors. Many Europeans still feared a further war between Germany and its neighbors; ensuring that two resources of great military strategic importance were available to all would make such an eventuality unlikely. In May 1950, Schuman famously called for the creation of a joint French-German coal and steel organization, as well as supra-national bodies to manage these resources. This arrangement was not limited to France and Germany but was also open to any other European states wishing to join. The newly created West Germany controlled the lion's share of these resources and thus had no real economic interest in responding to the initiative. Yet for political reasons the new Chancellor, Konrad Adenauer, viewed joining the enterprise as of the utmost importance—he believed that it would accelerate Germany's re-acceptance into the family of nations, enable the country to gain full sovereignty and allay the fears of its former enemy on the western border. Despite strong opposition to Schuman's plan among German industrialists, Adenauer was determined to enter the initiative and he was able to neutralize internal criticism through a sophisticated employment of the US's enthusiastic support.[10] This facilitated negotiations between the six West European states—France, Germany, Italy and the Benelux countries—which soon led to the birth of the European Coal and Steel Community (ECSC) (1951). The ECSC was founded upon two elements which recurred also as guiding principles in the communities which were established subsequently: the inter-governmental element, which reflected the division into European sovereign nation states; and the supra-national element, intended to allow the consolidation of a shared European policy and advance the process of integration, the new European framework.[11] Two bodies were created: the Council of Ministers, comprised of representatives of the member states, possessed legislative authority, while the supra-national executive High Authority was assigned managerial functions.[12] The latter was authorized to reach decisions directly connected with the topics covered by the community treaty. Only decisions regarding wider fields fell into the bailiwick of the Council of Ministers which, as was noted, represented the member states' interests. In addition, the High Authority enjoyed financial independence because its budget was funded by a special levy on profits from the steel and coal industries. These two factors endowed the High Authority with freedom of action, giving ECSC a noteworthy supra-national element.

The success of the ECSC encouraged efforts to establish additional common European bodies. In 1952, an attempt was made to create a united European army made up of forty divisions, while in 1953, European prominent figures endeavored to form a European Political Community (EPC), although neither initiative bore fruit. While states could relatively easily relinquish sovereignty on specific topics of economic consequence, such as shared control of natural resources, they found it far more difficult to compromise on topics regarded as closely connected to sovereignty: among them the right to determine and develop independent foreign and defense policies, as well as military control. Thus, it became evident that any attempt to accelerate European integration by tackling issues of high politics would not be a successful recipe for progress; in fact, the nations were likely to recoil from such efforts.[13]

Therefore, the architects of European integration returned to the original idea of gradual progress, focusing on areas where there was general agreement that cooperation was desirable.[14] Two areas appeared especially promising: accelerating the economic integration between the states—first and foremost introducing free trade, in addition to freedom of movement for capital and services—and the development of nuclear technology. Although the French government, seeking to advance the French nuclear project, was principally interested in the atomic field, it also discerned the benefits of agricultural liberalization. Germany, the Netherlands and Belgium, which were industrially developed nations, were attracted by the idea of a common market because this would enable them to increase their product exports. Italy's main concern was the free movement of workers as a solution to unemployment, as well as obtaining development funds to improve economic and social conditions in its weaker regions.[15] Thus the establishment of two parallel communities, the EEC and EURATOM, constituted a compromise between these various interests, a kind of "package deal." Interestingly, at the time EURATOM was perceived as the more important of the two communities, yet became marginal over the course of time. From West Germany's perspective, the decision to join the communities was of particular political significance: with this step, Adenauer tied the fate of his country even more closely to the West, reducing the chances of reaching an arrangement which would enable re-unification with East Germany in return for West German neutrality (as, for example, in the arrangement reached on Austria in 1955).[16] West Germany's business sector did not welcome the establishment of the EEC, fearing that it would negatively affect the country's exports outside Europe.[17] However, the Chancellor believed that the nation's future lay with Western Europe and considered the process of European integration as the surest way to ensure West Germany's democratic, peaceful and anti-Soviet nature. He perceived the establishment of the EEC as the most significant step in German history since Bismarck's unification of Germany in the mid-nineteenth century.[18] Ruling in favor of joining the community accorded well with the foreign policy which West Germany had followed since 1949 and in fact continued the political approach adopted by German governments since the end of the nineteenth century, all the more forcefully during the Weimar Republic.[19]

In June 1955, the foreign ministers of "The Six" met in Messina, Italy, and decided upon the establishment of an inter-governmental commission which would examine how to advance the establishment of two communities. The phrasing of the resolution clearly reflects the political impetus behind this decision, noting that the signatory governments

> consider that the further progress must be towards the establishment of a united Europe through the development of common institutions [. . .]. Such a policy appears to them to be indispensable in order to ensure Europe's global role, restore its influence and progressively raise the standard of living among its population.[20]

Indeed, alongside the economic and strategic advantages which the establishment of the two communities yielded, political incentives likewise played a major role. As Spaak commented:

> Europe, which once held a key position in international trade, both as a main purchaser of raw materials and as a supplier or industrial products, will become one of the most backwards regions in the world if it will not understand how to tear down the internal walls between its countries.[21]

The resounding failure of the Suez campaign in November 1956 revealed that the European nations had become a marginal element in comparison to the superpowers. In the wake of this humiliation, figures such as the French Prime Minister Guy Mollet welcomed the strengthening of European integration, viewing this as a means to renew France's influence on the global stage.[22] In March 1957, the negotiations concluded in the Treaty of Rome, which officially established the two communities,[23] significantly tightening the economic integration of the six Western European nations. Presenting the Treaty of Rome to the French legislature for ratification, French Foreign Minister Morris Faure informed the members of the house that "today we have two powers in the world: the USA and USSR. Soon a third power will join them—China. You will decide whether there will be a fourth: Europe."[24] Likewise, the "Federalists"—the idealists dreaming of a united Europe—considered the treaty a step towards a more complete process of integration, both in terms of depth (political and military integration) and breadth (additional European states joining the community over the course of time).[25] For these visionaries, the common market was from the outset a tool, a stage in a long process, the outcome of which no one was able to predict.

The European Community institutions

The Treaty of Rome was a lengthy document, made up of 248 articles, 4 appendices, 13 protocols and 9 accompanying declarations. The Preamble and Part One established various institutions to manage the community's affairs. As a natural continuation of the ECSC, the structure of the EEC reflected the dual elements of the European integration process, and each one of these received tangible expression in the new community's institutions. The Council of Ministers was to reflect sovereign nation states: as the highest authority in the community, it was staffed by representatives of the member states, each representative acting in accordance with his nation's interests. Unsurprisingly, this council was the most powerful body in the community—it was responsible for reaching key decisions. In fact, many councils of ministers—more than 20—existed in parallel, in accordance with the topic on the agenda: for example, councils of Foreign Ministers, Agriculture Ministers, or Finance Ministers met according to need. On many occasions, more than one minister from each country participated in meetings due to the varied topics under discussion. Thus, the concept of a single Council of Ministers with a fixed staff was in fact a fiction. Among the various "councils," the Council of Foreign Ministers and Council of Agriculture Ministers were without doubt the most important.[26] For example, in 1967 the former met seven times and the latter convened on eight occasions, while all the other councils together met only five times.[27] The Council of Ministers possessed a great deal of power but had precious little time.[28] Therefore, between ministerial sittings, the Committee of Permanent Representatives (COREPER) met to prepare for the ministers' discussions. The member states were represented in this committee according to their relative size and importance—Germany, France and Italy each had four representatives, Belgium and the Netherlands two, while Luxembourg had one representative. The member states appointed as representatives professional diplomats who would serve as a link connecting Brussels with The Six: among their other duties, they were tasked with ensuring that their nation's opinions were heard and considered in Brussels.[29] Officially, this body was not endowed with decision-making authority. However, its opinion carries significant weight even today and indeed, the Council of Ministers has almost always ratified its decisions. The appointments of the Permanent Representatives are for extended periods, during which they become well acquainted and consolidate a team spirit, forming bonds of mutual trust which help them to overcome disagreements and compromise within the negotiated agenda. Although they are ostensibly mere agents, carrying out the policy dictated in the capitals of The Six, in reality they enjoy significant room for maneuver because the instructions they receive are often hazy or open to interpretation.[30] Usually the COREPER reaches a decision concerning various proposals, which it then submits to the approval of the Council of Ministers. In reality, this means that the Council only discusses those issues upon which the COREPER did not reach agreement. Furthermore, this implies that decisions were made according to the lowest common denominator—the most conservative stance—leading to repeated and frequent clashes with the Commission, which demanded more vigorous progress.[31]

The European Commission, in contrast, embodied the future vision: a supra-national body staffed by bureaucrats identifying with the interests of the new entity—Europe—rather than those of their home countries. It is surprising to discover with what speed and fervor they adopted European thinking. However, the Commission's weakness in comparison to the Council of Ministers was a clear indication of reality triumphing vision; the priority of the present over dreams of the future. The Treaty of Rome did not grant the Commission responsibilities similar to those of the High Authority or the same amount of independence which it had enjoyed.[32] Although the Commission was to be a partner in the EEC's decision-making process, it would not make final decisions and was certainly not the highest authority. Its members could make recommendations, voice opinions, write reports and prepare programs but the final decision remained in the hands of the Council of Ministers and, therefore, the member states. As a body appointed by the member states, the Commission was not endowed with the same degree of financial independence as the High Authority. However, the Treaty of Rome designated three central roles for the Commission: 1) initiating and phrasing proposals for authorization by the Council of Ministers; 2) overseeing the implementation of the Treaty of Rome, and 3) using its comprehensive perspective to reconcile disagreements arising between the representatives of states in the Council of Ministers. Walter Hallstein, the first President of the Commission, described its role perfectly: it was "at once a motor, a watchdog and a kind of honest broker."[33] He later defined the Commission as "the conscience and the voice of the Community as a whole."[34] In addition, the Commission was to manage trade negotiations with states outside the EEC, in accordance with articles 113 and 238 of the Treaty of Rome. This was a significant concession on the part of the member states: by transferring responsibility for trade negotiations to the Commission, they relinquished an important tool not only in terms of external trade but also within the wider context of foreign policy.[35] Although the Commission did not possess legislative authority and was likewise not an operative body, it was involved to some degree in both these processes. Indeed, the Commission fulfilled a kind of intermediate function.

The development of the European Commission was at a significant and sensitive stage in the first days of the EEC—it sought to mold its character and determine its status within the Community framework. In the early days, it was not yet sufficiently clear what authorities the Commission would eventually be granted, in which areas it would be active and what real powers it would possess. Throughout 1958, the Commission established various mechanisms and filled its new positions, drawing some staff from the political echelons of the Community's six member states—of 14 commissioners that served between 1958 and 1967, seven were former government ministers—while the remainder were civil servants, academics or "experts."[36] The Commission's junior officials usually originated within the administrative ranks of The Six. The average Commission official was highly educated, fluent in a number of languages, experienced in European matters, prepared to work far longer hours than his counterpart in the national administration (in return for a higher salary and the rights reserved for diplomatic staff).[37] At first, the Commission employed a few hundred workers, but its staff soon grew, reaching 5,000 employees by 1965: ten times the size of the Council's staff. Each one of the Big Three (France, Germany and Italy) was permitted to staff 25% of the Commission's positions, while the Benelux states provided manpower for the remaining 25%. Despite this meticulous distribution according to nationality, the Commission was a supra-national institution and the new staff needed to consolidate a fresh identity, distinct from their national affiliation. They were required to act in accordance with the interests of the new entity—the EEC—and advance the status of the body which employed them—the Commission. Article 157 of the Treaty of Rome explicitly demanded that the Commissioners act completely independently of their nations' influence. Thus, for example, upon taking up their positions, Commissioners were required to swear that they would refrain from advancing their country's interests.[38] Indeed, they adopted the new identity surprisingly quickly, even taking into account that those recruited to work as Commission officials were "good Europeans," who viewed European integration positively.[39] These officials, in particular the most senior among them—the President, Commissioners and Secretary-General—attributed great importance to achieving an independent and noteworthy status for the Commission in the framework of the Community's institutions. It was clear to them that they themselves would need to provide the content for the new roles which had been established; it would be their responsibility to determine the place and status of the Commission among the other Common Market institutions; they would necessarily constitute the foundations for advancing the EEC towards supra-nationality and therefore must not accept a merely inter-national framework.[40] The possibility that the Commission would eventually become the government of the EEC did not seem outrageous at all.[41] Indeed, it appears that the Commission leadership held this opinion.[42]

Walter Hallstein was appointed as the first President of the European Commission. In his youth, Hallstein was a promising lawyer and outstanding scholar, receiving an academic post at the age of 29—an exceptional feat. His lack of affection for the Nazi Party was well known and threatened to impede his professional progress. During the Second World War, he served as a junior artillery officer in France and was taken captive by the Americans after the invasion of Normandy. Following the war, he returned to academic life—he served as Rector of Frankfurt University, until the West German Chancellor, Konrad Adenauer, asked him to serve in the new German Foreign Office, leading the German delegation at the negotiations regarding the establishment of the ECSC. In March 1957, Hallstein was among the parties to sign the Treaty of Rome. At the beginning of 1958, he was selected as President of the Commission. This was a surprising choice because Sicco Mansholt, the Dutch Minister of Agriculture, and Jean Rey, the Belgian Finance Minister, were considered more certain candidates (both would later serve alongside Hallstein as Commissioners). The decision to appoint a German to this position so soon after the Second World War was remarkable and testified to Hallstein's personal prestige, as well as the dramatic improvement in French-German relations over the previous decade.[43] Hallstein was famed for his serious nature, smiling only rarely, and known to be completely devoted to his work. He demanded that his assistants demonstrate commitment similar to his own; in Brussels stories concerning his "tyranny" abounded, although he was never accused of acting unfairly.[44] At an early stage, Hallstein became convinced that in order to respond to the political challenges facing the continent's countries in the long term, Europe must be consolidated into one federal framework.[45] Although in his position alongside the other Commissioners he was ostensibly the first among equals, he in fact possessed great power due to the President's responsibility for making appointments to various positions, as well as the privilege of chairing Collegium sessions—the Commission's managing committee. Hallstein sought to ensure that the integration process advanced according to the timetable determined by the Treaty of Rome, even seeking to accelerate it. He urged the Commissioners to gallop forwards; when negotiations between The Six reached an impasse he instructed them to take vigorous action in order to resolve the crisis.[46] Indeed, Hallstein viewed the Commission as the surety to fortify the EEC. He was aware of the fragility and weakness of the Commission in its early days and believed that for this exact reason the Commission needed to advance its agenda in an effective and uncompromising manner.[47] A case in point is the EEC's external trade policy. Hallstein perceived the molding of a common trade foreign policy as one of the EEC's central aims, yet discovered that the Treaty of Rome did not provide the tools necessary to achieve this.[48] While in his opinion the Commission was the body best suited to manage this policy, in reality the Council disputed the Commission's authority to decide on external trade policy.[49] In order to emphasize the supra-national basis of the Community and the independent status of the Commission vis-à-vis the six member states, Hallstein was punctilious in ensuring meticulous ceremonial etiquette. One diplomat complained that the rules of ceremony which the Commission dictated to new representatives presenting their credentials were "the most severe in all Europe, including the royal families on the continent."[50]

Jean Rey, former Belgian Finance Minister, was appointed as Commissioner responsible for foreign relations. Rey too was famed as a devoted European who considered European integration a goal of vast importance. His views generally accorded with those of Hallstein, although on occasion the relations between the two became tense due to Hallstein's interest in foreign policy, which Rey perceived as an invasion of his territory.[51]

Another figure of influence in the Commission, who likewise discerned the central importance of integration, was the Commissioner for agricultural affairs, Sicco Mansholt from the Netherlands. Mansholt was born into a family of farmers and from a young age devoted his life to agriculture. In his youth, he spent two years on the island of Java working on tea plantations. During the Second World War, he joined the Dutch resistance movement. Mansholt was a socialist and played an active role in the Cooperative Party. A tall man, exceptionally energetic and renowned for his love of sailing, he was most famed for his commitment to the idea of integration. In Brussels it was commonly believed that he pursued this aim even more zealously than Hallstein.

Article 113 of the Treaty of Rome outlines the procedure for trade negotiations with third-party countries, designating a number of stages. In the first stage, the Commission was to submit a recommendation to the COREPER suggesting that the community embark on negotiations with a certain country. The Permanent Representatives would then amend the proposal and submit it to the Council of Ministers for authorization. The Council of Ministers would determine the framework of any agreement, its aims and the topics it would cover. On many occasions, this decision reflected a compromise between the various interests of different member states. After reaching a decision, the responsibility for managing the negotiations fell to the Commission's Directorate General for Foreign Relations, which was required to report regularly to a special supervising committee of the Council to ensure that the Commission did not exceed its mandate. Upon reaching an agreement between the negotiating parties, the Commission was to submit it to the Council of Ministers, which alone possessed the authority to authorize it.[52]

The Commission discernibly pursued a number of goals in its earliest days. Firstly, it sought to advance all elements of European integration. Although vague, this goal arose frequently in the rhetoric of the Commission's staff. Alongside this aim, the Commission also desired to advance its own position and increase its power within the Community's institutions.[53]

Together with the Council of Ministers and the European Commission, the Treaty of Rome established a European Parliament located in Strasbourg, France, with 142 delegates from the six member states. The ECSC's Common Assembly formed the origins of the Parliament, which constituted a continued attempt to accord European integration with democratic elements and credibility. The power of the European Parliament differed from that enjoyed by legislatures in democratic countries: at the time, it possessed no legislative power or control over the Community's budget but was principally to act as an advisory body whose decisions were not binding. Its representatives were elected in their own countries and therefore were familiar with the particular interests of their electorates. Yet the Parliament had a certain leverage as the body which supervised the Commission: the Commission was obliged to answer questions addressed to it by the Parliament. Likewise, the Parliament alone was authorized to disperse the managing committee of the Commission. In general, the European Parliament proved to be a rather politically weak institution, and its powers increased only after the 1992 Maastricht Treaty.[54]

To facilitate member states' transition and adaptation to the new economic reality of a common market, a reasonably lengthy timetable was drawn up for the process of adjustment and implementation. The Treaty of Rome determined that from January 1, 1959 the member states would gradually reduce tariffs between them by small percentages in three stages, removing them completely only after twelve years (article 8). Beginning from January 1, 1962, a simultaneous process to establish a common external tariff vis-à-vis third-party countries would begin. The common external tariff towards other parties was determined using a simple arithmetic mean of the tariffs which all six countries imposed on a certain product.

Thus, for example, the common tariff for oranges would be 20%, the mean average of the six member states' tariffs on oranges (France—35%, Germany—16%, Benelux—13%, etc.).[55] In addition, the EEC decided to implement a Common Agricultural Policy, the declared aim of which was to cultivate agriculture in the EEC's countries (article 38), although it was clear that one of its central aims was to prevent external competition. The transition towards a common market also implied that fostering competition within a unified European market would generate new winners and losers. The potential impact of such a process on the agriculture sector was profound and therefore it required political and social sensitivity. It was particularly important to give special consideration to the agricultural sector due to the probable implications of restructuring on a labor-intensive sector, the unemployment effects on social and political stability, and concerns that adverse consequences for farmers may push them towards communist and fascist ideologies.[56] The countries which principally benefited from this policy were France, Italy and the Netherlands, all three of which were relatively significant exporters of food products, and thus pressured for the inclusion of a common agriculture policy in the Treaty of Rome. Likewise, at the insistence of the French, the Treaty included the possibility of granting trade concessions (meaning reduced tariffs) at preferential conditions to former colonies of the six member states.[57] Similarly, a Community aid fund was created to aid the development of former colonies.

From the outset, one of the market's aims was to draw additional West European members. However, many nations were hesitant, either due to considerations of political neutrality (Switzerland, Austria, Sweden) or economic reasons (Britain's preferential links with the Commonwealth countries).[58] Therefore it was decided that new candidates would be accepted by the unanimous agreement of the members (article 237 of the Treaty of Rome). At the same time, countries which had close trade relations with the market but did not wish to or were not able to apply for membership, could connect themselves with the market through an association agreement (article 238). Such status granted many of the economic privileges which the members themselves enjoyed, although this was not clearly defined at the time. Furthermore, articles 111 and 114 allowed certain kinds of trade privileges between the members of the market and third-party countries. These articles enabled the existence of "preferential relations," on a level lower than actual association. It is superfluous to note that some countries in the international community did not welcome the establishment of the Common Market, fearing that it would have detrimental effects on their trade. For these countries, the Common Market would not only reduce their competitive ability but also result in the loss of tariff preferences which they had previously obtained with the states now forming the EEC. The Common Market similarly generated certain tensions between EEC member states and their obligations as members of the General Agreement on Tariffs and Trade (GATT). The GATT was a formal agreement regulating international trade through mutual liberalization, transparency and shared trade rules. The GATT served as the international trade regime prior to the establishment of the World Trade Organization in 1995, and de facto operated as an international organization. Since 1947, under US leadership, the GATT attempted to remove trade barriers between its member states and encouraged international trade through multilateral trade negotiations. At the signing of the agreement, the GATT included 23 countries but within 15 years (1962) this number had risen to 70, encompassing 80% of global trade.[59] The key principle of the GATT was the most-favored nation (MFN) principle, which obligated countries to grant all members of the organization any privilege accorded to one member, thus treating all countries as "most favorable." However, article 24 of the agreement permitted countries to form free trade areas and customs unions as a framework of regional economic integration. Under article 24, in such cases, countries were permitted to grant preferential access to other member states of the regional economic integration framework, thus discriminating against other GATT members outside the regional economic framework. The rationale behind this deviation from the MFN principle was that countries form regional economic integration for reasons beyond economic interests (making it politically acceptable), and regional integration may act as a stepping stone for future multilateral liberalization (economically consistent with the long-term aims of the GATT). Nevertheless, to prevent exploitation of these privileges, a number of severe limitations were imposed. First, import restrictions towards countries outside the customs union could not be higher than those in existence in the individual states prior to its creation; a customs union could not impose new restrictions; a customs union must be implemented according to a reasonable timetable; and, finally, the agreement on a customs union required authorization by the GATT.[60]

The EEC was not the only integrative framework in existence in Europe at the end of the 1950s, although in retrospect it was doubtless the most successful. Among the other frameworks which, to a certain extent, competed with the EEC was the OEEC, a body comprised of 18 countries (including the six members of the EEC). As was noted, the OEEC was established in 1949 with the aim of coordinating distribution of the generous aid granted by the US to European countries under the Marshall Plan (known officially as the European Recovery Program). The OEEC continued to exist after the American aid had been exhausted, serving as a framework for coordinating trade policy and the reduction of protective quotas among its members. Likewise, the OEEC coordinated its members' economic policy, encouraged industrial development and policies by arranging educational seminars and circulating technical reports, as well as closely monitoring economic developments among the member states.[61] Between 1956 and 1959, negotiations were conducted within the framework of this organization regarding the establishment of a free trade area among its member states. However, due to the tensions which the establishment of the EEC had generated among the European countries—first and foremost differences of opinion between the UK and France—the negotiations were largely unsuccessful. Britain, which headed the camp of European countries outside the EEC, sought to minimize the adverse consequences to its trade likely to result from the Common Market by establishing a free trade area between all OEEC countries.

France vigorously opposed the idea, demanding at the very least a customs union. Finally, seven of the OEEC states which remained outside the EEC and felt concerned by its possible ramifications on their economies, decided to create their own free trade area—the European Free Trade Area (EFTA). EFTA consisted of the UK, Austria, Portugal, Ireland, Denmark, Switzerland and Sweden, with the UK assuming a pivotal role. In contrast to the EEC's six founding members, Britain conducted most of its trade with the Commonwealth, not continental Europe. Although British trade patterns were beginning to change, for both political and psychological reasons Britain found it difficult to make the change in foreign policy which entrance to the EEC necessitated. Britain insisted that a common market was likely to fail due to France's protectionist tradition; thus the Treaty of Rome came as a sad surprise to the British leadership.[62] From their perspective, the establishment of EFTA was to some degree a means to pressure The Six, while The Six perceived it as a step of defiance.[63]

Alongside the OEEC (which in 1960 was renamed as the OECD), the Council of Europe, established in 1949, fulfilled a legal rather than economic function. The Council of Europe was largely focused on issues of democracy, promoting human rights and developing best practices. It is important in the context of this book because in the early stages of European integration some believed that it would eventually become the European Parliament for the 18 OEEC states.[64]

The economies of The Six: the effects of establishing the EEC

European post-war economic recovery was in many respects astonishing. Much of his growth can be attributed to the US's Marshall Plan, the work of the OEEC, domestic economic policies (e.g. Keynesian policies), the reconstruction of previously existing industries and capacities and the GATT.[65] Yet it became evident that the creation of the Common Market yielded substantial rewards for The Six, and that the economic performance of EEC members outstripped that of the US and Britain. Within a short time, their economies blossomed: between 1958 and 1964, the Community's GDP rose by 39% while in the same period the US GDP rose at a rate of 28% and that of Britain was lower, increasing by 23%.[66] During these years, wages and consumption rates in each of The Six rose at an annual average rate of 4.5%.[67] The industrial sectors reaped the most benefits from this growth. In this period, the Community's industrial output increased by 52%, compared with US and British growth rates of 41% and 27% respectively.[68] Agriculture also thrived, despite the significant decrease in manpower within the West European agricultural sector, due to the evident improvements in production processes.[69] While the number of people employed in agriculture throughout The Six declined at an annual rate of 2.5%, the rate of agricultural production rose by 2% per annum.[70]

The level of agricultural mechanization serves as a standard indicator in assessing the degree of development. Accordingly, in 1955 there were 59 tractors for every 1,000 farmers in the Community. By 1970, this number had grown to 364.[71] No less indicative is the extent to which fertilizers and pesticides are used. This rose at a rate of 85% in the two decades between 1939 and 1959.[72] Nevertheless, the rate at which the agricultural sector grew lagged behind that of the industrial sector: the former's share of the Community's GDP decreased by half.[73]

Each member state benefited economically from the establishment of the EEC. At the end of the 1950s, France was experiencing severe economic problems resulting from the costs of attempting to maintain a declining empire, the war in Algeria, and the ongoing political instability under the Fourth Republic. Inflation peaked at 8% in 1957 and 9% in 1958.[74] France suffered from a constant deficit in the balance of payments and needed to depreciate significantly the franc's exchange rate in order to increase the competitive ability of its country's exports. EEC entry had a profound effect on the French economy. Indeed, France's intra-EEC exports rose significantly within a decade: from 22% of the country's entire exports in 1958 to 41% in 1968. The growth in the country's agricultural exports was even more dramatic. Since half of the Community's agricultural lands were located in France, it relied on its agricultural exports more than any other state in the EEC. During the 1950s, the French agricultural sector experienced a severe crisis: in fact, the establishment of the EEC saved it from annihilation, with France becoming the supplier of 40% of the Community's agricultural produce.[75] However, the growth of France's industrial sector was less significant and French industry mainly focused on three pillars: cars, trains and airplanes. Quality of life in the country rose during this period more than in any other of The Six. Yet concurrently the cost of living increased sharply—there was a price rise of 45%—and the country experienced the highest inflation in the EEC.[76]

The establishment of the EEC was no less important for Germany. While France was the community's produce barn and vegetable garden, Germany became its factory. In 1948, Germany imported most of its commodities, financed largely by the occupying powers (about two-thirds). However, from the end of the 1940s, Germany underwent a process of economic rehabilitation so swift that it became known as "the German economic miracle." The main architect of this process was the Finance Minister, Ludwig Erhard, assisted by senior economist Alfred Müller-Armack.[77] Erhard constructed an economic model combining aspects of a capitalist market economy, centralized planning and a social safety net. This policy, combined with amenable conditions, resulted in an extraordinary economic take-off. Between the years 1948 and 1963, the German GDP sharply rose at an annual average of 7.6%, more than any other European state (compare: France—4.6%, Italy—6%, UK—2.5%). Unemployment rates declined steeply from 11% (1950) to 3.7% (1958). Half a million new homes were built every year and welfare spending per citizen multiplied by 2.5.[78] This take-off was largely based on exports. In the mid-1950s German exports already greatly exceeded the country's imports: this resulted from the swift recovery of Germany's existing industrial infrastructure following the destruction of the war, the fall in the price of raw materials in the world market, and the outbreak of the Korean War, which led to a sharp (though short-lived) commodity boom.[79] Devastated Europe desperately needed machines that would once again set in motion the wheels of the economy; Germany, with its experienced human resources, work ethic and suitable material infrastructure, supplied them,[80] enabling German exports to forge ahead and increase at an average annual rate of 16.2% (France—7.6%, Italy—12.1%, UK—1.8%).[81] Ironically, Germany, which had caused the war, now reaped the fruits of reconstructing the continent's ruins. The country produced final goods at an unprecedented rate in comparison to any other period in its history and the establishment of the Common Market allowed Germany to sell them undisturbed in geographically close markets, giving the country an advantage over distant competitors, for example in the US. However, in the 1960s, the rate of growth slowed to some degree, falling to around 5.5%, due to the difficulty in maintaining such a high rate of growth in an economy which had already reached a significant level of development. Likewise, the Berlin Wall halted the flow of immigrants from Eastern Europe who worked in the most highly demanded professions.[82] Yet generally, the Germany economy continued to blossom in this period and unemployment declined to below 3%. The establishment of the EEC played a significant role in this boom, enabling Germany to expand its industrial exports.

The relatively weak Italian economy made the most impressive leap following the establishment of the Common Market. Like Japan, the Industrial Revolution reached Italy relatively late, although Italy's rate of development remained moderate over an extended period of time, a trend which continued under the fascist regime.[83] The end of the Second World War brought about a rise in the rate of Italy's economic growth, although only at the end of the 1950s did the real take-off begin. Italy's industrial production doubled between 1958 and 1966—a true economic miracle. At the beginning of the 1960s, Italian growth exceeded that of any other country, including the USSR and Japan. The most impressive advances occurred in the car industry, office equipment and the electricity industry: in 1967, every third refrigerator manufactured in Europe was Italian.[84] By contrast, the boom barely touched some regions and sectors. For example, Italy's South remained largely impoverished, and reducing the gap between that region and the developed North swiftly became one of the greatest challenges facing Italian governments.

When the Benelux states entered the EEC, they had already taken some steps towards economic integration, more than the other three member states. Even before the end of the war, in 1944, the Netherlands and Belgium signed a customs union agreement (Luxemburg joined as a result of its existing economic union with Belgium).[85] This integration was positive because the countries' economies complimented one another: Belgium focused on manufacturing, while the Netherlands's main income was from agriculture (mainly milk and poultry). At first, the Belgian economy dominated the union. Indeed, in the second half of the 1940s, Belgium's exports experienced an impressive jump as a direct result of the temporary disappearance of its biggest rival—Germany.[86] However, very soon Germany began to renew its exports and the Belgian economy entered a recession. Concurrently, an "industrial revolution" began in the Netherlands, giving the Dutch economy a jump-start. Over the next two decades the Netherlands's rate of economic growth was the highest in Western Europe[87] and it replaced Belgium as the most important economy among the Benelux nations. Among other developments, the Netherlands's exports rose dramatically in this period. Already in the 1950s, the economy had grown impressively, at the rate of 8.3% per annum, yet following the creation of the EEC it rose even further, reaching a peak in the 1960s—annual growth of 10.4%.[88] Thus, the Netherlands's exports were the most positively influenced by the establishment of the Community. The coordination between the Benelux countries was not only limited to the economic field, but also possessed political dimensions. The three countries conducted close consultations and frequently presented a united front in the Community institutions. The Netherlands enjoyed great influence in this forum, which is of vital importance in the tale told herein.

For marketing reasons, The Six made great efforts to present regional integration as a process encouraging global trade and therefore contributing to the economic wellbeing of countries outside the EEC. However, without doubt the establishment of the EEC was in reality a withdrawal inwards. Between 1958 and 1965, exports between the members of the Community rose three times more than exports between The Six and external countries.[89] In 1958, French agricultural exports to the EEC countries totaled 18% of the country's entire exports in this sector; ten years later no less than 50% of France's agricultural products were dispatched to the EEC's markets.[90] In fact, trade between The Six had expanded in comparison to trade with other European countries even before the EEC was founded. For example, in 1953, 20.6% of Italian exports were already to EEC countries and by 1956, this volume had risen to 25.3%.[91] A similar trend was evident in each one of the other five states which made up the EEC. Thus the increase in economic interactions between The Six was not only an outcome of the Treaty of Rome, although there can be no doubt that this agreement speeded up the trend. Indeed, regarding agriculture, the EEC's protectionism replaced national protectionism within each member state. From 1961, the EEC budgeted $4 million per annum to the Common Agriculture Policy, which was intended to ensure that the agricultural sectors of The Six would enjoy preference in marketing their produce,[92] as will be discussed at length later.

Notes

1 For simplicity throughout this book, West Germany is referred to as Germany, with the exception of places where reference to West Germany is relevant or when East Germany is discussed.

2 For a thorough explanation of the various types of economic integration and the differences between them see: Bela Balassa, *The Theory of Economic Integration (Routledge Revivals)* (Oxford: Routledge, 2013); Miroslav N. Jovanović, *The Economics of International Integration* (Cheltenham: Edward Elgar Publishing, 2015).

3 Removing barriers (trade, migration, capital and services) constitutes "negative" integration while coordinating policy on various issues is known as "positive" integration. See Jan Tinbergen, *International Economic Integration* (Amsterdam: Elsevier, 1954); David Coombes, *Politics and Bureaucracy in the European Communities: A Portrait of the Commission of the EEC*, ed. Institute Policy Studies (Beverly Hills: Sage, 1970).

4 On the factors leading to the creation of the European Coal and Steel Community, the first stage in European integration, see Alan S. Milward, *The Reconstruction of Western Europe, 1945–51* (London: Routledge, 2003).

5 Geoffrey Parker, *The Logic of Unity: A Geography of the European Economic Community*, 2nd ed. (London: Longman, 1975), 5, 78.

6 See: Walter Hallstein, *United Europe: Challenge and Opportunity* (London: Oxford University Press, 1962), 4.

7 Concerning the variety of approaches and motivations at the basis of the European integration process, see: Leon N. Lindberg and Stuart A. Scheingold, *Europe's Would-Be Polity: Patterns of Change in the European Community* (Englewood Cliffs: Prentice-Hall, 1970), 4–9.

8 Regarding the attempt to transform the OEEC into a basis for European Unity and the failure of this endeavor, see: Hallstein, *United Europe*, 7–9.

9 Stanley Hoffmann, "Obstinate or Obsolete? The Fate of the Nation-State and the Case of Western Europe," *Daedalus* 95, no. 3 (1966): 245–9; Amy Verdun, "Economic Growth and Global Competiveness: From Rome to Maastricht to Lisbon," in *The Sage Handbook of European Studies*, ed. Chris Rumford (Los Angeles: Sage, 2009), 245–9; Ernst B. Haas, *Beyond the Nation-State: Functionalism and International Organization.* (London: ECPR Press/Stanford University Press, 2008).

10 Desmond Dinan, *Europe Recast: A History of European Union* (Basingstoke: Palgrave Macmillan, 2004), 51–3; Peter Hans Merkl, *German Foreign Policies, West and East: Toward a New Balance of Osptolitik* (Santa Barbara: ABC-CLIO, 1974), 83–4.

11 David Weigall and Peter M. R. Stirk, *The Origins and Development of the European Community* (Leicester: Leicester University Press, 1992), 93.

12 Additionally, two further bodies were created: the Common Assembly and the Court of Justice.

13 Although others argue that the failure of these two initiatives in fact led to progress in the process of economic integration and speeded up the signing of the Rome Treaty. See: Dinan, 63–4.

14 Michelle Cini, *The European Commission: Leadership, Organisation, and Culture in the EU Administration* (Manchester: Manchester University Press, 1996), 24–5; Brian White, *Understanding European Foreign Policy* (Houndmills: Palgrave, 2001), 48.

15 See: I. Bach, "The European Common Market," *The Economic Quarterly* 6, no. 23 (1959) [in Hebrew]. Concerning the negotiations between France and Germany on this matter, see: Dinan, 66–70.

16 Deborah Welch Larson, "Crisis Prevention and the Austrian State Treaty," *International Organization* 41, no. 1 (1987).

17 Werner J. Feld, *West Germany and the European Community: Changing Interests and Competing Policy Objectives* (New York: Praeger, 1981), 37.

18 Dennis Bark and David Gress, "A History of West Germany: From Shadow to Substance, 1945–1963," (Oxford: Blackwell, 1993), 355–7; Merkl, 102; Hans-Peter Schwarz, *Konrad Adenauer: From the German Empire to the Federal Republic* (Providence: Berghahn Books, 1995), 228–9.

19 Christian Hacke, "Traditions and Stops in the German Republic: 1949–1987," in *The Germans 1945–1990*, eds. Oded Heilbronner and Moshe Zimmermann (Jerusalem: Magnes [in Hebrew], 1998).

20 Resolution adopted by the Foreign Ministers of the Member States of the ECSC at the Messina Conference, 1–2 June 1955

21 Quoted in: Bach.

22 Weigall and Stirk, 90–1.

23 Ostensibly the two agreements were the result of a compromise between the various interests of the member states. However, many claim that France succeeded in extracting the most significant concessions and to a great extent the agreement was designed to meet French requirements. See, for example, Alan S. Milward, *The European Rescue of the Nation-State* (London: Routledge, 1992), 220.

24 Quoted in Miriam Camps, *Britain and the European Community, 1955–1963* (Princeton: Princeton University Press, 1964), 88.

25 The idealistic motivation for their actions is clearly demonstrated by their declarations and writings. See: Paul-Henri Spaak, *The Continuing Battle: Memoirs of a European, 1936–1966* (Boston: Little Brown, 1971), 251.

26 Hence, the term Council of Ministers refers to the Council's Foreign Affairs Ministers configuration.

27 Wolfgang Wessels, "The EC Council: The Community's Decisionmaking Center," in *The New European Community: Decisionmaking and Institutional Change*, eds. Robert O. Keohane and Stanley Hoffmann (Boulder: Westview Press, 1991), 139.

28 John Peterson and Elizabeth E. Bomberg, *Decision-Making in the European Union* (London: Macmillan, 1999), 34.

29 John McCormick, *Understanding the European Union: A Concise Introduction*, 3rd ed. (Houndmills: Palgrave Macmillan, 2005), 98.

30 Peterson and Bomberg, 36.

31 Walter Hallstein, *Europe in the Making* (London: Allen and Unwin, 1972), 70–1.

32 Derek W. Urwin, *The Community of Europe: A History of European Integration since 1945* (London: Routledge, 2014), 81.

33 Hallstein, *United Europe: Challenge and Opportunity*, 21.

34 Cini, 14.

35 Francesca Martines, "Foreign Commercial Policy," in *Italy and EC Membership Evaluated*, ed. Francesco. Francioni (New York: St. Martin's, 1992), 158–75.

36 Neill Nugent, *The European Commission* (Houndmills: Palgrave, 2001), 26.

37 David Lipkin, "The Technocrats of the Common Market," *Davar*, July 30, 1965.

38 McCormick, 89.

39 Nugent, 29.

40 Christoph Sasse, *Decision Making in the European Community* (New York: Praeger, 1977), 184–6.

41 Cini, 21–2.

42 Wilfried Loth, William Wallace and Wolfgang Wessels, *Walter Hallstein: The Forgotten European?* (Houndmills: Macmillan, 1998), 115.

43 François Duchêne, *Jean Monnet: The First Statesman of Interdependence*, ed. Jean Monnet (New York: Norton, 1994), 309.

44 H. Bleich, "The Politician Who Never Won an Election," *Ma'ariv*, 1966.

45 Hanns Jürgen Küsters, "Walter Hallstein and the Negotiations on the Treaties of Rome 1955–57," in *Walter Hallstein: The Forgotten European?*, eds. Wilfried Loth, William Wallace and Wolfgang Wessels (Springer, 1998).

46 Peter Ludlow, "The European Commission," in *The New European Community: Decisionmaking and Institutional Change*, eds. Robert O. Keohane and Stanley Hoffmann (Boulder: Westview Press, 1991), 97.

47 Emile Noël, "Walter Hallstein: A Personal Testimony," in *Walter Hallstein: The Forgotten European?*, eds. Wilfried Loth, William Wallace and Wolfgang Wessels (Springer, 1998), 133.

48 Hallstein, *United Europe: Challenge and Opportunity*, 67.

49 Karl-Heinz. Narjes, "Walter Hallstein and the Early Phase of the EEC," in *Walter Hallstein: The Forgotten European?*, eds. Wilfried Loth, William Wallace and Wolfgang Wessels (Springer, 1998), 124.

50 Bleich.

51 Hans Von der Groeben, "Walter Hallstein as President of the Commission," in *Walter Hallstein: The Forgotten European?*, eds. Wilfried Loth, William Wallace and Wolfgang Wessels (Springer, 1998), 106.

52 White, 51.

53 Cini, 17; Hallstein, *Europe in the Making*.

54 Bernard Steunenberg and Jacobus Johannes Adrianus Thomassen, *The European Parliament: Moving toward Democracy in the EU* (Lanham: Rowman & Littlefield, 2002), 1–15

55 This is to some extent a simplification. In reality, certain agricultural projects, including citrus fruits, were included in category F, meaning that The Six negotiated the tariff rate for them. For a comprehensive analysis see: Gerald W. Dean and Norman R. Collins, *World Trade in Fresh Oranges: An Analysis of the Effect of European Economic Community Tariff Policies* (Berkeley: University of California Division of Agricultural Sciences, 1967).

56 Paul-Henri Spaak, "A New Effort to Build Europe," *Foreign Affairs* 43, no. 2 (1965); Ann-Christina L. Knudsen, *Farmers on Welfare: The Making of Europe's Common Agricultural Policy* (Ithaca: Cornell University Press, 2009); Ian R. Bowler, *Agriculture under the Common Agricultural Policy: A Geography* (Manchester: Manchester University Press, 1985).

57 Concerning the French pressure on this issue see Milward, *The European Rescue of the Nation-State*, 218–20.

58 John Singleton and Paul L. Robertson, "Britain, Butter, and European Integration, 1957–1964," *The Economic History Review* 50, no. 2 (1997); George Wilkes, ed., *Britain's Failure to Enter the European Community, 1961–63: The Enlargement Negotiations and Crises in European, Atlantic, and Commonwealth Relations* (London: Frank Cass, 1997).

59 Ivan T. Berend, *An Economic History of Twentieth-Century Europe: Economic Regimes from Laissez-Faire to Globalization* (Cambridge: Cambridge University Press, 2016), 193; Bernard M. Hoekman and M. M. Kostecki, *The Political Economy of the World Trading System: The WTO and Beyond*, 2nd ed. (Oxford: Oxford University Press, 2001).

60 M. J. Trebilcock and Robert Howse, *The Regulation of International Trade*, 3rd ed. (London: Routledge, 2005); Hoekman and Kostecki.

61 See Dov Genohovski, "The OEEC: Structure and Activities," *The Economic Quarterly*, no. 17/18 (1957): 191–7. In 1950, the architects of the EEC, Schuman and Monnet, tried to transform this framework into the basis for the integration of Western Europe. However, Britain and the Scandinavian countries halted this initiative, leading to the search for an alternative, more limited, framework: McCormick, 65.

62 Dinan, 70–1.

63 The British did not have much to gain economically from the establishment of EFTA because the external duty of the Scandinavian countries was low at any rate. However, as was noted, this was a means in the battle against the EEC. On the creation of EFTA, see Thomas Pedersen, *European Union and the EFTA Countries: Enlargement and Integration* (London: Pinter, 1994).

64 Urwin.

65 Nicholas Francis Robert Crafts, "The Golden Age of Economic Growth in Western Europe, 1950–1973," *The Economic History Review* 48, no. 3 (1995); Barry Eichengreen, ed., *Europe's Postwar Recovery* (Cambridge: Cambridge University Press, 1995); Barry J. Eichengreen, *The European Economy since 1945: Coordinated Capitalism and Beyond*, The Princeton Economic History of the Western World (Princeton: Princeton University Press, 2007); Douglas A. Irwin, "The GATT's Contribution to Economic Recovery in Post-War Western Europe" (Cambridge: National Bureau of Economic Research, 1994).

66 Eshkol's speech at the Industry Club, ISA, FM, file 4294/4, January 1967.

67 McCormick, 70.

68 Eshkol's speech at the Industry Club, ISA, FM, file 4294/4, January 1967.

69 The process of urbanization characterizing European society since the beginning of the nineteenth century increased dramatically in the 1950s. In France, for example, the pace reached 90,000 people every year.

70 Anthony Sampson, *The New Europeans: A Guide to the Workings, Institutions and Character of Contemporary Western Europe* (London: Hodder and Stoughton, 1968).
71 Wyn Grant, "Agricultural Policy and Protectionism," in *The Sage Handbook of European Studies*, ed. Chris Rumford (Los Angeles: SAGE, 2009), 260–76.
72 Michael Moïssey Postan, *An Economic History of Western Europe 1945–1964* (Oxford: Routledge, 2013), 175.
73 McCormick, 70.
74 Gilles Saint-Paul, "Economic Reconstruction in France: 1945–1958," in *Postwar Economic Reconstruction and Lessons for the East Today*, eds. Rudiger Dornbusch, Wilhelm Nölling and Richard Layard (Cambridge: MIT Press, 1993), 86–7.
75 Grant; Sampson.
76 Walter Laqueur, *Europe since Hitler* (London: Weidenfeld and Nicolson, 1970), 166–7.
77 Bark and Gress, 392–8; Geoffrey Keith Roberts, *West German Politics* (London: Macmillan, 1972), 32–3.
78 Heinz Lampert, "The Social Market Economy in the German Republic: Origin, Perception, Development and Problems," in *The Germans 1945–1990*, eds. Oded Heilbronner and Moshe Zimmermann (Jerusalem: Magnes [in Hebrew], 1998).
79 Nicholas Kaldor, "Inflation and Recession in the World Economy," *The Economic Journal* 86, no. 344 (1976).
80 Herbert Giersch, Karl-Heinz Paqué and Holger Schmieding, "Openness, Wage Restraint, and Macroeconomic Stability: West Germany's Road to Prosperity 1948–1959," in *Postwar Economic Reconstruction and Lessons for the East Today*, ed. Rudiger Dornbusch, Wilhelm Nölling and Richard Layard (Cambridge: MIT Press, 1993), 18–23.
81 Postan, 12, 92.
82 Alun Jones, *The New Germany: A Human Geography* (Chichester: Wiley & Sons, 1994), 48–9.
83 Grant Amyot, *Business, the State and Economic Policy: The Case of Italy* (London: Routledge, 2004), 11–17; Laqueur, 171–2.
84 Jan Luiten van Zanden, ed., *The Economic Development of the Netherlands since 1870* (Aldershot: Edward Elgar, 1996), 187–203.
85 The Benelux Customs Union came into effect in January 1948. Jacob Viner, *The Customs Union Issue* (Oxford: Oxford University Press, 2014 [1950]), 91.
86 Jan Luiten van Zanden, "The Economic Development of the Netherlands and Belgium and the 'Success' of Benelux, 1945–1958," in *The Economic Development of the Netherlands since 1870*, ed. Jan Luiten van Zanden (Aldershot: Edward Elgar, 1996), 187–203.
87 Richard T. Griffiths, "The Dutch Economic Miracle," in *The Economic Development of the Netherlands since 1870*, ed. Jan Luiten van Zanden (Aldershot: Edward Elgar, 1996), 173–86.
88 Jan Luiten van Zanden, *The Economic History of the Netherlands, 1914–1995: A Small Open Economy in the "Long" Twentieth Century* (London: Routledge, 1998), 135.
89 McCormick., 70.
90 Laqueur., 166–7.
91 Milward, *The European Rescue of the Nation-State*, 167–71.
92 Laqueur, *Europe Since Hitler*, 157–8.

References

Amyot, Grant. *Business, the State and Economic Policy: The Case of Italy*. London: Routledge, 2004.
Bach, I. "The European Common Market." *The Economic Quarterly [in Hebrew]* 6, no. 23 (1959): 197–209.

Balassa, Bela. *The Theory of Economic Integration (Routledge Revivals)*. Oxford: Routledge, 2013.

Bark, Dennis, and David Gress. "A History of West Germany: From Shadow to Substance, 1945–1963." Oxford: Blackwell, 1993.

Berend, Ivan T. *An Economic History of Twentieth-Century Europe: Economic Regimes from Laissez-Faire to Globalization*. Cambridge: Cambridge University Press, 2016.

Bleich, H. "The Politician Who Never Won an Election." *Ma'ariv*, 1966.

Bowler, Ian R. *Agriculture under the Common Agricultural Policy: A Geography*. Manchester: Manchester University Press, 1985.

Camps, Miriam. *Britain and the European Community, 1955–1963*. Princeton: Princeton University Press, 1964.

Cini, Michelle. *The European Commission: Leadership, Organisation, and Culture in the EU Administration*. Manchester: Manchester University Press, 1996.

Coombes, David. *Politics and Bureaucracy in the European Communities: A Portrait of the Commission of the EEC*. Edited by Institute Policy Studies Beverly Hills: Sage, 1970.

Crafts, Nicholas Francis Robert. "The Golden Age of Economic Growth in Western Europe, 1950–1973." *The Economic History Review* 48, no. 3 (1995): 429–47.

Dean, Gerald W., and Norman R. Collins. *World Trade in Fresh Oranges: An Analysis of the Effect of European Economic Community Tariff Policies*. Berkeley: University of California Division of Agricultural Sciences, 1967.

Dinan, Desmond. *Europe Recast: A History of European Union*. Basingstoke: Palgrave Macmillan, 2004.

Duchêne, François. *Jean Monnet: The First Statesman of Interdependence*. Edited by Jean Monnet New York: Norton, 1994.

Eichengreen, Barry, ed. *Europe's Postwar Recovery*. Cambridge: Cambridge University Press, 1995.

Eichengreen, Barry J. *The European Economy since 1945: Coordinated Capitalism and Beyond*. The Princeton Economic History of the Western World. Princeton: Princeton University Press, 2007.

Feld, Werner J. *West Germany and the European Community: Changing Interests and Competing Policy Objectives*. New York: Praeger, 1981.

Genohovski, Dov. "The OEEC: Structure and Activities." *The Economic Quarterly*, no. 17/18 (1957): 191–7.

Giersch, Herbert, Karl-Heinz Paqué and Holger Schmieding. "Openness, Wage Restraint, and Macroeconomic Stability: West Germany's Road to Prosperity 1948–1959." In *Postwar Economic Reconstruction and Lessons for the East Today*, edited by Rudiger Dornbusch, Wilhelm Nölling and Richard Layard. Cambridge: MIT Press, 1993.

Grant, Wyn. "Agricultural Policy and Protectionism." In *The Sage Handbook of European Studies*, edited by Chris Rumford, 260–76. Los Angeles: SAGE, 2009.

Griffiths, Richard T. "The Dutch Economic Miracle." In *The Economic Development of the Netherlands since 1870*, edited by Jan Luiten van Zanden, 173–86. Aldershot: Edward Elgar, 1996.

Haas, Ernst B. *Beyond the Nation-State: Functionalism and International Organization*. London: ECPR Press/Stanford University Press, 2008.

Hacke, Christian. "Traditions and Stops in the German Republic: 1949–1987." In *The Germans 1945–1990*, edited by Oded Heilbronner and Moshe Zimmermann. Jerusalem: Magnes [in Hebrew], 1998.

Hallstein, Walter. *Europe in the Making*. London: Allen and Unwin, 1972.

———. *United Europe: Challenge and Opportunity*. London: Oxford University Press, 1962.

Hoekman, Bernard M., and M. M. Kostecki. *The Political Economy of the World Trading System: The WTO and Beyond*, 2nd ed. Oxford: Oxford University Press, 2001.

Hoffmann, Stanley. "Obstinate or Obsolete? The Fate of the Nation-State and the Case of Western Europe." *Daedalus* 95, no. 3 (1966): 862–915.

Irwin, Douglas A. "The GATT's Contribution to Economic Recovery in Post-War Western Europe." Cambridge: National Bureau of Economic Research, 1994.

Jones, Alun. *The New Germany: A Human Geography*. Chichester: Wiley & Sons, 1994.

Jovanović, Miroslav N. *The Economics of International Integration*. Cheltenham: Edward Elgar Publishing, 2015.

Kaldor, Nicholas. "Inflation and Recession in the World Economy." *The Economic Journal* 86, no. 344 (1976): 703–14.

Knudsen, Ann-Christina L. *Farmers on Welfare: The Making of Europe's Common Agricultural Policy*. Ithaca: Cornell University Press, 2009.

Küsters, Hanns Jürgen. "Walter Hallstein and the Negotiations on the Treaties of Rome 1955–57." In *Walter Hallstein: The Forgotten European?*, edited by Wilfried Loth, William Wallace and Wolfgang Wessels, 60–81: Springer, 1998.

Lampert, Heinz. "The Social Market Economy in the German Republic: Origin, Perception, Development and Problems." In *The Germans 1945–1990*, edited by Oded Heilbronner and Moshe Zimmermann. Jerusalem: Magnes [in Hebrew], 1998.

Laqueur, Walter. *Europe since Hitler*. London: Weidenfeld and Nicolson, 1970.

Larson, Deborah Welch. "Crisis Prevention and the Austrian State Treaty." *International Organization* 41, no. 1 (1987): 27–60.

Lindberg, Leon N., and Stuart A. Scheingold. *Europe's Would-Be Polity: Patterns of Change in the European Community*. Englewood Cliffs: Prentice-Hall, 1970.

Lipkin, David. "The Technocrats of the Common Market." *Davar*, July 30, 1965.

Loth, Wilfried, William Wallace, and Wolfgang Wessels. *Walter Hallstein: The Forgotten European?* Houndmills: Macmillan, 1998.

Ludlow, Peter. "The European Commission." In *The New European Community: Decisionmaking and Institutional Change*, edited by Robert O. Keohane and Stanley Hoffmann. Boulder: Westview Press, 1991.

Martines, Francesca. "Foreign Commercial Policy." In *Italy and EC Membership Evaluated*, edited by Francesco Francioni, 158–75. New York: St. Martin's, 1992.

McCormick, John. *Understanding the European Union: A Concise Introduction*. 3rd ed. Houndmills: Palgrave Macmillan, 2005.

Merkl, Peter Hans. *German Foreign Policies, West and East: Toward a New Balance of Osptolitik*. Santa Barbara: ABC-CLIO, 1974.

Milward, Alan S. *The European Rescue of the Nation-State*. London: Routledge, 1992.

———. *The Reconstruction of Western Europe, 1945–51*. London: Routledge, 2003.

Narjes, Karl-Heinz. "Walter Hallstein and the Early Phase of the EEC." In *Walter Hallstein: The Forgotten European?*, edited by Wilfried Loth, William Wallace and Wolfgang Wessels, 109–30: Springer, 1998.

Noël, Emile. "Walter Hallstein: A Personal Testimony." In *Walter Hallstein: The Forgotten European?*, edited by Wilfried Loth, loc>William Wallace and Wolfgang Wessels, 131–4: Springer, 1998.

Nugent, Neill. *The European Commission*. Houndmills: Palgrave, 2001.

Parker, Geoffrey. *The Logic of Unity: A Geography of the European Economic Community*. 2nd ed. London: Longman, 1975.

Pedersen, Thomas. *European Union and the EFTA Countries: Enlargement and Integration*. London: Pinter, 1994.

Peterson, John, and Elizabeth E. Bomberg. *Decision-Making in the European Union*. London: Macmillan, 1999.

Postan, Michael Moïssey. *An Economic History of Western Europe 1945–1964*. Oxford: Routledge, 2013.

Roberts, Geoffrey Keith. *West German Politics*. London: Macmillan, 1972.

Saint-Paul, Gilles. "Economic Reconstruction in France: 1945–1958." Chap. 4 In *Postwar Economic Reconstruction and Lessons for the East Today*, edited by Rudiger Dornbusch, Wilhelm Nölling and Richard Layard, 83–114. Cambridge: MIT Press, 1993.

Sampson, Anthony. *The New Europeans: A Guide to the Workings, Institutions and Character of Contemporary Western Europe*. London: Hodder and Stoughton, 1968.

Sasse, Christoph. *Decision Making in the European Community*. New York: Praeger, 1977.

Schwarz, Hans-Peter. *Konrad Adenauer: From the German Empire to the Federal Republic*. Providence: Berghahn Books, 1995.

Singleton, John, and Paul L. Robertson. "Britain, Butter, and European Integration, 1957–1964." *The Economic History Review* 50, no. 2 (1997): 327–47.

Spaak, Paul-Henri. "A New Effort to Build Europe." *Foreign Affairs* 43, no. 2 (1965): 199–208.

——. *The Continuing Battle: Memoirs of a European, 1936–1966*. Boston: Little Brown, 1971.

Steunenberg, Bernard, and Jacobus Johannes Adrianus Thomassen. *The European Parliament: Moving toward Democracy in the EU*. Lanham: Rowman & Littlefield, 2002.

Tinbergen, Jan. *International Economic Integration*. Amsterdam: Elsevier, 1954.

Trebilcock, M. J., and Robert Howse. *The Regulation of International Trade*. 3rd ed. London: Routledge, 2005.

Urwin, Derek W. *The Community of Europe: A History of European Integration since 1945*. London: Routledge, 2014.

van Zanden, Jan Luiten. "The Economic Development of the Netherlands and Belgium and the 'Success' of Benelux, 1945–1958." In *The Economic Development of the Netherlands since 1870*, edited by Jan Luiten van Zanden, 187–203. Aldershot: Edward Elgar, 1996.

——, ed. *The Economic Development of the Netherlands since 1870*. Aldershot: Edward Elgar, 1996.

——. *The Economic History of the Netherlands, 1914–1995: A Small Open Economy in the "Long" Twentieth Century*. London: Routledge, 1998.

Verdun, Amy. "Economic Growth and Global Competiveness: From Rome to Maastricht to Lisbon." In *The Sage Handbook of European Studies*, edited by Chris Rumford. Los Angeles: Sage, 2009.

Viner, Jacob. *The Customs Union Issue*. Oxford: Oxford University Press, 2014 [1950].

Von der Groeben, Hans. "Walter Hallstein as President of the Commission." In *Walter Hallstein: The Forgotten European?*, edited by Wilfried Loth, William Wallace and Wolfgang Wessels, 95–108: Springer, 1998.

Weigall, David, and Peter M. R. Stirk. *The Origins and Development of the European Community*. Leicester: Leicester University Press, 1992.

Wessels, Wolfgang. "The EC Council: The Community's Decisionmaking Center." In *The New European Community: Decisionmaking and Institutional Change*, edited by Robert O. Keohane and Stanley. Hoffmann. Boulder: Westview Press, 1991.

White, Brian. *Understanding European Foreign Policy*. Houndmills: Palgrave, 2001.

Wilkes, George, ed. *Britain's Failure to Enter the European Community, 1961–63: The Enlargement Negotiations and Crises in European, Atlantic, and Commonwealth Relations*. London: Frank Cass, 1997.

2   The Israeli economy confronts the Common Market challenge

A blooming economy

During the first decade of its existence (1948–58), Israel made significant strides in developing its economy: for example, doubling the extent of cultivated land and more than trebling its industrial products.[1] Israel succeeded in absorbing huge waves of immigration, thus quickly trebling the country's population from 850,000 inhabitants in 1949 to 2.5 million in 1965—demographic growth of unprecedented dimensions in modern history.[2] The vast majority of immigrants arriving during these years possessed no appreciable capital, and occasionally they arrived with nothing at all. Thus, immigration obviously constituted a huge challenge for the nascent state, forcing the Israeli government to adopt an austerity policy until 1951, which consisted mainly of strict price supervision, as well as the rationing of food and other basic necessities.[3] At the same time, the government sought to solve the growing problem of unemployment—the result of large waves of immigration and soldiers returning home from war—by means of extensive public investment. This was financed by the unrestrained printing of money, causing runaway inflation.[4] Up until 1954, the demographic surge continued to constitute a difficult challenge and caused the Israeli economy serious difficulties: considerable unemployment, mainly among new immigrants; inflationary pressures due to the government's propensity to cover the deficit by printing money, and a shortage of the foreign currency necessary to finance imports and repay debt. However, in 1954, the situation changed, with the beginning of a rising economic tide that continued until the mid-1960s. The gross national product (GNP) rose dramatically during that period: 9% annually, while GDP per capita rose by 5% per annum.[5] In the years 1952–1954, GDP per capita stood at $445 per year, which ranked Israel as a moderately high-income developing country (compare with Argentina—$460, and Ireland—$410), yet still far from the conventional level for developed countries (Britain—$780, the US—$1,870). Within two years (in 1956) GDP per capita jumped to $596, one of the steepest rises during the period,[6] and by 1965 had reached $1,100. In 1964, the government budget was 23 times (!) larger than it had been a decade and a half earlier: rising from 360 million Israeli pounds in 1950 to 8 billion Israeli pounds. This improved the standard of living in the country: average per capita meat consumption rose by 38%, while consumption of fresh fruit increased by 50%. In 1965, some 90% of Israeli households owned a radio, 75% possessed a refrigerator and 30% had a washing machine.[7] Unemployment fell so much that by the end of the 1950s the Israeli economy enjoyed virtually full employment.[8] Inflation declined to 5%, in line with the concurrent Western world standard.[9] Israeli exports also blossomed at a dizzying pace. While in 1950, Israel exported goods worth $46 million, by 1962, the value of Israeli exports had risen to $480 million.[10] Yet at the end of the 1950s, Israel was still forced to import a large portion of the country's necessities, among them weapons, cars, consumer goods and raw materials (especially fuel). Indeed, the domestic market could not provide for the existing food demands.[11] As a result, despite the persistent growth of Israeli exports, the gap between expenditures on imports and export revenues remained. In 1956, Israeli imports totaled $560 million while exported goods totaled $170 million—a ratio of more than 3:1 in favor of imports. Seeking to reduce Israel's trade balance deficit and thus attend to the foreign currency shortage, decision makers needed to increase exports while simultaneously reducing imports. Among the measures adopted to achieve this end was a promotion campaign urging the public to reduce consumption. This was doomed to failure from the outset and decision makers were soon forced to employ more "coercive" tools, such as a wage freeze.[12] However, these efforts too proved ineffective. The key lay in ensuring that Israel would become an exporting country similar to small developed countries such as the Netherlands and Norway.

Agriculture—Israel's most important export sector

From the moment of Israel's birth, agriculture occupied a central place in its economy. The lion's share of new immigrants arriving in Israel between 1949 and 1961 were referred to the agricultural sector for clearly ideological reasons: the national ethos revered the cultivation of the land. Many, including Prime Minister David Ben-Gurion and Finance Minister Levi Eshkol, viewed the "return to the land" as an important Zionist value,[13] a symbol of the Jewish People's new life. However, other incentives also drove this policy of encouraging agriculture. The flight of the Arabs during the War of Independence had vacated abundant arable lands, an available resource worth exploiting.[14] The Israeli population's food requirements exceeded the capabilities of domestic production, thus generating a need for additional farmers. Furthermore, dispatching new immigrants to agricultural settlements helped to disperse the population and ensure its settlement in locations of strategic importance.[15] At the end of the 1950s, a large portion of the Israeli economy continued to rely on the agricultural sector. While some of Israel's decision makers viewed industrial development as the key to the country's future, agriculture continued to occupy a significant place in domestic production. Considerably greater national resources were funneled into developing the agricultural sector than those directed to the industrial sector—more than double.[16] In 1948, more than 110,000 inhabitants lived in 326 agricultural settlements, while by 1962, this number had trebled, reaching 303,000, with the number of agricultural settlements rising to 706. In 1958, 17.6% of Israel's labor force was employed in agriculture—a figure higher than that in industrial countries such as Germany and Belgium but lower than agrarian countries like France and Italy.[17] While agriculture commanded a fairly important, though not dominant, position in the Israeli economy, its share of exports was particularly significant: at the end of the 1950s, Israeli exports were largely centered on agricultural products. Of $140 million worth of exports in 1958, some $56.6 million were agricultural produce, $49.6 million were industrial products and $34.3 million were refined diamonds.[18]

Among Israeli agricultural sectors designated for export, one was by far the most conspicuous: citrus fruits. Despite accounting for only 8% of the volume of Israeli agricultural production, almost all exports prior to the state's establishment and in its first years were citrus products. Within ten years, from 1948 to 1957, the land area utilized for growing citrus fruit doubled from 120 thousand decares (46.33 sq miles) to 250 thousand decares (96.52 sq miles).[19] Yet at the end of the 1950s, the importance of growing citrus fruit had already declined; due to the development of other export sectors it accounted no more than 25% of Israeli exports. However, citrus fruit remained Israel's number one export product and indisputably its most important agricultural export—almost 80% of total exports in this sector. The pinnacle of Israeli citrus fruits was the Shamouti orange, best known by its popular name, the "Jaffa orange." Although the Israelis marketed the Jaffa orange as a symbol of the success of the Zionist enterprise, Palestinian Arabs had in fact improved the fruit and should be credited with the worldwide reputation which it enjoys to this very day. The Shamouti was born at the beginning of the nineteenth century as a result of a fortuitous event: Palestinian growers identified a random mutation of a different variety of orange and, recognizing its advantages, decided to cultivate it. Indeed, the Shamouti enjoys three significant advantages over other varieties of orange: its peel is easily removed, its thickness protects the fruit from pests, and its flesh has no seeds, offering a more pleasant eating experience. Due to this combination of factors developed several years after its first cultivation, the Shamouti became a hit among orange lovers and the fruit quickly found its way to overseas markets. The location of its cultivation, in Israel's central plain, gave the Shamouti its nickname, drawing on the largest and most recognizable city of that region, from which the fruit was exported to destinations all over the world: the port city of Jaffa. Rapidly, Jaffa orange cultivation grew to such proportions that unemployed individuals from neighboring countries descended on Palestine during the fruit-picking season, knowing they would find abundant work at reasonable wages. The Jews arriving in Palestine in the first waves of immigration quickly integrated into this already thriving sector, enjoying its success. The Jaffa orange became a symbol of coexistence between Jews and Arabs and its cultivation fostered particularly close cooperation. Jews worked in Arab orchards and vice versa, while in many cases cooperation in sorting, packing and marketing enabled the producers to reduce their costs.

Following the flight of Palestinian Arabs during the 1948 war, the Israeli government expropriated abandoned orchards, encouraging Israeli farmers to replace the Arabs in this agriculture sector. A central government body was established to facilitate the marketing of the Jaffa orange, named "The Citrus Marketing Board of Israel" (in fact, the continuation of a body established by the British). The marketing board was responsible for coordinating sales of the fruit, for both export and the domestic market. Farmers sent all their produce to Board-authorized contractors who sorted and designated, based on quality, for export, domestic consumption or industry. Only a small quantity of the produce—7%—was earmarked for the domestic market—these were relatively small fruits or those less attractive in appearance—while more than two-thirds was designated for export. The rest of produce, approximately 25%, was intended for industry.[20] The export of Israeli citrus fruit was geographically limited, and competed directly with other exporting countries. Israel's climate was similar to that of Southern European and North African countries which likewise exported citrus fruit. The tropical nations of equatorial Africa were too poor to purchase Israeli fruit in large quantities and satisfied themselves with the abundance of tropical fruit grown in their own lands. The US, with its huge citrus output from California and Florida, was the leading global citrus exporter and therefore had no need to import Israeli products. East European countries constituted only a limited market for Israeli citrus fruit; for both economic and political reasons, no more than 7% of Israel's citrus production went to those countries.[21] Therefore, the most important destination for Israeli citrus fruit were Western and Northern European countries, which imported 90% of the citrus fruits they consumed.[22] Among the six Common Market countries, only Italy grew citrus fruits; however, 70% of its produce was designated for internal consumption and only 30% for export.[23] Italian orchards were able to supply only around 6% of the demand for oranges among the EEC's population, leaving a large vacuum, which their competitors (such as Israel) filled. Thus, unsurprisingly the majority of Israeli citrus fruit was dispatched to Western Europe: Britain absorbed approximately one-third of Israel's citrus exports, while The Six purchased 40%.[24] Nevertheless, citrus fruits were never considered a "basic" commodity with an inelastic or solid demand. Despite Europe's appetite for juicy oranges (average consumption in the Netherlands and Germany was respectively 18 and 13 kilograms of oranges per person per year),[25] many alternatives existed, such as fruits grown abundantly in Europe (apples, pears and so forth) and industrially produced sweets, making the demand for oranges subject to constant fluctuation. Moreover, the Israeli orange had formidable competitors. The Maghreb countries and Spain exported oranges and enjoyed greater proximity to European markets, as well as lower labor and packaging costs. Although the Israeli orange remained competitive thanks to its quality and efficient marketing methods,[26] Israeli growers and marketers needed to strive constantly to maintain the Jaffa orange's share of the European market, typically among the more prosperous sectors.[27] Aside from citrus fruits and related products (such as juice), Israel also exported large quantities of wheat, eggs, oils and peanuts. However, these are of lesser important to our story.

The future of Israel's economy lies in industry!

In 1955, Pinchas Sapir was appointed Minister of Trade and Industry, an important reference point in the evolution of the Israeli economy.[28] Sapir was known for the miracles he had performed as assistant CEO of Mekorot.[29] After the establishment of the state, he served in several senior positions, such as Director General of the Ministry of Defense and later Finance Minister. Sapir was endowed with an extraordinary level of energy; he worked most of the day and demanded similar dedication from his employees. He was a "bulldozer," tirelessly striving to achieve his objectives, and often did not hesitate to employ manipulative politics and personal connections to advance his professional goals, as well as his own career, thus creating the image of an uninhibited politician. Yet he led an extremely modest life; both his public dedication and incorruptibility were exemplary. Although a politician and not a professional, he nevertheless insisted on learning the technical aspects of his domain, made possible by his phenomenal memory. However, at times this proved to be a stumbling block, because he tended to rely too greatly on his knowledge and intervene in matters that called for genuine expertise.[30] Sapir understood that Israel's economy was suffering from a severe problem and that it was his responsibility to find a solution to this. Israel imported much more than it exported, generating a sharp deficit in its trade balance and a constant need for foreign currency. The country's balance of payments remained in a state of equilibrium only thanks to the external assistance it received from the US and reparations in the form of final products from Germany. It was clear to Sapir that Israel's reliance on these "training wheels" could not continue and that the massive imports which the country required must be financed by other means: clearly this could only be achieved by dramatically increasing exports. He was also convinced that the country needed to assume a central role in funneling capital to predetermined investment channels:[31] yet it was unclear exactly which sectors were worthy of investment. Despite the significant contribution of agricultural exports in the 1950s, in the long term Israel lacked the land resources necessary to become a major exporter of agricultural products, and in addition did not possess sufficient quantities of water to increase its agricultural yield significantly. The latter problem was especially acute: Israel could barely supply sufficient water to irrigate half of its 5 million dunams of arable land, according to the most optimistic assessments,[32] without considering the expenses of conveying the water: most of the country's water sources were situated in the north, while its arable land was located in the center and south.[33] Moreover, two of Israel's major crop exports—citrus fruits and cotton—required large quantities of water.[34]

Ironically, in a country, which suffers from chronic water shortages, the export of oranges and cotton was equivalent to exporting water. Along with its limited agricultural infrastructure, Israel possessed scant raw materials (with the exception of Dead Sea minerals). Unable to compete with the cheap labor costs of countries which enjoyed a plentiful labor force, such as India and Japan, Israel could not hope to become a supplier of cheap industrial products (i.e. sustain mass industry). Its advantages lay in high technology and skilled manpower which, nevertheless, worked for lower wages than laborers in Western and Northern Europe and the US. Sapir understood that economic rationale dictated focusing on the export of high-quality goods such as luxury products, targeting markets in developed countries.[35]

Yet a major problem in the Israeli industry necessitated that a solution be rectified before the country's factories could become a competitive force in the global market: the majority of Israeli factories suffered from severe production inefficiencies. Most of them worked one shift per day—below the accepted standard for successful factories in the developed world, which operated two or even three shifts daily—because the products they manufactured were too expensive or too low quality for export.[36] Naturally, the first victims of this method were Israeli consumers, who necessarily purchased low-quality products at high prices. Numerous economic experts argued that the only way to boost the economy of a small country such as Israel was to develop its exports via specialization in several key sectors.[37] Sapir intended to advance this approach using strategic industrial policy, granting government assistance that would enable leading factories to reduce their manufacturing expenses and become internationally competitive. To this end, together with Finance Minister Levi Eshkol, Sapir implemented three primary measures: surcharges on imports, protecting Israeli products from foreign competition, and providing export subsidies via a mechanism of variable exchange rates.[38] Furthermore, they employed additional measures such as establishing a fund for extending loans to exporters and granting customs exemptions and discounts on payments of property tax. Aside from direct assistance, the government supported projects which were intended to facilitate export, such as organizing overseas fairs and exhibitions, publishing professional catalogues and advertisements, providing commercial advice, and conducting market research.[39]

Thanks to Sapir's policy of industrial support, this sector was responsible for most of the progress made in the Israeli economy: between 1956 and 1961, employment in the Israeli industry grew by 50% and industrial output rose by 80%.[40] Numerous factories were established in a range of sectors: diamond refinement, clothing, quarries (potassium, bromine, copper) and others. Three industries received particular support: food, textiles and metal processing. By the mid-1960s, there were more than 10,000 factories in Israel, four times the number in existence before the establishment of the state. In 1952, some 98,000 workers were employed in industry, 56% of them in large factories (i.e. with more than ten workers); by 1965, these figures rose to 223,000 and 74% respectively.[41] In 1965, around 434 million Israeli pounds were invested in Israeli industry,[42] compared with only 20 million pounds in 1950.[43] The significance of industry was also expressed in the volume of the young country's total exports: between 1948 and 1961, Israel's industrial exports grew by a factor of 18(!) while parallel growth in agriculture rose only by a factor of 2.5.[44] In 1959, industrial exports surpassed agricultural exports for the first time, making it universally clear that Israel's economic future depended upon industry.

While Israeli-refined diamonds were making their way mainly to the American market,[45] Israel exported a very broad variety of industrial products in small quantities to Western and Northern European countries. The Northern European market was particularly convenient for Israeli products for two reasons: in terms of climate they were very different, yet their standard of living was similar.[46] Many Israeli exports were high-quality luxury products (fashion and leather industry, diamonds, works of art) and naturally this required target consumers with relatively high purchasing power.[47] Dependence on this type of products is especially vital for a country such as Israel, which lacks natural resources, must import most of its raw materials and therefore its profits rely entirely on added value.[48] Europe's geographic proximity to Israel, in comparison to other more distant developed countries, was an additional consideration in directing Israeli products to Europe because proximity reduced transportation expenses. Export to nearby Arab markets was impossible due to the tension between Israel and its neighbors, as well as the low income levels in these countries.

At the end of the 1950s, Israel's economic decision makers attributed particular importance to the textile industry, which had been the steam engine driving the British Industrial Revolution in the second half of the eighteenth century and the first half of the nineteenth century. Traditionally, for several fundamental reasons, this was a comfortable transitional stage for developing economies en route to a modern economy: first, the textile industry requires a relatively simple level of mechanization compared with other industries, without any need for especially sophisticated technology to perform the processes involved, e.g., weaving, looms, knitting, finishing and coloring. Thus, the textile business can be maintained even in the absence of a labor force educated in engineering or technological proficiency. Second, the textile industry is labor intensive, requiring numerous pairs of working hands to perform the various tasks and therefore is especially suited to economies with an available labor force but relatively little capital. Third, the demand for textiles is extensive and steady: textiles are an essential product and willing buyers will always exist. Finally, many Jews in the Diaspora were traditionally employed in textile production and therefore Israel benefited from the knowledge and experience of many "experts," giving the country an advantage in this domain.[49] These attributes made the textile industry especially attractive for those who regarded the transition from agricultural reliance to an industrial-rich economy as Israel's economic future. First among them, as was mentioned, was Sapir, who considered the nurturing of the textile industry to be an important transitional phase on the path to modernizing Israel's economy.

Sapir's optimism was based on a success story with which every Israeli—man or woman, old or young, long-standing resident, or new immigrant—was well acquainted. In 1934, a Jewish-Austrian businessman named Erich Moller established a factory near Haifa which he named phonetically after the adjacent Arab village – Ata. Within several years, the Ata Textile Factory had become one of the most impressive economic successes in Mandatory Palestine. During the Second World War, Ata provided a respectable portion of the British Army's needs in the Middle East,[50] and following the establishment of the state, became the "national clothes supplier," creating the khaki clothes that had almost no competitor in the Israeli wardrobe. By the mid-1950s, the factory employed approximately 1,200 workers, making it one of Israel's economic giants; in 1952, it manufactured 40 million square meters of cloth per year, 50% of which was exported,[51] and by 1954, the total value of the factory's exports was one million dollars, 20% of all Israeli textile exports.[52] Ata was not the only example indicating the export potential of the textile industry. The Lodgia factory, which specialized in manufacturing socks, exported 70% of its products, valued in 1958 at $350,000.

These success stories inspired Minister Sapir, who believed that the new textile industry would provide a solution for unemployed immigrants with limited vocational training. Although it would require capital investment, the amount would be far less than other technology-intensive industries. Sapir planned to establish textile factories in border settlements across the country, staffing them with immigrants who had been in the country for some time, and in so doing realize dual goals: (1) guiding the Israeli economy on a path of intensified industrialization, and (2) downscaling the agricultural sector while at the same time settling peripheral regions or strengthening already existing but weak border settlements. With extraordinary energy, he began to coax rich individuals to invest in establishing textile factories at various locations in Israel. In one instance, he persuaded a Jewish investor to supply the capital for a large textile factory in Kiryat Gat, claiming that the city was situated on the outskirts of Tel Aviv, only a 30-minute drive from the metropolis. To prove how attractive the location was, he himself escorted the investor on a trip to Kiryat Gat during the early morning hours, a time when the roads were empty. Whether it was due to the success of this ploy or other factors, the investor supplied the necessary sum to establish the Polgat factory in Kiryat Gat.[53] In 1961, a similar enterprise was launched in a remote city in the heart of the Negev, 20 kilometers from Beersheva. Sapir succeeded in persuading the owner of the successful Kitan textile factory in central Israel to set up a branch in the distant development town of Dimona, which was populated by new immigrants, mainly of Moroccan origin. Many, including the leaders of the textile industry, doubted that the factory would succeed in view of its distance from the industry's hub (it is important to bear in mind that textile production typically requires several stages in different designated factories). Yet the skeptics were proven wrong: the factory succeeded in maintaining itself and even became profitable. Polgat and Kitan are only two examples of the momentum with which the textile industry advanced, encouraged by Sapir. Factories sprouted up like mushrooms after the rain—in Jerusalem, Kiryat Shemona, Afula, Beit She'an, Beersheva, Ashdod, Netivot, Ofakim and other locations.[54] This was in no small part due to particularly convenient conditions and government incentives: loans on preferential conditions, setting a special exchange rate for encouraging exports and providing incentives for increased output.[55] The government also made efforts to secure export markets to guarantee the future of this young industry because domestic demand was insufficient to support the number of factories established; selling products overseas was the only way to ensure profits. Israeli textile factories could not compete with their Asian counterparts (for example, in South Korea), yet the quality of their products was attractive to 'pampered' markets which enjoyed a high-income level. In this case too, Western Europe was an important potential customer. Already in 1955, textile products constituted 17.1% of all Israeli exports to The Six; this percentage grew in subsequent years as textiles became one of the chief industrial products exported to European markets. To increase profitability, the government began investing in growing cotton rather than importing it. In 1953, an initial trial, sowing cotton in over 2,800 dunams of land, yielded fairly good results, although from the outset the farmers faced a series of challenges, including a destructive attack of bollworms which destroyed a full season's harvest, and low labor productivity—cotton picking requires great skill and even an experienced Israeli worker was barely able to produce 50 kg per day (compared with 100 kg in the US). Yet in 1958 the extent of cotton sowed in Israel had reached 60,000 dunams, supplying almost 50% of the thread required for the blossoming textile industry.[56]

The Common Market challenge to Israeli exports

For Israel, the creation of the Common Market constituted a special problem. Until 1948, the Yishuv (the Jewish population in pre-state Israel) exported most of its goods to Britain and the Middle East. Following the War of Independence, Israeli exports were no longer welcome in the latter. While Britain continued to constitute an important export destination, Israeli exporters had to seek new markets for their goods.[57] The US was a tempting destination due to its size, however the great geographical distance, at a time when transportation costs were very high, significantly reduced the number of products which could be sold at competitive prices yet remain profitable. The most successful and most-sold Israeli products and services in the American market were refined diamonds and tourism. Western Europe became an alternate destination for those goods which were once sold to the Yishuv's neighbors. At the end of the 1950s, a considerable portion of Israeli exports, both industrial and agricultural, were dispatched to The Six – now a sizeable bloc populated by 160 million people, with the relative share of the market expected to grow in subsequent years. In 1955, EEC member states purchased 13.2% of all Israeli exports; by 1956, this figure had climbed to 17.5%, reaching 24% in 1957.[58] At the end of 1960, the EEC's relative share of Israeli exports passed 30%.[59] Citrus fruit was an important component, constituting almost one-half of all Israeli exports to The Six. As of 1957, more than 28% of Israeli citrus exports went to The Six, explaining the great importance which Israel ascribed to guaranteeing convenient conditions for continued Israeli citrus fruit exports to those countries. The establishment of the Common Market threatened to sabotage this, by imposing assorted customs duties on Israeli citrus fruits. France, seeking to protect the citrus growers in Algeria, increased customs duties to 35%. Countries that did not produce their own citrus fruits, imposed much lower customs duties: 0% in Germany and 13% in Benelux countries.[60] Israel expected that by the end of the EEC consolidation process, the common external tariff would be fixed at 20%. Israel sold very little fruit in France and thus the reduced customs rate in that country would have limited positive effect on its exports. However, Israel viewed the sharp rise in German customs duties (from 0% to 20%) as a harsh decree. If citrus exporters all over the world would be forced to contend with this customs rate, the problem would be considerably lesser. Yet some of Israel's competitors, i.e., Italian citrus growers, were part of the EEC and thus exempt from customs duties. Furthermore, it was expected that other competitors would enjoy similar benefits in the near future. At the Venice Conference of 1956, France stipulated as a condition for joining the emerging EEC that France's African colonies would be accorded a special status and benefit from the Common Market's commercial advantages. Therefore, it was presumed that Algeria, Tunisia and Morocco—all citrus exporting countries and therefore Israel's competitors—would sooner or later form association with the EEC. Spain too, another important exporter of citrus fruit, was likely to join the EEC at a later stage. These developments would reduce the competitiveness of Israeli fruit, blocking, or at least severely affecting, one of its most important markets. Significantly, Israeli citrus growers were highly sensitive to changes in overseas demand because almost 70% of their output was designated for export, whereas American or Italian citrus fruits were largely intended for the domestic market.[61]

Citrus fruit was the most important Israeli export threatened by the establishment of the Common Market, yet it was far from the only product in this position. The Economic Department at the Israeli Ministry of Foreign Affairs enumerated around a hundred additional products which would be affected by the creation of a common external tariff policy among The Six; for some, the damage was liable to be particularly serious. As was noted above, in the absence of raw materials, Israeli industry specialized in processing and upgrading imported raw materials, a significant portion of which originated from The Six. Therefore, as will be explained later, when Israel exported final products back to the EEC's countries, the impact of customs duties had an increased effect. The odds of Israeli exporters selling these products at competitive prices while still reaping a profit were very low.[62]

The threat to the future of Israel's exports to Western Europe was accompanied by an additional problem. Accessibility to potential markets was an important indicator in assessing the advisability of investing in Israeli factories. Potential investors needed to consider the export options for specific products when deciding whether to open a factory in Israel or at another location. While many investors in the nascent Israeli industrial sector were Jews whose motives were no less ideological than financial, they too were not prepared to risk their investment and sought to guarantee potential profit. Moreover, the government attempted to broaden the circle of investors, attracting also non-Jews. The impact of the Common Market on Israeli exports was liable to deter investors from choosing Israel as the destination for their foreign direct investment and capital, making it more profitable to invest in a factory situated in a EEC member state, or a country whose products were exempt from customs by virtue of their association with that body.[63] At the beginning of the 1960s, faced with the possibility that Britain would join the EEC, Israel was increasingly concerned for the future of its exports. Israeli decision makers reasonably assumed that all Western

European countries and the majority of former British territories in Africa would eventually join or form an association with the EEC.[64] If these concerns were to materialize, then the overall volume of Israel's exports to the EEC at risk would increase by at least 60%.[65]

Thus, the formation of the EEC presented a serious challenge to Israel. The young country's economy, just beginning to take off, was liable to crash into the new walls which the Common Market was rapidly erecting. Israeli decision makers and diplomats needed to find a way to break through these walls. There were a number of ways in which Israel could confront the challenges posed by the Common Market. The first was full membership in the EEC according to Article 237, a solution which would grant Israel all the economic and political advantages of the new framework. Indeed, immediately after the signing of the Treaty of Rome, certain Israelis expressed interest in a comprehensive investigation of this possibility, among them David Ben-Gurion, Israel's Prime Minister and Defense Minister, and Shimon Peres, Director General of the Ministry of Defense. In 1957, the latter conversed with one of the architects of European integration, Jean Monnet, who affirmed that this was a possibility, although it swiftly became evident that this assessment was not realistic.[66] A second option was to sign a limited commercial trade agreement meeting Israel's most urgent export needs. Israel's export structure was still centralistic, with ten main export products accounting for 90% of all exports to the EEC. An ad hoc arrangement ensuring the continued export of these goods was possible, even if it would involve significant problems, as will be discussed further below. A third option was a comprehensive agreement regarding a customs union or free trade area. It was believed at the time that such an arrangement necessitated association with the EEC based on Article 238 of the Treaty of Rome; this was perceived not only as the ideal solution in economic terms, but would also offer political advantages. "Association" was the closest possible connection with the EEC that a non-European country could achieve. Aside from preferential access to the Community's markets, association also involved technical and economic cooperation, financial assistance and perhaps even the prospect of full membership in the future.[67] Association also held political significance. In his book *Europe in the Making*, Walter Hallstein highlighted the differences between association and a regular trade agreement: "An association agreement consists of sustained institutional connections that constitute a sort of pact between the sides: a common goal materializes as countries associated with one another constitute one body, all made possible by common institutions and procedures."[68] Indeed, Israel's attraction to the EEC went beyond the economic sphere. Finding paths into this new entity—"Europe"—promised a reward far beyond mere economic benefits. It represented a solution to the existential problem, which gave the Israelis no rest—the persistent fear of a "second round" of hostilities in which Arab countries would seek to destroy the young state. "So long as the Arabs believe they have the power to destroy us, there will be no peace in the Middle East," stated a memorandum composed by the Israeli Ministry of Foreign Affairs at the end of 1956.[69] Thus, it is no wonder that the Israeli Foreign Minister defined an arrangement with the EEC as an existential Israeli interest, second only to the security issue in terms of importance.[70] Ben-Gurion too viewed this as critical to Israel's future.[71]

What assets were available to Israeli diplomacy in tackling the challenge of the emerging Common Market? It appears that Israel's bargaining power vis-à-vis The Six was quite meager. Israel suffered from three serious limitations: it was a tiny country, geographically disconnected from Europe and politically at odds with the Arab world. The Israeli economy was not large enough to make it an attractive economic partner. Under such conditions, the country's ability to draw concessions from the emerging EEC was very limited. When even far more substantial entities than Israel (the US, for example) faced difficulties in ensuring their interests vis-à-vis The Six, how could Israel possibly surpass them in this task? Moreover, Israel was neither situated along European borders nor a former colony of one of The Six: there was no apparent justification for special consideration and any concession or goodwill gesture toward Israel was liable to provoke similar demands from numerous other countries. In political terms, association with Israel was dangerous and could be detrimental to relations between The Six and Arab countries. This was an especially sensitive aspect for countries with a considerable presence in the Middle East, or that aspired to such a presence, such as France and Italy. Beyond Israel's specific limitations, other general factors concerning the EEC's structure and its decision-making procedures made it extremely complex for a country like Israel to achieve its aims. First, the EEC, in its early days, operated according to the "unanimous decision" principle. Each one of the six member states possessed the right of veto in the Council of Ministers, enabling it to quell any initiative or plan which seemed to oppose its own interests. Consequently, Israel would need to persuade all six countries, without exception, to assent to its requests. Second, powerful interest groups operating within the EEC opposed economic gestures toward Israel and did not hesitate to use all available means of influence to thwart them. For example, Italian orchard owners viewed Israeli citrus fruits as a threat to their exports, applying heavy pressure on the Italian government to oppose any concessions to Israel in this regard in the Community's institutions. Hence, Israel's chances of achieving a meaningful arrangement with the EEC appeared very low.

Yet Israeli decision makers and the administrative echelon alike were optimistic that it would be possible to obtain this goal. They based their optimism on the belief that they possessed a number of important assets, which they could utilize advantageously in this regard. The first asset was the moral argument and Israel's historic and cultural connection with Europe. Israel viewed Western Europe, primarily Germany, as owing a moral debt to the entire Jewish People and, consequently, the Jewish State. Numerous Jews who settled in Palestine and later Israel were of European extraction or were the descendants of Europeans. Admittedly, a significant portion of them willingly emigrated to Israel for Zionist reasons and were thus ostensibly not entitled to any special rights from the "Old Continent." Yet Jewish persecution in Europe, especially during the Holocaust, had created a moral (albeit not legal) basis for the view that Israel's population of European origin had been forcefully ejected. Would the European countries which had ousted their Jews now bring about their economic ruin? Although in geographical terms Israel was undisputedly not a part of the European continent, the Israelis sought to persuade the Europeans that, considering the country's historical and cultural ties, in essence Israel was European.

The second asset upon which the Israelis based their optimism was the belief that Israel could help European countries widen their influence in Asia and Africa. The Israelis argued that the former colonies were deterred and even disgusted by the prospect of European companies penetrating their economies, due to past ill feelings. Israel, as a developing country which had already established strong economic ties with numerous African countries, could serve as a convenient channel for renewed European penetration into Third World countries. The Israelis perceived the special relationship they had cultivated with France as a third asset. Since 1955, Israel and France had maintained close military and political cooperation; some viewed the relations between the two countries during that period as a sort of "tacit alliance."[72] For the French, Israel constituted a strategic asset at a time when their country was isolated from most Arab countries due to the war in Algeria. France wielded considerable influence in the framework of The Six, leading the Israelis to believe that they could exploit this influence to their advantage. In addition, the Israelis assumed that they were not completely without economic assets. Although the Israeli market, with its 2.25 million inhabitants, was not large, Israel imported far more from Western European countries than most other Middle Eastern countries. The trade balance (i.e. exports vs. imports) with The Six leaned sharply towards the latter and therefore Israel felt that it possessed an additional moral basis for demanding consideration of its interests.

As we shall see below, these "assets"—which infused Israeli hearts with confidence concerning their prospects with the EEC—were for the most part nothing more than pipedreams, a conspicuous case of wishful thinking. The Six never really viewed Israel as an economic or political asset but rather as a nuisance—not an opportunity to be exploited, but an obstacle to be surmounted. Nevertheless, in 1964, the EEC and its institutions agreed to sign an unprecedented agreement with Israel. Although limited in content, this was an extraordinary achievement for Israeli diplomacy—it had major implications, and created an undeniable connection between Israel and Europe, which served as the basis for future ties between the two.

Notes

1   ISA, FM, file 211/6, January 16, 1958. Hollis B. Chenery and Michael Bruno, "Development Alternatives in an Open Economy: The Case of Israel," *The Economic Journal* 72, no. 285 (1962).

2   In 1949, Israel's proportion of new immigrants stood at 266 new immigrants per 1,000 inhabitants; in 1950 this had declined to 154/1,000 and in 1951 was 132/1,000. For the sake of comparison, in 1854, the record year of immigration to the United States,

the proportion of immigrants to inhabitants was 16/1,000. In the record year of immigration to Argentina (1913) the comparative figure was 38/1,000: Don Patinkin, *The Israel Economy: The First Decade* (Jerusalem: Falk Institute for Economic Research in Israel [in Hebrew], 1960), 23.

3 Orit Rozin, "The Austerity Policy and the Rule of Law: Relations between Government and Public in Fledgling Israel," *Journal of Modern Jewish Studies* 4, no. 3 (2005).

4 Nadav Halevi and Ruth Klinov-Malul, *The Economic Development of Israel* (Jerusalem: Academin [in Hebrew], 1968).

5 Yoram Ben-Porath, "The Entwined Growth of Population and Product, 1922–1982," in *The Israeli Economy: Maturing through Crises*, ed. Yoram Ben-Porath (Cambridge: Harvard University Press, 1986); *The Israeli Economy: Growth Pangs* (Tel Aviv: Am Oved [Hebrew], 1989).To gain an impression of Israel's rate of growth during those years, one must consider the growth rate in other countries during the same period: 5% in Canada and France, 4% in the US and 3% in Britain. Even relative to developed countries experiencing booms, Israeli growth was unprecedented. Between the years 1950 and 1970, Israel's gross national product (GNP) rose at a rate of 9.7% per annum, while in Taiwan and Japan, the rise was more moderate, 8.4% and 8.6% respectively. See: Moshe Sirquin, "Economic Growth and Structural Change: An International Perspective," in *The Israeli Economy: Maturing through Crises*, ed. Yoram Ben-Porath (Cambridge: Harvard University Press, 1986).

6 Patinkin, 48.

7 See memorandum: Israël et la CEE, ISA, FM, file 3154/5, October 1966.

8 At the end of 1959, the number of unemployed workers fell to only 3,870, no more than 3% of the labor force. See: Yosef Goldstein, *Eshkol: A Biography* (Jerusalem: Keter, 2003), 410. Other sources indicate somewhat higher rates, i.e., 3.6% in 1961. See: Nadav Halevi and Ruth Klinov, *The Economic Development of Israel* (New York: Praeger, 1968).

9 Dan Giladi and Haim Ofaz, *Israel's Economy: Development, Characteristics, Policy* (Jerusalem: Ministry of Education, 1998).

10 *Davar*, July 19, 1963.

11 The surplus of imported food products and agricultural products in 1959 was 29.7%, a considerable improvement from the time of the state's establishment, when the surplus was 66.4%. See: Samuel Pohorilles, *Development and Planning in the Israeli Economy* (Tel Aviv: The Center for Agriculture Planning and Development [in Hebrew], 1969), 103.

12 David Horowitz, *Life in the Spotlight* (Ramat Gan: Masada, 1975), 140.

13 Baruch Kimmerling, *Zionism and Economy* (Cambridge: Schenkman Publishers, 1982).

14 The terminology "flight" is disputed. Nevertheless, this book does not engage with different narratives concerning the Israeli–Palestinian conflict. For more concerning the narratives and this conflict, see: Robert I. Rotberg, ed. *Israeli and Palestinian Narratives of Conflict: History's Double Helix* (Bloomington: Indiana University Press, 2006).

15 Halevi and Klinov.

16 In Israel during the mid-1950s, 72% of all government investments were funneled into the agricultural sector whereas 26% were invested in the industrial sector. A. Kidan, "Extension of Production and the Trade Balance," *The Economic Quarterly*, no. 13/14 (1956). Only after Pinchas Sapir became Minister of Trade and Industry in 1955 did the funds earmarked for encouraging industry increase, by 600%: David Levi-Faur, *Pinchas Sapir and Israel's Economic Development* (Tel Aviv: Sapir Development Center at Tel Aviv University, 1993), 13–19.

17 Rapport intérimaire: les relations entre la Communauté européenne et l'État d'Israël, EUA, BAC 7/1973-12, March 28, 1965.

18 Memorandum, ISA, FM, file 1953/5, December 18, 1959. In the context of diamond exports, the export of refined diamonds is an important sector, but its scope may be misleading in terms of other economic implications because the economic

value of diamonds increases significantly after the refinement stage. Therefore, the significant added value does not necessarily imply a corresponding comprehensive manufacturing activity.

19 One decare (1,000 square meters) is equivalent to the local Ottoman unit of the *dunam* in use since 1928 (prior to this, the size of a dunam was 919.3 square meters). The increase in land areas for growing citrus fruits, combined with the adoption of various measures for increasing yield and reducing production costs, elevated the Israeli citrus industry to a very competitive position in world markets. See: Government of Israel, "Ministry of Agriculture Report," in *Israel Government Yearbook 1962/3*, ed. Government of Israel (Tel Aviv: Information Center [in Hebrew], 1963).

20 Shimon Ravid, *Agriculture in Israel: Detailed Planning in a Mixed Economy* (Rehovot: Center for Agriculture Economics, 1979).

21 M. Klebanski, "Israel Foreign Trade in the European Free Trade Area," *The Economic Quarterly*, no. 17/18 (1957).

22 Memorandum of the Ministry of Agriculture, ISA, FM, file 1954/12, December 21, 1961. It is important to bear in mind that agricultural products are especially sensitive to geographical distance from the target markets because the shelf life of these products is particularly short. For this reason too, Europe was a preferred destination for Israeli agricultural exports.

23 Citrus Promotion Board Bulletin, ISA, MA, file 2423/2, August 31, 1958.

24 Rapport intérimaire: les relations entre la Communauté européenne et l'État d'Israël, EUA, BAC 7/1973-12, March 28, 1965.

25 Yosef Canan, "Our Standstill at the British Citrus Market," *Davar*, 1963.

26 S. Dubiner, "Promotion Board Rather Than a Citrus Board," *Davar*, 1957; Ezra. Zohar, *Sodom or Chelem* (Tel Aviv: Dvir [in Hebrew], 1987).

27 Itzhak Minerbi, "The European Common Market and Export of Oranges," *The Economic Quarterly*, no. 29/30 (1961); A. Pines, "Costs of Production in the Orange Industry," *The Economic Quarterly*, no. 25/26 (1960).

28 Minerbi.

29 Founded in 1937, Mekorot is Israel's national water company.

30 See David Horowitz's account: Horowitz, 179.

31 Yossi Beilin, *The Hebrew Industry: Origins* (Jerusalem: Keter, 1987), 126; Horowitz.

32 Despite immense efforts to increase available water for irrigation. In the first decade of the country's existence, water output increased from 250 cubic meters per year (1948) to 1,100 million (1958). Yet Israel's water system suffered from a shortage relative to need. See: A. Amir, "Agricultural Development in 1958," *The Economic Quarterly*, no. 21/22 (1958).

33 Halevi and Klinov.

34 Itzhak Galnoor, "Water Policymaking in Israel," *Policy Analysis* 4, no. 3 (1978).

35 85% of Israeli exports were directed to developed countries. See: *Davar*, July 19, 1963.

36 See: Kidan.

37 E. M. Bernstein, "Some Aspects of Economic Policy in Small Countries," *The Economic Quarterly*, no. 15 (1957): 189–92; Yehuda Horin, "Planning of Export," *The Economic Quarterly*, no. 17/18 (1957): 51–5.

38 Amnon Lamfrum and Hagai Tzoref, eds., *Levi Eshkol—the Third Prime Minister: Selected Documents (1895–1969)* (Jerusalem: National Archives [in Hebrew], 2002), 373.

39 Pinchas Sapir, "Export Policy," *The Economic Quarterly*, no. 13/14 (1956).

40 Beilin, 135.

41 CBS, *Sixty Years in Statistics* (Jerusalem: Israel Central Bureau of Statistics, 2008).

42 If figures are shown here in Israeli pounds rather than US dollars, it is because we could not find a reliable source to convert the currency from the (old Israeli currency) of the pound to the US dollar. For example, neither the Bank of Israel nor the US Federal Reserve publish historical exchange rate tables/data that goes as back as 1965.

43 See Memorandum, Israël et la CEE, ISA, FM, file 3154/5, October 1966.

44 Minister of Industry's speech in the Knesset, ISA, FM, file 948/17, December 29, 1961.

45 Richard Pomfret, *Export Policies and Performance in Israel* (Kiel: Kiel Institute for the World Economy, 1975).

46 Ilan Greilsammer and Joseph Weiler, eds., *Europe and Israel: Troubled Neighbours*, vol. 9 (Berlin: Walter de Gruyter, 1988); Richard. Pomfret, "Main Economic Trends in EC-Israel Economic Relations since the Creation of the Common Market," in *Europe and Israel: Troubled Neighbours*, eds. Ilan Greilsammer and Joseph Weiler (New York: Walter de Gruyter, 1988). While the US and Canada purchased 41% of Israel's refined diamonds (1958), the combined purchasing of The Six totaled 18%. However, the European Community was not an insignificant market for this sector. See: M. Bartur, "Israel and the Economic Integration of Europe," *The Economic Quarterly*, no. 28 (1960); Rouhollah K. Ramazani, *The Middle East and the European Common Market* (Charlottesville: University of Virginia Press, 1964).

47 Memorandum, ISA, FM, file 1953/5, December 18, 1959. It is no coincidence that 85% of Israel's exports were dispatched to developed countries. See: Horowitz, 11–16. Sapir focused on developing the textile industry in particular because he thought it suited the Israeli economy well. See: Beilin, 131.

48 Horowitz.

49 A. Markus, "Prospects of Industrial Export," *The Economic Quarterly*, no. 17/18 (1957): 145–54.

50 Shachar Atuan, "Me, You and Ata," www.mouse.co.il/gallery/1.3310756.

51 Ibid.

52 Shani Litman, "Come, Hebrew Fabric," www.mouse.co.il/gallery/1.3310754.

53 Davar, "Polgat—a Success Story," *Davar*, September 26, 1980.

54 Arie Ben Meir Arieli, *45 Years in the Service of Textile in Israel* (Tel Aviv: Israeli Textile Association, 1993). In 1965, no less than 29% of the workforce in Israel's periphery was employed in the textile industry. See: Beilin, 127.

55 Ayala Raz, "Israel's Fashion Industry—Stops in Time or 'Ata' as an Example," *Textile and Clothing Collection* 150, no. 39 (1997).

56 Amir.

57 Halevi and Klinov.

58 Memorandum, ISA, FM, 1946/19 December 23, 1957; Letter to The Six, ISA, FM, file 1946/21, October 1958.

59 ISA, FM, file 1954/5, August 18, 1961.

60 Customs rates prior to the unification were as follows: Oranges/clementines—16% for Germany (in practice—0%), 13% for the Benelux countries, 35% for France. Grapefruits—16% for Germany (in practice—0%), 12% for the Benelux countries, 20% for France. Lemons—16% for Germany (in practice—0%), 15% for the Benelux countries, 15% for France. The final customs rate following unification was expected to be 20%. The attractiveness of Israeli fruit in the French market was limited and thus the reduction of customs duties in France was insufficient to compensate Israel for the expected detrimental effects to its markets in Germany, the Netherlands, and Belgium. See: Ministry of Foreign Affairs, memorandum of the Economic Planning Committee at the Ministry of Agriculture, ISA, FM, file 1946/21, November 7, 1958.

61 Israel Citrus Board Bulletin, ISA, PM, file 2423/2, August 31, 1958.

62 Article by Michael Rom, ISA, FM, file 1958/8, January 5, 1962,

63 Ilan Greilsammer, *Israël Et l'Europe: Une Histoire Des Relations Entre La Communauté Européenne Et l'État d'Israël* (Lausanne: Fondation Jean Monnet pour l'Europe, Centre de Recherches Européennes, 1981), 22.

64 Britain constituted the most important destination for Israeli exports, with about one-third of all exports dispatched to that country. See: ISA, FM, file 211/6, February 20, 1958.

65 This data appears in the memorandum composed by the Economic Department at the Israeli Ministry of Foreign Affairs. See: ISA, FM, file 948/17, January 10, 1962. See also: Israel Government Yearbook 1963. Rapport of the Ministry of Industry and Trade.
66 Sharon Pardo, "The Year That Israel Considered Joining the European Economic Community," *JCMS: Journal of Common Market Studies* 51, no. 5 (2013).
67 Brian White, *Understanding European Foreign Policy* (Houndmills: Palgrave, 2001), 49.
68 Walter Hallstein, *Europe in the Making* (London: Allen and Unwin, 1972), 283.
69 ISA, FM, file 3111/31, December 1956.
70 ISA, FM, file 948/17, December 29, 1961.
71 State of Israel, ed. *State of Israel's Foreign Policy Documents* (Jerusalem: National Archives, 1981)., Vol. 14, Doc. 307, January 12, 1960
72 Gadi Heimann, *The End of a Wonderful Friendship: Israel-French Relations During De Gaulle's Presidency 1958–1967* (Jerusalem: Magnes, Hebrew University Press, 2015); Benjamin Pinkus, *From Ambivalence to an Unwritten Alliance* (Sede Boker: Ben-Gurion University [in Hebrew], 2005); Sylvia K. Crosbie, *A Tacit Alliance: France and Israel from Suez to the Six Day War* (Princeton: Princeton University Press, 2015).

References

Amir, A. "Agricultural Development in 1958." *The Economic Quarterly*, no. 21/22 (1958): 135–46.
Arieli, Arie Ben Meir. *45 Years in the Service of Textile in Israel*. Tel Aviv: Israeli Textile Association, 1993.
Atuan, Shachar. "Me, You and Ata." http://www.mouse.co.il/gallery/ 1.3310756.
Bartur, M. "Israel and the Economic Integration of Europe." *The Economic Quarterly*, no. 28 (1960): 353–62.
Beilin, Yossi. *The Hebrew Industry: Origins*. Jerusalem: Keter, 1987.
Ben-Porath, Yoram. "The Entwined Growth of Population and Product, 1922–1982." Chapter 1 In *The Israeli Economy: Maturing through Crises*, edited by Yoram Ben-Porath, 27–41. Cambridge: Harvard University Press, 1986.
———, ed. *The Israeli Economy: Growth Pangs*. Tel Aviv: Am Oved [in Hebrew], 1989.
Bernstein, E. M. "Some Aspects of Economic Policy in Small Countries." *The Economic Quarterly*, no. 15 (1957): 189–92.
Canan, Yosef. "Our Standstill at the British Citrus Market." *Davar*, 1963.
CBS. *Sixty Years in Statistics*. Jerusalem: Israel Central Bureau of Statistics, 2008.
Chenery, Hollis B., and Michael Bruno. "Development Alternatives in an Open Economy: The Case of Israel." *The Economic Journal* 72, no. 285 (1962): 79–103.
Crosbie, Sylvia K. *A Tacit Alliance: France and Israel from Suez to the Six Day War*. Princeton: Princeton University Press, 2015.
Davar. *"Polgat—a Success Story."* *Davar*, September 26, 1980.
Dubiner, S. "Promotion Board Rather Than a Citrus Board." *Davar*, 1957.
Galnoor, Itzhak. "Water Policymaking in Israel." *Policy Analysis* 4, no. 3 (1978): 339–67.
Giladi, Dan, and Haim Ofaz. *Israel's Economy: Development, Characteristics, Policy*. Jerusalem: Ministry of Education, 1998.
Goldstein, Yosef. *Eshkol: A Biography*. Jerusalem: Keter, 2003.
Government of Israel. "Ministry of Agriculture Report." In *Israel Government Yearbook 1962/3*, edited by Government of Israel. Tel Aviv: Information Center [in Hebrew], 1963.

Greilsammer, Ilan. *Israël Et l'Europe: Une Histoire Des Relations Entre La Communauté Européenne Et l'État d'Israël*. Lausanne: Fondation Jean Monnet pour l'Europe, Centre de Recherches Européennes, 1981.

Greilsammer, Ilan, and Joseph Weiler, eds. *Europe and Israel: Troubled Neighbours* Vol. 9. Berlin: Walter de Gruyter, 1988.

Halevi, Nadav, and Ruth Klinov. *The Economic Development of Israel* [in English]. New York: Praeger, 1968.

Halevi, Nadav, and Ruth Klinov-Malul. *The Economic Development of Israel* [in English]. Jerusalem: Academin [in Hebrew], 1968.

Hallstein, Walter. *Europe in the Making*. London: Allen and Unwin, 1972.

Heimann, Gadi. *The End of a Wonderful Friendship: Israel-French Relations During De Gaulle's Presidency 1958–1967*. Jerusalem: Magnes, Hebrew University Press, 2015.

Horin, Yehuda. "Planning of Export." *The Economic Quarterly*, no. 17/18 (1957): 51–5.

Horowitz, David. "Between Israel and the Nations." *The Economic Quarterly*, no. 33/34 (1962): 3–16.

———. *Life in the Spotlight*. Ramat Gan: Masada, 1975.

Kidan, A. "Extension of Production and the Trade Balance." *The Economic Quarterly*, no. 13/14 (1956): 44–53.

Kimmerling, Baruch. *Zionism and Economy*. Cambridge: Schenkman Publishers, 1982.

Klebanski, M. "Israel Foreign Trade in the European Free Trade Area." *The Economic Quarterly*, no. 17/18 (1957): 46–50.

Lamfrum, Amnon, and Hagai Tzoref, eds. *Levi Eshkol—the Third Prime Minister: Selected Documents (1895–1969)*. Jerusalem: National Archives [Hebrew], 2002.

Levi-Faur, David. *Pinchas Sapir and Israel's Economic Development*. Tel Aviv: Sapir Development Center at Tel Aviv University, 1993.

Litman, Shani. "Come, Hebrew Fabric." www.mouse.co.il/gallery/1.3310754.

Markus, A. "Prospects of Industrial Export." *The Economic Quarterly*, no. 17/18 (1957): 145–54.

Minerbi, Itzhak. "The European Common Market and Export of Oranges." *The Economic Quarterly*, no. 29/30 (1961): 107–17.

Pardo, Sharon. "The Year That Israel Considered Joining the European Economic Community." *JCMS: Journal of Common Market Studies* 51, no. 5 (2013): 901–15.

Patinkin, Don. *The Israel Economy: The First Decade*. Jerusalem: Falk Institute for Economic Research in Israel [in Hebrew], 1960.

Pines, A. "Costs of Production in the Orange Industry." *The Economic Quarterly*, no. 25/26 (1960): 135–42.

Pinkus, Benjamin. *From Ambivalence to an Unwritten Alliance*. Sede Boker: Ben-Gurion University [in Hebrew], 2005.

Pohorilles, Samuel. *Development and Planning in the Israeli Economy*. Tel Aviv: The Center for Agriculture Planning and Development [in Hebrew], 1969.

Pomfret, Richard. *Export Policies and Performance in Israel*. Kiel: Kiel Institute for the World Economy, 1975.

———. "Main Economic Trends in EC-Israel Economic Relations since the Creation of the Common Market." In *Europe and Israel: Troubled Neighbours*, edited by Ilan Greilsammer and Joseph Weiler, 56–72. New York: Walter de Gruyter, 1988.

Ramazani, Rouhollah K. *The Middle East and the European Common Market*. Charlottesville: University of Virginia Press, 1964.

Ravid, Shimon. *Agriculture in Israel: Detailed Planning in a Mixed Economy* [in Hebrew]. Rehovot: Center for Agriculture Economics, 1979.

Raz, Ayala. "Israel's Fashion Industry—Stops in Time or 'Ata' as an Example." *Textile and Clothing Collection* 150, no. 39 (1997).

Rotberg, Robert I., ed. *Israeli and Palestinian Narratives of Conflict: History's Double Helix.* Bloomington: Indiana University Press, 2006.

Rozin, Orit. "The Austerity Policy and the Rule of Law: Relations between Government and Public in Fledgling Israel." *Journal of Modern Jewish Studies* 4, no. 3 (2005): 273–90.

Sapir, Pinchas. "Export Policy." *The Economic Quarterly*, no. 13/14 (1956): 3–8.

Sirquin, Moshe. "Economic Growth and Structural Change: An International Perspective." Chap. 2 In *The Israeli Economy: Maturing through Crises*, edited by Yoram Ben-Porath, 42–74. Cambridge: Harvard University Press, 1986.

State of Israel, ed. *State of Israel's Foreign Policy Documents.* Jerusalem: National Archives, 1981.

White, Brian. *Understanding European Foreign Policy.* Houndmills: Palgrave, 2001.

Zohar, Ezra. *Sodom or Chelem.* Tel Aviv: Dvir [in Hebrew], 1987.

3   Pursuing a range of options

Establishment of the Inter-Ministerial Committee

Israel was quick to identify the growing and developing challenge posed by the economic integration in Western Europe. As early as November 1956, a few months before the signing of the Treaty of Rome, Michael Rozenberg, an official in the Ministry of Trade and Industry, published an article noting the likelihood that Europe was en route to creating a free trade area and advising Israeli decision makers to begin preparing accordingly. In early 1957, Shimon Peres, then Director General of the Ministry of Foreign Affairs and one of Prime Minister Ben-Gurion's inner circle, composed a ten-page memorandum analyzing the range of reasons—security, political and economic—why Israel should seek to join the EEC. When Peres met with Jean Monnet in May 1957, the latter raised the possibility that Israel should apply for EEC membership—although counseling that it would be wise to advance slowly and first prepare the ground accordingly.[1] In April 1957, a month after the signing of the Treaty of Rome, Israel's leaders established a special inter-ministerial committee tasked with examining the problems likely to arise following the establishment of the EEC and the attempt to establish a free trade area among the OEEC states, and recommending how the decision makers should respond to these new challenges. The committee included representatives from those ministries affected by the EEC: the Finance Ministry, the Ministry of Foreign Affairs and the Ministry of Trade and Industry, along with a number of experts from the Hebrew University of Jerusalem and the Bank of Israel. At its first meeting, hovering in the air was the question of whether Israel should try to gain acceptance to the EEC, following Peres's suggestion. As was noted, such a step could prove extremely advantageous: it would deal a mortal blow to the Arab boycott, secure export markets, attract investments and, no less importantly, reduce the young state's feeling of isolation. While Israel's neighbors in the Middle East did not offer the country a warm welcome, entering the EEC could provide an alternative home and a degree of security. By contrast, there were serious economic arguments against entering the EEC: possible damage to Israel's emergent industry and the ensuing limitations on molding an independent trade policy. However, regardless of the claims in favor and against, the very fact that the question was raised in earnest and received general legitimization—all the committee members believed it deserving of a thorough investigation—is astounding, revealing the degree to which Israel diplomacy was at once daring and naive. How could a non-European country with a political can of worms around its neck imagine that it would gain acceptance to an exclusive regional body which was only recently established, with difficulty, and even view this as a practical possibility, allocating time and resources to it? It is difficult to believe that such an option was even considered by any other country with similar characteristics to Israel. As we will see below, this naivety, largely a result of the country's "can-do" mentality, cost Israel dearly.

During the first discussions in the inter-ministerial committee, disagreements erupted between the representatives of the Finance Ministry on the one hand, who feared the economic price of joining the EEC, and delegates from the Ministry of Foreign Affairs on the other, who viewed the issue largely through the political prism, yearning for the political advantages which EEC membership would bestow.[2] The question of EEC membership was considered complex and thus a thorough study was required: as a result, a sub-committee was created to examine the probable short- and long-term effects of the Common Market on the Israeli economy and the repercussions of Israel either joining or not joining the EEC. In the meantime, the Ministry of Foreign Affairs began discreetly investigating to what extent the political conditions were ripe for Israel to join the EEC. Clearly, Israel's only chance of joining or forming an association with the EEC was through the patronage of one of the member states, preferably an influential one.

The natural candidate for the role of patron seemed to be France. These were the golden years of Franco-Israeli relations. Since 1955, France had sold Israel significant quantities of its most advanced weaponry, thus guaranteeing the Jewish state's security; this included dozens of fighter planes and bombers, helicopters, light tanks and artillery. French armaments formed the backbone of the Israeli Defense Force (IDF) throughout the 1950s, until the Six Day War. At the peak of the cooperation between the two countries during the Suez Crisis of 1956, France granted military aid to Israel free of charge. Paris also endeavored to provide Israel with economic assistance, as much as was possible within the limits of the country's reduced means. Thus, for example, Israel received a massive loan of $30 million, in addition to the capital necessary to build an oil pipeline from Eilat to Ashkelon. France offered Israel significant political support: indeed, the French were largely responsible for Israel's achievements in the agreement following the Suez Crisis. In an act unprecedented in the international arena, France even agreed to help Israel in the highly sensitive domain of developing independent nuclear capabilities, including a plant to separate plutonium.[3] Thus, unsurprisingly, Jerusalem was optimistic that France would help to advance Israel's interests in the EEC. France constituted one of the central pillars of the European enterprise and wielded significant influence within the Community's institutions. However, initial talks between Israeli diplomats and their French counterparts, as well as conversations with French politicians and statesmen, in the spring of

1957, indicated that Israel had little chance of joining the EEC.[4] Moreover, these figures advised the Israelis that in the meantime they should refrain from advertising their desire for a connection with the then uniting Europe, informing them that it would not be well received in Paris and was liable to damage Israel's long-term likelihood of success.[5] These statements were not made without good reason because at the time, the Israeli press was replete with allusions and speculations concerning Israel's chances of joining the new European framework. Moreover, Knesset Members demanded a public debate in the legislature concerning the matter. The Foreign Minister halted these attempts;[6] along with the officials at the Ministry of Foreign Affairs, he desired a thorough investigation of the matter before consolidating a policy. In general, the Israeli government preferred to conduct such campaigns discreetly, using public diplomacy only when it encountered a dead end or insurmountable obstacles.

In the meantime, the sub-committee also concluded, for its own reasons, that joining the EEC was not the ideal solution for Israel. Indeed, most members concluded that membership would require Israel to abandon an economic toolbox which played a vital role in ensuring the Israeli economy's continued prosperity. The economic policy tools included for example, export subsidies, import tariffs and the existing market control regime. At the same time, the sub-committee determined that the establishment of the EEC would not seriously damage Israeli industrial exports: barely 10% of Israel's total exports were attributed to the Common Market. Indeed, they believed that the central problem was limited to one export sector—citrus fruits—and only this sector required immediate action. The sub-committee identified a solution: fostering ties with the OEEC would reduce the damage and accord far better with Israel's economic needs. The 18 OEEC member states purchased more than 60% of Israeli's exports (90% of citrus fruit exports) and since 1948, the OEEC had worked successfully to reduce import quotas (limits on the total amount of goods imported) between its members; by this stage (1957) such quotas had almost been eliminated.[7] It was generally expected that the OEEC countries would soon establish a free trade area amongst themselves, removing all trade restrictions and granting economic advantages to those involved. Israel was concerned that at a later stage Spain, Israel's main competitor in the citrus sector, would also enter the free trade area, making it essential that Israel join. Likewise, Israel anticipated that membership of the OEEC would accord the country financial aid to develop its industry. Among the ranks of the OEEC were also other countries with weak economies, at similar stages of development to Israel—Turkey, Greece, Portugal, Ireland and Iceland— which enjoyed comfortable arrangements to avoid damaging their sensitive economies. Why should Israel not achieve a similar status? The sub-committee's conclusions, together with the negative signals received from the French, persuaded Moshe Bartur, the Director of the Economic Department at the Ministry of Foreign Affairs, who served as chair of the inter-ministerial committee, that in the meantime Israel should abandon the idea of joining the EEC and instead focus on joining the OEEC. Eventually, membership of this body would also serve to facilitate the connection with the EEC. The committee finally resolved to pursue two parallel channels: a preliminary study of the advantages, which a connection with the EEC could offer, and an initial recommendation that the government initiate contacts with the OEEC.[8] Indeed, a recommendation to this effect was submitted a few days later to ministers concerned with economic matters: the Finance Minister, Foreign Minister and Minister of Trade and Industry.[9] The Israeli government at this time failed to agree on which path Israel should take. While Prime Minister David Ben-Gurion and Finance Minister Levi Eshkol, motivated also by political factors, viewed members of the EEC as essential, others, for example Minister of Trade and Industry Pinchas Sapir, believed that Israel's integration into European organizations—including the EEC and OEEC—would have detrimental effects on the Israeli economy.[10] These disagreements arose partly from their differing economic outlooks. Although Eskhol recognized the importance of developing industry, he considered continued cultivation of the agricultural sector vital.[11] Sapir, conversely, emphasized industrial development as the key to the country's future.[12] Sapir believed that because the country's industry was sensitive to external competition, assimilating too rapidly into large European economic organizations would endanger the Israeli economy. Nevertheless, the ministers agreed that the Ministry of Foreign Affairs would initiate preliminary contacts in order to investigate the practicality of joining the OEEC.

In November 1957, the sub-committee submitted a report on the ramifications of joining the OEEC; subsequently its recommendations were discussed once again in the inter-ministerial committee. It became apparent that the problems involved in making such a connection were greater than the supporters of this solution had previously realized. Joining the OEEC would require Israel to minimize or even cancel quotas on imported goods, to reduce the restrictions on the import of services, and to terminate exports subsidies. While the first demand was not viewed as especially problematic—the Israeli economy was at any rate progressing in that direction—members of the committee viewed the other two demands as sufficiently detrimental to cast doubt on the wisdom of joining this organization. Although Israel would possibly be able to secure special membership conditions permitting the continued implementation of these protective measures, this was a rather optimistic scenario and its success chances remained unclear. However, Meir, Eshkol and Sapir determined that Israel's basic policy should be to seek membership or association with the new European organizations.[13]

Israel remained obligated to this political decision for many years to come. At the same time, Bartur suggested a new-old idea of his own.[14] He proposed that Israel examine the possibility of joining the GATT and simultaneously continue searching for a suitable route into the OEEC. This was indeed a radical solution. For many years, Israeli economic decision makers had opposed joining the GATT due to the negative effects of such a step on the bilateral and discriminatory trade agreements, which Israel customarily signed with various states. The founding principle of the GATT was the "Most Favored Nation" principle (MFN), according to which tariff reductions granted to one country would be extended to all the organization's member states, making every member state a most favored nation. Israel's entry was therefore likely to reduce significantly the country's ability to grant tariff preferences to other states in return for reciprocal gestures on their part. Moreover, Israel already enjoyed most of the tariff reductions which GATT members possessed. Many states, for example the US, Britain and Scandinavian countries, automatically implemented the MFN principle also vis-à-vis non-GATT countries.

Israel's total exports to GATT member states in 1956 totaled $90 million, of which $84 million enjoyed similar privileges to those which Israel would receive as a signatory to the agreement.[15] Thus, Israel's direct economic incentive to join the GATT—immediate tariff reductions—was limited. However, the establishment of the EEC would, in the future, lead to the cancellation of bilateral agreements signed with the six member states. Therefore, joining GATT at this stage was expected to be less detrimental than in the past. It would also offer Israel valuable advantages: the massive GATT framework included all the Western nations, among them The Six, and the organization thus enjoyed no small degree of power vis-à-vis the EEC. GATT members were concerned by a number of articles in the Treaty of Rome, which they viewed as likely to undermine their rights; first and foremost the EEC's Common Agriculture Policy (CAP). The CAP was a protectionist policy, which would adversely affect opportunities to export agricultural products to the market. The Israelis were also concerned by this, fearing that their small country lacked the necessary bargaining power in dealing with The Six. However, GATT, with the influential bargaining power endowed by its size, would be able to pressure the members of the EEC. Indeed, by joining GATT, Israel would receive every concession that the organization extricated from the EEC. Similarly, it would ensure that issues of the highest importance for Israel would be included in negotiations with the EEC states, enabling Israel to guarantee that Israeli interests would be taken into consideration.

Israel's attempt to penetrate the Council of Europe and the initiative for a multilateral agreement

Joining the OEEC or GATT were not the only routes via which Israel could tackle the challenge posed by the EEC and future free trade area. A third option, marginal although with promising prospects, was joining the body known as the "Council of Europe," which was created in 1949. The aim of this organization was to foster unity and wider coordination among the European member states, ten in number when the body was created. For this purpose, it established two institutions: the Committee of Ministers, the highest authority, and the Parliamentary Assembly, a consultative body made up of 140 representatives. The latter was tasked with drafting proposals to be presented to the Committee of Ministers. The Assembly met three times each year in Strasbourg to discuss proposals for accelerating European integration in various domains.[16] Although trade agreements between the member states were outside the organization's remit, many believed that it enjoyed certain political influence. Likewise, it was generally believed that at the opportune moment, the Assembly would become the OEEC Parliament.

Thus, unsurprisingly, Israel was interested in association with this organization. However, the first step towards achieving this was not an Israeli initiative, but rather resulted from an approach by the Austrian representative to the Committee of Ministers. In February 1957, he approached the Israeli representative in Vienna asking whether Israel would be interested in attending the next meeting of the Committee of Ministers as an observer.[17] The Israeli Ministry of Foreign Affairs failed to agree on whether this was worthwhile. Indeed, some viewed membership of this framework as redundant, affording no practical benefit. By contrast others, among them Amiel Najar, director of the Western Europe Department, believed it extremely important to form ties with any European institution, however peripheral.[18] After considering all the opinions, Walter Eytan, Director General of the Israeli Ministry of Foreign Affairs, decided to respond positively and initiate contacts in this direction. It immediately became evident that the chances of entering the organization were not as promising as they had at first appeared. In talks with representatives of the Council of Europe, Israeli diplomats encountered little enthusiasm.[19] Yet in December 1957, the Committee of Ministers agreed to Israel's ad hoc participation at the Assembly's next meeting in Strasbourg (January 1958), mainly due to the enthusiastic support of Fernand Dehousse, President of the Parliamentary Assembly in the Council of Europe. Later the Israelis would repay Dehousse for his kindness, using their influence to ensure that he retained his position in the face of British-led attempts to depose him.[20]

Four representatives were selected for the delegation to Strasbourg: two General Zionist Knesset Members—Peretz Bernstein and David Lifshitz—along with two diplomats—Deputy Director General of the Ministry of Foreign Affairs, Maurice Fischer, and Bartur. Contrary to the protocol regarding the status of observers, the Israeli representation was permitted to give a speech in the Assembly's economic committee. It was no coincidence that this task was given to Bartur, who was considered the most senior economic authority in the Israeli Ministry of Foreign Affairs. Bartur was a unique figure in the bureaucratic landscape of the Ministry. An original thinker in possession of a degree of self-confidence rare even among diplomats, he was never afraid to voice his opinion, even when in the minority, and customarily approached senior levels directly, often resulting in bad feelings. Bartur was considered a difficult colleague and tensions often arose with his co-workers. Yet he was also much admired and thus it was logical that the responsibility for relations with international economic bodies should be placed in his capable hands. Bartur exploited the platform offered by the Assembly, attempting to persuade his audience that Israel's gradual association with West European economic bodies was of the utmost importance. The arguments which Bartur employed are particularly instructive for our purposes: indeed, they would recur repeatedly, in different forms, in Israel's contacts with European figures over the coming years. Bartur argued that although Israel was a developing country, in terms of technology and human resources it was no different to Western nations. Likewise, Israel's foreign trade was relatively sizeable and constantly growing. Therefore, Israel should be viewed as a serious partner, worthy of consideration. He continued, noting that 60% of Israel's foreign trade was with European states and that its transport routes (air and sea) were all directed towards Europe; thus Israel should be viewed as a European state to all intents and purposes: "Israel in this respect [foreign trade] is almost as European as Switzerland." Finally, Israel had excellent relations with developing Asian and African nations: these countries viewed the successful Israeli experience as a precedent upon which they could build. This Israeli asset, combined with the Western European states' technical and material resources, could contribute to building strong ties with these countries.[21] In fact, in his speech Bartur laid out the three pillars of what was to become the *Israeli argument* in favor of acceptance into European bodies: 1) the fundamental-moral argument—in terms of the structure of its economy and its economic ties, Israel was to all intents and purposes a European state; 2) the utilitarian-economic reasoning—Israel's developing economy and the extent of its trade made it a worthwhile partner, and 3) the utilitarian-political reasoning—Israel was a potential conduit and proxy for European penetration of Third World countries. This speech apparently made an impression on his audience. In the discussion following it, the economic committee decided to explore possibilities for Israel's cooperation in regional bodies. Over the course of 1958–59, Israel continued to send observers to meetings of the Council of Europe, despite occasional attempts to limit Israel's rights as an observer, arguing that, at the end of the day, Israel was not a European state. The Israelis viewed their involvement in these meetings, access to this platform and the positive welcome they received, as serious achievements. For the first time, Israel had been accorded free approach to a respected European forum, which recognized the country's right to make its voice heard. However, association with the Council of Europe was not the heart of the matter. Rather, Israel's main aim was to impart a message, which would slowly penetrate the consciousness of the architects of European integration: Israel was a branch of Europe and, therefore, a part of it. The Israelis argued that the division of the world into geographic areas was obsolete; the defining factor was not geography but affinity—historical, cultural, and moral—between nations and, in this respect, Israel was without doubt "European." According to Bartur, this concept of affinity between Israel and Europe had already begun to gain ground in the capitals of The Six, due to Israel's involvement in the Council: "With our first appearance we put a foot in the door, and with our second appearance the door opens a bit more. If we will persevere, the door may open completely, through a gradual process and with our constant cultivation".[22] In addition, Israel's presence at the Council enabled the Israelis to maintain contact with a range of key figures in European bodies. Thus, the Council served as a kind of diplomatic parlor or social network.

The Israeli campaign for multilateral negotiations with OEEC countries

In parallel to pursuing the involvement with the Council of Europe, the Israelis examined the option of joining the OEEC. During a conversation between Maurice Fischer and two of the organization's senior personnel in February 1958, the latter suggested that Israel relinquish the idea of formal association, instead seeking a de facto agreement: Israel would convert its mutual trade agreements with most OEEC countries into one multilateral arrangement. In this way, without joining the organization, Israel would benefit from the trade advantages offered by membership, among them comfortable monetary arrangements and an increase in Israeli export quotas to member states.[23] Such a precedent already existed: the OEEC had signed similar agreements with Brazil and Argentina. The Israelis, as we have seen, tended to reveal great flexibility on the tactical level and were persuaded to adopt this solution. Bartur believed that "in this way we can reach strong de facto association with the body and thereby [achieve] a determined and permanent status in the OEEC institutions."[24] This reflects the Israelis' priorities with regard to association with this organization: the main objective was opening the European door; concrete economic advantages were merely a welcome addition.

In June 1958, Israel began following the new path agreed upon with the OEEC officials. Letters were dispatched to 14 of the organization's member states (out of 18), requesting official confirmation that they were prepared to begin negotiations with Israel. The Israelis did not content themselves with these letters but embarked on a comprehensive lobbying campaign, within which diplomatic representatives conducted extensive talks with politicians and senior bureaucrats in all the states. Bartur was dispatched as reinforcement and, over the course of the coming weeks, he wandered from country to country, effectively employing his rhetorical talents and great expertise in the economic field. In most capitals, the Israeli request was received with understanding, although smaller states expressed some concerns that the new agreement would damage their ability to export to Israel. However, the large nations—Britain, Germany, France and Italy—were the deciding factor and they revealed little enthusiasm to accede to the Israeli request.[25] At a certain stage, the British expressed willingness to support Israel on condition that, within the framework of the multilateral agreement, any credit which Israel received from one of the participating countries could also be used to purchase goods from other parties to the agreement.[26] The motivation behind this demand was clear: since the beginning of the 1950s, Western Germany had paid Israel large sums—reaching $750 million—as reparations for the Nazi atrocities in the form of credit to purchase German products, such as ships. The other European states gazed with longing at the significant sums involved and the Israelis, well aware of this, hoped to exploit the "carrot" of reparation payments to improve their bargaining power.[27] They hinted that within the framework of a multilateral agreement it would be possible to make the German credit available for general use; such allusions encouraged the British to respond positively. However, the Germans were not pleased by the idea, which had already begun to spiral through the corridors of European organizations. Indeed, the payments also helped the West German economy, providing orders for its factories. If the Israelis were able to use this credit to purchase merchandise from all OEEC states, the German economy would suffer a loss. Due to German opposition, the Israelis were forced to relinquish the idea of using reparation payments as an incentive to support their request.[28]

Although Israel pursued the issue with each OEEC member state separately, EEC members jointly coordinated their positions. In December 1958, the EEC's committee of experts discussed Israel's request for a multilateral agreement with OEEC states. The committee discerned no economic difficulty in responding positively to the request but recognized that the issue also possessed political dimensions, which exceeded its mandate.[29] An additional working group, appointed by the EEC to discuss trade aspects of the arrangements, did not detect significant problems but likewise saw no economic urgency to warrant haste on the part of The Six.[30] Despite these conclusions, and perhaps because of them, the European Commission was forced to admit that the root of the problem lay in "the especially sensitive character of the issue in *political terms*, which requires extremely careful steps on the part of The Six" (emphasis added).[31] In the meantime, many members of the OEEC outside The Six responded positively to Israel's request.[32] The Six did not wish to form the sole opposition to an agreement with Israel, yet at the same time did not desire a public announcement that the EEC as a body had reached a positive decision on the matter. Therefore, they decided that each country would give a positive answer separately in due course, as indeed occurred in February 1959.[33] The management of this relatively unimportant issue clearly reveals the degree of sensitivity that The Six accorded to any act, which Arab states could interpret as favoritism.[34]

In fact, almost none among the OEEC members were enthusiastic about the arrangement which Israel sought. Most had little, if anything, to gain in terms of trade. By contrast, the political and economic complications were very tangible: both in terms of conflict with Arab states and the fear that opening the dam with Israel would lead to a flood of states seeking similar arrangements.[35] OEEC countries were worried that behind the Israelis' ostensibly justified economic motivation lay a deeper political intention: obtaining legitimacy for the country and creating a rift between Europe and the Arab world. Such fears were not completely unfounded. The Israelis viewed a multilateral arrangement with the Western European states as far more than a limited trade agreement; it was a tactical step aimed to ease Israel's way into the consolidating European bodies—first and foremost the EEC—which would in turn serve a strategic purpose of the utmost import to the nascent state: breaking out of its political and economic isolation. The Israelis recognized that the European states would not rejoice at Israel's entry into their regional organizations and it was thus vital to find a way to sneak in, using cunning. Therefore, the Israeli request for negotiations of a multilateral agreement was a Trojan horse, intended to enable a crafty infiltration of Europe. Bartur expressed this explicitly:

> The pragmatic and moderate manner by means of which we have striven to reach a multilateral agreement is the only course with any chance of success in the current political situation. Meeting the basic principles of terminology, as well as the economic and trade techniques accepted in the OEEC, makes it very difficult to oppose our gradual penetration. If we will succeed, the path into economic unities such as the EEC will be open to us . . . hence

the defining practical, principle and psychological significance of the multilateral agreement . . . our entry into this wide West European circle [OEEC]
will provide a basis to launch—if it will be decided upon—into the close-
knit and cohesive inner circles of the economic, political economic unities
and in particular the European Community of The Six.[36]

In February 1960, the multilateral arrangement initiative died a natural death
due to the negotiations between the US and the OEEC concerning the creation of a new body incorporating the 18 Western European states as well as the
US and Canada (later called the Organization for Economic Cooperation and
Development, OECD). This body was intended to replace the OEEC; indeed, the
Americans advanced it specifically for this purpose. Washington was concerned
that the economic competition which had developed between the EEC and EFTA
was likely to have undesirable political ramifications and sought to establish a
new body—within which the US would play a central role—to serve as a basis
for general European cooperation. The US also sought to recruit European help
for their aid enterprise in developing countries, thus sharing the burden of this
to some degree.[37] They explicitly asked that during talks, the organization refrain
from negotiations concerning association with third parties, such as Israel; the
OEEC countries did not view this as a particularly great sacrifice. Members of the
working group appointed by the Council of Ministers of the EEC had no difficulty
in determining that, for the meantime, the examination of an arrangement with
Israel should be put aside, awaiting the outcome of these latest developments in
the OEEC.[38] Moshe Bartur, the driving force behind the Israeli campaign for a
multilateral agreement, was highly disappointed. Yet he was comforted by the
fact that the exhausting negotiations had yielded at least one positive result: by
means of constant lobbying, stubbornness and perseverance, Israel had managed
to extract from European economic bodies the recognition that Israel possessed
a special status vis-à-vis these organizations and that there existed objective justifications for the country's association with them.[39] Israel eventually joined the
OECD as a full member half a century later, in 2010.

An examination of Israel's initial policy towards the new challenge posed by
the foundation of the EEC reveals an interesting trend. From the outset, there
was a consensus among the professional level regarding two principles: first, it
was vital to explore a number of options simultaneously and pursue a number
of parallel channels, thereby raising the chances of locating a satisfactory solution for Israel's problems. Second, there was the need to adopt the principle of
"progress via the easiest route," focusing on the solution which would be least
problematic in terms of the Israeli economy and which had the highest chances
of success.[40] The Israelis did not expect that they would be able to penetrate
the heart of the European fortress quickly or easily. Indeed, Israeli diplomats
understood that this would necessitate a lengthy, consistent and patient campaign. They felt that the key lay in persistent lobbying and gradually wearing
down the opposition.

Initial contacts with the EEC

While they were engaged in talks with OEEC states concerning a multilateral agreement, the Israelis needed to tackle a problem with far more serious long-term ramifications. According to the Treaty of Rome, the first stage in the removal of tariffs between the six members of the EEC was scheduled to take place on January 1, 1959: a reduction of 10% in the tariff rate on most products originating from these states. Viewed alone, this was a minor step, which did not yet constitute a serious threat to exports from countries outside the EEC. For instance, if the tariff on citrus fruits in the Netherlands was 13%, following January 1, 1959, the tariff on Italian or French citrus fruits in the Netherlands would be reduced to 11.7%, while the duty on citrus fruits from outside the Common Market remained unchanged. This change was not drastic enough to damage the competitiveness of American, Spanish, or Israeli citrus fruit and, therefore, from Israel's perspective the danger was not immediate. However, the Israelis decided not to wait until their exports would suffer and began to explore ways to overcome the problem. The fact that the 1958 season was particularly bad in terms of marketing Israeli citrus fruits to Europe may also have influenced this decision: this was a result of a bountiful harvest, which caused a surplus in supply and a steep drop in prices.[41] Understanding that the EEC institutions would find it difficult to grant Israel special privileges, the Israeli Ministry of Foreign Affairs initially sought to solve the problem through direct negotiations with countries, which constituted the main consumers of Israeli citrus fruits: the Benelux states and Germany. In so doing, it intentionally bypassed the EEC institutions, assuming that these states would be much more willing than the Community institutions to consider Israeli interests. An opportunity to pursue this avenue arose in the talks between the Israelis and representatives of the Benelux countries in the summer of 1958 concerning a bilateral trade agreement.[42] During these talks, Israeli officials requested an arrangement that would prevent negative discrimination against Israeli fruit compared to those originating among The Six. Despite their understanding of the Israeli position, the Benelux representatives did not agree to comply with this request, claiming that a decision on this matter could only be made in the framework of the EEC and suggesting that the issue be raised therein. They also advised the Israelis to "soften" the ground among the other three governments, thereby creating a "supportive atmosphere" for the adoption of such a solution.[43]

The method of circumvention thus failed, leaving the Israelis with no choice but to follow the advice of the Benelux representatives. In a series of talks held in Bonn, Paris and Rome, the Israelis tried to persuade their counterparts that it was of the utmost importance to find a solution for their problem. While the Germans seemed aware of the issue and tended towards a supportive stance, the French and Italians were much more hesitant. Indeed, the French responded dryly that this was precisely the purpose of the customs union: positive discrimination in favor of products originating among The Six. The Italians, for their part, offered an honest explanation for their negative stance—in the framework of the negotiations for the Treaty of Rome, Italy had agreed to open its markets to industrial products from the more industrialized countries among The Six in return for enlarging the markets for Italian agricultural exports. Italy viewed it as unjust that Israel sought to compete with Italy on equal terms and in so doing reduce its gains: any special arrangement with Israeli would entitle Italy to additional concessions from the other members of the EEC.[44] The Israelis perceived this position as petty, although in fact it was largely justified. In opening their markets to German and Belgian industrial products and removing quotas, Italy, and to a certain extent also France, paid a high price and it became difficult for them to protect their industries from competition. As compensation, they were offered increased opportunities to export their agricultural products. Therefore pursuing a course of action detrimental to their economies in consideration of the needs of another country, one which was not even European, was counter-intuitive. Furthermore, a far more serious justification for refusing any special gesture towards Israel on this issue was that Israel, despite its abundance of citrus fruits, was in reality a small supplier and therefore, any arrangement beyond the letter of the law would not in fact cause great damage to Italy. However, if Israeli oranges were to receive special consideration, the Spanish, Algerians and Americans would subsequently demand comparable consideration. Indeed, the US was entitled to ask for such consideration as a member of GATT. Clearly granting any special rights accorded to Israel to countries with larger export quantities, would trigger a domino effect that could lead to the collapse of the EEC. Therefore, the Israeli case was viewed primarily as a precedent, rather than receiving an examination on the basis of its own merits.

Yet the Israelis were still prepared to try their luck. In October 1958, they submitted a letter to The Six, as well as the European Commission, requesting some kind of arrangement to prevent damage to Israeli citrus exports and related products. A long memorandum was attached to the letter, analyzing the importance of this sector for the Israeli economy. Israel did not seek to portray itself as a pauper at the door begging for a handout, but rather as a partner of equal status asking for its share of a deal. Israel limited its request at this stage to the citrus problem, although the Israelis exploited the opportunity and at the end of the letter asked the Commission to update Israel regarding "the nature of the permanent relationship which can be established between Israel and the EEC to enable negotiations concerning economic and other matters." For its part, Israel announced that it would welcome the establishment of these relations as soon as possible.[45] The Israeli letter combined two positions. On the one hand, it presented the stance of bureaucrats in the economic ministries, among them the Economic Department at the Ministry of Foreign Affairs, the Finance Ministry, the Ministry of Agriculture and the Ministry of Trade and Industry, who sought to limit Israeli demands to tariff arrangements, presuming that it would be easier for the Europeans to comply on such topics. On the other hand, the political echelons desired a far more binding relationship, mainly for political purposes. Despite the bureaucrats' fears regarding the potential ramifications of pretentious demands at such an early stage, they were eventually forced to accept a phrasing, which accorded with the will of the politicians.[46]

At the end of November 1958, the Israeli request was presented to the COREPER, which reached an unequivocal decision: Israel could not be granted special consideration because this case was no different to other expressions of similar concerns by GATT members. The council also articulated a fundamental message for the future: in contacts with third-party countries, the EEC must not behave as though it were guilty of some crime. Demands for "positive discrimination" were unjustified.[47] The position expressed by the Europeans at this stage fundamentally negated any Israeli pretention that the country was entitled to special treatment. If the Europeans would continue to adhere to this line in coming years, any Israeli attempt to achieve tariff preferences on a special basis was doomed to failure. However, the Europeans would later abandon this position.

Following this, matters developed in an unexpected direction. In the wake of the COREPER's discussion, the request was transferred to the care of the European Commission. The Commission was tasked with examining the request and drafting a reply reflecting the spirit of the Council's decision. The Commission would present the draft of the reply to the Council of Ministers for approval. Rey understood that the Commission had a significant interest in conducting direct, permanent and continuous relations with countries outside the EEC. First, the very existence of such relations would constitute a sign of sovereignty, thus making the Commission "Europe's" representative vis-à-vis the rest of the world. Second, foreign countries would understand the need to approach the European Commission to advance their interests with The Six, at least concerning trade affairs, thus endowing the Commission with institutional power.[48] The strong link between the depth and extent of European integration and the Commission's organizational power gave the Commission a strong incentive to advance integration. As any other bureaucratic institution, the Commission sought to strengthen its status and influence within the framework of the EEC. Indeed, the ostensible ethos of technocratic bureaucracy, devoid of favoritism and politicization, never really existed.[49] It is the nature of a bureaucratic body to seek to maximize its resources and authorities; it will not be satisfied with blindly implementing the orders of its superiors.[50] Therefore, Jean Rey, now Commissioner for Foreign Affairs at the European Commission, and the officials in his department encouraged foreign diplomats to establish representations in Brussels to conduct relations with the EEC, or at least to accord a special department within the country's Embassy in Belgium for this purpose. There had been no decision in the Council of Ministers authorizing the Commission to carry out such actions and therefore Rey attempted to play down the role of his department in this matter. In April 1958, the Israeli Ambassador in Brussels, Gideon Rafael, met with Rey for the first time. Rafael's aim in this meeting was to establish good relations with an influential figure in the EEC's institutions and outline Israel's problems to him. He did not submit any formal request on his government's behalf for direct relations with the Community institutions and did not even informally raise this as a possibility. Yet, towards the end of the conversation, Rey suddenly asked Rafael whether the Israeli government had directed him to ask for the meeting, being interested in a connection and cooperation with the EEC; this was a clear hint that the Commission would welcome a formal connection between Israel and the EEC. Rafael seized this unexpected opportunity, replying that his approach was indeed at the instruction of the Israeli government and an expression of its policy. According to Rafael's testimony, Rey found it difficult to conceal his satisfaction at this answer. He expressed with certainty that many countries would soon establish permanent representations to the EEC. All signs indicated that Brussels would be chosen as the center of the EEC and Rey expressed his hope to cooperate with Rafael in the future.[51] However, in his report of the conversation, Rey dryly noted that the request to establish formal relations with the Commission came from Rafael, emphasizing that he expressed no opinion on the matter.[52] While Rey sought to advance the establishment of an Israeli representation, he was careful to avoid giving the impression that he had played a part in this or even fostered any special interest in it. This pattern of covert cooperation with Israel, denied to the Council, recurred on numerous occasions over the coming years. Six months later, in a further conversation between Rafael and the President of the European Commission, Hallstein, the latter clearly stated that he would be very pleased if Israel would appoint the Israeli Ambassador in Brussels (that is, Rafael himself) as representative to the EEC, noting that a number of countries had already taken similar steps.[53] This enthusiasm, from a most senior figure representing the EEC, towards a politically "problematic" country such as Israel hints at the importance which the head of the European Commission attributed to cultivating formal relations between the EEC as a supra-national body and the countries of the world.

Indeed, at the end of November 1958, the Commission was asked to prepare a response to the Israeli request. As was noted, the request included two parts: finding a suitable arrangement for citrus exports to the EEC countries and establishing direct relations between Israel and the EEC. In fact, the second request was no more than Israel's positive response to the inviting messages which the country had received for some time from senior Commission figures. The Commission's officials discerned this immediately and therefore expressed a very positive attitude towards the Israeli approach in the memorandum which they prepared in response:

> The Commission notes with satisfaction the intention expressed by the Israeli government to establish with it permanent contact with the aim of studying the problems likely to arise. It will be pleased to respond positively to any step taken by the Israeli government in this regard.[54]

Regarding Israel's first request, the Commission's answer was more reserved, although it expressed willingness to embark on talks with Israel concerning the topic. In fact, Rey's department had already begun preparatory work for such talks, composing a memorandum regarding Israel's economic ties with the EEC countries; this was intended to ensure that the Commission would play an active role in future negotiations with Israel.[55] Due to the desire to proceed cautiously, it was decided to refrain from distributing it among other Community institutions. Now, the Commission needed to "market" this challenging response to the Council of Ministers, a task which was given to Guenther Seeliger, Director General of Rey's department. When presenting the memorandum to the meeting of the Council of Ministers on December 18, 1958, Seeliger minimized as much as possible the document's positive tone towards the Israeli requests. He claimed that "The Commission deemed it right to respond to Israel's request with the utmost caution. The proposed memorandum avoids taking a stance".[56]

This was a strange interpretation, which did not accord with the content of the document or its general tone. The ministers, angered by the freedom which the Commission had exercised in drafting proposals, which in no way accorded with the conclusions of the meeting of COREPER on November 27, were even more infuriated by this linguistic juggling. They noted that despite its "caution," the memorandum contained significant problems both fundamentally and procedurally. Furthermore, they reminded the Commission that the EEC was currently taking its first steps and this was a period of particular sensitivity: any solution adopted was likely to set a precedent for later cases and therefore it was vital to act with particular caution. "The Commission's memorandum suggests that it agrees with Israel's request to establish a permanent connection and also accepts the proposal to begin negotiations with that country," the Council members declared. However, the Commission was not authorized to make such decisions. It was only one among the bodies which made up the EEC and not the sole representative of the EEC. The decision regarding whether to establish permanent relations with Israel fell under the authority of member states' governments and they alone possessed legal authority in the EEC. Essentially, until then, the EEC had established relations with a very limited number of states; extending relations to other countries required the consideration of political and trade factors. Thus, the Council in fact stated that the establishment of an Israeli representation to the EEC was not a trivial matter and required consideration. Considering the situation, the Commission was asked to draft a new response reflecting the opinion of the Council of Ministers;[57] in this way, the Council severely rebuked the Commission. Although these bodies had very different opinions regarding how relations with Israel should be managed, this did not form the heart of the matter, nor did this aspect infuriate the foreign ministers of The Six. Rather the ministers were outraged by the Commission's pretension to manage the EEC's foreign affairs, as was expressed in the handling of the Israeli request. The ministers utilized the opportunity to send a clear message to the Commission regarding the balance of power and division of authority within the EEC.

The Israelis were totally unaware of the intense disagreement on this matter within the Community institutions. They had no idea that this had become a test of the balance of powers within the EEC. Likewise, they had no inkling which party supported their request and which sought to dismiss them empty-handed, as is evident by an additional tactical step employed by the Israelis to help them achieve their aim. Alongside the letter they dispatched to the European Commission at the end of October, the Israelis sent a missive to each of the capitals of The Six asking the governments to pressure the Commission to respond positively to Israel's request. The Israelis presumed that they enjoyed significant support among the governments of the member states (apart from Italy) and therefore it was worthwhile recruiting this support to pressure the Commission. Yet in reality, the situation was the opposite. Initially, the Israelis found it difficult to believe that the Commission assumed a positive attitude towards Israel, while the Council adopted a hesitant stance.[58] However, a conversation between Gideon Rafael and France's Permanent Representative to the Council revealed that indeed, France did not support Israel's requests.[59] Israel's blindness to the powers supporting and opposing its interests continued also in the coming years.

At the beginning of January 1959, the Commission submitted to the Council an edited version of the reply to Israel, far less positive than its earlier version. The French delegation still detected various defects and demanded that the sections which it deemed too positive be removed.[60] The final phrasing which was eventually sent to Israel was insipid and non-obligatory, to say the least. Regarding Israel's request for consideration of the country's citrus exports, the reply stated that the EEC found conceding to "individual" requests such as those presented by Israel problematic. The letter likewise expressed doubts concerning the real damage which Israel would sustain as a result of the elimination of internal tariffs. The response to the Israeli request for establish permanent and continuous negotiations with Community institutions was evasive.[61] The phrasing of the reply was intentionally hazy, seeking to ensure that not even one single line of the text could be interpreted as some kind of commitment to Israel. Indeed, Seeliger needed to harness all his powers of invention to persuade the Israeli diplomats that the letter also contained positive aspects. In his conversations with Israelis, he informed them using allusions that the Commission's Directorate for Foreign Affairs wanted to begin negotiations with Israeli experts to clarify various technical problems, such as the citrus fruit issue, and recommend solutions.[62] A month later, Rey confirmed to Bartur that the Commission intended to embark on informal talks with the Israelis that same September.[63] In fact, this constituted an informal positive response to Israel's requests in the letter. It is difficult to assess to what extent the Commission received permission to pursue a policy that contradicted the Council's decision. There is some basis to believe that the Commission, or at least Rey's department, exercised greater freedom than it possessed. This may have been a fundamental decision not to be satisfied with merely executing Council decisions and an expression of the Commission's desire to retain freedom of action.

As a basis for the future negotiations between the EEC and Israel, the Commission asked that Israel provide it with data concerning the losses its economy had sustained due to the removal of internal duties between EEC member states, which began in January 1959. This was a logical demand and was intended to make it easier to obtain the Council's agreement to talks with Israel. Some in the EEC doubted the extent of the damage to the Israeli economy and, as was noted, these doubts were expressed in the response letter. In an effort to prove that the trade negotiations were necessary and urgent, the Commission required exact statistics. The Israeli Ministry of Foreign Affairs set about this task seriously.

Its officials consulted with the management of the Citrus Marketing Board and, following clarifications, an embarrassing picture emerged: not only had Israel's citrus exports to The Six not suffered since January 1, 1959, but rather, in fact, exporters of Israeli citrus fruit had sold greater quantities in comparison to the same period in the previous year.[64] Although arguably the Israelis would sell more citrus fruit in the absence of the tariff reduction, this argument would not be sufficient in persuading the Europeans that a special arrangement with Israel was vital. Officials at the Israeli Ministry of Foreign Affairs found themselves in a difficult situation. The Commission continued to pressure the Israelis to provide the data, which was intended to advance Israel's interests. However, the Israelis were afraid to answer and chose to wait, hoping for a sudden fall in the extent of sales. Their hopes were in vain: steadily increasing quantities of Israeli fruit were sold in the markets of The Six. In their sorrow, officials at the Ministry of Foreign Affairs began to doubt the Commission's motivations; the demand to prove damage at such an early stage seemed none other than a trap, intended to give the EEC a justification for evading negotiations with the Israelis.[65] At a certain stage, they even considered informing the Commission that Israel would not provide the requested statistics. At any rate, the failure to provide the data was not the only reason for the delay in beginning negotiations. The Commission itself was not overly excited at this prospect. Despite being the most positive party towards Israel among the Community's institutions, it too was well versed in the problems and complications liable to result from special negotiations with a non-European country, not to mention the Arab factor. The Commission asked to await the results of the multilateral talks between Israel and the OEEC countries, due to begin in 1959; the success of these talks would in all likelihood release the EEC from the need to negotiate with Israel. Equally, it would ease the expected political pressure from Arab countries, should the talks would begin. Therefore, the Commission viewed it as preferable that the Israelis exhaust the OEEC channel before beginning talks with the European Commission.[66]

So too, the Israelis themselves were unsure what constituted the optimal solution for their problems. In the spring and summer of 1959, a number of alternative routes existed: a multilateral agreement with the OEEC; negotiations with the EEC in the framework of the GATT, which Israel had joined in March 1959, or an attempt to obtain economic gestures on a bilateral basis. Likewise, a further possible channel appeared at this juncture. On July 20, 1959, the seven European countries which remained outside the Common Market—Britain, Sweden, Norway, Denmark, Austria, Switzerland and Portugal—signed the European Free Trade Association Agreement (EFTA) in Stockholm. This organization was intended as a counterweight to the EEC, formed by countries, which mainly for political reasons, did not wish to join the Common Market yet feared the economic repercussions of remaining outside it. In contrast to the EEC, the members of EFTA did not intend to establish a common external tariff towards third-party countries but rather merely eliminate tariffs between themselves on industrial products (agricultural products were not included in the agreement). From a narrow economic perspective, this framework was even more important to Israel than the EEC: 34% of all the country's exports and 53% of its agricultural exports were to EFTA countries, in comparison to 22% and 33% to the EEC, respectively.[67] In addition, the conditions of association with this organization for new countries were much lighter than the demands of the EEC; so too the economic suitability required was far more limited.[68] Therefore, Israel seriously considered pursuing a form of association with this new framework. Thus, the negotiations with the EEC were not necessarily perceived as the most promising or effective route for solving Israel's trade difficulties. Yet it gradually became clear that other routes were closed to Israel or only of limited utility. The multilateral negotiations ran aground on the background of the establishment of the OECD. The idea of solving Israel's export problems vis-à-vis The Six in the framework of the GATT proved to be overly optimistic, for various reasons:[69] firstly, because the extent of the expected reductions from these negotiations was modest, at most 20%, and secondly because the talks were slow and the agreements would be implemented over extended periods. Finally, the negotiations focused on industrial products, while agricultural exports formed the heart of Israel's problem.[70]

Likewise, the parallel channel of an arrangement with "The Seven," i.e. the EFTA states, proved to be insufficient. EFTA developed slowly and, at this early stage, it was difficult to conduct serious negotiations. When the organization began functioning in Geneva on July 1, 1960, it employed no more than 15 individuals—compared to the 1,500 Commission officials working in Brussels at the time.[71] Furthermore, the Israelis concluded that the effectiveness of an agreement with EFTA would not be comparable to the benefits Israel would reap from an agreement with the EEC. The populations of the EFTA countries were equal to half the population of The Six. Clearly, in terms of potential, The Six were far more significant than The Seven. A further issue impaired the utility of an agreement of EFTA: the free trade area did not include agricultural products, which were of particular importance to the Israelis. Likewise, in contrast to the Treaty of Rome, the EFTA agreement did not include the possibility of economic aid packages for developing countries associated with the organization.[72] However, the most important consideration for preferring The Six over The Seven was the additional political dimension of the former. While EFTA offered a solely economic arrangement, association with the EEC in any form was of political significance.

Israel's repeated attempts to solve its problems through the bilateral channel—direct approaches to The Six—also proved ineffective. Even the countries which were more positively inclined towards Israel, such as the Netherlands, were not prepared to act outside the framework of the EEC and demanded that any agreement reached between the two countries be authorized by the Community institutions in Brussels.[73] In November 1959, the Israeli inter-ministerial committee responsible for examining ways to preserve Israeli trade interests in Europe decided to abandon the bilateral channel.[74] Therefore, in the final months of 1959, it increasingly seemed that direct negotiations with the EEC institutions constituted the most effective way to tackle the challenge, which the customs union between The Six presented. Yet unsolved questions remained: how could the Israelis persuade the EEC to begin these negotiations and what goal should Israel set out to achieve in these talks?

Notes

1 Pardo, S. "The Year that Israel Considered Joining the European Economic Community." *JCMS: Journal of Common Market Studies* 51(5) (2013): 901–15.
2 Kessler, Z. "Israel Continue to Run Importation Policy." *Herut*, December 31, 1958.
3 Concerning the cooperation between France and Israel in the final years of the Fourth Republic see: Bar-Zohar, M. *Bridge over the Mediterranean: French-Israeli Relations, 1947–1963*. Tel Aviv: Am Hassefer, 1964; Kassir, S. and F. Mardam-Bey. *Itinéraires de Paris à Jérusalem: la France et le conflit israëlo-arabe*. Washington, DC: Institut des études palestiniennes, 1993; Pinkus, B. *From Ambivalence to an Unwritten Alliance*. Sede Boker: Ben-Gurion University [in Hebrew], 2005; Schillo, F. *La politique fran-çaise à l'égard d'Israël, 1946–1959*. PhD, Institut d'études politiques, 2008; Rosman, M. *La France et Israël, 1947–1970: De la création de l'État d'Israël au départ des Vedettes de Cherbourg*. PhD, Paris 1, 2009; Crosbie, S. K. *A Tacit Alliance: France and Israel from Suez to the Six Day War*. Princeton: Princeton University Press, 2015.
4 See the conversations between Yaakov Tsur and Renee Meyer, Donnedieu de Vabre and Sebilleau of the French Foreign Ministry and Shimon Peres's conversation with Jean Monnet: ISA, FM, file 3111/33, July 3, 1957; July 23, 1957.
5 Tzur to Najar, ISA, FM, file 3111/23, July 17, 1957.
6 For example, proposals for the agenda by M. K. Vilensky and M. K. Sneh, ISA, FM, file 3111/34, July 1957.
7 By 1956, 90% of the import quotas between the members of the organization had been removed. Two countries were still allowed to apply these import restrictions due to their economic situations: Turkey and Iceland. See: Genohovski, D. "The OEEC: Structure and Activities." *The Economic Quarterly* (17/18) (1957): 191–7.
8 Protocol of the fourth meeting of the inter-ministerial committee, ISA, FM, file 1946/19, September 30, 1957.
9 ISA, FM, file 3111/34, October 20, 1957.
10 See, for example, Sapir's reply to Bartur, ISA, FM, file 1946/19, October 25, 1957.
11 Goldstein, Y. *Eshkol: A Biography*. Jerusalem: Keter, 2003; Goldstein, Y. "Eshkol and the 'New Economic Plan' in Historical Perspective: The Price and Return to the Recession Policy as a Solution to the Economy's Problems—The First Attempt." *The Economic Quarterly* 57(2–3) (2010): 241–53.
12 Greenberg, Y. *Pinchas Sapir: Economical-Political Biography, 1949–1975*. Tel Aviv: Resling, 2011; Sapir, M. *The Great Is: A Biography of Pinchas Sapir*. Tel Aviv: Yedioth Aharonoth, 2011.
13 Bartur to Shinnar, ISA, FM, file 294/6, November 27, 1957.
14 For some time Bartur had supported Israel joining the GATT. Indeed, in 1956, he acted to advance this matter without success (see: Kessler, Z. "Israel Continues to Run Importation Policy." *Herut*: December 31, 1958. In fact, the idea was first raised by Efraim Haran in a memorandum submitted to Bartur. See: ISA, FM, file 1946/19, November 14, 1957.
15 Halevi, N. and G. Hanoh. "Israel and G.A.A.T." *The Economic Quarterly* 5(17/18) (1957): 154–62.
16 Rom, M. *In the Path of Israel's International Commercial Policy: The Preferences and the European Common Market*. Tel Aviv: Tel Aviv University Press [in Hebrew], 1998.
17 Bentsur to Foreign Ministry, ISA, FM, file 3111/29, February 15, 1957.
18 Najar to Bandur, ISA, FM, file 3111/29, May 18, 1957.

19 Rom, *In the Path of Israel's International Commercial Policy.*
20 Shneerson to Fischer, ISA, FM, file 211/5, April 22, 1958; April 28, 1958.
21 ISA, FM, file 211/6, January 16, 1958.
22 Bartur's report to the Knesset Foreign Affairs and Defense Committee, ISA, Knesset, February 18, 1958.
23 The scope of the multilateral agreement was confined to quota reduction and did not address tariff reductions.
24 State of Israel, ed. *State of Israel's Foreign Policy Documents.* Jerusalem: National Archives, 1981.
25 Bartur to the Economic Department, ISA, FM, file 211/4, July 16, 1958; July 20, 1958. 34th conference of the Permanent Delegates Committee, EUA, CM2/1958-115, November 27, 1958.
26 State of Israel, ed. *State of Israel's Foreign Policy Documents.*
27 See Rafael's letter to Bartur, ISA, FM, file 1946/21, February 28, 1958. And in addition Bartur to the Knesset Foreign Affairs and Defense Committee, ISA, Knesset, February 18, 1958.
28 State of Israel, ed. *State of Israel's Foreign Policy Documents.*
29 Note of the secretariat, EUA, CM2/1960-662, December 9, 1958.
30 EUA, BAC 17/1969-15, December 16, 1958.
31 EUA, CM2/1968-120, December 18–19, 1958.
32 The list included Britain, Sweden, Denmark, Norway, Switzerland and Austria. Portugal and Greece expressed readiness to join at a later stage, after the talks would mature into an agreement.
33 A positive response was received from the French and Italians in March 1959, see: ISA, FM, file 211/4, March 5, 1959; file 1946/10, March 12, 1959.
34 The Italians were especially fearful of the Arab reaction. Egypt, Yemen and Saudi Arabia had placed diplomatic pressure on Rome to block the Israeli initiative. See: Segreteria Generale-Archivio Storico, Direzione Generale Affari Politici III, 1959–62, file 33, July 9, 1959; file 28, November 15,1959; November 25, 1959.
35 In principle, increasing the quotas for Israeli exports would require a similar growth for the other GATT countries.
36 Bartur to Israeli representations in Western Europe: State of Israel, ed. *State of Israel's Foreign Policy Documents.*
37 Winand, P. *Eisenhower, Kennedy, and the united states of Europe.* London: Macmillan, 1996.
38 EUA, BAC 3/1978-321, February 23, 1960.
39 Bartur to Eytan, ISA, FM, file 937/12, March 20, 1960.
40 In Bartur's words, "It is necessary to sneak in." See: Bartur's survey to the Knesset Foreign Affairs and Defense Committee, ISA, Knesset, February 18, 1958.
41 *Herut*, November 30, 1958
42 Beginning January 1, 1958, the Benelux counties pursued a common trade policy and therefore negotiations were conducted with the three as one entity.
43 Memorandum, ISA, FM, file 1946/21, July 8, 1958.
44 Report of the Economic Department, ISA, FM, file 211/4, August 17, 1958.
45 ISA, FM, file 294/4, October 31, 1958.
46 Gideon Rafael later claimed that the disagreements among various decision makers in Israel regarding the desired agreement with the EEC led to an unfocused drafting of the memorandum. He believed already at this stage that the aim of association was not realistic. See: Rafael, G. *Destination Peace: Three Decades of Israeli Foreign Policy: A Personal Memoir.* New York: Stein and Day, 1981.
47 34th conference of the Permanent Delegates Committee [PMC], European Union Archive [EUA], CM2/1958-115, November 27, 1958.
48 During his visit to Israel, Petrilli, Commissioner for Social Matters in the European Commission, testified to the importance which the Commission attributed to the

appointment of representations to the EEC and its desire to achieve recognition in this manner. See: ISA, FM, file 1953, March 28, 1960.
49 Curtin, D. and M. Egeberg. "Tradition and Innovation: Europe's Accumulated Executive Order." *West European Politics* 31(4) (2008): 639–61. On the classical model of bureaucracy see: Putnam, R. D. "The Political Attitudes of Senior Civil Servants in Western Europe: A Preliminary Report." *British Journal of Political Science* 3(3) (1973): 257–90; Weber, M. "On Sociology." in *Max Weber: Essays in Sociology.* H. H. Gerth and C. W. Mills, eds. New York: Oxford University Press, 1946.
50 Ellinas, A. A. and E. Suleiman. *The European Commission and Bureaucratic Autonomy: Europe's Custodians.* Cambridge,: Cambridge University Press, 2012.
51 Rafael to Bartur, ISA, FM, file 1946/21, April 18, 1958.
52 EUA, BAC 3/1978-321, April 14, 1958.
53 Rafael to Bartur, ISA, FM, file 1946/21, October 31, 1958.
54 EUA, BAC 3/1978-321, December 3, 1958.
55 This is explicitly noted in the source: EUA, BAC 3/1978-321, December 4, 1958.
56 EUA, BAC 3/1978-321, December 17, 1958.
57 EUA, CM2/1958-120, December 18–19, 1958.
58 Bartur to Shneerson, ISA, FM, file 211/6, December 28, 1958.
59 Rafael to Bartur, ISA, FM, 1946/22, January 7, 1959.
60 EUA, CM2/1959-47, January 8, 1959.
61 EUA, CM2/1960-662, January 13, 1959.
62 State of Israel, ed. *State of Israel's Foreign Policy Documents.*
63 See Bartur's testimony in this regard: ISA, FM, file 1946/6, August 27, 1959.
64 Boaz to Nirgad, ISA, FM, file 1946/23, May 10, 1959.
65 Bartur to Boaz, ISA, FM, file 1946/23, June 11, 1959.
66 EUA, BAC 3/1978-321, June 1959.
67 State of Israel, ed. *State of Israel's Foreign Policy Documents.*
68 Judt, T. *Postwar: A History of Europe since 1945.* New York: Penguin, 2010.
69 Regarding these negotiations and the problems involved see: Report on Israel joining the GATT, ISA, FM, file 211/9, June 4, 1959; Boaz to Nirgad, ISA, FM, file 1946/23, July 16, 1959.
70 See the memorandum concerning Israel-GATT and the Common Market: ISA, FM, file 1954/12, December 28, 1961.
71 Y. Elizur. "Europe is United—and Israel Isolated?" *Ma'ariv,* October 11, 1960.
72 For example, the European Community development bank granted a huge loan of $125 million to Greece upon its association with the Common Market..
73 It should be noted that in principle The Six were still permitted to reach bi-lateral arrangements until 1962. However, in reality the states ensured that the Council approved any such arrangement. See: Cidor to Baron Ittersum, ISA, FM, file 1946/23, April 2, 1959; Cidor to the Economic Department, ISA, FM, file 1946/23, May 8, 1959.
74 Economic Department to Boaz, ISA, FM, file 1946/24, November 27, 1959.

References

Bar-Zohar, M. *Bridge over the Mediterranean: French-Israeli Relations, 1947–1963.* Tel Aviv: Am Hassefer, 1964.
Crosbie, S. K. *A Tacit Alliance: France and Israel from Suez to the Six Day War.* Princeton: Princeton University Press, 2015.
Curtin, D. and M. Egeberg. "Tradition and Innovation: Europe's Accumulated Executive Order." *West European Politics* 31(4) (2008): 639–61.
Elizur, Y. Europe is United—and Israel Isolated? *Ma'ariv,* October 11, 1960.

Ellinas, A. A. and E. Suleiman. *The European Commission and Bureaucratic Autonomy: Europe's Custodians*. Cambridge: Cambridge University Press, 2012.

Genohovski, D. "The OEEC: Structure and Activities." *The Economic Quarterly* (17/18) (1957): 191–7.

Goldstein, Y. *Eshkol: A Biography*. Jerusalem: Keter, 2003.

Goldstein, Y. "Eshkol and the 'New Economic Plan' in Historical Perspective: The Price and Return to the Recession Policy as a Solution to the Economy's Problems-The First Attempt." *The Economic Quarterly* 57(2–3) (2010): 241–53.

Greenberg, Y. *Pinchas Sapir: Economical-Political Biography, 1949–1975*. Tel Aviv: Resling, 2011.

Halevi, N. and G. Hanoh. "Israel and G.A.A.T." *The Economic Quarterly* 5(17/18) (1957): 154–62.

Judt, T. *Postwar: A History of Europe since 1945*. New York: Penguin, 2010.

Kassir, S. and F. Mardam-Bey. *Itinéraires de Paris à Jérusalem: la France et le conflit israëlo-arabe*. Washington, DC: Institut des études palestiniennes, 1993.

Kessler, Z. "Israel Continues to Run Importation Policy." *Herut*, December 31, 1958.

Pardo, S. "The Year that Israel Considered Joining the European Economic Community." *JCMS: Journal of Common Market Studies* 51(5) (2013): 901–15.

Pinkus, B. *From Ambivalence to an Unwritten Alliance*. Sede Boker: Ben-Gurion University [in Hebrew], 2005.

Putnam, R. D. "The Political Attitudes of Senior Civil Servants in Western Europe: A Preliminary Report." *British Journal of Political Science* 3(3) (1973): 257–90.

Rafael, G. *Destination Peace: Three Decades of Israeli Foreign Policy: A Personal Memoir*. New York: Stein and Day, 1981.

Rom, M. *In the Path of Israel's International Commercial Policy: The Preferences and the European Common Market*. Tel Aviv: Tel Aviv University Press [Hebrew], 1998.

Rosman, M. *La France et Israël, 1947–1970: De la création de l'État d'Israël au départ des Vedettes de Cherbourg*. PhD, Paris 1, 2009.

Sapir, M. *The Great Is: A Biography of Pinchas Sapir*. Tel Aviv: Yedioth Aharonoth, 2011.

Schillo, F. *La politique française à l'égard d'Israël, 1946–1959*. PhD, Institut d'études politiques, 2008.

State of Israel, ed. *State of Israel's Foreign Policy Documents*. Jerusalem: National Archives, 1981.

Weber, M. *On Sociology. From Max Weber: Essays in Sociology*. H. H. Gerth and C. W. Mills, eds. New York: Oxford University Press, 1946.

Winand, P. *Eisenhower, Kennedy, and the united states of Europe*. London: Macmillan, 1996.

4 A covert understanding between the Commission and Israel

The Commission pushes Israel towards the solution of association

In January 1959, the Israelis were convinced that the conditions were ripe to request diplomatic relations with the EEC; thus, at the end of the month, the Israeli Foreign Minister, Golda Meir, submitted an official application to appoint an Israeli representation to the Community's institutions. A few days later, after Brussels authorized this step, Gideon Rafael was appointed to serve as the first Israeli representative to the EEC, in addition to his main role as Israeli Ambassador to Belgium. Later it was a source of pride for the Israelis that they had been among the first to identify the future significance of the EEC and the fourth nation to appoint a special representative to manage relations with it. In fact, they took greater credit than they deserved: the idea did not originate among the Israelis, but rather they were pushed towards it. Indeed, the Ministry of Foreign Affairs was in no hurry to furnish the means that would endow the new position with any significant content. It was clear that Rafael could not effectively fulfill two positions simultaneously and that an official responsible for maintaining relations with the Community institutions was needed. However, the Israeli Ministry of Foreign Affairs, suffering from severe budget difficulties, did not believe that such an appointment was justified at this stage.[1] Therefore the task was given to an official in the Israeli reparations delegation in Germany: he was to divide his time between Cologne and Brussels. All Rafael's protests that such an arrangement would be unsatisfactory were ignored. Despite recognizing the importance of the EEC, many continued to view it as of limited political significance, particularly given the budgetary constraints faced by a ministry of restricted means, such as the Israeli Ministry of Foreign Affairs.

Upon receiving permission to appoint a representative to the EEC, in February 1959, the Director General of the Israeli Ministry of Foreign Affairs, Walter Eytan, his deputy Moshe Bartur, and the Israeli representatives to The Six attended a special meeting in Brussels at which they sought to establish a unified policy towards the new entity. This step, as others, was the initiative of Gideon Rafael. Due to his geographic proximity to the EEC institutions, he had become principally responsible for managing contacts with them. However, he was not authorized to co-ordinate and correlate policy and was unable to determine a uniform policy line, which he could then implement. In fact, the Israeli representations in each one of the capitals of The Six managed Israel's policy towards the EEC in a decentralized fashion; thus, unsurprisingly, chaos ensued. Rafael keenly felt the inefficiency resulting from the duplications and, at times, contradictory political stances adopted by each one of the representatives in their contact with the European institutions. Therefore, in November 1958, Rafael suggested hosting a conference of ambassadors in Brussels: the Israeli representatives would share their opinions and impressions, consolidating agreement and understanding regarding a common approach and means of coordination.[2] His suggestion was welcomed by the Ministry of Foreign Affairs in Jerusalem and three months later the most senior Israeli diplomatic echelons in Western Europe met at the Israeli Embassy in Brussels to discuss the important question: *Which way now?* Moshe Bartur, who in the meantime had been appointed Deputy Director General of the Ministry of Foreign Affairs, and was without doubt the highest authority in the Ministry on matters concerning Israel's economic ties with Europe, delineated three possible aims for Israel vis-à-vis the European organizations: integration—an attempt to achieve full membership, association—according to article 238 of the Treaty of Rome, or close relations—embarking on talks with European bodies regarding concrete matters, although apparently not of the utmost importance, with the aim of creating an opportunity for future association. Bartur warmly recommended the third option. He, as the rest of those present, was aware that persuading the Europeans to grant Israel association would be extremely difficult; so too, he was highly conscious that the chances of achieving full membership were miniscule. Bartur had previously opposed including overly pretentious demands in Israel's first letter to the EEC. He believed that the unrealistic and evasive answer issued by Brussels was a direct result of this pretention. Thus, he was convinced that conducting talks regarding "minor" technical issues presented the optimal path for progress. First, this tactic would reduce the danger to the Israeli economy by tightening economic ties with Europe. Secondly, and perhaps more importantly, the European institutions, particularly the Council, would struggle to dismiss the Israelis empty-handed. Indeed, the Europeans would find it far more difficult to reject a limited trade request (such as a demand for tariff relief regarding a certain product) than an application for comprehensive association. Surprisingly, the conference participants comprehensively supported this suggestion. Bartur's path was pragmatic and sophisticated, yet modest. As such, it did not accord with the nature of contemporary Israeli diplomacy, that of setting high goals, confident that any obstacle could be overcome using creativity, consistence and belief in the justice of the cause. Therefore, while accepting Bartur's argument, Director General Eytan cautioned: "I must warn against setting aims which are too modest [in our contacts with the European bodies]. the minimalist approach does not accord with the country's spirit."[3]

Considering the consensus among the participants at the conference of ambassadors in February 1959, it is amazing to discover that within only a few months Israel's approach had undergone a complete turnabout. In fall 1959, the minimalist line decided upon at the conference was abandoned, replaced by a general agreement that Israel should seek the ambitious solution of association. Leading the supporters of this revolution was none other than the architect of the minimalist approach: Moshe Bartur. What brought about this sudden change? In July 1959, Mapai Party Knesset Member David Lifshitz sent a long memorandum to the Israeli Foreign Minister. For almost two years, Lifshitz had served as one of the Knesset's observers in the Council of Europe. The Speaker of the Knesset, Yosef Sprinzak, chose Lifshitz for this role as one of the most influential figures in the ruling party and among the few fluent French speakers. Lifshitz's mission enabled him to establish close contact with various Western European figures who held central positions in their countries and the new economic bodies: statesmen, politicians, senior bureaucrats and high-ranking officials. In his conversations with them, Lifshitz was surprised to discover the extent to which they seemed to favor strengthening the relationship between Israel and the new EEC.[4] However, he was most surprised by two senior officials in the European Commission— Robert Marjoline, Vice President of the Commission and Economics and Finance Commissioner, and Émile Noël, the Secretary-General—who informed Lifshitz that while Israel would not be able to become a full member of the EEC, association in the framework of article 238 was a possibility.[5] Furthermore, the two Europeans handed the shocked Lifschitz a Commission memorandum containing an official interpretation of the association article from the Treaty of Rome, drawing his attention to those sections concerning the great degree of flexibility which an association arrangement offered both sides. Ostensibly, according to them, this would protect Israel from any economic damage. It was difficult to avoid the impression that the two Europeans had done their utmost to market the idea of Israel's association. Indeed, they claimed that it was important to connect Israel with the EEC not only due to the tariff issue but also because this could contribute to Israel's aid enterprise among developing African and Asian nations. Joining this endeavor would be a blessing for Israel, the EEC and the Third World. The Europeans concluded with satisfaction that, from the EEC's perspective, this was a decisive factor in favor of Israel's association. The bait had been carefully chosen to whet Israeli appetites. At the end of the 1950s, Israel had embarked on a full-swing diplomatic campaign, expending extensive resources, to conquer the hearts of African and Asian countries. Motivated by political, economic and psychological factors, the Israeli Ministry of Foreign Affairs, with the Minister at its head, accorded this endeavor great significance:[6] they believed that obtaining the faith and goodwill of the African and Asian peoples would also serve to improve relations with Western states, among them European countries. Israeli diplomats and statesmen seized every possible opportunity to show their counterparts in the West how Israel could help advance their nations' interests in the Third World. The formula was simple: European countries possessed the resources, while Israel had at its disposal the public relations necessary to open the door to these countries. The Israelis enjoyed the idea that their country's moral virtue constituted a desirable commodity in Europe. However, to a great extent, this was an illusion.

The Europeans did not view themselves as retired colonialists bearing the mark of Cain and thus in need of Israel's agency to make them acceptable to the Africans. Although at times Israeli activities in Africa did not contradict Europeans interests—as in the case of France, for example—the Europeans were generally in no hurry, to say the least, to create ties with Israel in this respect. Presumably, Marjoline and Noël did not really believe that Israel's association with the EEC was essential in cultivating relations with Third World states. However, they knew that this explanation would appeal to and flatter the Israelis.

If these two Commission figures had not yet sufficiently sold the idea of association with the EEC, one of them, half-jokingly, commented to Lifshitz that

> without exceeding the bounds of my "economic" profession, I will satisfy myself with another point, which is certainly no less important for you: the political-security aspect of the "little European" organization. And I presume that your people in Jerusalem know how to accord this aspect suitable consideration.

Furthermore, they noted that association with the EEC was likely to enable Israel's eventual membership in NATO.[7] Lifshitz certainly found it difficult to believe his ears. The political-security motivation at the foundation of Israel's efforts to form a connection with Europe was a taboo: it was common knowledge but never mentioned to external parties. On more than one occasion, in internal discussions the Israelis had admitted that association with European bodies would represent a vast asset in fortifying the future of the young country. Many perceived becoming part of Europe—economically, politically and militarily—as an insurance policy for the state. Indeed, Ben-Gurion viewed this as the primary reason for the approach to Europe. However, clearly the link between Israeli-European relations and the Arab–Israeli conflict constituted the most sensitive point for the Europeans and the main reason for their hesitancy to form close ties with Israel. Therefore, in conversations with Europeans, the Israelis endeavored to avoid mention of anything which could give rise to suspicions that their demands for a tariff arrangement or proposals for Israeli-European cooperation in Africa were motivated by political considerations. Of course, this caution was unable to allay entirely European suspicions that Israeli requests were driven by political interests; indeed, in their internal discussions, the Europeans expressed this concern repeatedly. However, the Europeans too usually endeavored to act with appropriate tact and avoided voicing their doubts to the Israelis. Thus, it was shocking that Marjoline and Noël admitted to understanding Israel's motivations for association with Europe and deemed them legitimate. Even if their comments did not necessarily reflect the official EEC line, or even that of the Commission, it was surprising to hear such statements from two senior figures in the EEC. The two European officials hinted at the reason for their generous stance towards Israel in their concluding words when they noted that despite Israel's desire to consider joining EFTA, they did not view this as a suitable alternative to ties with the EEC. Lifshitz's report continued:

Indeed, it has recently been announced that the "organization of The Seven" (EFTA) is being established in Europe. However, those with understanding view this organization as an artificial amalgamation, without sufficient continuity, integrity or mutual harmony, and they do not consider this declaration [the Stockholm Agreement] as anything other than a means to pressure the EEC.

The Ministry of Foreign Affairs in Jerusalem was unsure how to react to Lifshitz's astonishing report. Ministry officials wondered whether it evidenced a change in the Commission's stance. Indeed, until this point, the Commission had not been overly enthusiastic towards Israel's cause, not even with respect to realizing the modest guarantee given by Seeliger and Rey that talks would begin to clarify technical trade issues. Was it possible that the Commission now supported Israel's association with the EEC? It appears that officials at the Ministry of Foreign Affairs in Jerusalem failed to grasp the allusion in the concluding comments of the two Europeans. Their comments seemed too strange to be taken seriously and therefore the report remained buried among piles of documents in the Economic Department at the Foreign Ministry.

However, a few weeks later, increasing evidence complementing Lifshitz's report began to reach Jerusalem. At the beginning of September, Ram Nirgad, the same Israeli diplomat who had been tasked with serving as Rafael's assistant for relations with the EEC—in addition to his main position in the reparation delegation located in Cologne—conversed with Alfred Mozer, the Head of Cabinet of Sicco Mansholt, European Commissioner for Agriculture. Mozer asked Nirgad whether Israel was considering association with the EEC, noting that Israel could seek such an arrangement, in particular considering that Greece and Turkey had recently approached the EEC regarding this same matter. He believed that the chances of success were good; the fact that Israel was not a European country should not present an obstacle. He advised Israel not to approach the officials in the Commission offices but to go directly to the most senior echelon: Rey, Mansholt and Hallstein. Mozer admitted that matters did not depend solely on the Commission: the Foreign Ministers of The Six would need to authorize the recommendation, reaching a unanimous decision after consulting with the Council. However, he reiterated that he was confident regarding the chances of success, particularly with a positive recommendation from the Commission. The Israeli diplomat wondered if his European conversant was not a little too optimistic. What could explain this eruption of enthusiasm for Israel's association? Indeed, once again, ostensibly in a different context, Mozer added:

> Israel's place is with The Six (the EEC) and not The Seven (EFTA) if Israel wishes to integrate into the European economy. The US offers political support to The Six and not The Seven. As a more organized body, which can grant economic aid to countries associated with it, the Six can give Israel more . . . The Six is a union aspiring to economic, social and political integration, a body, which will wield increasingly significant political power as it consolidates.[8]

Thus, there is little room for doubt regarding the forces behind the attempts to sell the idea of association to Israel: competition with EFTA. Nirgad relates that the day before his conversation with Mozer, he had attended a festive reception for senior EEC officials and delegations to the EEC from other countries. Hallstein, President of the Commission, caught Nirgad as he entered the reception hall, and asked him to join him at his table to discuss an important matter, a great honor for a junior Israeli diplomat serving as the representative of a small country on a part-time basis. Upon taking his seat, Nirgad discovered that Hallstein placed him alongside a man named Jean-François Deniau who, he discovered, served as the head of the section for association agreements within Rey's department.[9] Following the conversation with Mozer, Nirgad began to wonder whether it was a coincidence that he had been seated next to this person.[10]

Moshe Bartur was one of the first to understand the situation, concluding that a golden opportunity had emerged and that this necessitated a re-examination of the strategy which he had molded. However, determining whether or not to change strategy required a direct conversation with the highest echelons in the European Commission. Only a few days after receiving Nirgad's report, Bartur informed the Commission of his intention to visit Brussels for a round of talks with Hallstein and Rey and indeed, at the beginning of October 1959, Bartur arrived in the city. His first conversation was in fact with relatively low-ranking officials in the Commission: Seeliger, Rey's Director General for External Affairs, and Robert Faniel, Director of the Bilateral Relations Section in the same directorate. When Bartur asked whether article 238 of the Rome Treaty could serve as the basis for cooperation between Israel and the EEC, Seeliger revealed no enthusiasm for the idea whatsoever. He made no attempt to beat around the bush and conceal his doubts under the mantle of procedural excuses, but revealed what in his opinion constituted the greatest obstacle: the Arab nations were not likely to accept Israel's association with the EEC amiably. The Arab–Israeli conflict could not be separated from the ongoing global hostilities between East and West and therefore such association was likely to have sweeping ramifications. If Seeliger thought that Bartur would appreciate his honesty, he was gravely mistaken. The Israelis would never graciously accept the treatment of their country as a "political problem." In this period, the Israelis were extremely sensitive to revelations of submission to Arab pressure. Therefore, Bartur angrily demanded to know what alternative arrangement the EEC was willing to offer Israel, especially because any other solution, for example an ad hoc agreement, would constitute a breach of the GATT agreement. To this, Seelinger had no real answer and admitted that an association constituted the only legal possibility for a special and differential tariff arrangement with Israel. Yet, he remained convinced that the time was not right for an association agreement between Israel and the EEC.[11]

Based on this conversation, the Israelis understood that any sympathy within the Commission for the idea of Israeli association was not all-embracing.[12] In contrast to the Commission leadership, the professional bureaucrats belittled the advantages of closer relations with Israel and were more sensitive to its possible complications. Certainly, it appears that this disparity between Commissioners and bureaucrats characterized the Commission throughout the period under discussion herein. Following this conversation with the officials in the Directorate for External Affairs, the Israelis began to question their interpretation of the signals ostensibly received by Lifshitz and Nirgad. However, Bartur's talks over the coming days with Hallstein and Rey indicated that there had been no error. Upon hearing of Israel's desire to investigate the prospects of association, Rey's reaction was totally at odds with the stance displayed by the director of his office. He welcomed the initiative, adding that the time was ripe for such initial talks. Turkey, Greece and Tunisia were already at the door, so why should Israel not join them? Echoing Mozer, Rey expressed confidence that Israel's interests would receive support among the governments of The Six. However, the task of preparing the ground in the various capitals fell to Israel. In the meantime, he suggested discussing the matter unofficially with Commission officials, without publicizing it. He noted that Hallstein likewise deemed this approach acceptable.[13]

The Israelis decide in favor of association

The talks between the Israelis and Commission officials left no room for doubt: the European Commission, or at least its highest levels, was interested in association with Israel. The time had now come for Israeli leaders to decide upon strategy: should they abandon the gradual approach, with its modest goals, in favor of aiming higher—association with the EEC? At this juncture, Bartur completely revised his opinion. The chances of an immense leap forwards, obtaining association with the EEC at an early stage, was too tempting to resist, even for a man as wise and careful as Bartur. In a memorandum to the Foreign Minister he recommended examining the option of association.[14]

However, the decision to strive for association required preliminary research. In the coming weeks, various Israeli ministries concerned with economic affairs—the Finance Ministry, Ministry of Agriculture and Ministry of Trade and Industry—conducted technical investigations, assessing the ramifications which association would have on the Israeli economy. They concluded that Israel could withstand the economic price of this step: the reward reaped would be greater than the cost. Therefore, at the beginning of January 1960, Bartur felt sufficiently confident to submit a detailed memorandum to the Prime Minister which concluded with an unequivocal recommendation in favor of association.[15] Bartur desired limited association, minimizing as much as possible the economic price Israel would pay: this would include removal of a number of tariffs on what Israel and The Six considered the most important key products. Israel, as a developing nation, would request special consideration: the right to phase out tariff levels more gradually (24 years rather than the 12 years allocated to The Six), thus protecting its infant industry. The desire to protect Israel's industry was not the only reason for Bartur's recommendation that the extent of association be limited. He similarly understood that despite the European Commission's goodwill and optimism, the negotiation of an association agreement would be lengthy and difficult:

We must presume that association with Israel will not cause the countries of the Common Market the same difficult economic problems [as Greece, Turkey and Tunisia], but at the same time, understandably, they do not have the same political desire for Israel to join the family. Rather the opposite: there is serious reluctance due to the Arab–Israeli conflict and it will not be easy to overcome this. The conclusion is that the only possibility must be limited association, which will restrict as far as possible the political significance, and which will be founded on maximum reciprocity in terms of rights and obligations with respect to tariffs and trade.[16]

Thus, Bartur's approach evidently remained cautious. Although convinced that it was advisable to strive for an ambitious aim such as association, he remained faithful to the principle that the political barrier could be overcome most effectively via a business-focused approach, utilizing economic-technical terms, a tactic which would minimize the ability of those opposing a closer relationship with Israel to obstruct the process. Likewise, Bartur recommended that Israel undertake a diplomatic campaign to pressure the countries among The Six. He understood that the Commission's support would be insufficient, and Israel would also require the backing of senior statesmen and politicians in the EEC. So too, Bartur viewed US support of Israel's interests as vital, because the Americans enjoyed significant influence among The Six. Finally, Bartur recommended to the Prime Minister that Israel continue concurrently with the talks concerning association, advancing along other routes: the negotiations regarding a multilateral agreement (which at this stage still remained on the table), joining GATT and, in particular, waiting to see the fate of EFTA. He emphasized that examining the possibility of association with the EEC did not tie Israel's hands; the country remained free to choose the path best suited to its needs. This approach would not only leave open all options but also, and perhaps mainly, improve the country's bargaining power vis-à-vis the EEC. Bartur was well aware that the possibility of association had arisen on the background of the blossoming rivalry between two economic blocs in Western Europe and he hoped that Israel would continue to enjoy the benefits of this situation in the exhausting negotiations ahead.

Persuading Ben-Gurion to adopt this path was relatively easy: since the establishment of the EEC, the Israeli Premier had believed that therein lay the solution to the young state's survival. In discussions with Bartur and Yaacov Tsur, then Deputy Foreign Minister, in January 1960, Ben-Gurion stated that it was vital for Israel to reach an association agreement with the EEC and every effort should be made to achieve this.[17] Indeed, he believed wholeheartedly that this ambitious goal was attainable. Thus, Ben-Gurion accepted Bartur's recommendations. To understand why the politicians abandoned their cautious policy of probing a limited economic treaty with the EEC and instead opted to strive for an association agreement, we must first understand the contemporary climate among Israel's political hierarchy. In January 1960, when the Israeli government resolved to seek an association agreement with the EEC, Ben-Gurion convened a special cabinet meeting to discuss Israel's security problems. He opened the meeting by saying, "Here is an assessment of the security situation and related issues which are giving me *concern and anxiety*," admitting that "This anxiety is giving me no rest" (emphasis added). The Prime Minister, as everyone else present, was concerned that the balance of power between Israel and the Arab nations would soon shift to such a degree that it would threaten Israel's very survival.[18] Ben-Gurion reminded his colleagues that Israel's past military victories were no guarantee of similar triumphs in the future. Moreover, Israel's qualitative edge was being eroded, and the quantitative power imbalance was constantly growing to the Arabs' advantage. Ben-Gurion believed that within 3–4 years Egypt would be positioned to attack Israel and had no doubt that President Nasser of Egypt, would seek to annihilate Israel. Internationally, the situation seemed bleak: efforts to gain acceptance into NATO had failed; the US was refusing to supply Israel with large quantities of high-quality arms; de Gaulle's new regime in France, Israel's main weapons supplier at the time, sought to implement a more balanced policy vis-à-vis the Arabs. In the long term, Israel would not be able to depend upon France for a continued supply of weapons. Ben-Gurion cautioned that the West was courting Nasser and could well abandon Israel to its fate, as the Egyptian President waited impatiently in the wings. Thus, Israel needed to make a preemptive move. One step that Ben-Gurion recommended was strengthening ties with the consolidating EEC; he felt this was the only way to guarantee the resources necessary for Israel's survival and fully believed this ambitious goal to be attainable. Some weeks later, Ben-Gurion informed US Undersecretary of State Douglas Dillon that Israel was seeking association with the EEC, explaining in the following manner why a simple economic trade agreement would not suffice: "Our interest in the EEC is not just economic. In light of our political and economic isolation in the region we are interested in maintaining a vital relationship with Europe."[19]

Ben-Gurion was not the only Israeli figure who regarded close ties with Europe as a solution to the country's security issues. Indeed, this belief was widespread at the time. Lifshitz's argument in his above-mentioned report recommending association with the EEC was based on the political and security implications of such a step: Israel would gain an indirect gateway to integration with Western organizations, following its failed NATO bid.[20] Bartur likewise frequently commented that European membership would bring political, as well as economic, advantages.[21]

In a memorandum written in 1965, he explained in detail the logical link between association and Israel's security problems:

> Our relations with the countries of Western Europe in general and the members of the Market in particular are based on "imponderability" rather than strong, tangible shared interests . . . our good relations with these countries are a result of natural sympathy, a similar political philosophy, feelings of guilt—especially Germany. In a few cases circles within the Market countries claim that a conflict of interests exists: moving closer to Israel is liable to harm and impair political ambitions in the Arab world and

Middle East . . . Association with the Common Market would create the "contractual" and organic link, which is currently lacking. Without such a connection, even the friendliest relations with one state or another will be left without any protection or formal defense against changes in internal and foreign policy . . . thus association with the Community has great significance for relations with all its member states. It will bring us substantially closer to the center of political decision-making, which is likely to become one of the central pillars of international policy in the present day . . . association with the Market means almost a complete stabilization of Israel's international status, it is likely to deal a fatal blow to the Arab illusions concerning the possibility of annihilating Israel . . . it is impossible to exaggerate the tangible and psychological value of association for Israel. The political ramifications, and accordingly also the security ramifications, of such association, are likely to be truly crucial. Therefore, association with the Market should be viewed as a deciding factor in terms of security.[22]

The press echoed this view: "EEC membership might be exceedingly important for Israel's security because, as recent rapid developments demonstrate, Israel may have problems buying arms in future," warned *Davar*, a prominent newspaper which identified with the ruling party.[23] The Israelis realized that the Europeans were conscious of the political motives behind their desire to join the EEC. In a report to the Knesset Foreign Affairs and Defense Committee, Bartur noted, "It is clear to everyone, Europeans and Israelis alike, that if Israel becomes the first ever non-European state [in Europe], this economic agreement would have great political implications." He believed that precisely for this reason Israeli ministers unanimously supported the membership solution.[24] The government was worried that a perceived political motive would deter the Council of Ministers from approving Israel's request and therefore, in all dealings with the EEC, Israel consistently sought to disguise its real motives. For example, suspecting that a document from the Ministry of Foreign Affairs could give the impression that Israel foresaw political gain, a ministry official quickly demanded that the document be re-written, "[t]o avoid the impression that Israel is interested in more than just an economic treaty and that it has political goals."[25]

Israel's political and security challenges were not the only reasons for the new state's anxiety. The leadership was no less afraid of economic collapse. Israel verged on the point of bankruptcy during the early 1950s; this was only avoided by means of US aid and German reparations. During the early 1960s, there was a prevailing sense of economic insecurity, especially as the end of the reparation payments loomed. "It is abundantly evident that our funds, especially those originating outside the country and which allow us to meet our budget requirements, are dwindling," warned Finance Minister Levi Eshkol.[26] The Israeli economy was suffering from the effects of the Arab boycott and this, combined with the arms race, constituted another factor which could lead to Israel's destruction. The Israelis believed that an association agreement with the EEC would deal a death blow to the Arab boycott. As Bartur wrote to the Foreign Minister, "If we succeed in joining one of the united European organizations, the Arab boycott would break down psychologically and utterly collapse."[27] Several members of the Foreign Affairs and Defense Committee agreed with this assessment.[28] In his discussions with European parliamentary representatives, Levi Eshkol noted two possible means that could bring about Israel's destruction: a military offensive, and economic strangulation caused by the creation of the EEC.[29] Thus, the Israelis perceived both the security and economic threats as equally dangerous, describing them in apocalyptic terms. Joining the EEC would combat both these evils at once and, therefore, was viewed as a solution to the nascent state's desperate needs.

In January 1960, Ben-Gurion and Foreign Minister Meir began their cam-paign to advance Israel's relations with the EEC in the US and Europe. Israeli advocacy was not restricted to the senior political echelons in The Six but also attributed great importance to fortifying their position among EEC officials. In October 1959, Hallstein and Rey were invited to visit Israel, ostensibly to view first-hand the structure of the Israeli economy. The Israelis were experts at effectively exploiting the opportunity of a foreign visit to win the hearts of their guests, taking visitors to see Israel's most precious treasures: a kibbutz, the Dead Sea factories, meeting with young soldiers at a military base, visiting the Holocaust Museum at Yad Vashem. The guests were lavished with continuous attention, accompanied from one site to the next, all the while absorbing a large dose of Zionism. At every step, they encountered the achievements of the young nation, accomplished not by means of material abundance but through the power of the spirit: self-confidence, determination, diligence, initiative and creativity. This propaganda campaign was often highly successful and many visitors left Israel's borders captivated by the country's magic. However, regardless of whether the guest yielded to the country's thrall, the Israelis viewed the visit itself as a great blessing. Since its establishment, Israel's Arab neighbors had waged a de-legitimization campaign, negating the state's right to exist, casting aspersions on the morality of the entire Zionist enterprise and trying to isolate the country politically and economically via means such as the Arab boycott. For both politi-cal and psychological reasons, it was important for the Israelis to win the world's acceptance, to receive external validation, countering the Arab de-legitimization campaign, and thus Israelis viewed the visits of world leaders as very important for this exact reason. Figures invited to visit Israel were well aware that this was not simply another foreign trip but rather a political statement; indeed, many feared that acceding to the Israelis' insistent pleading would embroil the body they represented—be it a state, international organization, or economic firm—in complications. Therefore, Hallstein and Rey warmly thanked the Israelis for the invitation, expressing their apologies that due to prior obligations and their heavy workload they would not be able to accept. However, at the end of 1959, one of the Commissioners, the Italian Giuseppe Petrilli, a professor of political science who was responsible for social affairs in the EEC, expressed a desire to visit Israel. Indeed, his office was tasked with developing employment and improving work-ing conditions in the EEC member states and, as such, he wished to view the

Israeli model. Petrilli was especially interested in Israel as a developing state, characterized at once by a liberal economic orientation and a socialist nature. The Israelis pounced on Petrilli as though they had unearthed a treasure chest, seeking to endow the visit with as much official character as possible, whereas the Commission endeavored to ensure the utmost modesty, emphasizing that Petrilli was travelling in his professional role as Commissioner for Social Affairs, rather than representing the Commission in a wider capacity.[30] The Director General of Petrilli's office informed the Israelis that the Commissioner was highly sensitive to matters of honor and accordingly, the Israeli Ministry of Foreign Affairs was briefed to lavish upon him as many honors as possible. When Petrilli arrived in Israel, the Israelis welcomed him in the manner usually reserved for the leaders of important nations. The Israelis were apparently successful: the Commissioner for Social Affairs became one of Israel's most impassioned advocates in the Commission. For their part, the member states of the EEC were punctilious in avoiding the impression that they had any part in Petrilli's visit, to the extent that no representative of The Six attended a reception which he hosted in Israel on the eve of his return to Brussels.[31]

In fall 1959, the parties agreed to hold initial talks between the Commission and Israeli representatives regarding the possibility of an association agreement, scheduled to begin six months later. At the beginning of April 1960, Bartur visited Brussels and met with the highest echelons in the Commission. He received the impression that "among everyone there is a feeling of great support and positivity towards our matters."[32] However, shortly after Bartur's visit, the Commission's approach to Israel underwent a dramatic change. On the agenda of the meeting of the Council of Foreign Ministers in May 1960 was the question of the EEC's position regarding the association of third-party countries. During the debate, the Foreign Ministers of Italy and France expressed their hesitancy to grant association to countries, which were neither European nor former colonies of The Six.[33] It suddenly became clear to the Commission that, in opposition to their presumptions, the Council of Ministers was not open to the idea of Israeli association. There was no real chance that the Council would authorize formal negotiations regarding association in the foreseeable future, not only due to fear of the Arab response but also because they were concerned that this would call forth a deluge of approaches from additional countries. Likewise, association talks with Greece and Turkey, which had appeared promising and encouraged the Commission to search for a similar solution with Israel, had become embroiled in complex difficulties;[34] there was no great yearning for similar entanglements with another nation. In the meantime, the concern that Israel would decide to form an association with EFTA had also diminished; it seemed that EFTA was not seeking to expand its ranks.

Therefore, the Commission concluded that it needed to find a way out of the situation it had created a year earlier, when it had pushed Israel towards the solution of association. The Commission could not simply renege on the under-standings which it had reached with the Israelis, and therefore sought to minimize the content of the issues under negotiation, perhaps even evading talks about association, replacing it with a limited trade agreement. The Commission also wanted to ensure that the agreement to conduct initial talks would not become public knowledge. Although the leadership of The Six, as well as the Council of Ministers, knew about the talks between the Commission and Israel regarding ongoing important trade issues, they were unaware that the Commission and Israel had reached a verbal understanding that the talks would investigate the possibility of association. Therefore, Israel was asked to agree that the talks would not be managed by a special delegation of experts but rather by the country's diplomatic representatives to the EEC in Brussels. The Israeli economic experts required for the clarification of various matters arising in the talks would be temporarily seconded to the Embassy. In this way, no one would suspect the Commission of engaging in special negotiations with Israel outside the remit of the trade talks then underway with all delegations in Brussels. It was agreed that externally the talks would be presented as technical clarification regarding a relatively inconsequential topic occupying the EEC in those days.[35] The Commission approached the talks as though they were being forced upon it; this was evident at the first meeting between the Israeli and Commission representatives, during what were known as "the preliminary talks." At the request of the Commission, this meeting was held in a restaurant over lunch, illustrating the extent to which the Commission desired to give the talks an official stamp. At the meeting, the two Commission officials—Seeliger and Deniau—tried to persuade the Israelis to renounce the idea of a customs union and accept a more limited arrangement, an idea which the Israelis completely rejected. Seeliger and Deniau also sought to find a comfortable procedure that would allow them to receive technical data regarding the Israeli economy without this appearing as "convicting evidence" that official talks with Israel were underway. The natural method was to send a detailed questionnaire for Israel to answer. However, dispatching a questionnaire on official paper could be viewed as a Commission initiative to search for a path towards association with Israel. It was finally resolved that the questionnaire would be printed on blank paper and thus devoid of any incriminating link to an EEC body.[36]

Lobbying in the capitals of The Six

The Israelis were furious at the Commission's attempts to avoid giving the talks any kind of official nature. When the questionnaires were sent to Israel, not only without any reference to the Commission but with no title whatsoever, Amiel Najar, the new Israeli Ambassador in Brussels (replacing Rafael), felt that the time had come to approach two of Israel's friends in the Commission leadership: Mansholt and Marjoline. They in turn protested to Rey, who was forced to admit that matters had lost all proportion and agreed that Israel's answers could be written on official paper of the State of Israel and addressed directly to him.[37] However, these minor gestures were insufficient to dissipate the uncomfortable sensation among the Israelis that the Commission's approach had changed and that the latter was trying to dissolve the negotiations. While believing that the

Commission remained as supportive of association with Israel as it had been in the past, it seemed that fears of the Council's response had led it to exercise exaggerated caution. The Israelis had for some time feared that "covert" talks with the Commission would harm the chances of success; it was now evident that this concern was justified. Therefore, at the beginning of 1960, Najar recommended a change of tactics, approaching the Council of Ministers to receive its blessing for negotiations with the Commission. If the Council would authorize the Commission to conduct negotiations with Israel regarding association, the Commission would no longer have any reason or excuse to proceed sluggishly and cautiously. Likewise, the Council would not be able to claim that the preliminary talks had been conducted behind its back and therefore did not obligate it in any way.[38]

Najar did not wait quietly for the policy line he suggested to be accepted in Jerusalem, but had been acting to advance it for some time. He met with Permanent Representatives of the Council and consulted with them regarding Israel's chances of achieving association with the EEC. The responses he received were almost always chilly; he was informed that Israel should use the normal diplomatic channels in the capitals of The Six and, only after receiving unanimous agreement, would there be reason to vote on the matter in the Council.[39] This trick was intended to cause the failure of the Israeli initiative but free the Council from any responsibility for it. Therefore, it transpired that the key to success lay in persuading the political echelons in each of The Six to favor association with Israel. The Benelux countries were considered clear supporters of Israel and their backing was almost always guaranteed. The three big countries were highlighted as "problematic" and therefore the main efforts were directed towards them. The German attitude was considered hesitant, the Italians opposed the idea mainly due to economic considerations, whereas the French were also cautious for political reasons. However, Israel had excellent relations with the French leadership and it was only natural to believe that the Israelis would be able to persuade them to help in this matter.[40] However, French-Israeli relations had altered since the events in Algeria had returned Charles de Gaulle to power in June 1958. The Fifth Republic did not feel the same level of commitment to Israel as its predecessor. Although the background to the alliance with Israel remained unchanged—the war in Algeria was still far from over—the French government did not hesitate to dismiss Israel empty-handed when it felt that acceding to Israel's requests conflicted with French interests.

In this same period, the French attempt to thaw tensions with Egypt led to a cooling in its policy towards Israel. Nevertheless, in the first months of 1960, the hostility between Paris and Cairo once again intensified; simultaneously Franco-Israeli relations flourished. The French government, with the personal involvement of De Gaulle, decided to sell to Israel 72 Mirage fighter planes, the most modern weapon produced by the French military industry.[41] The Israelis hoped that if they could successfully exploit this renewed "honeymoon period" between Israel and France to acquire support for Israel's association request, France could in turn pressure Germany and Italy. Therefore, Paris became a focal point in the Israeli campaign, which endeavored to recruit the country's elite to the cause. In June 1960, Ben-Gurion flew to France; among other matters on the agenda (including nuclear cooperation between Israel and France), he expressed to French Prime Minister Michel Debre Israel's desire for association with the EEC. To the Israeli premier's great pleasure, his French counterpart supported this idea.

Debre's positive response finally persuaded Ben-Gurion that an association agreement was an attainable short-term goal. The Israeli bureaucrats, strained by the prolonged talks with the Commission, rejoiced as they prepared for the final offensive on the fortress of the Council of Ministers—the last barrier to Israel's association with the EEC. Some, including Bartur, viewed this step as a mistake. Bartur doubted the wisdom of an approach to the Council at this juncture. His cautious tactics dictated that the Israelis first exhaust the Commission channel, slow and frustrating as it may be, before requesting a Council decision on Israeli association. He had no illusions concerning Israel's chances of success in persuading The Six that Israeli association was in their interest. Slogans such as "Israel as a bridge between Europe and the countries of Asia and Africa" or talk about "Israeli purchasing power" were all very well on paper—indeed it was essential to present Israel's demands as a deal benefitting both sides[42]—but a realist such as Bartur was not deluded regarding the true power of such arguments. When the Israeli Ambassador to The Hague, Hanan Cidor, proposed that Israel adopt a stricter negotiating strategy vis-à-vis the Community institutions, Bartur's department instructed him to stop talking such nonsense.[43] Cidor was gently informed that in light of Israel's economic weakness and the country's "political" stigma, "we must mainly follow the paths of lobbying—as respectably as possible."[44] In simple terms, Israel had no real ability to reward or punish The Six for supporting or denying of its requests. The only effective weapon available to Israel consisted of the following: on the one hand, due to the country's exceptional political circumstances, Israel really and truly depended upon Europe in terms of its foreign trade; on the other hand, the moral sensitivity which the states of Western Europe felt towards the fate of the Jewish nation. Only if Israel could prove that special arrangements with the EEC were essential for the state's continued existence, and if no arrangement other than association would be found, was there a reasonable chance that the Council would vote in favor of this solution. Bartur believed that The Six would not dare to bar Israel's way purely for political reasons—this would be an admission of surrender to Arab pressure. However, he was likewise convinced that they would not hesitate to use any plausible economic excuse to extricate themselves from the problem. Bartur viewed the negotiations with the Commission as an opportunity to prevent the Council from employing such "practical" economic excuses: for this precise reason, the talks were of great significance.[45] Bartur understood that arguments persuading The Six of the expected economic profit or political benefit would not lead to a ruling in favor of association with Israel; the only way to bring them to take a step which they considered as counter to their own interests was to exhaust the legitimate arguments buttressing their refusal,[46] forcing them to recognize the unfair and illogical nature of such a rejection. The decision to abandon utilitarian arguments regarding the profitability of association with Israel, replacing them with a "strategy of argumentation," perhaps constitutes the most significant development in the episode at the heart of this book. In the long term, this would enable Israel to reap success, despite the poor resources at the country's disposal.

However, it was widely presumed—Bartur too eventually succumbed to this belief—that Israel possessed the required tools to advance the solution of association already at this stage. This conviction was based on two foundations: complete confidence in the Commission's support for association and the latter's willingness to do its utmost to advance this cause; and the belief that the political elite in most of The Six could be persuaded to support Israel—reinforced by Ben-Gurion's talks with Debre. The Israelis had no doubts concerning the Commission's support: indeed, the Commission had suggested the very idea at the outset and encouraged Israel to take this route. Although in the past few months its bureaucrats had revealed a certain lack of enthusiasm towards the preliminary talks with Israel, this was perceived as tactical caution, intended to maximize the chances that the Council of Ministers would eventually approve the association option. The Israelis remained positive that they and the Commissioners were playing on the same team—a belief which had no basis in reality. In fact, the Commission was to a certain degree playing a double game. On the one hand, it encouraged Israel to strive for association because this served its own needs, implying to the Israelis that it was a partner in the campaign to advance association. However, on the other hand, the Commission was not really prepared to become embroiled in complications with the Council for Israel's sake. To the Council of Ministers, the Commission's representatives did not hesitate to portray themselves as doing everything in their power to halt Israeli demands for association. A perfect example of this occurred in a meeting of the COREPER on July 26, 1960. Each one of the representatives of The Six in turn updated their colleagues regarding the contacts initiated by Najar concerning the possibility of Israeli association with the EEC. The atmosphere was far from supportive of the Israeli initiative. When his turn came, Noël, the Commission's representative, did not hesitate to follow the line adopted by his colleagues. "Indeed, Najar approached a number of people in the Commission regarding possible association," Noël laconically reported, failing to note that a dialogue with the Israelis concerning this topic had been underway for some months, involving the highest echelon of the Commission. He also omitted to mention that he was among the first to plant the dream of association in the hearts of the Israelis. Noël continued, stating that the Commission had responded guardedly to Najar's approaches ("we advised him to proceed with caution"), counseling Israel that it was first necessary to gain the backing of the governments of The Six, before approaching the Council of Ministers. This account, although not a complete fabrication, was doubtless misleading. The members of the Council were not aware of the exact reality, but felt uncomfortable with Noël's testimony; indeed, rumors of talks between the Commission and Israeli representatives regarding matters that exceeded the bounds of trivial trade concerns had reached them. Therefore, one of the representatives requested an explanation for the questionnaires sent to the Israeli Embassy. Noël hastily sought to calm any concerns, stating that the contacts were "with the employees at the Israeli Embassy only" and of a technical nature, intended to clarify the future effects of the establishment of the EEC on Israel's trade with the continent. The questionnaires, which were sent to the Israelis "on plain white paper only," did not obligate the Commission in any way.[47] Noël determinedly sought to allay any fears that the Commission was involved in the Israeli initiative for association, and was not averse to telling white lies; this reveals that the Commission's willingness to take risks and expose itself for the sake of the Israelis was highly limited. It is amazing to discover the limited responsibility which the senior Commission echelons exhibited after having pushed Israel, with both hands, towards the solution of association. At any rate, the Israelis continued to believe that the Commission supported their interests wholeheartedly.

The Israelis clung to a further illusion: they were sure that it would not be overly difficult to garner the political support among The Six necessary to pressure the Council of Ministers into a positive decision regarding Israeli association. However, here too existed a great disparity between the Israelis' conviction and reality, as was abundantly evident, although the Israelis consistently ignored the facts. Following his visit to Paris at the end of June, Ben-Gurion traveled to the Netherlands and Belgium. There the Israeli Prime Minister sought to replicate the success of his talks with Debre, hoping to use the positive stance of the French as leverage to gain additional support for Israel among The Six. This should not have been difficult in the cases of the Netherlands and Belgium: their support of Israel was guaranteed. Yet in his conversation with the Dutch Foreign Minister Joseph Luns, who was also serving as the rotating President of the Council of Ministers, the latter expressed pessimism regarding the chances of a positive decision in the Council. France and Germany would not agree to this, he argued, although his country's support was assured.[48] Luns's hesitancy should have alerted the Israelis to the warning signs. Since the establishment of Israel, the Dutch had constituted one of the friendliest countries towards the young Jewish nation. If Israel hoped to obtain unrestricted support for its interests from any of The Six, The Hague would offer this. In his conversation with the Belgian Foreign Minister Pierre Wigny, Ben-Gurion encountered an even chillier reception. Wigny evaded the Israeli Prime Minister's request to support Israeli association, voicing serious doubts as to whether the time was right for such a step. Even the French card was of no help: the Belgian Foreign Minister refused to believe that Debre intended to keep his word and help Israel form an association with the EEC. The only promise that the Israeli Prime Minister succeeded in extracting from his Belgian colleague was a loose pledge that it might be possible to find suitable arrangements which would avoid any economic damage to Israel resulting from the Common Market. In fact, the Belgians were concerned about the possible ramifications of Israel's request on their relations with Arab nations, mainly Egypt, wherein Belgium had important interests.[49]

Ben-Gurion's conversation with Hallstein and Rey was no more encouraging. Hallstein assumed a cautious and non-obligatory approach, claiming that the decision was reserved for the Council of Ministers. To enable the submission of a recommendation to the Council regarding association with Israel, the Commission needed to receive the answers to the questions previously dispatched to Israel. Ben-Gurion complained that the entire process was too slow for his liking. "I do not get very excited when people tell me that the problem must be studied before any decision," the Israeli premier replied to an embarrassed Hallstein, "it is better to decide and then afterwards learn how to implement."[50] For some reason, the Israeli Prime Minister failed to understand the clear signals that the Europeans were not overly excited by the idea of Israel's association. In his report to the Knesset's Foreign Affairs and Defense Committee, he stated that "everyone with whom I discussed the matter [Israel's EEC association] expressed a positive opinion."[51] This was not a lie: no one with whom Ben-Gurion met wanted to give the impression that he personally opposed the idea, finding it comfortable to pass the blame onto others. Although the Israeli Premier was no stranger to the diplomatic world and certainly knew how to interpret the messages imparted to him, it seems that in this case he clearly chose not to understand them.

Further convicting evidence regarding the Europeans' lack of enthusiasm continued to accumulate on the desk of the Department for Western Europe and the Economic Department at the Ministry of Foreign Affairs in Jerusalem. Above all, one thing was abundantly clear: German antagonism to the possibility of an association agreement with Israel.[52] Since the mid-1950s, West German foreign policy had followed the Hallstein Doctrine (the same Hallstein who served as President of the European Commission from 1958): the country severed diplomatic ties with any state that recognized East Germany. However, this was a double-edged sword, exposing Germany to parallel sanctions. Indeed, the Arab nations seized this opportunity to demand that West Germany avoid instigating diplomatic relations with Israel, resulting in a "diplomatic balance of terror." The Arab nations refrained from establishing diplomatic relations with East Germany, while West Germany rewarded this by avoiding the establishment of official diplomatic relations with Israel. However, this simple formula was not unproblematic and, due to its unofficial nature, its boundaries were unclear.

Some West Germans feared the Arabs might consider an association agreement with Israel as hostile and in violation of their mutual understandings. Beyond the political factor, there were economic reasons for Germany's reluctance to aggravate the Arabs. In the late 1950s, the Germans had established extensive commercial ties with Arab nations, which were eager for German expertise and anxious to buy high-quality Germany industrial products. German firms naturally found the vast potential of the Arab market, with populations numbering dozens, if not hundreds of millions, extremely attractive.[53] The German government dared not risk an economic opportunity of this scope.

Once the Israeli Ministry of Foreign Affairs realized that Germany was the main obstacle to an association agreement, it moved quickly. In such cases, its modus operandi was to approach the highest-ranking decision makers, assuming that they would adopt a more positive attitude toward Israel than narrow-minded officials; likewise, they possessed the ultimate authority to decide. Thus, the Israeli representative in Germany, Felix (Eliezer) Shinnar, received orders to raise the question with Adenauer.[54]

The decision to approach the highest West German authority was motivated by the belief that the German Chancellor was a friend of Israel and regarded it as his country's moral obligation to help the Jewish state. The reparations agreement signed between the two countries in 1952, in the framework of which West Germany obligated to pay Israel the enormous sum of $750 million (mainly in final products), was largely his achievement. Adenauer's motivations were mainly practical: he recognized the importance of the payments in rehabilitating Germany's international image—although also principled—he viewed fortifying the security and economy of the Jewish state as a historical debt which the Germans must pay.[55] In March 1960, the Israeli Prime Minister and the West German Chancellor met for the first time while the two were visiting New York. The historic meeting took place in the luxurious Waldorf Astoria Hotel. Ben-Gurion asked the Chancellor for a special loan of $500 million to develop the Negev, to be paid over ten years. He also asked the German politician to authorize a military aid deal, which had been drawn up previously by Defense Minister Strauss. Adenauer agreed in principle to both requests,[56] an additional indication of the obligation he felt towards Israel. Israeli leaders hoped that it would be possible to harness Adenauer's goodwill to support Israel's bid for association with the EEC.

Shinnar knew exactly how to play on the elderly German statesman's heartstrings. He emphasized the tremendous consequence of the arrangement for Israel's future. The German Chancellor was unable to dismiss him empty-handed and promised that Germany would support an association agreement with Israel if the other five countries gave their backing.[57] Adenauer used the same tactic which the Israelis had encountered among other European statesmen: he appeared to respond positively to Israel's request while making his backing contingent on his counterparts, assuming (and hoping) that Israel would find it difficult to gain their support. This tactic was not a good sign, although the Israeli Ministry of Foreign Affairs deemed even his qualified consent as a major triumph.

Adenauer knew that he could rely upon the other European leaders to oppose Israel's request. Italy's stance was no less hostile, although for different reasons. As was noted, the Italians were mainly concerned about the economic price they would pay if Israel were to join the Common Market. Italy was the most agrarian nation among The Six. While in 1960, agriculture accounted on average for 9% of the GDP of EEC member states, there were significant differences between the various countries in this respect. In Germany, the most industrialized nation, agriculture accounted for 6% of GDP. By contrast, in Italy, the number was 13%.[58] Indeed, 6.5 million Italian workers were employed in agriculture, constituting 40% of the country's workforce, compared to 30% in France, 12% in the Netherlands and 9% in Germany.[59] Although this figure decreased constantly—by the beginning of the 1970s, the percentage of Italian workers engaged in agriculture had fallen to 20% of the workforce—throughout the period, Italian agriculture remained a central economic sector. In particular, Italy enjoyed a comparative advantage over the other EEC member states in the cultivation of fresh fruit. In the years 1958–59, Italy harvested 4.1 million tons of fruit, compared to 3.8 in Germany, 1.4 in France and 0.7 in the Netherlands.[60] A significant amount of this was citrus fruit and therefore Israeli agricultural products competed directly with the Italian produce, mainly Sicilian citrus fruit. Italian farmers were frustrated that while Italy was the only member of the EEC to export citrus fruit, its products accounted for a mere 5%–6% of the market volume among The Six. Italian oranges and lemons were barely seen in Belgium, the Netherlands and France; only in German markets did the Italian farmers acquire a significant portion of the market (11%). In this constellation of severe competition, there was little motivation to grant trade gestures to a competing country such as Israel.[61] In addition, Israeli exports competed with other sectors of the Italian economy, for example the textile industry, which in contrast to Germany and France was based on small factories producing luxury products at relatively high prices—very similar to the Israeli exports in this sector. The political structure in Italy was very helpful to those sectors, which felt threatened by external competition, and they successfully pressured the government in Rome. Italian governments tended to be weak, based on loose coalitions with an insubstantial majority. The Christian Democratic Party, for example, a central element in Emintora Fanfani's coalition in the years 1960–63, relied to a great degree on the agricultural sector and therefore Italian farmers had effective leverage to ensure that no competitor would get a foot in the EEC's door. Likewise, the trade unions in Italy enjoyed exceptional power; some referred to their influence as a kind of left-wing "shadow government."[62] They did not hesitate to use the threat of strikes when seeking the weak government to accede to their demands and in influencing the Italian stance in Community institutions. Furthermore, the Italians shared the "usual" political and economic motivations for hesitancy towards Israel: fear of the Arab response. Fanfani's government sought to play a more central role in the international arena, viewing the country as perfectly positioned to serve as a mediator between East and West. The deterioration in relations between France and the Arab states following the war in Algeria, as well as the tensions between these countries and the UK after the Suez Crisis, had generated a certain vacuum; one which Italy hoped to fill. Similarly to Germany, Italy lacked a colonial past in the Middle East (apart from its rule in Libya), a fact which constituted an advantage in the contemporaneous climate. Likewise, a large community of Italian expatriates lived in Egypt, according Rome with an advantage in this important Arab nation. Italian exports to Arab states in 1960 reached the impressive value of $177 million, while exports to Israel were far lower, totaling only $20 million. Italian companies won highly desirable tenders in North Africa (mainly in Morocco and Egypt) to search for oil, extract minerals, build factories, establish television networks and provide training and advice, while the extent of Italian investment in the Arab world reached a few million dollars.[63] Thus, the Arab factor influenced Italian policy during this period. It should likewise be noted that the Arab nations often made Italian economic penetration conditional on minimizing economic ties with Israel. For example, when an Italian group signed a $24 million contract with Egypt to construct refineries, the government in Cairo stipulated that the contract would be canceled in the eventuality that Italian companies were found to be supporting the Israeli economy. The weapon of the Arab boycott was especially effective vis-à-vis Italy because the public and private industries in this country were the most concentrated in Western Europe: a number of giant corporations almost completely controlled the large factories, all of them with diverse businesses among the Arab states.[64] The Italian Foreign Ministry did not encourage, to say the least, Italian business ties with Israel.[65] Likewise, it was in Italy's economic interest to present itself as the most stubborn opponent of Israel's association with the EEC. The basis upon which Israel sought association with the EEC was already legally shaky, thus providing the Italian government with a convenient justification for opposing it. This matter was clarified to Najar in the most explicit manner by the Italian Permanent Representative in the Council.[66]

There was clear evidence that politicians and officials of The Six were strongly antagonistic towards an association agreement between Israel and the EEC. Yet the Israelis continued to believe that their chances of success were high. At the meeting of the Cabinet for Economic Affairs in August 1960, those present decided to persist with the campaign and continue lobbying in the various capitals to gain support for Israel's quest. Germany and Italy were highlighted as the main countries to be won over. No one suggested examining the actual chances of success and the consequences of failure. The die was cast in September 1960, when Israel presented a lengthy document to the Commission providing detailed answers to the questionnaire it had been given a few months earlier. The document summary explicitly stated that Israel was applying for association under Article 238 of the Treaty of Rome:

> The significant similarity of Israel's economic and social aims with regard to social, political and wage structure, as well as the wage level and social charges, serve as a suitable basis on which *an association agreement* can be founded. It is believed that such an association agreement confirming the Article 238 of the Treaty of Rome should take the form of a customs union and include provisions pertaining to participation in the agricultural arrangements envisaged by the EEC and the harmonization of social and economic policies [emphasis added].[67]

There could now be no turning back, as the Commission acknowledged first and foremost. Having read the document that Israel had submitted, Hallstein and Rey informed the Israelis that in their view the Council of Ministers needed to authorize formal preliminary talks with Israel.[68] In fact, Israel had left them with no choice. The informal talks that the Commission had conducted with Israel at its own initiative, without the approval of the Council of Ministers, had been possible under the title "a clarification of the commercial issues dividing the parties." The agreement that the purpose of the talks was to explore the option of an association agreement with Israel was no more than a verbal understanding between the Commission and Israel, essentially a kind of conspiracy. When the Israelis presented an official document declaring their desire for an association agreement, the Commission could no longer maintain this pretense. The decision to open formal talks examining the question of association could only be made by the Council of Ministers. Thus, the Commission needed the Council's explicit agreement before it could resume talks with the Israelis.

For its part, Israel prepared for a final attack on the EEC fortress, engaging the heaviest artillery in its possession. The multi-talented Bartur was sent to Italy in September because a person with great talents of persuasion was needed to overcome the fiercest stronghold of opposition. His conversations led him to conclude that the situation was not as bad as those in Jerusalem feared and that it would be possible to change the Italian government's position. He was especially encouraged by interest among the economic ministries in Rome regarding various kinds of economic cooperation with Israel.[69] For example, the Director General of the Italian Ministry of Agriculture was interested in a proposal for cooperation between citrus growers in the two countries;[70] translating this into action would require the direct involvement of the Italian political echelon. Therefore, at the beginning of October, Foreign Minister Meir met with the Italian Foreign Minister Antonio Segni at the UN Convention in New York. At this meeting, Meir tried to depict Israel not as a trade competitor but rather as an economic opportunity for Italy,[71] suggesting that Italian companies should invest in the Israeli economy. She proposed that an Italian delegation visit Israel to study the range of opportunities for cooperation. Segni's response was positive, although he offered no guarantees regarding association.[72] A few days later, the Israeli Agricultural Minister Moshe Dayan arrived in Italy. Dayan was under great pressure from farmers and lobbyists in the Citrus Marketing Board of Israel to ensure the continued export of Jaffa citrus to the EEC. The Israeli citrus sector was experiencing accelerated growth, a result of planting new orchards and the Israelis' agronomic success in overcoming the two greatest enemies of the orange tree: the black aphid and the Mediterranean fly. Predictions indicated that within five years, production would increase by a rate of 50%. A new port was to be constructed in the city of Ashdod, close to the citrus orchards, to facilitate the transport of millions of crates of oranges all around the globe. There were also plans to build three new packaging factories every year, in addition to the thirty existing ones. Trucks and freight wagons were being imported to transport the produce to the ports.[73] Yet all these efforts would be in vain if continued exports to Europe's markets could not be guaranteed. In a conversation with his Italian colleague, Marianz Rumor, Dayan raised the possibility of cooperation between Israel and Italy in the agricultural sector in return for a more positive Italian stance towards Israel in the framework of the EEC. He proposed that Israeli experts would participate in development programs in southern Italy, an endeavor to which the Italians attribute great importance.

While the Israeli political echelon was working with vigor to persuade their Italian colleagues of the great benefits which Italy would gain from Israel's integration into the EEC, behind the scenes other forces were at work to advance Israel's interests. Commissioner Petrilli, a personal friend of Italian Premier Fanfani, agreed to persuade the Prime Minister that Israel's association with the EEC would be beneficial and received the impression that Fanfani's reaction was positive.[74]

However, the optimism regarding signs of change in Italy's position was premature. The Italians scattered many pleasantries, seasoned with generalized promises about improving economic ties between the nations, but were unwilling to alter their position on the concrete question of association. The Italians, as the rest of The Six, did not want Israel to consider them as responsible for the failure of Israel's association bid, and therefore resorted to the usual tactic. They were willing to reconsider their position upon receiving clear indications from the other countries that they too supported Israel's application. A brief investigation by the Italian Foreign Ministry proved what it already knew: all the other countries, with the exception of the Netherlands, opposed Israel's association. Not without satisfaction, the Italian Foreign Ministry presented the results of its fact-finding to the Israeli diplomats.[75]

In fact, the Italian enquiry was not entirely fair: when asking their European counterparts to indicate their stance on the matter, they made clear their own opposition to the Israeli request, detailing the political and economic reasons.[76] However, the Israelis could no longer blame Italy for obstructing their association agreement with the EEC. They were forced to confront a frustrating reality: they were like a person trying to cram his belongings into a suitcase; every time he manages to arrange one side, he discovers that the other side is in chaos. In Paris, officials at the Quai d'Orsay (the French Foreign Ministry) sought to find a way to evade fulfilling Debre's hasty promises to Ben-Gurion. Having failed to deny Debre's statements, Israel proved that the words were recorded in the protocol of the conversation; they adopted a new line of defense, doubting that Debre's promises were valid as he had been unaware of the full complexity of the matter.[77] Following significant Israeli pressure on Olivier Wörmser, the Director of the Department of Economic Affairs at the Quai d'Orsay, he agreed not to oppose the Israeli request in the Council of Ministers, although hinting that he would not support it in the face of opposition from others.[78]

The Israelis began to understand the difficulties they were facing. Their campaign of persuasion had not yielded the sought-after results. A large question mark remained regarding Israel's chances of achieving the necessary support in the Council of Ministers. Maurice Fischer, Deputy Director General of the Ministry of Foreign Affairs, was the first to regain his composure. He understood that Israel was racing towards a reverberating failure and needed to stop the wagon before the final collision. He ordered the representation in Brussels to prevent the discussion of Israel's association in Council of Ministers, arguing that Israel needed additional time for preparations.[79] However, it was too late: Israel had already stated its desire for association in an official request and matters were now beyond its control. The Commission required the Council's agreement to continue its preliminary talks with Israel. However, in view of the accumulating evidence regarding the difference of positions in the capitals of The Six concerning Israeli association, it was logical to presume that the Council would respond negatively to the Commission's request. Therefore, Najar and Bartur devised a new plan. They recommended that Israel itself submit to the Council of Ministers an official request to open talks regarding association. The logic behind this was simple: while it would be easy for the Council of Ministers to respond negatively to the question when presented discreetly by the Commission, it would be much more difficult to reject an official Israel appeal.[80] This was an all-or-nothing bet: if, despite everything, the Council would reject the Israeli request, the door to association with the EEC would be slammed in Israel's face for the foreseeable future. The Israelis faced a difficult decision. Before reaching any resolution, the Minister for Trade and Industry, Pinchas Sapir, met with Rey, who promised that the Commission would informally consult with the Council of Ministers; nothing would be submitted in writing and therefore there would be no damage to Israel, even in the case of a negative response.[81] Rey's words persuaded Sapir not to gamble with such high stakes; together with the Foreign Minister he opted for the discreet Commission approach. In so doing, it appears that Sapir avoided causing Israel more serious damage than that which it in fact sustained.

The failure of Israel's first attempt to achieve association

On October 19, 1960, the European Council met as planned. Off the record, Rey showed the Commission the memorandum from Israel, noting: "It seems that Israel seriously believes in the possibility of obtaining an association agreement with the EEC and therefore the Commission felt obliged to bring the matter before the governments."[82] Rey omitted to mention the Commission's role in the affair, even maintaining that "the Commission has always responded to Israeli requests [for association] with caution and reserve." Rey's attitude was unhelpful in generating an atmosphere sympathetic to Israel. One by one, Belgium, Germany and Italy spoke out against the idea, employing the following two arguments: discussing association with Israel could compromise the negotiations under way with Greece and Turkey; and Israel was not a European state or part of NATO and was therefore not entitled to special treatment from the EEC. France's representative at the meeting, Deputy Foreign Minister Georges Gorse, was the only figure who tried to moderate the rejectionist line, arguing that the Council should not assume a wholesale negative stance. The negative conclusion was nevertheless clear and the chairman, Luns, explicitly phrased this in the meeting's summary.

   This decision meant that negotiations between the Commission and Israel would cease immediately, at least until the talks with Greece and Turkey concluded. This morally released the Commission from its understandings with the Israelis. Therefore, Rey quickly notified Bartur that in view of the new situation, the Commission was no longer authorized to continue the talks.[83] The Israelis understood that the situation was hopeless and all their achievements over the past two years had been for naught. The Council had ruled that Israel was not a part of Europe, had no special ties to Europe, and therefore was not entitled to preferential treatment from Europe. It is easy to imagine the atmosphere of gloom that engulfed those involved in cementing Israel's ties with the EEC.

Yet, precisely now, at the lowest ebb, help arrived from a seemingly unexpected source. On October 31, the foreign ministers of the six EEC member states met and, naturally, the subject of Israel arose. The ministers had now considered the matter and developed a clear policy line concerning Israel's request. They agreed that the time was not right for association with Israel and, as a matter of principle, European countries which were not yet full members should have priority rights to association. In the second stage, this right would be extended to African countries possessing past ties to Europe, implying that the EEC would only then consider an expansion of the framework to non-European countries such as Israel. The ministers were principally concerned that having closed the door to the Israelis, the latter might take the desperate step of filing a formal request to the Council for talks concerning association. Such a step would force The Six to oppose Israel's request directly and openly, placing them in an uncomfortable position. It was clear to the ministers that they needed to respond to Israel's request with special sensitivity, particularly when collectively speaking on behalf of Europe, a continent which shared a complicated past with the Jewish People. In this regard, Israel was different to all the other nations.

Thus, the ministers dispatched an urgent and confidential message to Israel, asking that Israel not apply for association at present.[84] The Israelis discerned that this development altered the balance of power between Israel and The Six instantly. Israel had not considered submitting a formal request for association, a step which would have sealed its chances for the foreseeable future. However, given that it had been asked so frantically to avoid this step, Israel could now pretend that it had been denied a basic right and was therefore entitled to compensation. "We have been handed an important card," Najar wrote to Foreign Minister Meir, suggesting that Israel should exploit the Council's anxiety to limit the damage caused by the suspension of talks with the Commission. He proposed composing a memo to Luns demanding that, in return for not submitting the formal application for association, the Commission would be authorized to conduct a comprehensive and discrete inquiry with Israel concerning the entire problem of the relationship between Israel and the EEC. This time Israel would not state that its ultimate goal was an association agreement with the EEC but would be content with the general wording "negotiation without any limits or definition of its goals."[85] The Israeli Ministry of Foreign Affairs embraced Najar's proposal warmly and the memorandum was filed.

In those same days, the French newspaper *Le Monde* published an article reporting that, in a closed meeting of the six Foreign Ministers (on October 31), little enthusiasm was expressed regarding the possibility of association with Israel, due to fears of damage to relations with the Arab states. It also noted that the European ministers considered the option of association limited to European states or former European colonies.[86] This information was evidently leaked by an "inside" source. The foreign ministers of The Six were embarrassed at this leak and the exposure of the real reason for their opposition to Israeli association with the EEC. They had argued that their objection was not a result of political motivations, but rather institutional considerations, including: the desire to avoid expanding the ranks of the EEC too hastily, while the body was still in its infancy and searching for its own way, as well as the need to conclude the negotiations with Turkey and Greece, and other such arguments. Now it seemed that the real reason for their opposition had been revealed. Israel had every right to be angered by the article in *Le Monde*. Indeed, since their earliest contacts with EEC institutions, the Israelis had been asked to act discreetly, and had made sure to do so; yet the matter had been publicly exposed in its entirety, in a most humiliating manner. This episode gave Jerusalem additional ammunition: the Israelis intended to exploit the embarrassment it caused to EEC foreign ministers. A memorandum was sent to The Six claiming that

> after the meeting of the foreign ministers of the six member countries last 31 October, unverified, contradictory, and in many respects harmful information was published in several leading newspapers on the subject of relations between Israel and the EEC. The government of Israel deemed it to be in the interest of all parties to detach these relations from the climate thus created, and to return to conducting these relations in a pragmatic fashion.[87]

On November 15, Najar met with Luns, carrying the memorandum in his briefcase. The Israeli Ambassador was full of righteous anger. The Dutch Minister found himself in a weak position, which required a generally apologetic tone to his comments. Najar began by complaining at how the Council had treated Israel—in his words, without respect. Israel proposed to the EEC an honorable solution: the Council of Ministers would allow the Commission to continue preliminary talks with Israel. Najar deemed it important to clarify that even in this case Israel did not promise to renounce the right to approach the Council with an association application when it would deem this suitable; the agreement to postpone the application was temporary. Najar also complained that Israel had been pushed to the end of the line of those waiting for association (after other European countries and former colonies), as the newspaper article stated. Israel would be willing to wait until the conclusion of the negotiations with Greece but not one moment longer, Najar made abundantly clear. The Israeli was well aware of how to apply pressure at the most sensitive points. "There is no need to emphasize the special relationship between Israel and Europe based on a past rich in events," he noted. Association with the EEC would have a dramatic effect on the future of the young nation, on both economic and political levels. The Israelis knew that Luns had been forced to accept decisions which countered his beliefs in the Council of Ministers, and offered him an opportunity to correct this: "I am approaching you as a Dutch Minister," Najar added. The Israeli diplomat identified clear signs of excitement in the Dutch Minister. "It was worthwhile for us to meet, if only for me to hear these things," were Luns's parting words to Najar. The Dutch Ambassador in Jerusalem reiterated the request that Israel for the time being reject the request for association because of the sensitivity of the negotiations between Turkey and the EEC.[88]

A week later Najar believed that he already felt the welcome effects of his initiative:[89] "the memorandum we sent has served our purpose well . . . the atmosphere which had begun to be hesitant and negative has become more friendly and positive."[90] Najar, as many other Israelis, interpreted the situation through the prism of his heart's desire. However, the Israelis were soon forced to acknowledge the harsh reality. Even if the Europeans felt particularly uncomfortable in dismissing the Israelis empty-handed, they would not consider sacrificing EEC interests for the sake of Israel.

Assenting to the Israeli request to renew the talks with the Commission on the basis of the memorandum would, in reality, mean investigating the option of association. Indeed, although the memorandum from the Israeli Foreign Ministry did not mention the word "association" explicitly—instead stating that "preliminary talks must address all the problems [facing Israel and the EEC] and consider every possible solution and agreement without discounting any one of them in advance"—this phrasing could not conceal Israel's aims. The Council would not consider an attempt at infiltration through the back door and likewise did not trust the Commission to serve as an effective brake on Israeli attempts to widen the content of the talks.[91] When, on occasion, an Israeli diplomat inquired discreetly about the fate of the memorandum, he was informed of the need to wait at least until the conclusion of negotiations with Greece and Turkey.[92] With great displeasure, the Israeli diplomats used the only weapon remaining in their arsenal. They announced that Israel sought to form association with *one* of the European bodies and in so doing hinted that if the path to the EEC was blocked, they would join EFTA as an alternative. In despair, they now tried to use this old bargaining chip. However, its chances of success were not great: it was clear that EFTA was not open to accepting non-European countries. Likewise, there is no proof that this consideration influenced any organ in the EEC, apart from the Commission. The Six feared closer ties between Israel and the EEC; they were not concerned by the opposite. If EFTA wanted to take on the political burden of association with Israel, it was welcome to do so. Fundamentally, the Israeli failure to force association upon the Europeans was unavoidable, because coercion cannot succeed when one side demands an action, which the other party views as the worst possible option. The Israelis sought to coerce Europe into association but did not possess a bargaining chip powerful enough to overcome the opposition of The Six.

The Israeli Ministry of Foreign Affairs utilized the interim period, waiting for the Council's response, to prepare: it was clear that the Israeli struggle to find a pathway into Europe had reached a crossroads and that a re-assessment was vital. The ministry therefore called a special senior management meeting to examine future strategy. The optimism which had swept through the ministry only a few weeks previously, a result of The Six's ostensible goodwill toward Israel, faded.

Yet at the same time, there was speculation that the Europeans felt uncomfortable in refusing Israel and were therefore adopting a tactic of procrastination, claiming that Israel must wait its turn. The participants concluded that Israel needed to bring maximum pressure to bear on the senior politicians in The Six and the US, feeling that Israel had not exhausted the range of options available in these countries. They likewise agreed to lobby European parliamentarians in an attempt to garner support for Israel.[93] Despite the blows they had received, the Israelis did not flinch, believing that an agreement was within arm's reach, if only they could effectively leverage their political influence. Even now, they refused to believe what was already clear: that The Six opposed an agreement with Israel. This opposition was unrelated to any special consideration of this or that country but was rather intrinsic and could not be changed by well-thought-out public relations or diplomatic subterfuge. Opposition emanated from the highest echelon within each country and not from a narrow-minded attitude among the ranks of EEC officials. The refusal to recognize these facts continued to block Israel's path in the future.

Notes

1   To understand the importance of this decision, it is important to note that at the end of the 1950s, Israel had only twelve embassies all around the globe.

2   Rafael to the office of the Foreign Minister, ISA, FM, file 1946/21, November 28, 1958.

3   Summary of the discussions at the conference of ambassadors in Brussels, ISA, FM, file 1946/22, February 1959.

4   Among the figures who expressed a positive stance towards closer relations between Israel and the EEC were Guy Mollet, former French Prime Minister, Jean Monnet, one of the architects of the European integration and Karl Schmidt, leader of the Socialist Part in Germany.

5   Lifshitz to the Foreign Minister, ISA, FM, file 1946/24, July 9, 1959.

6   See: Michael Curtis and Susan Aurelia Gitelson, eds., *Israel in the Third World* (New Brunswick: Transaction Books, 1976); Elinor Burkett, *Golda* (New York: Harper Collins, 2008); Mordechai E. Kreinin, *Israel and Africa: A Study in Technical Cooperation* (New York: Praeger, 1964); Zach Levey, *Israel in Africa: 1956–1976* (Dordrecht: Martinus Nijhoff 2012); Joel Peters, *Israel and Africa: The Problematic Friendship* (London: British Academic Press, 1992); Arye Oded, *Africa and Israel: A Unique Case of Radical Changes in Israel's Foreign Relations* (Jerusalem: Magnes [in Hebrew], 2011); Olusola Ojo, *Africa and Israel: Relations in Perspective* (Boulder: Westview Press, 1988); Tibor S. Rodin, "Political Aspects of Israeli Foreign Aid in Africa," PhD dissertation (University of Nebraska, 1969).

7   Lifshitz to the Foreign Minister, ISA, FM, file 1946/24, July 9, 1959.

8   Nirgad to Bartur, ISA, FM, file 1946/23, August 10, 1959A.

9   Jean-François Deniau was a French statesman and diplomat. He became a European Commissioner in Rey's time as President of the Commission (1967–70).

10   Nirgad to Bartur, ISA, FM, file 1946/23, August 10, 1959B.

11   Protocol, ISA, FM, file 1946/24, October 5, 1959.

12   Officials in the department for External Relations were apparently unaware of the signals that senior figures in the Commission imparted regarding their positive approach to an association agreement with Israel. They also failed to understand the aim of Bartur's visit to Brussels. See: EUA, BAC 3/1978-321, October 1, 1959.

13 Protocol, ISA, FM, file 1946/24, October 7, 1959.
14 Bartur to the Foreign Minister, ISA, FM, file 211/6, October 18, 1959.
15 ISA, FM, file 1953/5, January 3, 1960.
16 Memorandum, ISA, FM, file 1953/5, December 18, 1959.
17 State of Israel, ed. *State of Israel's Foreign Policy Documents* (Jerusalem: National Archives, 1981), Vol. 14, Doc. 14, 12.01.1960.
18 Concerning Israel's security concerns at the time see: Zach Levey, *Israel and the Western Powers, 1952–1960* (Chapel Hill: University of North Carolina Press, 1997); Zaki Shalom, *The Superpowers, Israel and the Future of Jordan, 1960–1963: The Perils of the Pro-Nasser Policy* (Brighton: Sussex Academic Press, 1999).
19 Memorandum of conversation, ISA, FM, file 1953/6, March 16, 1960.
20 Lifshitz to the Foreign Minister, ISA, FM, file 1946/24, July 9, 1959.
21 Bartur to the Foreign Ministry, ISA, FM, file 211/4, July 12, 1959; October 11, 1959; December 26, 1959.
22 Bartur to the Foreign Minister, ISA, FM, file 3147/10, April 6, 1965.
23 Davar, October 29, 1959.
24 Minutes No. 27 of the Knesset Foreign Affairs and Defense Committee, ISA, Knesset, file 7567/2, July 26, 1960.
25 Bendor to Levavi, ISA, FM, file 1958/10, February 16, 1962.
26 Minutes of Israeli Cabinet Meetings, ISA, PM, January 26, 1960.
27 Bartur to Foreign Minister, ISA, FM, file 3132/8, December 26, 1959.
28 See, for example, David Ha'Cohen and Zalman Eran, Minutes No. 28 of the Knesset Foreign Affairs and Defense Committee, ISA, Knesset, file 7567/2, August 3, 1960.
29 ISA, FM, file 1957/11, February, 1962.
30 ISA, FM, file 1953/5, January 26, 1960.
31 Boaz to Israel representations in Western Europe, ISA, FM, file 1953/6, March 28, 1960.
32 State of Israel, ed., *State of Israel's Foreign Policy Documents*, Vol. 14, Doc. 318, 25/04/1960.
33 For a long discussion of this matter see: Documents diplomatique françaises (DDF), 1960, tome I, pp. 596–600.
34 Among these difficulties were Greek-Turkish relations, as well as other trade matters. See: Selim Ilkin, "A Short History of Turkey's Association with the European Community," in *Turkey and the European Community*, eds. Ahmet Evin and Geoffrey Denton (Opladen: Leske Verlag, 1990); Roswitha Bourguignon, "A History of the Association Agreement between Turkey and the European Community," in *Turkey and the European Community*, eds. Ahmet Evin and Geoffrey Denton (Opladen: Leske Verlag, 1990).
35 Background survey for economic cabinet, ISA, FM, file 1953/7, May 26, 1960.
36 Nirgad to Bartur, ISA, FM, file 1953/7, June 3, 1960.
37 Najar to Bartur, ISA, FM, file 1953/7, July 26, 1960.
38 Najar to the Foreign Minister, ISA, FM, file 1953/7, July 8, 1960.
39 EUA, CM2-1960-157, July 26, 1960.
40 Memorandum from Bartur to the Prime Minister, ISA, FM, file 1953/7, June 12, 1960.
41 Gadi Heimann, *Franco-Israeli Relations, 1958–1967*, vol. 36 (Oxford: Routledge, 2016).
42 Bartur himself employed these arguments extensively, for example on his journey to Brussels in spring 1960. See: Leroy á Van Offel'n, AMAECEB, file 6.110/VI, May 6, 1960.
43 Cidor to Bartur, ISA, FM, file 1954/1, February 1, 1960; Bartur to Cidor, ISA, FM, file 1954/1, March 4, 1960.
44 Boaz to Cidor, ISA, FM, file 1953/6, April 20, 1960.
45 Bartur to Najar, ISA, FM, file 1953/7, July 20, 1960.
46 Bartur called this "the negative argument" in favor of Israeli association with the EEC and in his opinion it was the most effective. See: Protocol of the Knesset Foreign Affairs and Defense Committee, ISA, Knesset, file 7567/2, August 3, 1960.

47 EUA, BAC 3/1978-321, July 27, 1960.
48 State of Israel, ed., *State of Israel's Foreign Policy Documents*, Vol. 14, Doc. 327, 28/06/1960.
49 Association éventuelle d'Israël á la Cummunauté Européenne, AMAECEB, file 6.110/ VI, September 23, 1960.
50 Summary of the Prime Minister's conversations, ISA, FM, file 1953/7, July 1960. At the end of July, Luns reiterated a similar message to Najar. See: ISA, FM, file 1953/7, July 21, 1960.
51 Protocol no. 5 of the Knesset Foreign Affairs and Defense Committee, ISA, Knesset, file 7567/2, July 5, 1960.
52 State of Israel, ed., *State of Israel's Foreign Policy Documents*, Vol. 14, Doc. 330, 07/07/1960; Doc 332, 07/09/1960.
53 Memorandum of Economic Department,, File 1958/8, December 1961.
54 The reparations agreement between West Germany and Israel was signed in 1952 on the background of significant public protests in Israel and among world Jewry. As part of the agreement, an office was established in Cologne, headed by Felix Shinnar from the Israeli Ministry of Finance. Although the two countries established diplomatic relations only in 1965, the reparations office de facto became an Israeli diplomatic representation. These covert relations (which also extended to security cooperation) were conducted far from the eyes of the Israeli and German publics and were extensive, as this book attests.
55 Regarding the reparations and Adenauer's motives, see: Felix Eliezer Shinnar, *Between Needs and Feelings: Israel-German Relations, 1951–1966* (Jerusalem: Shocken, 1967).
56 Concerning Ben-Gurion's conversation with Adenauer see: State of Israel, ed., *State of Israel's Foreign Policy Documents*, Vol. 14. Doc 215, 14/03/1960.
57 Ibid., Vol. 14, Doc. 336, 08/07/1960.
58 Alan S. Milward, *The European Rescue of the Nation-State* (London: Routledge, 1992), 236–7.
59 Geoffrey Parker, *The Logic of Unity: A Geography of the European Economic Community*, 2nd ed. (London: Longman, 1975), 125–33.
60 Jacques Bourrinet, *Le Problème Agricole Dans L'intégration Européenne* (Paris: Éditions Cujas, 1964), 248.
61 *Giornale di Sicilia*, March–April 1962, ISA, FM, file 286/8.
62 Geoffrey Shepherd, "Textiles: New Ways of Surviving in an Old Industry," in *Europe's Industries: Public and Private Strategies for Change*, eds. Geoffrey Shepherd, François Duchene and Christopher Thomas Saunders (London: Frances Pinter, 1983), 42.
63 Ministry of Foreign Affairs Memorandum, "Israel-Italy relations in light of the economic relations between Italy and the Arab states," ISA, FM, file 280/14, May 1961.
64 Memorandum "Israel-Italy relations,, ISA, FM, file 286/2, September 1962.
65 See, for example, the Italian Foreign Minister's opposition to Italian companies participating in international trade fairs held in Israel: See: Elron to the Economic Department, ISA, FM, file 217/3, February 6, 1962.
66 State of Israel., ed., *State of Israel's Foreign Policy Documents*, Vol. 14, Doc. 332, 19/07/1960.
67 Ibid., Vol. 14, Doc. 340, 20/09/1960.
68 Ibid., Vol. 14, Doc. 341, 10/06/1960.
69 Bartur to the Ministry of Foreign Affairs, ISA, FM, file 2713/17, September 17, 1960; Elron to Nadivid, ISA, FM, file 280/18, September 20, 1960.
70 Elron to the Economic Department, ISA, FM, file 280/18, September 26, 1960.
71 The Israeli Embassy in Rome pressured Israeli politicians to initiate economic cooperation with Italy as a route to the hearts of the Italians. See: summary of the discussing regarding the need to cultivate relations between Israel and Italy, ISA, FM, file 280/18, July 25, 1960; State of Israel., ed., *State of Israel's Foreign Policy Documents*, Vol. 14, Doc. 281, 02/10/1960.
72 Ibid., Vol. 14, Doc. 281, 02/10/1960.

73 Protocol no. 29 of the Citrus Marketing Board of Israel, ISA, MA, file 2423/12, February 18, 1960; Memorandum "Planning of a citrus packing plant," ISA, MA, file 2424/4, August 8, 1960.
74 State of Israel., ed., *State of Israel's Foreign Policy Documents*, Vol. 14, Doc. 341, 06/10/1960.
75 Foreign Ministry tender, ISA, FM, file 1954/3 August 10, 1960.
76 Cassieres á Wigny, AMAECEB, file 6.110/VI, October 22, 1960.
77 Bartur to Yehil, ISA, FM, 1954/3, October 8, 1960.
78 Bartur to the Ministry of Foreign Affairs, ISA, FM, file 1954/3, October 11, 1960.
79 Fischer to the Embassy in Brussels, ISA, FM, file 1954/3, October 10, 1960.
80 Najar to Fischer, ISA, FM, file 1954/3, October 11, 1960.
81 Bartur to the Foreign Minister, ISA, FM, file 1954/3, October 13, 1960.
82 Bartur to the Foreign Office, ISA, FM, file 1954/3, October 27, 1960. Similar documentation of the meeting was not found in the EU archives. However, the report presented here was received by Nirgad. Nirgad obtained a confidential copy of the meeting's summary.
83 Bartur to the Foreign Minister, ISA, FM, File 1954/3, October 23, 1960.
84 ISA, FM, file 1954/3, November 3, 1960.
85 Najar to the Foreign Minister, ISA, FM, file 1954/3, July 11, 1960.
86 *Le Monde*, October 31, 1960.
87 Sharon Pardo and Joel Peters, *Israel and the European Union: A Documentary History* (Lanham: Lexington Books, 2012), 12.
88 NAN, Z111-238-240, 290, doc. 4220/915, December 1, 1960.
89 Najar to Bartur, ISA, FM, file 1954/3, November 15, 1960.
90 Najar to Bartur, ISA, FM, file 1954/3, November 25, 1960.
91 The Council was angered by the Commission's behavior throughout the affair. It was clear that the Commission had exercised freedom which exceeded the bounds of its authority. Fortunately, for the Commission leadership, the extent of the coordination with the Israelis was not revealed.
92 Najar to Bartur, ISA, FM, file 1953/8, February 14, 1961; Najar to Alon, ISA, FM, March 15, 1961.
93 Meeting Summary, ISA, FM, file 1954/3, November 16, 1960.

References

Bourguignon, Roswitha. "A History of the Association Agreement between Turkey and the European Community." Chap. 3 In *Turkey and the European Community*, edited by Ahmet Evin and Geoffrey Denton, 51–64. Opladen: Leske Verlag, 1990.

Bourrinet, Jacques. *Le Problème Agricole Dans L'intégration Européenne*. Paris: Éditions Cujas, 1964.

Burkett, Elinor. *Golda*. New York: Harper Collins, 2008.

Curtis, Michael, and Susan Aurelia Gitelson, eds. *Israel in the Third World*. New Brunswick: Transaction Books, 1976.

Heimann, Gadi. *Franco-Israeli Relations, 1958–1967*. Vol. 36, Oxford: Routledge, 2016.

Ilkin, Selim. "A Short History of Turkey's Association with the European Community." Chap. 2 In *Turkey and the European Community*, edited by Ahmet Evin and Geoffrey Denton, 35–50. Opladen: Leske Verlag, 1990.

Kreinin, Mordechai E. *Israel and Africa: A Study in Technical Cooperation*. New York: Praeger, 1964.

Levey, Zach. *Israel and the Western Powers, 1952–1960*. Chapel Hill: University of North Carolina Press, 1997.

―――. *Israel in Africa: 1956–1976*. Dordrecht: Martinus Nijhoff, 2012.

Milward, Alan S. *The European Rescue of the Nation-State*. London: Routledge, 1992.

Oded, Arye. *Africa and Israel: A Unique Case of Radical Changes in Israel's Foreign Relations*. Jerusalem: Magnes [in Hebrew], 2011.

Ojo, Olusola. *Africa and Israel: Relations in Perspective*. Boulder: Westview Press, 1988.

Pardo, Sharon, and Joel Peters. *Israel and the European Union: A Documentary History*. Lanham: Lexington Books, 2012.

Parker, Geoffrey. *The Logic of Unity: A Geography of the European Economic Community*. 2nd ed. London: Longman, 1975.

Peters, Joel. *Israel and Africa: The Problematic Friendship*. London: British Academic Press, 1992.

Rodin, Tibor S. "Political Aspects of Israeli Foreign Aid in Africa," PhD dissertation, University of Nebraska, 1969.

Shalom, Zaki. *The Superpowers, Israel and the Future of Jordan, 1960–1963: The Perils of the Pro-Nasser Policy*. Brighton: Sussex Academic Press, 1999.

Shepherd, Geoffrey. "Textiles: New Ways of Surviving in an Old Industry." Chap. 2 In *Europe's Industries: Public and Private Strategies for Change*, edited by Geoffrey Shepherd, François Duchene and Christopher Thomas Saunders, 26–51. London: Frances Pinter, 1983.

Shinnar, Felix Eliezer. *Between Needs and Feelings: Israel-German Relations, 1951–1966*. Jerusalem: Shocken, 1967.

State of Israel, ed. *State of Israel's Foreign Policy Documents*. Jerusalem: National Archives, 1981.

5 The end of the dream of association

A limited trade agreement?

The Council of Ministers' unanimous negative response to the question presented by the Commission at the meeting, which took place in October, lowered the curtain on negotiations between Israel and the EEC. However, at this stage Gorse, the French representative, suggested that instead of talks regarding association, Israel and the EEC could embark on negotiations for a special trade agreement. He proposed a goal more modest than a full customs union: that is, customs arrangements for a limited number of products. Gorse sought to help the Israelis minimize the damage caused by their attempts to achieve the ambitious goal of association. Had his proposal been accepted, it would have generated a new, although more limited, basis for renewing the talks. Yet his proposal was never addressed; none of the other representatives mentioned it, nor was it put to the vote. In fact, Gorse was not the first to suggest the idea of a special trade agreement as an alternative to a full customs union. The Commission had suggested this possibility to Israel in May 1960, when discussing the directions for the initial talks.[1] Already regretting pushing Israel toward the solution of association, the Commission sought to investigate whether a more modest solution could satisfy the Israelis. However, the latter stubbornly insisted on the solution of a customs union and this idea was not considered seriously.

In fact, the Israelis remained unsure to what extent a limited trade agreement was practical, even if they accepted such a solution. According to the GATT agreement, any tariff reductions granted to one country would necessarily be extended to all members. Only the framework of a customs union or a free trade area could release countries from this requirement. A limited trade agreement with Israel thus contradicted the GATT agreement unless the custom reductions were extended to other member states, making such a possibility impractical: every product, which Israel sought to include in the arrangement, was also exported by other countries.[2] Thus granting customs reductions to Israeli exporters would force the EEC to accord similar benefits to exporters from other GATT member countries, usually with far-reaching ramifications. It is important to remember that even in the country's leading export sector—citrus fruits—Israeli production was meager compared to other countries. For the sake of comparison:

during the 1957–58 season Israeli orchards yielded 350 thousand tons of fruit, while Spanish producers reaped 1.1 million tons and the Americans harvested close to 5 million tons.[3] Therefore, customs reductions for Israeli citrus exports would force the Europeans to extend similar benefits to American and Spanish fruits, dealing a death blow to the Italian citrus sector. Israel could only achieve customs reductions on a restricted group of products without exposing the EEC to the threat of flooding from other markets. Therefore, a limited trade agreement would necessarily be either too wide, and therefore dangerous for The Six, or too narrow and thus unsatisfactory from Israel's perspective.

Yet in the first months of 1961, various European figures began hinting to Israeli diplomats that while association was unattainable in the near future, it might be possible to examine the solution of a limited trade agreement. This idea was first raised by the Commission. In February 1961, Najar met with a Commission official who explicitly informed him that, to the best of his under-standing, Israel had no chance of achieving association with the EEC because of the political issues involved. However, it might be possible to find a less conspicuous path, for example, a trade and economic cooperation agreement. The Europeans could easily market such an agreement to the Arabs, enabling them to highlight their rejection of Israel's request for association.[4] A few weeks later, Najar spoke with Rey and Noël separately. Both of them reported on the progress of the talks with Turkey, noting that association with that country would apparently not be based on a customs union but rather a special trade agreement; they thus hinted to the Israeli diplomat that alternatives to a customs union existed.[5] At the end of April and again at the beginning of May, two senior German statesmen—Schaffenberg, the permanent German repre-sentative in the Council of Ministers, and Erhard, the West German Finance Minister—spoke with Shinnar, advising the Israeli to pursue the path of a trade agreement.[6] Likewise, a few days later, the Dutch Foreign Minister counseled the Israeli Ambassador in Brussels to abandon the dream of association and instead strive for an "ad hoc arrangement," stating that were Israel to bring consolidated proposals for such an agreement to the Council of Ministers, the Netherlands would be able to support them.[7] Even the Secretary General of the Italian Foreign Ministry, Italio Cattani, who was not considered a particularly enthusiastic supporter of Israel, noted that a trade agreement could constitute a possible alternative to association.[8] At the same time, the Europeans' com-plete and utter opposition to association with Israel was highly evident. Indeed, European bureaucrats and politicians clarified unambiguously at every opportu-nity that at this stage an Israeli request for association could not be considered. Even Hallstein, who in the past had given the Israelis cause for optimism about association, now declared his opposition to it.[9]

Considering these signals, the Israeli Ministry of Foreign Affairs discerned the existence of a new path that could prove more practical than association. However, one question remained unanswered: to what extent was it desirable for Israel to pursue this path? Association would offer Israel far more than mere trade benefits; it had far-reaching political and economic ramifications for the

state's future. The Israelis believed that association with the EEC could suf-
focate the Arab boycott, attract enormous investments for the Israeli economy
and perhaps even advance Israel's integration into NATO. In contrast, a trade
agreement was restricted to preventing the economic damage Israel was likely
to suffer following the establishment of the Common Market. All agreed that
it was a pale shadow of association. At this juncture, the Israelis necessarily
confronted the question of whether it was not preferable to pursue the chance
of obtaining a trade agreement, if association was an unattainable dream.

Some assumed this position, particularly those serving in the capitals of The
Six.[10] Among them was Walter Eytan, former Director General of the Ministry
of Foreign Affairs who was then serving as Israeli Ambassador in Paris. He concluded that the chances of obtaining association were slight and advised that
efforts be focused on reaching a trade agreement.[11] Likewise Felix Shinnar, the
Israeli delegate in Cologne, claimed that

> after the Common Market rejected our proposals for association and for
> negotiations to find an alternative to full association, it is vital for us to
> reach an 'ad-hoc' arrangement which will enable us to continue the impor-
> tant trade connection without discrimination and difficulties that will
> endanger this trade link and, in so doing, the battle for the State of Israel's
> economic stability.[12]

Najar sought to adopt an intermediate approach. He had previously been an
enthusiastic supporter of association, ready to wage a campaign to achieve it.
However, because of his close contacts with EEC bureaucrats in his official
capacity, he was among the first to discern how deep-seated European hesitancy
towards association truly was. Therefore, Najar suggested re-defining the goals:
association with the EEC would be Israel's maximum aim, but at the same time
the country would be prepared to settle for a minimum achievement – that is, a
trade agreement – if association proved impossible to obtain.[13]

The suggestion of relinquishing the aim of association and pursuing in its stead
a "normal" trade arrangement was a particularly important crossroads in the story
of negotiations between Israel and the EEC. It reflects the complexity and unique
nature of the relations between Israel and the EEC. The Europeans did not want
to enter into negotiations with Israel; they were even less desirous of reaching a
special arrangement with that country, first and foremost because this threatened
their important interests in the Arab world. However, for historical reasons, the
Europeans could not dismiss Israel using the most obvious justification: it was not
a European country, it was not a former colony of one of The Six, and therefore
Europe was not obligated to grant it any special arrangements beyond those given
to all GATT members. Moreover, the Europeans could not admit openly that
the central reason for their opposition was fear of the Arab response. Indeed, the
Europeans felt compelled to exercise special sensitivity in their dealings with the
Jewish state and were unwilling to respond with a clear and blunt negative; this
is evidenced by the request that the Council of Foreign Ministers communicated

to Israel via Luns, asking the Israelis to refrain from submitting a formal request for association. In so doing, the Europeans barred to themselves the easiest way of blocking Israel's path. Some Europeans, hoping that they would persuade Israel to abandon the ambitious aim of association and believing they would be forced to grant significant gestures at some point, were willing to offer a modest alternative. However, this very willingness constituted an admission that Israel was not "just another country"—that the EEC felt special moral responsibility towards the Jewish state and was obligated to find a way of solving the problems which the establishment of the Common Market had created for it. Later, when it became clear to the Europeans that the Israelis could not be satisfied with a few trade reductions, this admission would be inescapable.

Israel insists on association

However, Israeli leaders in Jerusalem found it difficult to renounce the idea of association. The Foreign Minister and the highest echelons in her ministry clung to the belief that only association offered a solution to Israel's problems. They opined that a trade agreement would not answer even Israel's most minimal demands and therefore could not constitute an alternative to association. The Israeli appetite for an association agreement increased following the successful conclusion of negotiations between Greece and the EEC (May 1961). The Greek economy, as Israel's, was in the early stages of development. Industry accounted for a tiny portion of the domestic product and was mainly based on small factories and simple products intended for the internal market. Most of Greece's exports, around 90%, were agricultural products.[14] The Greeks needed to continue the stream of constant agricultural exports to the European markets and simultaneously protect the country's infant industry. Indeed, the conditions that Greece obtained in the framework of the agreement were a cause for jealousy. Greece received all the tariff reductions The Six shared, including a 50% reduction on tobacco and raisins—its two main products. By contrast, Greece was given the right to reduce protective tariffs (caps) on industrial products gradually, in a long process planned to last for 22 years. Thus, Athens in fact received the export benefits of the customs union without paying the short-term price. In addition, Greece was granted a development loan of $125 million.[15] The Israelis viewed the agreement reached with Greece longingly, regarding it as a precedent that could be replicated in their case.

The Ministry of Foreign Affairs thus decided to dispatch without delay a formal request to the Council of Ministers to open negotiations with Israel. The phrasing was identical to that of the memorandum submitted in November 1960—it did not mention association explicitly as the final aim of the talks, but insisted on leaving "all the doors open." Golda Meir planned to visit Paris for talks with the French government echelons at the beginning of June 1961. In preparation for these meetings, she consulted with the officials most well-versed in the subject of the EEC, among them Eytan, Bartur and Najar, focusing on what line she should adopt in her coming conversation with

French Foreign Minister Couve de Murville. Despite the evidence of sweeping European opposition to association—and in opposition to the clear signs that the EEC was willing to consider positively a special trade agreement with Israel—it was decided that Meir would persist with the demand for association.[16] Their conclusion was that only this path could solve Israel's customs problems and, more importantly, constitute a political achievement; as Bartur wrote: "I do not care if they will camouflage this entry into the customs union [that is, not call it association], but we must not give up on the content."[17] Indeed, at her meeting with the French Foreign Minister, Meir informed Couve de Murville that the Israeli government was prepared to accept any phrasing—association or otherwise—that could safeguard Israeli economic interests. At the same time, she noted that Israel expected to be included in the EEC in some way. The French Foreign Minister responded noncommittally, emphasizing that it was necessary to search for the most *suitable* way to protect Israeli interests.[18]

At the end of June 1961, the Ministry of Foreign Affairs in Jerusalem convened a special meeting, attended by senior officials from all the country's ministries concerned with economic affairs, to reach a final decision regarding the path Israel should adopt. At the meeting, there was complete consensus regarding the necessity of Israel's association with the EEC; the special trade agreement was not even on the agenda. The only disagreement concerned tactics. While some argued that it was necessary to declare openly Israel's desire for association, others (mainly officials in the Ministry of Foreign Affairs) favored a more cautious approach that would not insist upon "terminology" but rather emphasize content. This approach had already been expressed in the draft of the request to the Council of Ministers, which was presented to the attendees. Eventually this draft was adopted.[19] Thus the Israelis reached the final decision to pursue a comprehensive solution in the form of association. On this occasion, too, there was no serious discussion of the chances of success, and once again they did not concern themselves with the possible ramifications of failure. The fact that the trade agreement was assessed as insufficient in terms of Israel's political and economic needs was enough to disqualify it immediately. No one considered returning to the measured tactics suggested by Bartur two years previously: slow progress while focusing on technical issues, with the aim of buttressing the affinity between Israel and the EEC and thus preparing the ground for a leap forward in relations.

Having decided on the solution of association, the Israelis resolved to increase political pressure, hoping to improve the chances of receiving a positive answer from the Council. As part of this political campaign, the Foreign Minister invited for a meeting the French, German, Dutch and Italian ambassadors, personally handing them the letter from the Israeli government to the Council of Ministers. This was an exceptional step: trivial matters such as delivering a letter were usually handled by lower-ranking officials. However, Meir sought to impart a message via this act, emphasizing how important this issue was for Israel. In particular, in her conversation with the Italian Ambassador, the Foreign Minister took the opportunity to speak about the topic at length. Repeating statements she had made to the Italian Foreign Minister one year earlier, she hinted that Israel was ready to grant Italy a series of economic benefits to minimize the damage Israel's association would cause to Italy. "We are ready for far-reaching cooperation," Meir emphasized.[20]

In mid-July, Israel's request for a discussion of this matter was conveyed to The Six. The French Foreign Ministry's analysis of Israel's letter reveals the extent of the disparity between Israel's assumptions and the European stance. The Quai d'Orsay had no doubt whatsoever as to the real motives behind Israel's efforts to negotiate an association agreement with the EEC: clearly, Israel sought to achieve political gains and to break the blockade against it by strengthening ties with Europe. They estimated that the mere opening of negotiations between Israel and the EEC institutions would constitute a tremendous political victory for the former and the country would exploit this for propaganda purposes. The Israelis' ostensible concern that a customs union would harm the Israeli economy was viewed as an excuse. Indeed, the French officials indicated that the opposite was true: over the preceding two years, Israeli exports to the Common Market had only increased. Although the citrus sector had experienced a significant decrease in the sale of the fruit to Western Europe in the years 1960–1961 (20%), this in fact resulted from an especially bad harvest that year rather than any difficulty in locating buyers. In fact, the Israelis sold their citrus fruits in European markets at higher prices than usual.[21] Whatever the truth of the matter, from the French ministry's perspective, the question of Israel's entitlement to preferential treatment was more pressing. Opening the door to Israel, even a crack, would invite a disastrous flood of similar requests. Two of the Israelis' main claims—that Israel was really a European country and could form a bridge to Africa and Asia—were not treated seriously and were even ridiculed.[22]

The French Foreign Ministry was not the only one in The Six to interpret Israeli motives in this manner. Whereas the Israelis were convinced that their lines of argument were effective—for example, concerning Israel's contribution to European penetration of Africa or Israel's special status vis-à-vis the EEC—these arguments actually caused more harm than good. They were regarded as an Israeli attempt (and an unsophisticated one at that) to deceive the Europeans and disguise the country's true motives. Still, it seems that most of The Six were willing to compromise to a certain degree. Many positive statements were heard in favor a special trade agreement; the multiple declarations of this nature from a variety of sources indicate that this was no coincidence but rather resulted from coordination between or perhaps even an express decision by The Six. If the Israelis had mentioned a trade agreement in their letter and formulated a concrete proposal for such an agreement, the Council of Ministers may well have received it positively.

The Six believed that the political and economic price of a limited trade agreement would be lower than constantly fending off Israel's approaches, which embarrassed The Six politically, forcing them to invest time in diplomatic maneuvers and internal discussions, and likewise entailed significant unpleasantness. Over the previous three years, the Israelis had acquired credibility for stubbornness: it was clear that they would not stop until they achieved their goal.

Of all the formulae Israel used, their persistence and optimism proved the most effective. It seems that their diplomatic nagging was a very valuable asset and was in part responsible for Israel's successes vis-à-vis the EEC in this period.

In a letter addressed to the Council of Ministers, Israel asked the Council to discuss its issue in its coming session, planned for July 24, 1961. The Germans requested that this be listed on the agenda under the paragraph "other business" and the other representatives agreed that it would be conducted in a limited forum to preserve maximum secrecy, once again indicating The Six's sensitivity regarding every public aspect of the EEC's relations with Israel.[23] At this meeting, the Council President, the German Müller Armack, sought to help the Israeli case: "My impression is that the Israelis are willing to settle for a trade agreement and their intentions are not necessarily association in every sense of the word," he said. However, Hallstein quickly corrected him: "I am under the impression from talking with them, that the Israelis are not limiting the talks to a defined solution. This is also how it seems from the memo they circulated." In view of Hallstein's comment, the Belgian Spaak felt forced to deem the Israeli application was premature; an assessment with which the Italian and Dutch representatives concurred. However, the French representative, Gorse, expressed solidarity with the president's view, agreeing that Israel was only interested in a trade agreement. He suggested passing a Council resolution ordering an in-depth study to clarify the trade relationship between Israel and the EEC: "That way the Council's response to Israel can include a positive element."[24] The others accepted his stance. While Israel's request was rejected, the Council instructed the Commission to carry out an internal study, without any obligation to negotiate formally with Israel.[25] For most of the Council delegates, the main goal of the study was not to examine the negative impact of the customs union on Israel's economic future, but to silence the Israelis for as long as possible. When Rey asked the Council about the time frame for the study, the latter stressed that the Commission should not feel bound to any specific timetable. Rey understood the hint, and instructed the members of his department accordingly, telling them "there is no special urgency to start working."[26]

At a crossroads

Israel's hopes of success had been great; thus their disappointment at the rejection of their approach was immense. A few saw the Council of Ministers' decision as almost hostile, arguing that it was now necessary to approach the two most senior figures within The Six—De Gaulle and Adenauer—and demand their personal intervention.[27] Others took comfort in the fact that the Council of Ministers had ordered the first official investigation of Israel's problems. One way or another, the Israelis were determined to exploit the Commission's investigation to establish continuous contact with the body, in itself a form of negotiations. For this purpose, it was necessary to decide whether they should continue striving for association. In August 1961, Israeli ambassadors to Western European countries gathered in Europe to assess the situation, decide on lines of action and coordinate their implementation. A substantial portion of the discussion concerned Israel's ties with European economic bodies, principally with the EEC. Naturally, the focus was on the most appropriate reaction in the face of the negative response issued by the Council of Ministers. The speakers were in almost complete agreement that the search for a comprehensive solution should not be abandoned—that is, association or at least a full customs union. Only this solution could ensure Israel's long-term aims and withstand the legal test of the GATT regulations. A limited trade agreement was neither desirable nor a practical possibility.

Despite this ostensible agreement, however, a gap began to emerge between those who viewed political profit as the main object and therefore refused to abandon the dream of association, and those who were prepared to settle for a comprehensive economic arrangement, less than association. Here, for the first time, it is possible to discern a significant fissure in the monolithic perception of association as the only possible option, a view that had reigned until this point. While the majority continued to oppose a limited arrangement, Walter Eytan dared to voice a different opinion. In an almost apologetic tone he noted that the "idea of a [limited] trade agreement with the market is also a possible form of association with it." Everyone present disagreed with him, citing various reasons. Alon, the economic director, rejected outright the option of even discussing a limited trade agreement, stating, "[T]here is no precedent of a trade agreement with the [common] market and therefore we will not be able to prepare a proposal because we do not know what to prepare."[28] The Ambassadors agreed that it was vital to persist with the tactic of ceaseless "nagging": "We must act in the political and diplomatic field . . . so that in the end they will have no choice but to accept us in one way or another for association," said Eytan. Shinnar emphasized that "we must not allow them [the Europeans] to let extended periods pass without meeting [with the Israelis]." Meanwhile Najar warned against actions that were liable to push the Europeans into a corner, hinting that the successes up to this point were due to a combination of moderation and persistence: "We have acted in a way that has put them in an uncomfortable position," he summarized. Finally, a number of speakers agreed that the moral argument constituted the most useful weapon in Israel's arsenal; it was more effective than claims about the benefits which association with Israel would bring to the Europeans. In this way, the recommendation submitted by Bartur one year previously—that the moral argument should form the heart of Israel's polemic strategy—became a permanent foundation of the Israeli approach.

At this point, understanding that association was unrealistic, the Israelis apparently renounced this goal. Yet in its stead, they sought a comprehensive arrangement in the form of a customs union that would de facto create a framework almost identical to association yet *without the political significance* of official association. Following the renewed opportunity for cooperation with the Commission, over the ensuing weeks increasing numbers of Israelis, figures from both the bureaucratic and political echelons, concluded that it was necessary to abandon the dream of association and reconcile themselves to a customs union.

In December 1961, Pinchas Sapir announced in the Knesset that "Israel does not want to be accepted into the Common Market . . . however Israel demands an arrangement which will ensure that no negative discrimination against it will result from the very fact of the Common Market's existence." Although this declaration did not signify a retreat from the demand for association, it alluded that the Israelis were ready to accept a different form of arrangement. In January 1962, the Director General of the Ministry of Trade and Industry voiced his opinion to the Association of Engineers' Club: while the dream of membership was unrealistic, a customs union with the EEC in specific sectors was definitely within the realm of the possible.[29]

Apart from the progress of talks with the Commission, another reason for accepting the idea of a customs union rather than association was the growing fear that destructive economic ramifications would ensue if a suitable arrangement with The Six was not found quickly. The first stage in the process of integration concluded at the end of 1961. During this stage, the internal tariffs on products were reduced at a faster rate than originally planned: 40% on industrial products and 30–35% on agricultural products. On January 1, 1962, the second stage in establishing the customs union was scheduled to begin: raising a unified customs wall toward non-members. France seized this opportunity to pressure the Germans with respect to the Common Agricultural Policy. They were later joined by the Dutch, and the pressure was successful. The Six decided that in the second stage of integration they would enact a special arrangement for agricultural products, defending their relatively vulnerable agricultural sector.[30] Originally, the Common Agricultural Policy was designed to achieve a number of aims: to raise the agricultural yield by allocating subsidies; to ensure a high standard of living for the agricultural community (both as part of the "welfare state" and to address fears that unhappy farmers could provide a support base for radical political parties on both the right and left of the political spectrum); to stabilize the markets in cases of insufficient or overproduction, and to ensure the continuous and undisrupted supply of agricultural produce by developing a market which would be as far as possible autarchic. This last goal of course had significant ramifications for food exporters outside Europe who sold their produce to the continent.[31]

In July 1958, an inter-governmental conference of The Six gathered in the city of Stresa, Italy, to endow this policy with real content. In 1960, the office of the energetic Commissioner for Agricultural Affairs, Mansholt, drew up a plan to re-organize the EEC's agriculture. However, Germany and Belgium, the Community's industrial nations, endeavored to protect their fragile agricultural sectors and opposed such a comprehensive reform. By contrast, France adamantly demanded the implementation of the agricultural reform as a condition for continued progress in integration.[32] Eventually, at the end of 1961, the Europeans decided to adopt a step more modest than Mansholt's plans, mainly concerned with determining minimum prices and levies toward external parties.[33] In practical terms, this instituted a long series of protective measures: for example, import levies to ensure that no external agricultural product which was also produced in one of the market's countries would enjoy any advantage over the local product.[34] This arrangement was especially protectionist toward products such as poultry and eggs; in these cases, the agricultural sectors of The Six were able to meet the demand entirely (or almost entirely). In fact, the Israelis estimated that Israel's export of these products to the EEC would become almost impossible, a harsh blow for the chicken coop sector in Israel. Eggs constituted one of Israel's most important exports to the Common Market—The Six received 250 out of 350 million eggs exported by Israel—with the value of this sector reaching 8 million dollars.[35] Moreover, the seriousness of the issue was exacerbated by the fact that the export of eggs was the main source of livelihood for the country's weakest kibbutzim and moshavim,[36] many of which were located in the periphery and the government viewed their economic survival as an important national interest.

Israel's fears concerning the ramifications of the failure to reach an arrangement with the EEC in the near future were rooted not only in current developments but were also, and perhaps mainly, connected to imminent changes. Indeed, two dangers alarmed Israeli politicians and bureaucrats alike. First, in August 1961, Britain applied to join the EEC, according to article 237 of the Treaty of Rome; it was generally assumed that this would come to fruition by the end of 1962. Fifteen percent of Israel's national exports were dispatched to this country alone (the British market absorbed almost half of the Jaffa citrus exports). Therefore, an even greater volume of Israeli exports was now under threat and the need to find an arrangement with the EEC became yet more pressing.[37] Second, it was rumored that Spain was poised to submit a request to join the EEC, or at least for association.[38] Since the end of the Second World War, the various organs of European integration had boycotted Spain because of Franco's dictatorial regime. However, Spain was slowly starting to emerge from isolation: in 1958, the country joined the OEEC and also became an observer at the Council of Europe. In 1959, the Spanish conducted successful negotiations to establish a representation in Brussels, and in 1960, the first Spanish Ambassador submitted his credentials to the President of the European Commission. However, Spain's pressing economic problems required more than mere symbolic recognition. Franco's government sought to integrate into the new economic space in Western Europe: geographically, Spain was a natural part of this space. In February 1962, the Spanish submitted an official request for "the status of association which is likely, at the right time, to become full membership."[39] Spain was the largest citrus fruit exporter in Europe and therefore Israel's main competitor. Spanish inclusion in the Common Market could have harsh implications for Israeli exports in this sector.

The Israelis' feeling that their country was standing on the brink of economic disaster can also be explained by the widening discrepancy in the balance of payments which developed during 1961 and at the beginning of 1962. The reparations from Germany, the main source for closing this gap, were scheduled to cease within two years. There was an apparent decline in the proceeds from the "Jewish Appeal," an enterprise to raise money from world Jewry that constituted an important additional source of foreign currency. Considering this combination of factors, it is not difficult to understand why in this period Finance Minister Eshkol was deeply concerned for the future of Israel's economy.[40] In February 1962, he and the Foreign Minister became convinced that it was necessary to abandon the goal of association. In the same month, the Cabinet for Economic Affairs passed a decision to "participate in negotiations which aim to attain Israel's inclusion in the Common Market's customs area by creating a *customs union* or *free trade area*" (emphasis added). Israel was relinquishing the goal of association according to article 238.[41]

Eshkol regarded renouncing the dream of association as a step that would ease the path to reaching an agreement with the EEC. He perceived such an arrangement as one of the most important steps for the future fortification of the Israeli economy and was therefore ready to make great sacrifices. Relinquishing the dream of association was not the only sacrifice or even the greatest of them. On Saturday night, February 11, 1962, the surprised Israeli public was informed that the Finance Ministry had implemented a depreciation of 66% in the exchange rate of the Israeli pound. The official rate had until this date been 1.80 Israeli pounds to one US dollar; this was now altered to 2.80 Israeli pounds to one dollar. This was a highly daring and unpopular step, especially because many Israelis made loan repayments linked to the dollar. It involved a steep rise in the prices of various commodities, among them fuel, due to increased import prices. It also incurred economic risks: it was expected to shock the entire economy, particularly certain manufacturing sectors. For this reason, Pinchas Sapir opposed the step and even abstained from voting on the matter.[42]

In Eshkol's view, however, Israel's chaotic monetary policy could no longer be allowed to continue. Since the establishment of the state, the Israeli government had zealously kept the Israeli pound at a high rate. This led to a significant gap between the official rate, which ranged from 0.3 Israeli pounds per dollar (1949) to 1.80 (1953 onward), and the rate at which it was sold by currency speculators on Lilienblum Street in Tel Aviv, who would happily pay almost three Israeli pounds for every dollar they received. In order to avoid harming exporters' opportunities to sell their wares abroad, and also as a means to "reward" the business circles close to the ruling parties, the government had implemented a policy of applying especially high exchange rates on particular sectors. Thus, for example, the Citrus Marketing Board could exchange the dollars it received in payment for oranges at a much higher price than the official rate. This policy of many different exchange rates—or, as it was popularly referred to, "*meah sha'arim*"[43]—was in fact the premium payment for exporters, in other words a protectionist measure. It also violated the rules dictated by the international monetary regime, which the International Monetary Fund (IMF) was responsible for enforcing. Indeed, the Israeli government was under pressure from both the IMF and GATT to cancel this policy of differential exchange rates.[44] Eshkol, Sapir and other government figures, however, did not want to pay the high economic price involved in canceling the "premiums" and were afraid of this dramatic step, which would instigate a single low rate for the Israeli pound (by depreciating it). However, at this juncture, Eskhol concluded that the policy of many rates was an obstacle, deterring The Six from acceding to Israeli requests. It was therefore necessary to adopt the unwanted and highly disputed step of reducing the exchange rate. Upon returning from a round of talks in Europe, Eshkol hinted that this unpopular step was on the horizon: "[W]e will need to do things that will obviously allow us to face the new reality," he said, adding

> our industry must reach a situation in which its products will be made cheaper by 25% in comparison to Europe's and I do not hesitate to determine that we will need to decide regarding some matters, due to a lack of alternatives.[45]

Presumably it was no coincidence that the announcement of the reduction was timed to coincide with the arrival of a large European Parliament delegation in Israel. This shrewd step was effective: the head of the delegation, Senator Alan Foher, announced that "there is no doubt that the depreciation of the Israeli Pound and the Israeli government's new economic policy remove one of the main obstacles on the way to Israel's association with the Common Market."[46] Eshkol's willingness to take the dramatic step he had avoided for so long serves as additional evidence indicating the importance, which the leaders of the Israeli economy attached to an arrangement with the EEC.

In February 1962, the government decided to approve the Israeli pound's depreciation. A month later, all that remained was for the government to pass a decision to abandon the association goal and replace it with the more realistic aim of a commercial agreement. In their meeting on March 11, 1962, almost all the ministers agreed that the country should aim to reach an economic arrangement and nothing more. "Our activity should be aimed at guaranteeing the interests of our exchange trade with Europe. The matter of the framework is a second and third degree issue," declared Transport Minister Yitzak Ben-Aharon. He acknowledged the tremendous importance of association for Israel, yet at the same time complained that for many months the Israeli public had been told its government was seeking a far-reaching arrangement. This change of tack would appear to signal a defeat. The only minister who was not convinced that Israel should give up the aim of association was the Religious Affairs Minister, Zerach Warhaftig. He reminded ministers, "[I]f we have an eventual aim, it is to be part of the Market, not just economically but also politically," adding that Israel could not exist as "a nation that dwells alone." Although Warhaftig deemed necessary reaching an economic agreement with Europe, he explained that integration was no less significant. Sapir, the only minister who had never fallen under the spell of association, spoke out now more bluntly than ever, declaring, "Talking about an eventual aim will complicate matters for us and distance us from solutions that are vital for us." Everyone waited to hear the response of Prime Minister Ben-Gurion, who had previously been an enthusiastic advocate of association with Europe, even stating that Israel's ultimate aim was full membership. He finally stated, "I think Ben-Aharon is right—and we all agree that the issue is in fact purely economic—namely to stop our exports being harmed," thus signaling that he himself had awoken from the dream of association with Europe. Yet he found it necessary to add that "many would agree with the Minister Warhaftig's comment that we do not rule out association with the market, if that were only a possibility."[47]

Israel's fixation on an association agreement, which, as we have seen, repeatedly caused the failure of every attempt to achieve a realistic arrangement with the EEC, requires explanation. Why did the Israelis remain unwilling to compromise and adopt a more modest solution even after their early optimism about the chances of obtaining association agreement had dissipated? Why did the many discussions in professional forums involving experts well-versed in European matters fail to consider seriously any other alternatives? The most logical answer is that only an association agreement could tackle the economic problems created by the EEC and therefore any other solution was deemed insufficient. Two facts, however, cast doubt on the claim that the Israeli desire for association was mainly motivated by economic concerns.

First, there was no consensus regarding the extent of damage Israel could expect to sustain following the deepening of European economic integration. While some professionals and politicians in Israel described it using terminology of destruction, others doubted the seriousness of the damage or that any negative effects would ensue.[48] Among the latter group was Dr. Michael Rom, a senior bureaucrat in the Ministry of Trade and Industry, who in the first half of 1961 composed a long document refuting the assumption that the establishment of the EEC posed a threat to Israel. Rom claimed that a large portion of the products which Israel exported to the EEC's member states would not be harmed by the Common Market. He demonstrated, using detailed tables and figures, that even the damage Israel was likely to sustain would be much less significant than was generally assumed at the time; furthermore, it could be minimized by modest government subsidies. Rom also claimed that association with the EEC would expose the Israeli economy to great, economically unjustified dangers. Thus, he concluded that the matter should be carefully considered and not accepted as self-evident.[49] While Rom's opinion was unconventional, he was regarded an expert in his field and there was no reason to doubt his analysis. Yet his recommendations were not taken seriously. The summary of the memorandum which was submitted to the Finance Minister and Minister of Trade and Industry in August 1961[50] had little effect—thus casting doubt on claims concerning the economic motivations behind the bid for association.

A second fact is yet more indicative. Even if the Israelis were certain that the establishment of a Common Market constituted a real threat, there was no reason to think that association could offer the only means of relief. As Rom indicated in his memorandum, and as the experts in various ministries well knew, the main problem concerned a limited group of items—no more than ten—which accounted for 90% of Israel's entire exports to the EEC.[51] An ad hoc arrangement regarding these items would in fact solve the economic problem.[52] Indeed, this was the logic at the basis of the European proposal to reach a special trade agreement according to articles 111–14 of the Treaty of Rome. The Israeli response to this argument was that such a trade arrangement contradicted the rules of the GATT (article 24) and was therefore impractical. This was a narrow legal interpretation because article 24 allowed regional preferential agreements on condition that they included most of the trade conducted between the parties to the agreement. The question of how to measure the extent of trade—according to the number of products traded or the amount of money changing hands—remained open. At any rate, the problem of justifying any trade arrangements to the GATT would, in the end, have fallen upon the Europeans and not Israel: they would be forced to tackle the legal complications and perhaps even take certain risks. It was illogical for the Israelis to view this as an obstacle to conducting serious talks about such an arrangement, which, as was noted, could solve the heart of their problem. If, during the process of negotiations, the Europeans concluded that the limited solution did not accord with the GATT agreement, then the Israeli demand for a wider agreement might be accepted.

Despite this, it is possible to detect economic logic in the lack of Israeli enthusiasm for a limited trade agreement. Israeli industry was engaged in a take-off. New economic sectors had been established and it was clear that products which accounted for the main chunk of Israeli exports would not preserve their status for long. For example, the new textile industry was already producing much more than the local market could absorb—a surplus production of 30% in 1960, growing to 100% in 1961. It was important to locate new export markets for this surplus.[53] Israeli economic decision makers found it difficult to predict the future and therefore they understandably sought to reach the most comprehensive possible agreement, one that would embrace the maximum number of sectors. However, this explanation alone cannot explain the Israeli fixation on association. First, as noted above, a customs union or free trade area could exist regardless of whether an association agreement is in place or not. Second, a trade agreement with the EEC, even if limited, did not need to be permanent but rather could be widened at a later stage to encompass other economic sectors, in accordance with the development of Israeli industry. Thus, it seems that this argument served to a certain extent as an excuse to negate the possibility of a trade agreement and did not constitute the main reason for Israeli leaders' fixation on association.

Israel's insistence on association was thus not only linked to economic issues, but involved also political and psychological factors. For a country that had faced an existential-security challenge since its birth, association was far too tempting to resist. Throughout its existence, Israel had sought temporary answers to its distress: finding a patron (the US and France), winning potential allies (the Alliance of the Periphery), and joining a regional alliance (NATO). Strengthening ties with Europe was simply a further action in the same pattern. It was a particularly attractive proposition because it offered a long-term solution, in contrast, for example, to a patron or an alliance, which could abandon Israel at any time due to changes in the political constellation. Moreover, the Israelis saw association with Europe as more than a temporary solution to its current problems—it confirmed the image they sought to project. If the Europeans agreed to embrace Israel, this would confirm that Israel was indeed a modern, cultured, Western state—a Jewish European state such as Theodor Herzl had envisaged.

It is important to bear in mind that the vast majority of the political, intellectual, and financial elite in Israel originated from Europe.

A letter that Ben-Gurion dispatched to the French President in June 1962 exemplified this approach:

> Israel as a state imbued with European culture and the western European way of life sees itself as an integral part of the free world, it bestowed one of the ideological foundations of this world and imbibes from it the cultural values close to the hearts of all men. Its geographical proximity to Europe and the origins of many of its residents [in that continent] contribute to this affinity and the close ties with Western Europe.[54]

Given this view, it is no surprise that Europe was perceived as Israel's natural neighborhood. Association was deemed the first necessary step in Israel's assimilation into Europe.[55] When Ben-Gurion was asked by a journalist at the French *Le Figaro* about Israel's intentions vis-à-vis Europe, the Prime Minister responded: "At present we want association like Greece. Although we will be happy to become a full member!"[56] Without doubt, Israel could not expect to become a full member of the EEC in the foreseeable future. However, association would be a dramatic step in this direction.

The winter of 1962 was a defining moment in the Israeli approach to the EEC. Emergent dangers—the accelerated process of integration among The Six, Britain's request for full membership, and Spain's explorations of association with the EEC—significantly heightened Israeli fears that without a trade agreement, the country's economy would sustain heavy damage. The political factor, while it did not disappear, became marginal. Clinging to the dream of association was now perceived as an obstacle to achieving burning Israeli interests. Therefore, this goal was renounced, making room for an aim, which was perceived as more realistic and likely to guarantee the economic future of the Jewish state—that is, a comprehensive arrangement in the form of a customs union or free trade area. A symbol of this turning point was the central role, which the Israeli Finance Ministry now began to play in managing policy vis-à-vis the EEC; in earlier stages, this was left in the hands of the Ministry of Foreign Affairs, with the Minister at its head. Ironically, suspicions persisted among the members of the EEC that Israel's desire for a trade agreement was motivated mainly by political motives. As we will discover, this view had a detrimental influence on the negotiations and was a repeated source of misunderstandings between the two sides.

Notes

1 Nirgad to Bartur, ISA, FM, file 1953/7, May 20, 1960.
2 Grapefruit was the exception to this: Israel was the main grapefruit supplier and therefore it was relatively easy to grant tariff relief on this product. See: Efraim Haran's lecture to exporters, ISA, FM, file 1954/5, August 10, 1961. With respect to other products in which Israel played a significant role—diamonds (30%), bromine (10%),

potash (5%)—the country was far from being the main supplier. See: article by Michael Rom, ISA, FM, file 1958/8, January 5, 1962.

3 "Season Summary: Citrus Production and Global Trade," ISA, MA, file 2423/2, August 17, 1958. However, American fruit was barely sold in the European market, in contrast to Spanish produce.

4 Najar to Bartur, ISA, FM, file 1953/8, February 14, 1961.

5 Najar to Alon, ISA, FM, file 1953/8, March 15, 1961.

6 Boaz to the Foreign Minister, ISA, FM, file 949/1, May 31, 1961.

7 Cidor to Levavi, ISA, FM, 1954/4, May 25, 1961.

8 Fisher to Levavi, ISA, FM, file 280/14, June 20, 1961.

9 Najar to the Ministry of Foreign Affairs, ISA, FM, file 1954/4, June 5, 1961.

10 One significant opponent was Michael Rom, Director General of the Ministry of Trade and Industry, who opposed association not because it was impossible to achieve but rather because he believed that it would harm the Israeli economy in the future. See: "Information and Response," ISA, FM, file 1958/8, January 5, 1962.

11 Eytan to Yehil, ISA, FM, file 949/1, May 9, 1961.

12 Shinnar to the Head of the Economic Department, ISA, FM, file 3328/10, June 7, 1961.

13 Najar to Levavi, ISA, FM, file 1954/4, May 15, 1961.

14 Susannah Vereney, "The Greek Association with the European Community: A Strategy of State," in *Southern Europe and the Making of the European Union, 1945–1980s*, eds. António Costa Pinto and Nuno Severiano Teixeira (New York: Columbia University Press, 2002).

15 Regarding the agreement, see: M. Maor, "The Common Market Necessitates Psychological Adjustments," *Ma'ariv*, October 31, 1962.

16 Shak to the Office of the Minister, ISA, FM, file 949/1, June 8, 1961.

17 Bartur to Levavi, ISA, FM, file 3328/10, June 6, 1961.

18 MAE, Afrique-Levant [AL]-Is-106, June 8, 1961.

19 Haran to Najar, ISA, FM, file 949/1, June 30, 1961.

20 Summary of the Foreign Minister's conversations, ISA, FM, file 949/1, July 16, 1961.

21 State of Israel, "Government Yearbook 1961/1962" (Jerusalem: Prime Minister's Office, 1962).

22 Note, AMAE, Communauté Européenne [CE]-IS-1467, July 21, 1961.

23 Boegner, AMAE, CE-IS-1467, July 21,1961.

24 The relative positive view of French political echelon to Israel's association with the EEC is also reflected in internal correspondence in the foreign ministries of the member states. For example: National Archives of the Netherlands, File 145-2397, Dossier 996, 11.06.1961.

25 EUA, CM2-1961-48, July 24, 1961.

26 EUA, BAC 3/1978-321, July 26, 1961.

27 Bartur to the Ministry of Foreign Affairs, ISA, FM, file 1954/5, August 4, 1961.

28 Protocol of the Conference of Israeli Ambassadors in Western Europe, ISA, FM, file 3328/9, August 28, 1961.

29 *Davar*, "A Custom Union with the Common Market—a Goal within Reach," *Davar*, January 7, 1962.

30 The 1961 arrangement included the following products: grains, pork meat, poultry, eggs, fruit, vegetables and wine. The 1963 arrangement, which was achieved after a long marathon of talks, included milk products, beef and rice.

31 Mark Blacksell, *Post-War Europe: A Political Geography* (Folkestone: Dawson, 1977), 148–60; Wyn Grant, "Agricultural Policy and Protectionism," in *The Sage Handbook of European Studies*, ed. Chris Rumford (Los Angeles: SAGE, 2009).

32 Maurice Couve De Murville, *Une Politique Étrangère, 1958–1969* (Paris: Plon, 1971), 313–15.

33 David Weigall and Peter M. R. Stirk, *The Origins and Development of the European Community* (Leicester: Leicester University Press, 1992), 136–7. Despite its modest nature, the agreement was a veritable achievement. Many believed that the agricultural issue would constitute an impassable obstacle and cause the collapse of the EEC. The discussions were intensive and extended. Those involved in the talks became so exhausted that three of Mansholt's assistants collapsed and needed medical attention. (See: *Ma'ariv*, "Sapir of the Common Market—to Israel," *Ma'ariv*, October 24, 1963.) Mansholt should be credited with the success of the negotiations, and it greatly improved his prestige.

34 Michael Tracy, *Government and Agriculture in Western Europe, 1880–1988*, 3rd ed., Agriculture in Western Europe (New York: Harvester Wheatsheaf, 1989), 255–6.

35 *Ma'ariv*, "Renewed Export of Eggs," *Ma'ariv*, September 27, 1962.

36 On this see the Memorandum of the Economic Department, ISA, FM, file 1959/1, March 1, 1962.

37 Regarding Israel's economic ties with Britain and its the commonwealth, see: Communication of the Anglo-Israeli Trade Office, ISA, MA, file 2432/24, February 1959. Another Israeli concern was that EEC enlargement would require the support of the new member states, and would make association even more difficult. These concerns arose, for example, in a conversation between the foreign minister and the Dutch ambassador. See: NAN, Files Z111-238-240,290, 706-48GS dossier 996, February 28, 1962.

38 Shaul Ben Haim, "Our Exports Are in Danger," *Ma'ariv*, January 15, 1962.

39 Juan Carlos Pereira Castañares and Antonio Moreno Juste, "Spain in the Centre or on the Periphery of Europe?," in *Southern Europe and the Making of the European Union, 1945–1980s*, eds. António Costa Pinto and Nuno Severiano Teixeira (New York: Columbia University Press, 2002).

40 Yosef Goldstein, *Eshkol: A Biography* (Jerusalem: Keter, 2003), 442.

41 Decision of the Ministerial Committee, ISA, FM, file 1958/10, February 1962.

42 Tzvi Lavi, "Back to the 'Black Sabbath': When the Pound Dropped by 66%," *Yedioth Aharonoth*, December 4, 2012.

43 One Hundred Gates (in Hebrew *Meah Sha'arim*) is the name of an old Jewish neighborhood in Jerusalem. The word "gate" is also used in Hebrew to refer to the exchange rate.

44 I. Zilber, "Is Depreciation of the Pound on the Horizon?," *Ma'ariv*, August 7, 1959.

45 Y. Shadmi, "We Expect a Merciless Campaign," *Ma'ariv*, January 23, 1962.

46 Tzvi Lavi, "The Depreciation of the Pound Paves Israel's Way for Association with the Common Market," *Ma'ariv*, November 2, 1962.

47 Protocol of government meetings, ISA, PM, Vol. 29, March 11, 1962.

48 See, for example, Oren to Gazit, ISA, FM, file 1958/9, January 18, 1962.

49 Report by Michael Rom, ISA, FM, file 1953/6, May 1961.

50 Michael Rom, *In the Path of Israel's International Commercial Policy: The Preferences and the European Common Market* (Tel Aviv: Tel Aviv University Press [in Hebrew], 1998).

51 These products include (in this order): citrus fruits, diamonds, eggs, wheat, potassium, olive oil, citrus fruit juices, concentrates, peanuts, swim suits. See: Report by Michael Rom, ISA, FM, file 1953/6, May 1961.

52 The main economic argument against an ad-hoc arrangement was the desire to attract investors for new industries and the fear that if these were not included in the arrangement with the EEC they would become far less attractive. However, it is difficult to discern in this excuse, which was hardly ever voiced, sufficient reason to reject an ad hoc arrangement. See Levavi to Eytan, ISA, FM, file 3328/10, November 12, 1961.

53 David Levi-Faur, *The Non-Invisible Hand: Politics of Industrialization in Israel* (Jerusalem: Yad Ben Zvi, 2001), 191–2.

54 ISA, FM, file 949/4, July 27, 1962.

55 In a highly similar manner, the Turks viewed association as confirming that their country was Western, secular, democratic and closely tied to Europe. Therefore, they refused to accept any other arrangement. On this see: DDF, 1962, tome I, doc. 197, June 28, 1962.
56 *Le Figaro*, January 5, 1962.

References

Ben-Haim, Shaul. "Our Exports Are in Danger." *Ma'ariv*, January 15, 1962.

Blacksell, Mark. *Post-War Europe: A Political Geography*. Folkestone: Dawson, 1977.

Castañares, Juan Carlos Pereira, and Antonio Moreno Juste. "Spain in the Centre or on the Periphery of Europe?" In *Southern Europe and the Making of the European Union, 1945–1980s*, edited by António Costa Pinto and Nuno Severiano Teixeira, 41–65. New York: Columbia University Press, 2002.

Davar. "A Custom Union with the Common Market— a Goal within Reach." *Davar*, January 7, 1962.

De Murville, Maurice Couve. *Une Politique Étrangère, 1958–1969*. Paris: Plon, 1971.

Goldstein, Yosef. *Eshkol: A Biography*. Jerusalem: Keter, 2003.

Grant, Wyn. "Agricultural Policy and Protectionism." In *The Sage Handbook of European Studies*, edited by Chris Rumford, 260–76. Los Angeles: SAGE, 2009.

Lavi, Tzvi. "Back to the 'Black Sabbath': When the Pound Dropped by 66%." *Yedioth Aharonoth*, December 4, 2012.

———. "The Depreciation of the Pound Paves Israel's Way for Association with the Common Market." *Ma'ariv*, November 2, 1962.

Levi-Faur, David. *The Non-Invisible Hand: Politics of Industrialization in Israel*. Jerusalem: Yad Ben Zvi, 2001.

Ma'ariv. "Renewed Export of Eggs." *Ma'ariv*, September 27, 1962.

———. "Sapir of the Common Market—to Israel." *Ma'ariv*, October 24, 1963.

Maor, M. "The Common Market Necessitates Psychological Adjustments." *Ma'ariv*, October 31, 1962.

Rom, Michael. *In the Path of Israel's International Commercial Policy: The Preferences and the European Common Market*. Tel Aviv: Tel Aviv University Press [in Hebrew], 1998.

Shadmi, Y. "We Expect a Merciless Campaign." *Ma'ariv*, January 23, 1962.

State of Israel. "Government Yearbook 1961/1962." Jerusalem: Prime Minister's Office, 1962.

Tracy, Michael. *Government and Agriculture in Western Europe, 1880–1988*. Agriculture in Western Europe. 3rd ed. New York: Harvester Wheatsheaf, 1989.

Vereney, Susannah. "The Greek Association with the European Community: A Strategy of State." In *Southern Europe and the Making of the European Union, 1945–1980s*, edited by António Costa Pinto and Nuno Severiano Teixeira. New York: Columbia University Press, 2002.

Weigall, David, and Peter M. R. Stirk. *The Origins and Development of the European Community*. Leicester: Leicester University Press, 1992.

Zilber, I. "Is Depreciation of the Pound on the Horizon?" *Ma'ariv*, August 7, 1959.

6 The decision to begin negotiations on a trade agreement

The bureaucrats in Brussels stand firm

The Council of Ministers gave the Commission a mandate to conduct an exclusively internal study. As already mentioned, this phrasing was carefully chosen to avoid any impression that talks were being conducted "through the back door." However, it was only natural to presume that the Commission would have some kind of contact with the Israelis in order to receive material and their help in studying the technical issues: the Israelis hoped to exploit this contact as an alternative to official talks.

The success of this new program depended upon obtaining the Commission's cooperation. Whether the Commission would be prepared to revive the old "conspiracy" with Israel and proceed without informing the Council of Ministers was far from certain. Ever since the Council of Ministers had responded negatively to the Commission's question in October 1960, Commission personnel had demonstrated a chilly attitude toward Israel's attempts to progress in the direction of association. This was evident in talks conducted with figures who, in the past, had exhibited the most enthusiastic attitude to Israeli association: Hallstein and Rey.

There were three main reasons for this change. First, the Council of Ministers had left the Commission no room for maneuver in continuing the talks with Israel; whereas previously it had been relatively easy to camouflage the form of the negotiations and their aim, this now became much more difficult. Second, the Commission had already been burned twice by the freedom it had exercised in managing contacts with Israel and on both occasions had been reprimanded for this; the officials did not want to expose themselves to any further embarrassment of this kind. Third, the Commission was less motivated to create closer ties between Israel and the EEC than it had been at the end of 1959, when the tension between the EEC and EFTA was at its pinnacle. Therefore, it was far from certain that the Commission would respond favorably to the Israeli initiative. However, the belief that beginning trade negotiations on behalf of the EEC with a non-European country such as Israel would advance integration and help to fortify the Commission's independent status within the EEC remained valid among the Commission leadership.

At the end of September 1961, Israeli Ambassador Najar spoke with Rey about the possibility of renewing the talks between Israel and his department, and was pleased when Rey expressed willingness for a certain degree of cooperation. Rey agreed that within the framework of the study, Israel would submit a document highlighting the problems expected to beset the country's economy following the establishment of the customs union, including possible solutions. Talks with Israeli representatives would then proceed based on this document. Finally, the Commission would compile an integrative study encompassing Israel's perspective. Apparently, Rey's positive approach was influenced by the encouraging stance adopted by Müller-Armack, the German representative in the Council of Ministers. In correspondence with Shinnar, Müller-Armack had agreed to continuous consultations with Israel in conducting the study[1]—correspondence that the Israelis were quick to show to Rey to persuade him.

However, the Israelis soon encountered difficulties from an unexpected source. When they approached Rey's officials to coordinate contacts, it became clear to them that the bureaucrats—exasperated that their superiors had reached covert understandings with the Israelis while leaving them to tackle the problems resulting from this arrangement—were stubbornly opposed to any Israeli involvement in their work.[2] Hallstein and Rey were well-practiced in camouflaging their role from the Council of Ministers—aided to a great extent by the Israelis—and they pretended that their approach towards Israel was diffident. However, it was impossible to conceal the role of the junior officials in these contacts with the Israelis, which the Council deemed too close. Thus, the bureaucrats were held responsible when the Commission exceeded the bounds of its authority.

Seeliger, the director of Rey's office, had been reprimanded after the Council of Ministers discussed the issue of Israel in October 1960 and had no desire to become the Commission's permanent scapegoat. He advised Rey to act with caution and not to respond hastily to the Israeli request for involvement in the survey. "You will surely remember the manner in which the Israelis exploited the initial talks we conducted with them [summer 1960], despite promising to maintain complete confidentiality," he wrote.[3] He also reminded Rey of the Council's explicit instruction that the survey was to be "internal." In a conversation with Nirgad at the beginning of October, Seeliger expressed his intention to conform entirely to the mandate which the Council of Ministers had given to the Commission. Despite citing Rey's comments and reading from the letters written by Müller-Armack, the Israeli diplomat was unable to change Seeliger's stance on this matter.[4]

The Israelis understood that they would likely encounter many more problems among the bureaucrats in the Commission's Directorate for External Affairs in the future. In the meantime, they relied on the arrangement with Rey and compiled a document presenting the problems that Israel was facing and suggesting possible solutions for them. The Commission officials, however, received the Israeli memorandum at the end of November with some anger. They had presumed that the Israelis would be satisfied with a limited trade agreement, an impression which the Israelis had intentionally given in their conversation with Rey. Yet the document explicitly emphasized that the anticipated arrangement must be of far greater compass, stating that "an arrangement regarding a limited number of products does not constitute an effective solution and is expected to encounter legal difficulties." Due to the varied range of Israeli exports, the writers of the memorandum claimed, the Common Market would negatively impact around a hundred different custom items. In conclusion, they noted that "only *comprehensive solutions* can respond to the problems described, although the option of gradual or partial implementation during the period of negotiations would not be excluded" (emphasis added).[5] Thus, the Commission officials understood that the Israelis sought to use the platform of a special trade agreement to advance a full customs union arrangement.[6]

This memorandum gave Seeliger and his officials exceptional artillery: they could easily convince Rey that the Israelis had violated his trust and were once again trying to smuggle in the solution of association via the back door, an act that was likely to embroil the Commission in complications yet again. At this point, Rey refused to advance according to the original plan: he declined to open talks with the Israelis to consolidate a joint document.[7] The Israelis viewed this as a further failure. An opportunity to include their perspective in the Commission's ostensibly objective study would have increased the chances of the Council of Ministers considering their interests. Despite the opportunity to participate in the study, they had been unable to resist the temptation to exploit the channel Rey opened to raise, once again, the solution of a comprehensive customs union that they so greatly desired—and in fact viewed as essential. They insisted that the arrangement must cover all the products which Israel exported to The Six, without reference to their weight within the total export volume. In defense of the Israelis, it must be noted that the structure and direction of the Israeli economy indeed made limiting the products on the list difficult. While the Argentinians could be satisfied with requests for tariff reductions on meat and the Brazilians found an arrangement for exporting coffee to be sufficient, Israeli exports were not only varied but in the process of developing, making it impossible to solve Israeli export problems by dealing with one or two products.

Following the submission of this memorandum including the over-extended list of export products, the Israelis embarked on feverish preparations for what they viewed as the most crucial stage in the campaign to find an arrangement with the EEC. The Cabinet for Economic Affairs meeting decided to apply significant political pressure on The Six to bring the Council of Ministers to decide in favor of opening official negotiations with Israel concerning an arrangement for its problems, even at the price of renouncing the term "association." In Jerusalem, a sense of imminent doom began to take root: if Israel failed to find a route into the EEC, this would lead to economic destruction. Senior ministers such as Golda Meir and Levi Eshkol repeated the mantra that an arrangement with the EEC was the most important issue for the future of the State of Israel, apart from security concerns.[8] Internal memoranda in the Ministry of Foreign Affairs began to claim that "Israel being left outside the market is like putting an economic noose around the country's neck"[9]—a discourse that trickled into talks between Israeli diplomats and foreign figures. At the beginning of February, a delegation from the European Parliament, including participants from all the member states, visited Israel.[10] During the visit, Eshkol informed the delegation that

> there are two routes that can lead to Israel's destruction: the first—a military offensive from outside; the second—an economic noose similar to the one which will probably be created by the new economic framework bourgeoning among the West European states.[11]

Similar sentiments were voiced during talks with The Six and the US; indeed, Abraham Harman, the Israeli Ambassador in Washington, deemed it necessary to warn his colleagues that overuse of terms such as "holocaust," "disaster," "collapse," and "death blow" was liable to cause more harm than good.[12]

In Jerusalem, the optimism that it would be possible to persuade the Council of Ministers to open negotiations with Israel over full association had dissipated; Israeli leaders no longer referred to a solution within the framework of article 238 of the Treaty of Rome, but instead discussed a customs union or free trade agreement between Israel and the EEC in the framework of article 24 of the GATT agreement. None of the Israelis mentioned a restricted trade agreement, which would encompass a limited number of export items; the general opinion was that such an agreement would be technically impractical and insufficient with regard to the country's long-term interests.[13] A few even found it difficult to renounce the dream of full association.

The most vociferous among the latter was Bartur who, now heading the Israeli delegation in Geneva, was no longer at the heart of activities regarding the EEC. Bartur had for some time been bitter regarding his successors' management of the campaign for association with the EEC. In the previous summer, even before submitting the official request to the Council of Ministers, he felt that they were not pushing the matter with sufficient rigor. In his opinion, the issue was of the utmost importance and therefore he requested that he be allowed to return and run the show:

> I believe completely that had a way been found to enable me to approach every plane and place, equipped with full authority from the governing powers in Israel (for example, a letter from the Prime Minister), I could have acted with chances of success, because I believe in it . . . the matter requires action with a different spirit and form, outside routine diplomacy.[14]

Now, from Geneva, Bartur watched as the dream of association was evaporating—a dream which he regarded as "the most important and greatest aim for fortifying Israel from the political, economic and security perspectives."[15] Bartur had been the greatest advocate of penetrating the EEC through roundabout ways, taking the route of least possible resistance. However, because Commission officials had persuaded him that association was attainable, Bartur remained faithful to this goal, even when everyone else abandoned it. Dispatching angry letters to various recipients, including all the ministers involved in the matter, he demanded that they reconsider what was, in his opinion, the destructive decision to relinquish the aim of association. When he felt they were not taking his opinion seriously enough, he did not hesitate to quarrel with those who had replaced him in office.[16]

Another persistent advocate of association was Knesset Member David Lifshitz. Similarly to Bartur, he was a victim of the illusions planted by Commission leaders that association was attainable. He viewed accepting a trade arrangement, even a comprehensive one or one that was an intermediate aim, as a serious tactical error. In a long article published in the Labor Party newspaper *Davar*, he severely criticized those who held with "the trade approach": "Association . . . this is the last border to membership inside the Market, membership that incurs demanding obligations and grants evident benefits . . . beyond this border lies a domain with one meaning: remaining outside, without any special rights."[17] He censured those charged with conducting the negotiations, claiming that instead of making association their clear aim, "out of over caution or hesitancy [they] were satisfied with raising the neutral demand to remove obstacles to our exports, without defining the basis upon which we submit this argument."

Apart from those few individuals, such as Bartur and Lifshitz, who felt that Israel was asking for too little—and others, such as Rom, at the other end of the spectrum, who held that an arrangement with the EEC was unnecessary—officials and leaders of the Israeli economy widely agreed on the benefits of a comprehensive arrangement that amounted to less than association. To achieve this aim, they underlined the main targets to be "captured" by Israeli diplomacy: Washington and Paris.

Lobbying for negotiations

The US was believed to wield significant influence over The Six; thus the Israelis believed that US government support of a special agreement between Israel and the EEC would remove a severe obstacle from their path. Articles 111–14 of the Treaty of Rome, which constituted the basis for the desired arrangement between Israel and the EEC, were relatively vague. It was unclear to what extent they enabled circumvention of the Most Favored Nation principle in the GATT agreement, without which Israel could not hope to achieve significant reductions on its export products. Likewise, there was no precedent for an arrangement between the EEC and a third-party country based on these articles. Therefore, the Israelis preferred to rely on article 24 of the GATT agreement, which allowed tariff reductions in the framework of a comprehensive agreement, such as a customs union or free trade agreement. This was another reason why Israel preferred a comprehensive solution over a limited trade agreement, which would ostensibly contradict article 24. This notwithstanding, the Israelis were concerned that other GATT members would censure a special arrangement between the EEC and Israel. Given the US's leading role in the GATT, its agreement was of prime importance.

The most senior figure in managing the Israeli economy—Finance Minister Levi Eshkol—assumed this diplomatic task. In January 1962, before arriving in Europe, Eshkol flew to Washington together with the Governor of the Bank of Israel, David Horowitz, to obtain the US government's blessing for a trade arrangement between Israel and the EEC. His first conversation with Secretary of the Treasury, Douglas Dillon was encouraging. It was commonly known that Dillon favored increasing the liberalization of global trade; on more than one occasion he had pressured The Six to adopt a less protectionist policy vis-à-vis countries outside the EEC. At his initiative, for the past two years (1960–62) a round of negotiations had been under way in the framework of the GATT, which would later be named after him ("the Dillon Round"). However, Dillon referred Eshkol to George Ball, Deputy Secretary of State of Economic Affairs, who was responsible for EEC matters in the US government. Here disappointment awaited the Israeli Finance Minister. Ball was unenthusiastic at the idea that Israel be granted a special status in its relations with the EEC. He expressed certainty that the economic difficulties Israel was facing due to the establishment of the unified customs wall would be resolved within the framework of the negotiations which the US was then conducting in the framework of the GATT. He refused to accept Eshkol's argument that Israel could not wait for the completion of these negotiations, and was skeptical when informed that Israel had already sustained heavy economic damages following the first stage in the integration process.[18]

Ball's negative response to Eskhol's request ought to be understood in the context of the US administration's negative attitude towards Israel's desire for a special arrangement with the EEC. The US's opposition was not motivated by a conflict of economic interests; indeed, Israeli exports did not compete in any significant way with American products. Rather, the US's stance on the consolidation of the EEC was generally dictated by political interests. Although the establishment of the Common Market could harm American exports to The Six, the government in Washington welcomed the deepening integration between Western European countries, believing that this would strengthen the ranks of the West in the face of the Soviet threat. It is important to note in this regard that the government's support of the integration process played a major role in its success; on more than one occasion, the Americans pulled "the Community wagon out of the mud" (for example, pushing the Germans into the Coal and Steel Community). In contrast, the Americans opposed EFTA, regarding it as a solely protectionist economic arrangement, harmful to their economic interests and without any political profit.[19] The administration's opposition to the Israeli process, as was evident in Ball's comments to Eshkol, thus stemmed first and foremost from honest concern about the international status of the EEC and the desire to avoid difficulties with the Arab countries. This conversation made it clear to the disappointed Israelis that the US government would not support their appeals for an arrangement with the EEC. Therefore, Israel decided upon a more modest aim: employing all the leverage it had with America to persuade the US government to adopt a neutral position, one which would not harm Israel's interests.[20]

Israel also tried to obtain British support.[21] At a World Bank meeting in Vienna, the Israeli representative approached his British colleagues in an attempt to find out whether Britain would support an Israeli association with the European Community. The Israelis thought was that Britain was expected to become a full member of the community soon. The Israelis understood that since the process of association with the European Community will continue for some time, it is important to invest in recruiting support from countries that may become future Community members. Israel believed that although it was not clear whether the British would be members at the time of the decision, it was highly likely that the British position would have a bearing on the matter. The British, for their part, responded with reservations.

While Eskhol and Horowitz encountered failure in the US, they hoped for more success in another domain of similar importance. Within the EEC, France had been spotlighted as the deciding factor, able to tip the scales in Israel's favor. Israel enjoyed widespread support in France, reaching the highest echelons of power. The Israelis believed that if France adopted a supportive stance towards Israel in the Council, its status in the EEC would also convince the more hesitant Italy and Germany to accept the outcome. Georges Gorse had twice intervened in Israel's favor in the Council of Ministers, ostensible proof that it was possible for a pro-Israeli element to sway the remainder of the representatives. Already by August 1961, the Cabinet for Economic Affairs decided to utilize military personnel and politicians in the French government who were supportive towards Israel, and no longer limit themselves to contact with the more hesitant Foreign Ministry and Trade Ministry.[22] In November 1961, the director of the Western Europe department at the Israeli Ministry of Foreign Affairs outlined the aims: "We must obtain from the French not only a positive attitude, but their agreement to be the best man in our relations with the Market."[23]

In January 1962, the Commission had almost completed its survey of the Israeli case; now was the time to launch an assault on the government in Paris. The Israeli Ministry of Foreign Affairs assessed, correctly, that the main problem lay in the Quai d'Orsay, in particular in the Department for Economic Affairs headed by Wörmser.[24] According to their strategy, the Israelis would persuade senior French politicians to instruct officials in the Department for Economic Affairs to vote in favor of negotiations with Israel in the Council of Ministers. Presumably, those politicians supportive of Israel, such as Prime Minister Debre, would require little pressure; the Israelis would merely need to coordinate meetings to ensure they were acting with the necessary intensity. Couve de Murville, in contrast, was highlighted as problematic, and it was presumed that only serious and incessant pressure would persuade him to give clear instructions to his officials in Brussels. Therefore, in the second half of January, Eshkol visited Paris to discuss arrangements with the EEC.[25] As the Israelis had anticipated, in Eshkol's conversation with the French Foreign Minister, the latter remained unenthusiastic: in Eshkol's eyes, he was "as cold as ice and as immovable as steel."[26] Couve de Murville was only willing to promise to enter Israel's interests on the agenda of the coming meeting of the Council of Ministers in March.

It was clear that direct pressure on the French Foreign Minister was not sufficiently effective: other means were evidently required. One of these was to recruit the senior political echelon, President Charles de Gaulle and Prime Minister Debre, so that they would instruct the French Foreign Minister to cooperate with Israel. It was easy to persuade Debre, who indeed spoke to Couve de Murville about the matter.[27] Accessibility to de Gaulle was more limited and could be achieved only via a series of people close to him, such as Pierre Maillard, de Gaulle's advisor, and Raymond Schmittlein, head of de Gaulle's party in the legislature and chairman of the Israeli-French Parliamentarian Friendship Committee.[28] These figures promised that they would try to convince the President to make a positive decision regarding Israel. A further means was to pressure the French Foreign Minister through political and public elements supportive of Israel. Maurice Schumann, head of the Foreign Affairs Commission in the legislature, undertook to bring up Israel's interest in the EEC for discussion in his commission, and indeed succeeded in passing a unanimous decision in favor of negotiations with Israel. Edgar Pisani, Minister of Agriculture and Minister Responsible for the EEC, promised his aid and vowed to speak with Couve de Murville on the topic.[29] The Israelis campaigned among the representatives in the French legislature, asking them to send letters to the Foreign Minister which called upon him to support Israel. This was even more successful than expected: more than a hundred letters reached the office of the French Foreign Minister (who was not particularly pleased by this).[30] Likewise the Israeli-French Parliamentarian Friendship Committee was recruited to the battle, and influential figures such as Schmittlein, Kosta-Flora and General Marie Pierre Koenig helped by approaching the Foreign Minister, Prime Minister and President.[31] Concurrently, efforts were made using the French media. A special conference was organized, attended by 250 participants from the French media, devoted to the problem of Israel and the EEC. The Quai d'Orsay spokesman complained bitterly to an Israeli diplomat that Israeli journalists were bothering him on a daily basis with irritating questions, as though this was France's central problem. Indeed, the Israeli Ambassador in Paris admitted, "We have harassed the French, perhaps even to the extent of annoying them."[32]

Although France was the central target of Israeli pressure in this period, it was not the only one. The European Parliament delegation that visited Israel at the beginning of February received unremitting attention. The Israelis were likewise able to use their excellent relations with socialist parties in Western Europe to issue a joint call for a suitable arrangement to Israel's problems.[33] The socialist faction in the European Parliament, which accounted for around one-fifth of all the seats, acted with fervor to advance Israel's interests under the direction of the chair of the faction's activities committee, who viewed Israel's association with the EEC as defraying a historic moral debt. On his journey to Europe in January

1962, Eshkol also visited the Netherlands and Belgium, speaking with the political elites in both countries. In most of the meetings, his conversants expressed great caution and a non-obligatory standpoint.[34]

Eshkol also exploited his visit to Brussels to speak with various high-ranking figures in the Commission, among them Rey and Marjoline. Rey refused to share with Eshkol the results of the survey which the Commission had just completed, although he hinted that according to the findings, the establishment of the Common Market would not have a negative impact on Israeli exports to the EEC; in fact, it seemed exports would even increase. This angered Eshkol, who tried in vain to prove, using statistical evidence, that this was not the case.[35] As in the past, proof of real damage proved to be the Achilles' heel of Israeli propaganda.

The Israelis had further reason to be angry with the Commission officials. Although more than six months had passed since the Council of Ministers had ordered the Commission to start working on the survey, it had not yet been completed. The Israelis had made great efforts to bring their matter onto the agenda of the upcoming meeting of the Council of Ministers in March; however, without the survey, there would be nothing to discuss. They therefore pressured Hallstein to hasten his officials to finish their task,[36] mistakenly thinking that the delay was caused by certain governments which sought to sabotage discussion of the topic in the Council of Ministers. In fact, Rey's department had followed the Council of Ministers' "recommendation" that there was no urgency to finish the survey. Despite everything, however, the Israelis continued to view the Commission as an ally. In Najar's conversation with Hallstein at the beginning of February, the Israeli said, completely unprompted, "We have acted significantly [in various circles] to strengthen the hand of the Commission so that you will be able to write a positive survey."[37]

In Germany too, the Israelis had little success. Among those countries which were unenthusiastic towards Israel, Germany's position was influenced most clearly by political interests. While France, and in particular Italy, could rightfully claim that Israel's inclusion in the customs union would harm their economic interests, this did not apply in Germany's case. There was no doubt that the Arab consideration dictated Bonn's line on this issue; the Germans themselves admitted this on more than one occasion. Historical residue made this stance seem even more outrageous to the Israelis. They believed that the new Germany owed a great moral debt to the Jewish people and this should be more important than any consideration outside of Germany's most fundamental interests. Jerusalem regarded the Arab threats as toothless and the Israelis were unwilling to accept German claims regarding the political necessity of taking their view in consideration. As evidence, the Israelis highlighted the fact that Germany's trade relations with Arab states had improved during the implementation of the reparations agreement.

In August 1961 the Israelis decided to pressure politicians, professional associations, the clergy and university professors with the declared aim of generating "a moral crisis in Germany" which would lead to a change of policy.[38]

Eshkol recruited Nachum Goldman, chair of the World Zionist Organization and President of the World Jewish Congress, to persuade the Finance Minister, Ludwig Erhard. The German complained that the Israelis were nagging constantly, noting their failure to understand that the EEC needed first to decide on the status of neighboring states, a matter that was currently on the agenda: first and foremost, Britain, and following this the three neutral states, Sweden, Austria and Switzerland. The Israelis needed to be patient— "How is it possible that the eternal people do not have the time to wait?" he replied. But Goldman was not outwitted: "If the Jewish nation has merited being eternal, this is because it has always known how to fight for its place and to push."[39] Unintentionally, Goldman had summarized Israeli diplomacy regarding the EEC: a battle of attrition waged through constant nagging. The Germans continued to display a hesitant stance in the following days. In a rare moment of candor, Germany's Permanent Representative to the Council of Ministers admitted the deciding role played by the Hallstein doctrine in molding the German government's approach toward Israel. Germany would not be able to support Israel due to fear of the Arab reaction.[40]

Thus, at the end of February 1962, Israel's situation seemed unpromising; additional pressure was needed to tip the scales in its favor. Eshkol set out on a second round of lobbying in Western Europe—a last opportunity to prepare the ground before the country's fate would be decided in the Council of Ministers. He decided to take the bull by the horns and visited Italy first.

The Israelis had certain reasons to hope that Rome's hostile approach to a special agreement between the EEC and Israel had changed somewhat. Between 1958 and 1962, Israel had tripled its exports to Italy and more than doubled imports from that country.[41] One of the central factors urging the Israelis to tighten economic relations with the Italians was the desire to change Rome's attitude to the link between Israel and the EEC. The Israeli government pressured public Israeli companies to place orders with Italian firms. Tzim, for example, was persuaded to purchase two Italian cargo ships, even though the company could obtain them on better terms elsewhere. Similar pressure was exerted on Kur, Delek and the Dead Sea Factories.[42] Government representatives, not satisfied with this, also demanded that private companies sign contracts with Italian companies and meet their stipulations. In one case, officials at the Israeli Ministry of Foreign Affairs asked their counterparts in the Defense Ministry to pressure a private company specializing in optics which had signed an agreement with a large Italian company but, for various reasons, had delayed ordering from it.[43] The Israelis invited a series of Italian figures to visit Israel, tempting them with joint economic projects and seeking to convince them that there was no serious conflict of trade interests between the two states. The most important among these was a visit by Professor Saraceno, one of two Directors General of the giant government corporation IRI, which controlled a long line of government companies. The guest met leaders of the Israeli economy, entrepreneurs, company managers, officials at the Finance Ministry and Bank of Israel, as well as economists at the Hebrew University of Jerusalem.

He was taken to all four corners of the country, exposed to the extent of Israeli development and business opportunities.[44] The second Director General of IRI needed no such persuasion—this was the same Petrilli who, in his former role as Commissioner for Social Matters, had fallen in love with the young country. In order not to damage the goodwill of those among the Italian leadership who supported Israel, the Israelis, in the GATT plenary, did not raise justified complaints that Italy was failing to abide by the GATT rules with respect to Israel, despite an assessment that the Israeli case was solid.[45]

The Israelis also offered Italy guidance in modernizing its citrus sector. In March 1962, a delegation of Italian citrus growers arrived in Israel, among them many Sicilians, to view the successful marketing methods implemented in Israel. The delegation visited orchards, packing factories, research institutes, factories for the production of citrus-derived products (for example juices), government offices and more. They met with senior figures on the Citrus Marketing Board and raised suggestions for coordinating export timing and goals to ensure good prices.[46] Only a few months later, the Israeli company Asis, encouraged by Minister Sapir, began managing a large factory processing citrus fruits in Sicily.[47] These tactics had a certain degree of success: when the Italian Finance Minister visited Israel, he declared there was no real competition between the Israeli and Italian citrus growers because the two countries specialized in different types—the Italians in lemons and blood oranges, while the Israelis focused on grapefruits and Shamouti oranges.[48] The Italian minister only admitted half the truth, however. Although the types of fruit the Italians grew were different from those grown in Israel, the products were still considered competitors. Moreover, Italy intended in the coming years to plant another million dunams of orange orchards in the south of the country to combat the severe unemployment problem in this impoverished region.[49] While at the time Italy did not meet the full citrus demands of the EEC member states, it intended to use the opportunity of the customs union to increase its share of this market significantly.

Moreover, Israel and Italy were competitors in other fields: one of Israel's central export products to the EEC was bromine; in fact, 90% of the bromine imported to the EEC was Israeli in origin, produced from the saline-rich waters of the Dead Sea. Within the EEC, the Italians were the main buyers of a bromine derivative used as a fuel additive (ethylene dibromide). In 1958, the Dead Sea Factories established an Italian company, Mediterranean Products, which was tasked with marketing bromine products in Italy. The Dead Sea Factories owned half the shares in this company, while the Italian public owned the remainder.[50] The company signed an agreement obliging it to purchase 3,000 tons of this substance every year at a value of $1,250,000—almost the entire Israeli production.[51] However, simultaneously a plant was established in Sicily to produce bromine from sea water. The Dead Sea—with a concentration of bromine eleven times higher than in normal sea water—is ideal for producing bromine, and the Italian factory could not compete with Israeli prices. The Italian government was under heavy pressure to protect the new bromine industry. Therefore, Italy ignored Israeli requests to lower the high level of tariff which the EEC placed on this product in the Treaty of Rome (23%).[52] Even in these limiting conditions, the import of Israeli bromine was profitable; therefore, various stakeholders pressured the Italian government to impose a cap on its import. In 1962, the government in Rome limited the import of bromine from Israel to 50 tons (the Israeli exports to Italy had until then stood at 200 tons) and the import of ethylene dibromide to 1,000 tons, one-third of the quantity the Italian company had committed to purchase.[53] During Eshkol's talks with all Italian ministers concerned with financial matters, it became evident that Italy's support for an arrangement with Israel was far from assured.[54]

In Paris, Brussels and Bonn, Eshkol was more successful. In Brussels, Spaak expressed doubts that Israel would be able to reach a comprehensive arrangement with the EEC, but he was at least willing to guarantee support for the opening of talks between the Community institutions and Israel.[55] Eshkol extracted a similar promise from Erhard in Bonn who, like Couve de Murville, had been harassed unceasingly in the preceding months by Israel's many friends in Germany.[56] In Paris, Eshkol was pleased to discover that the Israeli pressure had borne fruit: Couve de Murville had softened and appeared highly receptive, guaranteeing France's support in the EEC. However, he added that he was not sure whether the matter appeared on the agenda of the Council of Ministers, a strange comment considering that he himself was head of the Council and therefore not only able to put the matter on the agenda but had promised to do so in the past. Eshkol's final conversation was with Hallstein. The President of the Commission did not omit any details in describing the difficulties awaiting Israel: fear of the Arab reaction was important, but the principal concern was the undesirable consequences which the Israeli precedent would set. While this did not necessarily rule out a solution to Israel's problems, discretion was a top priority, and Israel would need to be satisfied with preliminary talks rather than official negotiations. With a wink, he claimed that a thin line separated the two kinds of talks and it would be possible to cross it in the future. "Israel needs to be tactically flexible," advised Hallstein. Likewise, he noted that "the Commission is doing all we can to move the governments, although it is going slowly."[57] These words were encouraging. The report that Rey's department compiled (which had been secretly leaked to the Israelis) was quite positive from Israel's perspective, emphasizing its problems vis-à-vis the EEC. The Israelis thus had reason to hope that the entente with the Commission was not dead after all.

The chances of a positive decision at the coming meeting of the Council of Ministers seemed higher, as the appropriate constellation had finally emerged. The Commission appeared supportive once again. In France, Israeli diplomacy had succeeded in placing significant pressure on decision makers, even if it was not certain that this would indeed translate into a positive stance in the Council. The Netherlands, Belgium, Luxembourg and Germany promised to vote in favor of opening of talks. However, more than anything else, it was Israel's fatalistic approach to the necessity of finding a comprehensive and immediate arrangement for its problems that pushed the country to race forward. Few were ready to ask whether the intensive diplomatic battle had indeed achieved its aims and prepared the ground for the decisive discussion in the Council.[58]

The adaptation of the "tactical approach"

In February 1962, the Commission, as was noted, finished composing the survey which the Council of Ministers had requested the preceding July. Rey refused to include in it the Israeli theses submitted in the memorandum of November 1961. Instead, the Israeli memorandum in full was added as an appendix to the survey. This not only failed to serve the Israeli case, but harmed the country's interests: the obvious differences between the data presented in the Commission's survey and the statistics in the Israeli appendix created the impression that the Israelis were distorting the facts.[59] Yet the survey was not completely negative towards Israel. It included many of the arguments raised in the Israeli memorandum concerning the structure of the Israeli economy and its problems. However, in contrast to the Israelis' conclusion that their case was within the realm of a *sui generis* and therefore deserved a special arrangement, the survey determined that Israel's problems vis-à-vis the EEC were similar to those of other developing countries. Israel's demand for a comprehensive agreement in the form of a customs union was not realistic, the survey concluded, for political and economic reasons. Therefore, any solution would necessarily be restricted to articles 111–14 of the Treaty of Rome.

At this stage, Levi Eshkol concluded that, at least in tactical terms, Israel should not reject any possibility out of hand. His recent contacts in Europe had finally persuaded him that the Europeans would accept nothing but a partial arrangement concerning individual products as the foundation for negotiations.[60] He therefore believed that Israel's main aim should be to pass a decision in favor of negotiations in the Council of Ministers. Such a decision would constitute a victory in itself, enabling Israel to exploit the stage to advance a wider agreement. Israel would eventually achieve the customs union it desired, and perhaps even association. When, in their meeting at the beginning of March, Erhard informed Eshkol of the solution suggested by Rey's officials in the survey, Eshkol thus expressed a positive attitude—that is, it was most important for the two parties to begin talks. The Israeli Ministry of Foreign Affairs also supported the practical approach outlined by the Finance Minister. However, it did not hurry to agree entirely to solutions that seemed less than satisfactory, and preferred to maintain a non-binding stance.[61] These differences of opinion were sufficiently evident for the Europeans to notice them.[62]

However, this was no more than a tactical argument: on the strategic level, there was almost complete consensus among the Israelis that it was necessary to exploit the Europeans' willingness to negotiate a limited trade agreement as a platform to advance their real interest—a full customs union. The Israelis now referred to this as the "tactical" approach,[63] a whitewashing that in fact concealed a cynical decision to take advantage of the goodwill of people such as Luns, Spaak, Debre, Hallstein and Rey, in addition to many others, who did not feel comfortable rejecting Israel's requests outright and therefore suggested the solution of a limited trade agreement. The Commission was aware that Israel sought to achieve the most inclusive arrangement possible. Commission personnel—commissioners and bureaucrats alike—on more than one occasion informed their Israeli contacts that Israel's consent to a limited trade agreement was obviously only a temporary arrangement.[64] However, they never imagined that the Israelis would be unwilling to compromise on a limited arrangement even in the short term and were, in fact, planning to exploit the talks to attain their real aim.

Many among The Six, mainly the foreign ministries of "the big three," considered negotiations over a limited trade agreement too great a concession. They were convinced that Israel's considerations were mainly political; therefore, the country would view negotiations with Community institutions as a victory, while this was likely to embroil the Europeans in complications with the Arabs. The "big three" had a wide range of political and economic interests in the Arab world; France's position in particular was extremely sensitive. The negotiations with the FLN in Algeria were in their final stages (the Evian Agreement was signed at the end of March 1962), and it was evident that the conditions would soon be ripe for France's return to the Arab world. The decision to open talks between the EEC and Israel at such a moment was especially inopportune. Moreover, in the same period, the Arab states had noticeably increased their pressure on The Six to refrain from signing a trade agreement with Israel. Until 1961, the Arab states had not been overly concerned by Israel's attempts to achieve association with the EEC, probably the result of fastidious European secrecy and the absence of real results. However, following a growing number of Israeli and European newspaper articles divulging the contact between the two sides and the possibility of Israeli association, in June 1961 the Arab League's Economic Council established a special committee tasked with examining the expected implications of Israel's association with the EEC. The conclusions indicated that Israel would reap palpable economic benefits, largely neutralizing the weapon of the Arab boycott. The committee therefore advised that both the Arab League and the member states individually embark on a series of actions. Indeed, at the beginning of 1962, the number of Arab meetings with The Six regarding this matter sharply increased. Particularly diligent were the Iraqis who, through various channels, approached the Foreign Ministries of The Six on numerous occasions demanding that they shun association or any other agreement with Israel.[65] Echoes of this Arab pressure appeared in newspapers published in the EEC member states and in the American media.[66] Thus, "the big three" were plainly apprehensive about the very act of negotiating with Israel, not just the content of the talks. The solution which the Commission suggested was modest enough to make it doubtful that a flood of similar demands from other countries would ensue. Yet the Europeans continued to regard it as imperative to delay the negotiations for as long as possible.

As was noted, Rey was instructed that there was no need to hurry in preparing the report. Rey's department followed this instruction meticulously: despite the original assessment that it would be ready by November 1961, he did not present the final report to the COREPER until February 1962. At this stage, some representatives of The Six in the Council attempted to highlight defects in the report that would justify an additional study. On March 7, topic was discussed in the Council, with appropriate caution, under the paragraph entitled "various." Rey promised the members that the Commission alone had prepared the report, despite repeated Israeli requests to assist in its drafting. Although the report included guidelines for a concrete solution, the discussion was delayed until the next meeting of the Council of Foreign Ministers.[67] However, the delay this afforded was minimal: the meeting was planned for April.

Rey's officials were now asked to prepare proposals for a possible arrangement with Israel, which Rey would submit orally to the Council. Rey opposed the approach of his officials, who sought to minimize as much as possible the EEC's involvement in an arrangement with Israel, and therefore he instructed Seeliger to endeavor to expand it, including some of the Israelis' requests. Seeliger decisively disagreed; indeed, he viewed the solution which he and his officials had presented in the report as the most that could be offered. He was convinced that Israel would accept this solution, and assumed that the country was interested in negotiations for political reasons as well as economic ones.[68] In parallel, Seeliger's officials made active efforts to persuade their Israeli colleagues that the outline proposed in the report was the most Israel could hope for, hinting that if Israel agreed to accept this solution, the door would finally be open for the Council of Ministers to rule in favor of official negotiations.[69]

Rey too believed that no further obstacles remained to opening talks.[70] However, in conversations between representatives of The Six and the Israelis, the former made it abundantly clear that there was still a long way to go before the conditions would be ripe for negotiations: the Community institutions were overloaded with work; many pressing issues required a solution, for instance, the question of Britain's membership; and The Six were contending with internal difficulties, including government political crises in Germany and Italy.[71]

It was easy to understand that these were mere excuses. The Israelis did not anticipate good news. Would the great pressure they had applied in the capitals of The Six, mainly France and Germany, bear fruit this time? The Israelis had received explicit promises of support from politicians who were especially sensitive to pressure from the interest groups and various bodies supporting Israel's cause. However, the Israelis had already learned from bitter experience that promises of support offered no guarantee when the matter was discussed in the Council. "The Market has a special kind of arithmetic," noted Levavi to the Knesset Foreign Affairs and Defense Committee. "It appears that 1+1+1+1+1+1 do not equal 6 but rather 0. You can receive a positive answer from each member of the Common Market, but then they gather together, discuss [the topic] and reach a negative decision."[72]

On April 3, the question of negotiations with Israel was again raised in the Council of Ministers. Once more Rey was asked to present the tentative solution which his department had prepared. It is evident that at this stage he was beginning to lose patience. The Council of Ministers did not favor negotiations with Israel. Many European states were assembling at the EEC's door, seeking either membership (Britain and Denmark) or association (Austria, Switzerland, Spain, Turkey); this threatened administrative collapse and endangered the economic achievements made so far. Israel was thus a low priority on the Council's agenda.[73] At the same time, the Council of Ministers did not dare reject the Israeli request out of hand and had repeatedly used the Commission as a means of delay.

Rey decided to force the Council once and for all to take responsibility in this matter rather than continually shifting it to him. Therefore, he laid out the facts: the damage which the Israeli economy could be expected to sustain as a result of the establishment of the EEC was not as severe as Israel sought to portray, although no doubt the country would encounter certain problems. The Council needed to decide whether this was the appropriate time to look for a complete solution to this problem or whether the political constraints which had prevented it until now remained valid: "as we can learn from the fact that the issue is not found officially on the Council's agenda," he said. Rey noted that even if the Israelis were aiming for a comprehensive arrangement, they would in fact be willing to accept a limited and more realistic solution, as the Israeli Finance Minister's most recent declarations evinced. At any rate, a dialogue with Israeli experts was indispensable to reaching a solution, and the Commission was ready to facilitate this. Rey suggested that if the Council was interested in playing down the importance of the talks, then there was no need at present for representatives of the Council of Ministers to become involved, as the rules ostensibly required. He was referring to article 111 of the Treaty of Rome, which stipulated that upon deciding to begin talks with a third party, the Council of Ministers would appoint an accompanying advisory committee, ensuring that the interests of The Six were represented in the negotiations.[74] Rey believed that The Six would, at this stage, prefer to relinquish the privilege guaranteed by article 111 in order to avoid any impression that the preliminary talks with Israeli experts were a form of negotiations.

Thus, the decision was in the hands of The Six. Gorse, serving as president of the session, expressed support for Rey's proposal. Likewise, the Belgian Spaak and German Müller-Armack, who had both promised the Israelis that they would support their cause, followed his approach. The Italian representative did not dare to break rank, and he too, although weakly, agreed that contacts could be initiated with the Israelis, although these must remain unofficial. For a moment, it seemed that the Council was about to rule in favor of beginning preliminary talks with Israel.

However, the French Permanent Representative in the Council, Boegner—in contrast to Gorse—opposed negotiations with Israel before the completion of a comprehensive study on the expected damage to the latter's economy. Boegner was a bureaucrat and thus was not subject to the same pressures that had been exerted on the political echelon. Rather, he faithfully represented the French Foreign Ministry's stance, a position that even the French Foreign Minister himself had difficulty in expressing openly under the weight of political pressure. Indeed, officials in the Economic Department at the Quai d'Orsay and political figures were governed by different constraints. Many of the former were educated at the École Nationale d'Administration, where the French political and economic elite trained and socialized.[75] They were a group of expert technocrats who reached decisions based on purely professional considerations. They felt themselves far less bound by political constraints and therefore did not hesitate to send Boegner explicit instructions ordering him to oppose negotiations with Israel at this stage. At the very least, they hoped to cause a delay, during which time it would be possible to open negotiations with another Middle Eastern state (Iran) and thus soften the blow for the Arabs.[76] Accordingly, Boegner firmly opposed the talks with Israel, arguing that the required study had not yet been completed to determine the extent the European customs union and CAP would have a detrimental effect on the Israeli economy. The Commission first needed to carry out such a study, examining each product individually, and only afterwards would it be possible to consider Israeli cooperation. "The difference between preliminary talks and formal negotiations is a fine line," Boegner warned the Council.

Boegner's words immediately changed the direction of the discussion. Each representative in turn espoused their opinion, apart from the Dutch representative, who remained loyal to Rey's proposal. The strange phenomenon which Levavi had highlighted—that the Europeans tended to unite around the most cautious approach—came to pass yet again.

French politicians had borne a great deal of pressure in the weeks preceding the session, and indeed it appeared that the Israeli endeavors had paid off. Thus, Boegner's reticence is surprising and requires an explanation. Was the initiative to delay the decision an independent step on the bureaucratic level, or did it originate from higher ranks? The instructions sent by Wörmser, director of the Department of Economic Affairs at the French Foreign Ministry, to Boegner on April 2 contained severe criticism of the Commission's report. Wörmser argued that the document was nothing more than a survey of Israel's economic data and it did not portray the concrete damage the Israeli economy had sustained following the establishment of the EEC. Its conclusions were vague and appeared inclined toward a comprehensive agreement with Israel, such as an association agreement. Wörmser concluded that a further, detailed, study, focusing on the damage anticipated to each individual product, was required.[77]

It was clear that the bureaucrats in the French Foreign Ministry opposed talks with Israel at this stage. Was this in response to instructions from the Foreign Minister? Couve de Murville was obviously unenthusiastic regarding the Israeli cause, as was apparent in his speech to the Committee for Foreign Affairs in the French legislature—although, as was noted, the committee decided to support the negotiations. In his speech, Couve de Murville avoided any obligation regarding the stance that France would adopt in the coming session of the Council of Ministers, in fact arguing that it was first imperative to verify how UK membership would affect the EEC.[78] However, it is impossible to determine with any certainty that the Foreign Minister himself issued these instructions; it is conceivable that in this case, as in others, the bureaucrats exercised freedom and acted in accordance with how they interpreted France's interests. Regardless of the origins of the directions, the French stance in the Council was no less hesitant, and perhaps even more, than those adopted by the Italians and Germans; therefore, in terms of results, the Israeli pressure on Paris must be declared a failure. Yet from a certain perspective, the Israeli endeavor could be considered a success: Israel succeeded in recruiting to its side an impressive group of statesmen, politicians, officials and other influential figures. The pressure this group exerted forced the opponents of the negotiations with Israel to pay lip service to the matter and be content with implementing delaying tactics and technical excuses. However, these tactics could not be effective indefinitely.

Rey was not pleased by this development. As in the past, the Commission would pay the price of The Six's unwillingness to deal with the Israeli nuisance. Rey also did not understand how the Commission could carry out this new assignment: it did not have access to the statistics needed for the extensive research the Council demanded, in particular data concerning the ramifications of the economic reform under way in Israel, announced only a few days earlier by Finance Minister Eshkol. Therefore, Rey asked for permission to establish contact with Israeli experts to facilitate a joint study of the concrete problems. Hallstein, who was present at the meeting, supported his suggestion. This technical justification left the Council of Ministers no choice but to compromise: the Commission would conduct *covert* interactions with Israeli experts through the representation in Brussels, disguising the talks under the garb of "conventional" diplomatic contact. This was exactly the same system that the Commission had used to manage contacts with Israel two years previously. At the same time, it was agreed that the Council would not sent representatives to the talks, as it had done in the case of negotiations with Turkey. This step was similarly intended to avoid any suspicion that formal negotiations were under way.[79]

The Israeli response was predictable. Rey went out of his way to lessen their disappointment and paint the Council's decision in the best possible light. "Although a decision has yet to be reached to open negotiations with Israel," he noted, "the Commission has been authorized to establish contacts with the Israelis without limitations and the procedure can be flexible."[80] As a token of appeasement, Rey gave Najar the secret report that had been presented to the Council (a few weeks previously, Rey had adamantly refused to share any of its content with the Israelis).[81] He also expressed willingness to visit Israel, having rejected the Israelis' invitations on a number of occasions in the past.

The Israelis were less angry than he had imagined they would be. Their awareness that the battle would be difficult, along with the past failures they had suffered, made them somewhat immune to another disappointment. Even before the discussion in the Council, Levavi had predicted that "the official status of the talks will be problematic, the rate of their progress will not be fast, and the results this year will probably be rather modest."[82] Therefore, the most recent step backwards was not viewed as a failure but rather the opposite: an opportunity. The Israelis viewed the permission to initiate contacts with their experts as a first step in negotiations that would soon assume an official character. The Economic Department at the Ministry of Foreign Affairs instructed its representatives in Western Europe to undertake serious preparations, conducting precise and thorough groundwork. It was well understood that it was necessary to seize the opportunity and act. Other countries were already knocking at the Community's door and it was important to maintain Israel's place at the front of the line.[83]

For their part, the Europeans sought to minimize the political damage of contact with Israel. The Arab states continuously heightened their pressure in this regard. At the beginning of April 1962, the technical committee established by the Arab League to fight any arrangement between Israel and the EEC met in Cairo. It advised all League members to establish contacts with The Six to prevent any kind of agreement with Israel; various Arab states, among them Iraq, Lebanon and Jordan, responded to this call.[84] In response, the Council of Ministers adopted a number of cautionary steps. It ordered that the talks between Israeli experts and the Commission be delayed for a period long enough to avoid any suspicion that these followed a decision in the Council of Ministers (at its April meeting). Rey received clear instructions not to begin the contacts before the end of May, even if the Commission were to complete its preparations beforehand. Likewise, the Council sought to limit the number of Israeli experts as far as possible ("one or two") and ensure that they would be assigned to the Embassy in Brussels, thus maintaining the disguise of normal diplomatic contacts.

Rey believed that these conditions were too stringent. The Israelis asked permission to send four to five experts, a number which seemed to him logical and even necessary. However, he was mainly infuriated by the Council's apparent prohibition against the Commission contacting any person not officially appointed to the Embassy.[85] This would narrow the Commission's room for maneuver and challenge its operational independence, something Rey was not prepared to accept. In terms of the content and framework of the agreement, The Six were interested in the most limited possible arrangement, with minimal involvement of the EEC as an independent body. For their part, it was optimal that each individual state sign the agreement separately and that the role of the Community institutions be limited to behind the scenes coordination.

Within this conflict of interests, on May 17, 1962, a delegation of four Israeli experts arrived in Brussels to manage—in reality, although not in name—the first round of trade negotiations between the EEC and Israel. Very quickly, and unsurprisingly in view of the great disparity between the goals of the two sides, the talks encountered difficulties. The first point of disagreement concerned the essence of the talks. Rey's officials (Seeliger, Russel and Faniel) insisted on implementing the instructions of the Council of Ministers precisely, minimizing Israel's role in analyzing the implications of the data and almost completely excluding the Israelis from the search for solutions.[86] The Israelis protested, claiming that this contradicted earlier agreements with the Commission leadership. There was no justification for the delegation's presence if its function was restricted to providing raw data. Indeed, Rey accepted this argument and forced his officials to conduct comprehensive talks, including various forms of potential agreements between Israel and the EEC. Already, in the first days of the talks, Israel attained a serious achievement. For the first time, Commission officials accepted, completely and with almost no reservations, Israel's claim regarding the anticipated threat to the country's economy due to European economic integration. Even more importantly, they also recognized that a full response to Israel's problems necessitated a comprehensive solution, apparently in the framework of a customs union with the EEC.[87] However, this acknowledgment did not imply that the Commission viewed such an outcome as realistic, at least in terms of the EEC's interests.

Indeed, the *realistic* solution became the cause of the most serious disagreement between the negotiating parties. The Commission officials endeavored to create a basis for the most limited possible arrangement, asking the Israelis to provide details of the items that would suffer the most serious damage once the common external tariff and the Common Agricultural Policy were implemented. The Israelis, seeking a comprehensive arrangement—not a trade agreement for a few products—vacillated, arguing that it was very difficult for them to pinpoint individual items because the sum total of Israeli exports was likely to be affected. The Israeli economy was engaged a dynamic process of development; products which were exported only minimally today could in a very short time become the locomotives of the Israeli economy. When the Commission officials insisted that the Israelis highlight the most sensitive products, the delegation compiled a list of 116 items: all the products which Israel exported to the EEC member states and which incurred any custom whatsoever. This was an Israeli attempt, although not particularly sophisticated, to achieve a comprehensive arrangement through the back door.

Needless to say, this did not please the Commission representatives. However, they endeavored to check the long list, confirming their expectations; Israel was a central supplier to the EEC of only two products on the list: bromine (90%) and grapefruits (43%).[88] The Commission officials discerned that it would not be possible to reduce customs because the Most Favored Nation principle of the GATT agreement obligated them to grant any custom benefits accorded to Israel to all the other GATT members. The Israelis argued, in contrast, that paragraph 24 of the GATT agreement confers a legal basis on a preferential agreement between two countries if this incorporates a *substantial portion* of the export trade between them—a fact of which the Commission was, of course, well aware. Yet this would necessitate a comprehensive preferential agreement in the form of a free trade area or customs union. The EEC felt unable to justify granting privileges to Israel that other states outside Europe would be happy to receive. Indeed, any gesture, concession, or benefit granted to Israel would expose the EEC to similar demands from other states in the future,[89] quite apart from the concern over how Arab nations would react to such an exceptional gesture.

The optimal answer for the Europeans was to find a solution to Israel's problems within the framework of a multilateral agreement between the EEC and a large group of countries, avoiding the political damage of an agreement with Israel. For many months, The Six tried to persuade Israel that its demands would be met within the framework of the negotiations under way with the GATT—that is, the Dillon Round. Yet it was difficult for them to tackle the justified Israeli claims that this arrangement would not effectively respond to the needs of the Israeli economy—mainly the issue of agricultural exports—because the GATT was principally concerned with industrial products.

In an attempt to overcome these problems, the Commission officials now proposed a new plan. They suggested that Israel's problems would be solved in the framework of relief steps that the EEC would grant to all developing countries. Such an arrangement was not expected to encounter serious difficulties vis-à-vis the GATT because one of its fundamental principles explicitly concerned aid and preferential treatment to underdeveloped countries. The Commission officials proposed a number of ideas regarding the kind of gestures that the EEC could offer to developing countries and which Israel could also enjoy.[90] The Israelis did not view this as a solution to their problem. They believed that it would be a slow process involving many difficulties, and it was not clear what final form an arrangement of this kind would assume.[91]

At the beginning of July, the Commission submitted to the Council of Ministers the detailed report which the latter had requested. Although it accepted many of the arguments regarding the unique nature of the Israeli case, the report itself was cautious, presenting these claims as Israel's arguments. As promised to the Israelis, the Commission recommended beginning trade negotiations on the basis of articles 111–14, the main principles of which included, first, liberalization according to the OEEC criteria and increasing the quotas; and second, establishing a follow-up commission that would meet regularly to follow the development of trade relations between the two sides, propose solutions to custom problems on a non-discriminatory basis, and discuss options for financial and technical cooperation, also among developing countries.[92]

The Commission sought to market the proposal to the Council by emphasizing that the EEC would not need to make any economic gestures of significant proportions because Israel was mainly interested in the positive "psychological effect" of such an agreement.[93] This argument was not only ineffective—indeed, The Six were particularly worried by exactly this psychological effect—but also an erroneous assessment of the reality. The Europeans tended to dismiss how the establishment of the Common Market would affect the Israeli economy. They were unaware of the apocalyptic lens through which the Israelis regarded this issue, or refused to believe in the authenticity of this outlook. However, the Israelis truly and wholly believed that the establishment of the EEC was liable to endanger their economic future. They saw a comprehensive arrangement as the only way to overcome this challenge, never abandoning their obligation to achieve such an arrangement; they were prepared to accept the Commission's proposals as a tactical step in the short term, hoping that during negotiations it would be possible to widen the content of the agreement. Although the Israelis viewed the EEC's willingness to enter negotiations as significant, also in political terms, they did not consider this the heart of the matter and certainly would not be satisfied with this achievement.

The decision to open negotiations

In Jerusalem, in the meantime, preparations were under way for a final lobbying campaign to ensure that this time the Council of Ministers would decide in favor of talks with Israel. The focus of the new diplomatic campaign was Paris. Israeli failure to ensure the support of the French representatives in the Council the preceding April required a re-assessment of the situation. Opinions were divided in Jerusalem and Paris over why French officials had acted in this manner. In the Israeli Foreign Ministry, the West European Department and the Research Department commonly believed that the French hesitation was mainly a result of the "Arab factor." France was at this exact moment closing its Algerian chapter and would be able to return to the Arab world. Officials in Jerusalem also feared that the French were playing a double game with Israel: while the senior political echelon paid lip service to the negotiations between the EEC and Israel, it was secretly instructing the technocrats to cause difficulties or alternatively avoid any involvement and thereby allow officials to maintain their negative stance.[94] Thus, presumably decision makers, no less than the officials at the Quai d'Orsay, were hesitant towards Israel. By contrast, the Embassy in Paris was of the opinion—based on close acquaintance with the reality on the ground—that the political echelon indeed supported Israel's interests and issued instructions accordingly to the lower ranks. Yet, the officials, well versed in the technical difficulties and aware of the wide range of problems likely to ensue in the EEC's relations with other countries following the Israeli precedent, succeeded in persuading their superiors of the need for caution.[95] Likewise, the Embassy believed that the reasons for this cautious approach mainly concerned the future of the EEC and not the Arab factor. These differences of opinion led to a variety of inferences regarding the best route of action. In Jerusalem, officials believed it necessary to exert more pressure on the decision makers; but the Embassy advised opening a direct and technical dialogue with expert officials. "The right to speak should be given to the technocrats and them alone," recommended the economic advisor at the Paris Embassy. "We will stop talking now about historical, cultural and transportation affinity and what else connects Israel with Europe, and we will talk about oranges, eggs, goose meat, peanuts, grapefruit segments, black metal and white metal etc."[96] Documents in the archive in Paris provide no evidence to indicate clearly which side was correct, although the historical reality accords better with the Embassy's version. The officials in Brussels, at the center of the web of technical issues, were in a better position than the statesmen to assess the entire range of problems that a trade agreement with Israel, the first of its kind, would entail. They knew, for example, that the only feasible legal basis for offering special gestures to Israel was so narrow that it would not satisfy even the most minimal Israeli ambitions. Unlike the political echelon, which clung to the illusion that it could placate Israel by simply agreeing to come to the negotiating table, these officials were aware that the other party's ambitions remained as far-reaching as in the past. Any discriminatory arrangement in favor of Israel contradicted the GATT agreement and therefore was not legally practical. Non-discriminatory trade gestures for any more than a tiny list of products were impossible.

Certainly, officials such as Boegner saw no common ground for agreement if Israel continued to demand a comprehensive agreement. From their perspective, negotiations that began in such circumstances were destined to failure;

therefore, it was logical to avoid them.[97] Thus, so long as Boegner received no explicit instruction from his superiors to vote in favor of the talks, he considered himself as authorized to ask questions, express concerns, highlight difficulties and, in so doing, delay the decision.

Given the extreme limitations on the ability of Israeli diplomats to influence the professional French bureaucrats in Brussels, the only means at their disposal was to pressure the political ranks in Paris. The endeavors made in the preceding April led Israeli diplomats to doubt that pressuring the French Foreign Minister alone would have the desired outcome. Couve de Murville displayed an impressive ability to withstand ceaseless nagging by various people on Israel's behalf, and had so far refused to instruct his officials to force the opening of official negotiations. Therefore, the Israelis directed their efforts at other avenues in the French government, such as the Minister for Economic Affairs.[98] In the meeting of the Israeli Cabinet for Economic Affairs, the Agriculture Minister Moshe Dayan counseled a direct appeal to the highest authorities in France and West Germany—de Gaulle and Adenauer—asking them to issue clear orders that their representatives should respond positively to the Commission's recommendation. The seed of this idea was sown by the Commissioner for Agricultural Affairs, Mansholt, at a meeting with Dayan.[99] The cabinet endorsed this suggestion, and thus, at the end of June 1962, Ben-Gurion dispatched a personal letter to the two European statesmen, in which he wrote, "I ask that you extend your aid so that we will reach the agreement we desire with the European Community, one which is so vital to our existence."[100]

The appeal to the highest political rank in these two countries brought immediate results. Adenauer instructed his representatives in Brussels to support the Commission's recommendation. In his letter of response, de Gaulle expressed explicit support for a trade agreement between Israel and the EEC, although at the same time noting the obstacles liable to arise on the way, mainly "the fact that the EEC is now in a process of expansion which is likely to bring about an evident change in its character."[101] The French President's express support for a trade agreement between Israel and the EEC apparently also initiated a change in the Foreign Minister's position: at the beginning of July, Couve de Murville expressed France's unreserved obligation to endorse the opening of official talks with Israel.[102]

The Israelis hoped that their matter would be discussed in the coming session of the Council of Ministers on July 23, 1962. However, because the Commission submitted its report to The Six only on July 10, the Permanent Representatives in the Council claimed that this left insufficient time for a thorough examination of it and they therefore postponed the discussion to the next meeting, scheduled for September.[103] The Israelis were by this stage frustrated by the numerous postponements. Suspicions about the Europeans' motivations in causing these delays led them to interpret this latest move as an intentional step to impede the arrangement with Israel once again, for political reasons. The Israeli representatives in each of the capitals of The Six complained at this seeming attempt to avoid the Israeli issue due to fear of the Arabs.[104] Ben-Gurion and Golda Meir imparted their personal disappointment to the French Ambassador in Israel.[105] On this occasion, too, the Israelis chose to approach the senior political echelon, asking them to instruct the professional bureaucrats in Brussels. Eshkol was sent to Paris in September 1962 to talk with the new French Prime Minister, Georges Pompidou. In this conversation, he did not relent until the French politician personally guaranteed that he would explicitly order Boegner to withdraw his objection.[106]

On September 24, 1962, the topic of Israel appeared on the agenda of the Council of Ministers. For the Europeans, the moment of truth had arrived. None of The Six rejoiced in the idea of trade negotiations with Israel; the talks were of no economic import for the EEC and involved many risks,[107] for the EEC's relations with both the Arab world and other countries outside the Community, which would demand a similar arrangement.[108] Nevertheless, at this juncture, many Europeans believed that some kind of trade arrangement with Israel was inevitable. For four years, Israel had been knocking on the doors of the EEC. The Community had not initially dismissed the Israeli claim that the country constituted a special case, deserving of special consideration, but instead employed delaying tactics. In so doing, it set a trap for itself. The benefits of diplomatic delaying tactics are clear in the short term: they enable the party to avoid undesirable actions without generating a crisis. However, in the long term, this strategy incurs a heavy price, imparting a message that the claims of the other side are ostensibly legitimate. Thus, the Europeans could no longer continue to delay without giving the impression that the repeated postponements had, from the very beginning, been an exercise to conceal a lack of desire to help Israel. In view of the extremely modest—compared with the original Israeli demands—outline of the arrangement which the Commission had agreed upon with Israel, many felt that they could no longer morally justify holding back. They felt it impossible to postpone the decision any further with a clear conscience; the only option was to agree to the Israelis' request.[109]

Among those who were in favor of official negotiations with Israel was the Commission, which now promoted the framework it had proposed. Having managed contacts with Israel for the previous two years, the Commission felt a moral obligation to support Israel's appeal to begin negotiations, especially considering the latter's agreement to limit the contents of a future arrangement.[110] However, the Commission had two additional reasons for endorsing the talks. First, the negotiations were expected to accelerate the development of EEC's joint foreign trade policy.[111] Whereas the rate of establishing the custom union had been faster than expected, the consolidation of a joint trade policy towards third parties had not progressed. Certain areas, such as quotas, remained entirely within the remit of national governments. The Commission was tasked with deepening integration of the EEC and therefore viewed progress in this regard as significant. Second, consolidating a shared trade policy would strengthen the status of the Commission within the EEC by according it new functions. The Commission had conducted the negotiations with Turkey and was to manage the talks with Israel.

Following this, it was expected that other non-European countries would approach it, asking it to regulate and conduct their affairs with the EEC; thus, the Commission discerned great potential for political capital.

Alongside the Commission, other players supported negotiations with Israel. The Benelux countries were always more amenable to Israeli requests, and now were the three clearest proponents of the talks among The Six. There were two main reasons for this. First, the Arab consideration was less central for these three small countries. While the "big three" possessed political interests in the Middle East and North Africa, the interests of the three smaller countries in this region were mainly limited to financial-trade aspects.[112] Although highly dependent on Arab oil, the Europeans, in the period under discussion, did not yet feel that their relations with Israel constituted a threat to the continued and constant supply of this important resource.[113] Second, the Netherlands enjoyed great influence among the three small states and, as was noted, was the most positively inclined towards Israel. Likewise, among The Six, the Dutch government was least hesitant about the deepening process of integration. Among the "big three," Germany was the greatest advocate for Israel, because the highest levels of German decision makers—first and foremost Adenauer—was convinced that Germany could not form an obstacle to what the Israelis perceived as a vital interest.[114] Although Italy remained, for both economic and political reasons, stubbornly opposed to the talks, the Italians were not willing to prevent the negotiations with Israel at any price. "We will not be the *bête noir* in this matter," Eguidu Ortona, a leading figure in the Italian Foreign Ministry, promised the Israeli Ambassador in Rome.[115]

In this constellation, France continued to play the deciding role. As was noted, Israel was France's client, an important purchaser of products made by its military industry, and a loyal political partner that had repeatedly voted in favor of France's interests in the UN Assembly. Israel possessed many friends in France's political parties and the security establishment. From such perspective, it would be inconvenient for France to find itself responsible for the failure to reach a trade agreement. However, two considerations led France to hesitate. First, France, even more than its partners, feared the ramifications of negotiations on relations with the Arabs. At the end of 1962, France was at the peak of a diplomatic campaign to win renewed influence in the Middle East. This led the French to restrict the public dimension of relations with Israel to a minimum, even though security cooperation continued as usual. The public character of a decision to begin negotiations would therefore contradict the general line of French policy.[116] The French Foreign Ministry was especially hesitant concerning the Commission's suggestion that it examine options for economic and technical cooperation in developing countries, additional evidence of its refusal to accept the argument that Israeli would constitute an asset in advancing European relations with Africa.[117] Second, given that such negotiations would change the equilibrium within the Community institutions, France saw this as an additional test of the balance of power between the supranational element and the governments of The Six. If the Commission was given sole responsibility for managing the negotiations with Israel, as it had in the past, this would strengthen the supranational element, a development Paris did not necessarily view positively.[118] The French were also concerned that negotiations conducted by the Commission bureaucrats, without the supervision of the member states, could lead to unwanted obligations in the name of the EEC. The French Foreign Minister felt that in its negotiations with Greece the Commission had exceeded the bounds of its authority and acted too freely.[119] France did not intend to allow this pattern to recur in negotiations with Israel, in particular when on more than one occasion the Commission had revealed a tendency to accede to the Israeli requests.

Therefore, the French made their agreement to the negotiations dependent on two conditions. First, alongside the negotiations with Israel, the EEC would announce negotiations with an additional non-European country, preferably a Middle Eastern state such as Iran.[120] Second, representatives of the Council of Ministers would participate in the talks together with Commission officials.[121] While the first stipulation received general agreement in the session of the Council of Ministers, the second provoked an argument between Couve de Murville and Hallstein, the latter seeking to ensure that the Commission would retain the central position in conducting the talks. Indeed, the French request exceeded the bounds of article 111, which stipulated that the role of the accompanying committee appointed by the Council was to supervise the negotiations and offer counsel, without detracting from the Commission's responsibility to manage the talks in practice.

Unsurprisingly, the heads of the Commission regarded this request as a setback in European integration, and likewise as a challenge to the authority and status of the Commission within the EEC. However, the other states accepted France's conditions, and Rey and Hallstein were forced to concede. It was decided that a joint delegation, including representatives from both the Commission and the member states, would be sent to the negotiations. The positive response to the French provisos had dramatic ramifications for future negotiations, as we will see in the following chapters.

The Italians were the only ones who expressed opposition to beginning the talks. Israeli efforts to change the Italian attitude on the issue, tempting them with offers of economic cooperation, had no significant effect. The Italians remained highly suspicious, belittling the gains they could expect from such cooperation. A memorandum from the Italian Foreign Ministry reveals how unimpressive Israeli endeavors were in the eyes of Rome.[122] However, as guaranteed to the Israelis, the Italian Foreign Minister Colombo followed the majority line and assented.

Four years after Israel first approached the EEC seeking an arrangement for its problems, the Community agreed to begin official talks. Considering the modest outline of any future arrangement, this achievement may appear limited. However, the agreement to official talks of this kind—in particular with Israel, which was weighed down by potential political complications, of negligible economic importance to the Common Market, and had no affinity with the EEC apart from a historical-moral debt—was an exceptional step.

Notes

1 Shinnar to Levavi, ISA, FM, file 3328/10, September 26, 1961.
2 See: Nirgad to the Ministry of Foreign Affairs, ISA, FM, file 1954/6, September 26, 1961; Nirgad to Alon, ISA, FM, October 4, 1961.
3 EUA, BAC 3/1978-321, September 25, 1961.
4 Nirgad to Alon, ISA, FM, file 1954/6, October 4, 1961.
5 Memorandum, ISA, FM, file 1954/7, November 1961.
6 EUA, BAC 3/1978-321, November 30, 1961.
7 Najar to the Economic Department, ISA, FM, file 1954/7, December 2, 1961.
8 Levavi to Eytan, ISA, FM, file 948/17, December 29, 1961.
9 Memorandum of the Economic Department, ISA, FM, file 1958/10, February 5, 1962.
10 At the end of the visit, the parliamentary delegation published a summarizing announcement which determined that "the Israeli economy's lines of development are parallel to those of the EEC and it is necessary to find a formula to solve the problems affecting Israel which are linked to the establishment of the Community." Regarding this visit see: Israel Government Yearbook (1962/1963), Report of the Ministry of Foreign Affairs.
11 See: ISA, FM, file 1957/11, February 8, 1962.
12 Harman to Levavi, ISA, FM, file 1958/10, February 12, 1962.
13 Resolution of the Cabinet for Economic Affairs. See: ISA, FM, file 1958/10, February 4, 1962.
14 ISA, FM, file 3328/10, June 7, 1961.
15 Bartur to Levai, ISA, FM, file 1959/1, March 6, 1962.
16 ISA, FM, file 1958/10, February 1, 1962; file 1959/3, February 17, 21, 27, 1962.
17 David Lifshitz, "The Path to the European Common Market," *Davar*, August 17, 1962.
18 Protocol of Eshkol's conversation with Ball, ISA, FM, file 1958/8, January 10, 1962.
19 Pascaline Winand, *Eisenhower, Kennedy, and the United States of Europe*, vol. 6 (London: Macmillan, 1996), 134.
20 Levavi to Gazit, ISA, FM, file 1959/9, January 15, 1962.
21 NAN, De Gemeenschappelijke Markt wenst Israel niet op te neme, Files Z111-238-240, 290, 27 September, 1961.
22 Bar-Romi to Bendor, ISA, FM, file 3328/10, August 25, 1961.
23 Bendor to Levavi, ISA, FM, file 3328/10, November 14, 1961.
24 The Israelis were suspicious that he was trying to overcome his "Jewish complex" by assuming an especially reticent stance towards Israel.
25 In addition to the meeting with Couve de Murville, Eshkol met with Maurice Schumman (chair of the commission for foreign affairs in the French legislature), de Latre (supervisor of foreign currency), and other figures concerned with the EEC. Apart from Couve de Murville, who expressed a chilly position, Eshkol encountered great understanding. See: ISA, FM, file 948/17, February 17, 1962.
26 Protocol of the Knesset Foreign Affairs and Defense Committee, ISA, Knesset, file 7568/2, March 27, 1962.
27 The Embassy in Paris received a report concerning this conversation. See: ISA, FM, file 948/18, February 15, 1962.
28 Shmittlein had a long-established relationship with de Gaulle. During the Second World War, he acted as mediator between de Gaulle and the Free French Army on the one hand and the Jewish Agency and Hagana organization on the other to estab-lish a broadcasting station in Haifa that would send out messages to the Vichy soldiers stationed in Syria and Lebanon encouraging them to desert. See: Eliahu Sacharov, *Out of the Limelight: Events, Operations, Missions, and Personalities in Israeli History* (Jerusalem: Gefen, 2004).

29 ISA, FM, file 949/3, March 28, 1962.
30 This was Schmittlein's initiative, not that of the Israeli Embassy, and was done without the latter's knowledge. Reports from the Embassy indicate that it greatly angered the Quai d'Orsay. See: ISA, FM, file 948/18, March 1, 1962. A sample letter can be found in the files at the Quai. See: AMAE, CE-IS-1467, March 1, 1962.
31 ISA, FM, file 948/18, February 14, 1962.
32 Eytan to Levavi, ISA, FM, file 949/3, March 6, 1962.
33 Horam to Levavi, ISA, FM, file 948/17, December 16, 20, 1961
34 Economic department to Israeli representations in The Six, ISA, FM, file 1958/9, January 23, 1962. See also: NAN, Files Z111-238-240,290, Memorandum 3/62, January 22, 1961
35 Ibid.
36 Najar to Levavi, ISA, FM, file 1958/10, February 8, 1962.
37 Ibid.
38 Bar-Romi to Bandur, ISA, FM, 3328/10, August 25, 1961.
39 Eytan to Levavi, ISA, FM, file 1958/10, February 6, 1962.
40 Najar to the Economic Department, ISA, FM, file 1958/10, February 17, 1962.
41 Israeli exports to Italy: 1958—$3.7 million; 1959—$7.1 million; 1960—$11.6 million; 1961—$12.1 million. Italian exports to Israel: 1958—$7.7 million; 1959—$12.9 million; 1960—$19.8 million; 1961—$18 million. See: Elron to the Economic Department, ISA, FM, file 1959/1, March 1, 1962.
42 Elron to Minerbi, ISA, FM, file 286/1, February 7, 1962; ISA, FM, file 286/4, May 26, 1962.
43 Elron to Karni, ISA, FM, file 286/8, September 27, 1962.
44 Report on the visit of Prof. P. Saraceno, one of the financial directors of IRI, ISA, FM, file 286/4, March 10, 1961.
45 Haran to the Economic Department, ISA, FM, file 286/2, November 12, 1962.
46 "Evidence and thoughts on the visit of the Italian delegation to Israel", ISA, FM, file 286/8, March 1962.
47 Bejarano to Dinstein, ISA, FM, file 286/8, July 3, 1962.
48 Memorandum of the Economic Department, ISA, FM, file 1958/8, December 1961. In the 1960–61 season, Italy exported 235,155 tons of lemons while Israel exported only 7,670 tons. In contrast, Israel exported 42,422 tons of grapefruit, a fruit which Italy did not export at all. The destinations for orange exports from the two countries were also different: Italy exported its blood oranges to Central Europe, while Israel's Shamouti oranges went to the north of the continent—to Germany, Britain and Scandinavia. See: "The competition between Italy and Israel with regard to citrus exports," memorandum of the Economic Department, ISA, FM, file 1960/9, March 15, 1963.
49 *Davar*, December 9, 1962; January 4, 1963
50 Brochure of the Dead Sea Factories, ISA, MIT, file 6962/12, June 27, 1961.
51 Davar, "Violation of Bromine Export Agreements," *Davar*, November 14, 1962.
52 Note, AUE, BAC 26/1969-668, January 5, 1963.
53 "Survey of Trade Relations between Israel and Italy", ISA, FM, file 286/2, August 20, 1962.
54 Fisher to Levavi, ISA, FM, file 1959/1, March 1, 1962.
55 Najar to the Ministry of Foreign Affairs, ISA, FM, file 1959/1, March 4, 1962.
56 Economic department to Israeli embassies, ISA, FM, file 1959/1, March 6, 1962.
57 Najar to the Ministry of Foreign Affairs, ISA, FM, file 1959/1, March 6, 1962.
58 One of them was Maurice Fisher, Israeli Ambassador in Rome, who cautioned that by pushing the Europeans to raise Israel's matter in the Council of Ministers in March, the Israelis would be "shooting themselves in the foot." He discerned that the position of the ministers was currently even more diffident than it had been in the preceding July. See: Fischer to Levavi, ISA, FM, file 1957/11, January 24, 1962.

59 Rey referred to the document as "cunning," deliberately exaggerating the extent of the danger to Israel in order to extort concessions. See: ISA, FM, file 1959/1, March 13, 1962.

60 Kokhav to Bartur, ISA, FM, file 1959/2, March 19, 1962.

61 For example, the director of the Western Europe Department instructed representatives in The Six, to emphasize that Israel was aiming for talks with no limitation on content and to fight against the tendency to restrict negotiations to articles 111–14. See: Bandur to Levavi, ISA, FM, file 1959/1, March 15, 1962.

62 AMAE, CE-Is-1467, March 21, 1962.

63 See Levavi and Eshkol's comments to the Knesset Foreign Affairs and Defense Committee: ISA, Knesset, file 7568/2, March 27, 1962.

64 Note au sujet des relatines des l'état d'Israël avec la C.E.E, EUA, BAC 3/1978-322, February 22, 1962.

65 See for example: EUA, BAC 38/1984-73, March 26, 1962; Querton á Brasseur, Démarche de la Fédération des Chambres de Commerce des pays Arabes, AMAECEB, file 6.110/VI, May 4, 1962.

66 See Memorandum of the Ministry of Foreign Affairs, ISA, FM, file 949/3, March 19. 1962.

67 EUA, CM2-1962-6, March 7, 1962.

68 EUA, BAC 3/1978-322, March 20, 1962.

69 See, for example, the conversation between Faniel and Najar, ISA, FM, file 1959/1, March 14, 1962

70 Najar to the Economic department, ISA, FM, file 1959/2, March 31, 1962.

71 Najar to the Economic department, ISA, FM, file 1959/2, March 17, 1962; Shak to Levavi, ISA, FM, file 949/3, March 29, 1962; Kitron to the Economic Department, ISA, FM, file 1959/2, April 2, 1962.

72 ISA, Knesset, file 7568/2, March 27, 1962.

73 DDF, 1962, tome I. doc. 89, March 17, 1962.

74 On this matter see David Coombes, *Politics and Bureaucracy in the European Communities: A Portrait of the Commission of the EEC*, ed. Institute of Policy Studies (Beverly Hills: Sage, 1970), 178–9.

75 Alfred Grosser, *French Foreign Policy under De Gaulle* (Boston: Little Brown, 1967), 83–4.

76 Regarding this matter, see the memorandum by Wörmser, head of the Economic Department at the Quai d'Orsay: Wörmser à la delegation Français à Bruxelles, AMAE, CE-IS-1467, April 2, 1962.

77 AMAE, CE-IS-1467, April 2, 1962.

78 The Embassy received a report on this from a first-hand source. See: ISA, FM, file 949/3, March 29, 1962. In a conversation between Schmittlein and Couve de Murville a few weeks later, the content of which was imparted to the Embassy in Paris, the latter claimed that he fervently supported Israel and that Gorse, not Boegner, represented France's position. It is unclear how honest these comments were. See: ISA, FM, file 949/4, July 6, 1962.

79 EUA, CM2/1962–51, July 2–4, 1962.

80 Najar to the Economic department, ISA, FM, file 949/3, April 5, 1962.

81 Of course, he could not have known that a copy of the survey had for some time been in the hands of the Israeli Ministry of Foreign Affairs; a senior official in the Commission ensured that internal confidential documents were transferred to Israel on a regular basis.

82 Levavi to Harman, ISA, FM file 1959/1, March 13, 1962.

83 Economic Department to Israeli embassies, ISA, FM, file 949/4, April 9, 1962.

84 EUA, BAC 3/1984-73, May 3, 1962; AMAE, CE-Is-1467, June 12, 1962.

85 Rey to Seeliger, EUA, BAC 3/1978-322, May 10, 1962.

86 The delegation to the Ministry of Foreign Affairs: ISA, FM, file 1959/3, May 23, 1962.
87 Faniel's memorandum to Rey, a copy of which was passed on to Israel. See: ISA, FM, file 1959/3, May 22, 1962.
88 Étude des échanges CEE/Israël, EUA, BAC 17/1969-15, June 21, 1962
89 See, for example, the reference to this in the session of the Council of Ministers which met in April: EUA, CM2-1962-13, April 3, 1962.
90 Seeliger to Rey, EUA, BAC 3/1978-322, June 5, 1962.
91 Cohen to Alon, ISA, FM, file 1959/4, June 20, 1962.
92 Étude des échanges CEE/Israël, EUA, BAC 17/1969-15, June 21, 1962.
93 Boegner to Wörmser, MAE, CE-IS-1467, December 29, 1962.
94 These matters were expressed particularly bluntly in a letter written by the deputy Director General of the Ministry of Foreign Affairs, Y. Levavi, to the Ambassador in Paris: "The obstacle is that there is no instruction to Boegner and he, lacking orders, will never vote in favour of something clear but rather will support only foot-dragging, until he receives an instruction." See: 949/5, 30/08/196: ISA, FM, file 949/5, August 30, 1962.
95 Eytan to Levavi, ISA, FM, July 30, 1962, See, for example, Moshe Shak's comments in his answer to the letter from Deputy Director General Levavi, as quoted in the previous footnote: "Again I ask myself who is deceiving whom here? Is it possible that de Gaulle, Debre, Pompidou, Schmmitlein and so on will all enter into a conspiracy with the technocrats such as Wörmser, Boegner etc.? Such a thing could not be kept secret in Paris and certainly there would be someone who would tell us that in the utmost secrecy a decision had been reached for the politicians to feed the Israelis nice words while the technocrats say that the time is not yet right. I do not believe in the existence of a 'conspiracy' between the technocrats and the statesmen." See: ISA, FM, file 949/5, September 12, 1962.
96 ISA, FM, file 949/4, April 24, 1962.
97 See: Boegner's comments to Najar, ISA, FM, 949/5, July 19, 1962.
98 ISA, FM, file 949/4, June 29, 1962.
99 Meeting of the Economic Cabinet, ISA, PM, June 24, 1962.
100 ISA, FM, file 949/4, June 27, 1962.
101 ISA, FM, file 4315/12, July 25, 1962.
102 ISA, FM, file 949/4, July 6, 1962.
103 EUA, CM2/1962-57, July 23, 1962.
104 ISA, FM, file 949/5, July 31, 1962.
105 AMAE, CE-Is-1467, July 31, 1962.1962.
106 Eytan to Levavi, ISA, FM, file 1959/6, September 7, 1962.
107 See, for example, the comments by the Italians during the meeting of the Council of Permanent Representatives concerning the undesirable psychological ramifications of such negotiations. EUA, Note sur les relations entre la communauté et Israël, CM2/1964-899, September 15, 1962
108 On this occasion, Hallstein admitted to Najar that the official explanation citing internal Community issues as delaying the opening of negotiations between the EEC and Israel was to a large extent an excuse. The real reason was indeed the Arab factor. See: Najar to Levavi, ISA, FM, file 1959/6, October 2, 1962.
109 As the Dutch Permanent Representative at the Council noted, "[T]he commercial agreement with Israel must precede any other, since Israel's appeal is the oldest and dates back to 1958." See: EUA, Note sur les relations entre la communauté et Israël, CM2/1964-899, September 15, 1962.
110 Rey promised Najar that the Commission would push the proposed outline and not be satisfied with presenting it to the Council (Ministry of Foreign Affairs to Israeli representatives in the capitals of The Six, ISA, FM, file 1959/6, September 11, 1962).

A document that the Commission submitted to the Council of Ministers stated, "[T]here can be no escape from acceding, at least in part, to Israel's request due to the situation of this country, the special importance of the Common Market for it and because the development of contacts with it until now makes it difficult to refuse outright." See: EUA, BAC 17/1969-15, September 18, 1962.

111 See Rey's comments in this regard during the meeting of the Council of Ministers: EUA, CM2/1962-64, September 24, 1962.

112 See, for example, the stance of the Belgian Foreign Ministry on this matter: Aide-memoire: Israël, AMAECEB, file 6.110/VI, July 19, 1962.

113 Nevertheless, Arab countries exerted heavy pressure on the Netherlands. For example, in the summer of 1961, the Egyptian Ambassador demanded from the Dutch Foreign Minister that the Netherlands will not support Israel's request for association and protested that the Netherlands leads the support of Israel among The Six. Moreover, the Ambassador even threatened the Netherlands that the Arab League countries would take extreme measures against EEC member states if Israel associates with the organization. The minister played down the Netherlands's role in promoting Israel's interests. See: NAN, Files Z111-238-240, 290, July 31, 1961.

114 However, at the same time the German Foreign Ministry prepared a circular for its representatives instructing them how to present the expected decision to the Arabs. See: ISA, FM, file 1959/6, October 10, 1962.

115 ISA, FM, file 1959/6, September 12, 1962. In a conversation between an Israeli diplomat and another official at the Italian Foreign Ministry, Cesidio Guazzaroni, the latter said that "Italy will not be an exception and will not veto the proposed decision on negotiations if and when signs of this will appear in consultations with The Six". Elron to Levavi, ISA, FM, file 1959/6, September 12, 1962.

116 See: Gadi Heimann, "From Friendship to Patronage: France-Israel Relations, 1958–1967," *Diplomacy & Statecraft* 21, no. 2 (2010).

117 MAE, Ce-Is-1467, September 11, 1962.

118 See for example Wörmser's comments to Eytan: "France's approach on this particular matter reflects its traditional and continuous stance on the European Commission and its responsibilities/authorizations. The Commission is always trying to see itself as a kind of seventh state in the EEC, deciding on a certain line and passing decisions to the Council of Ministers as though the Council were nothing more than a parliament discussing the decisions of this seventh government, merely required to authorize them. France never agreed to allow the Commission to act as it sees fit with only a fundamental general authorization from the Council of Ministers. This does not refer to a matter between France and Israel but rather the fundamental French approach to the role of the Commission and its authority. Agreeing to grant a general, fundamental authorization to the Commission to begin negotiations with Israel without defining from the outset the topics of the negotiations and their aim opposes French policy on the relations between the Commission and the Council" Eytan to the Economic Department, ISA, FM, file 949/5, September 12, 1962. It should be noted that this was the constant approach of the French Foreign Ministry which, among other matters, opposed the Commission's management of negotiations with former African colonies. See: DDF. 1960, tome II, doc. 135, September 22, 1960.

119 DDF, 1961, tome I, doc. 166, March 31, 1961.

120 EUA, Note sur les relations entre la communauté et Israël, CM2/1964-899, September 15, 1962.

121 Couve de Murville's words at the meeting of the Council of Ministers, EUA, CM2/1962-64, September 24, 1962.

122 SGAS, "Sviluppi trattative CEE Israele", Direzione Generale Affari Politici III, 1959–62, file 277, November 22, 1962.

References

Coombes, David. *Politics and Bureaucracy in the European Communities: A Portrait of the Commission of the EEC*. Edited by the Institute of Policy Studies, Beverley Hills: Sage, 1970.

Davar. "Violation of Bromine Export Agreements." *Davar*, November 14, 1962.

Grosser, Alfred. *French Foreign Policy under De Gaulle*. Boston: Little Brown, 1967.

Heimann, Gadi. "From Friendship to Patronage: France-Israel Relations, 1958–1967." *Diplomacy & Statecraft* 21, no. 2 (2010): 240–58.

Lifshitz, David. "The Path to the European Common Market." *Davar*, August 17, 1962.

Sacharov, Eliahu. *Out of the Limelight: Events, Operations, Missions, and Personalities in Israeli History*. Jerusalem: Gefen, 2004.

Winand, Pascaline. *Eisenhower, Kennedy, and the United States of Europe*. Vol. 6, London: Macmillan, 1996.

7 The low ebb of Israel-EEC negotiations

Stalemate in the first round of negotiations

The Israelis received the Council of Ministers' decision with great satisfaction and even excitement. However, the announcement to the media was phrased with restraint, clearly intended to maintain low expectations because of past experience.[1] Nevertheless, officials commonly believed that despite the anticipated difficulties and the restricted content of the talks, The Six were willing to invest significant efforts in finding a solution for Israel's problems—otherwise, they would have avoided authorizing the negotiations.[2] Decision makers and officials shared a general feeling that a real chance had emerged to reach a comprehensive arrangement solving most of the problems facing Israeli trade following the creation of the Common Market.

However, disagreement remained regarding the optimal tactics to widen the scope of the arrangement as much as possible. The optimism among some bureaucrats, mainly in the Finance Ministry, the Ministry of Agriculture and the Ministry of Trade and Industry, was so great that they recommended insisting on a comprehensive agreement in the framework of a customs union or free trade area. They doubted that a more limited arrangement could respond to Israel's export needs and believed that the GATT agreement could only be overcome through a comprehensive arrangement. Bureaucrats at the Ministry of Foreign Affairs were more cautious, being better acquainted with the barriers in Community institutions and the capitals of The Six. They advised that it would be best to advance using a less direct approach: by agreeing to discuss every item individually, thereby gradually expanding the list to include most of Israel's export products. The Israelis eventually decided on a combination of tactics—they would begin by demanding a customs union or comprehensive agreement and retreat to an "item by item" tactic if the EEC representatives were unreceptive to the former.

It is important to emphasize that the two solutions were based on the same discriminatory principle: Israeli products would be given preferential treatment and they would win significant tariff benefits or even complete customs exemption. Officials in the financial ministries and those at the Ministry of Foreign Affairs assumed that the EEC was filled with goodwill toward Israel and therefore would search for creative and legal means by which they could overcome any obstacles to granting the country's goods significant benefits.[3] This assumption was completely wrong, as we will see shortly.

One might wonder how the Israelis, who had for so long been engaged in close interactions with their European counterparts, could misinterpret their intentions so entirely. This is especially surprising because the Israelis received information clearly indicating that the Europeans felt little enthusiasm regarding the idea of real trade gestures to Israel. The Dutch representatives informed the Israelis that although they had tried to persuade their colleagues to find ways to respond more positively to the Israeli requests, they had received the cold shoulder. "Our endeavors to convince our partners concerning Israel's unique situation and the need to give it special treatment have failed completely," they admitted to the Israelis.[4] Similarly, in covert talks between a member of the Israeli delegation in Cologne and a German representative in the delegation to the upcoming negotiations with Israel, the latter described the unsympathetic mood among the other representatives, principally the Italians, and advised Israel to moderate its demands from the outset.[5]

Israel's illusions were to a certain extent rooted in a natural tendency to imagine and hope for the best. Following such a long and difficult battle, the Israelis did not want to believe they had obtained so little. Furthermore, the Israelis had an exaggerated faith that the Europeans recognized the damage which the Israeli economy had already sustained due to European integration. In fact, the Europeans remained rather skeptical about the extent of real damage to Israel and perceived Jerusalem's cries of catastrophe as a tactical maneuver to extort concessions. The third reason for Israeli optimism was, as in preceding cases, the encouraging messages they received from the highest echelon of the Commission. Immediately following the positive decision in the Council of Ministers, Hallstein and Rey noted that despite the limited contours of the negotiations, their interpretation of articles 111–14 remained flexible, and therefore the Israelis could achieve much more than they expected.[6] Hallstein even advised the Israelis on how to conduct the negotiations: they should refrain from demanding a comprehensive arrangement and instead battle over each item, "so that the logical conclusion will be the widest possible agreement."[7] As would become clear, the Commission leadership was almost as blind as the Israelis to the real stance of The Six and would later regret the optimism it had instilled in the Israelis.

The EEC viewed the opening of official talks as a serious gesture towards Israel. Now, believing that this was the most important aspect as far as the Israelis were concerned, some of The Six—mainly France and Italy—deemed that the EEC could adopt a more rigid position and avoid endowing the negotiations with any content granting Israel real trade benefits. Italy had opposed negotiations from the outset; and France had voted in favor of the talks only because of political pressure from the highest echelons, whereas the professional bureaucrats continued to maintain that it had been a mistake to do so. Following an examination of the possible benefits that could be proposed to Israel, the French Foreign Ministry concluded that it would be possible to offer

Israel almost nothing within the framework of the talks.[8] It must be added that France and Italy were especially concerned about the eventual reaction of Arab states when the trade negotiations with Israel opened.[9] Therefore, already at the first preparatory meeting of the EEC's negotiating delegation, the French representative asked that they postpone the negotiations indefinitely. The German delegate rejected this proposal, arguing that it would contradict a decision made by the Council of Ministers.[10]

Obviously, the uncooperative line of the French government surprised the Commission, which understood that the Israelis were unlikely to accept the extremely narrow framework of the negotiations, even as a starting point, and that a crisis would soon ensue. At the next meeting of the joint delegation, the Commission representative urged the representatives of the member states that "it is necessary to do something for Israel." He expressed concern about comments in the press which noted "the meager generosity which the Community is demonstrating towards Israel."[11] Given the diffidence among the representatives of The Six, the heads of the Commission realized it had been a mistake to foster Israeli hopes that the negotiations would realize a significant portion of their goals. Setting far-reaching aims at the beginning of the talks would provide artillery for those seeking to postpone the talks indefinitely; at the same time, the Commission's assertion to the Council that the Israelis were mainly interested in the psychological and symbolic aspects of the decision would thus appear dishonest.

Israeli Finance Minister Levi Eshkol planned to attend the opening ceremony of the negotiations and deliver a speech. This embarrassed the Commission leadership, but at least accorded with the claim regarding Israel's ostensible "psychological needs". However, rumors that he intended to cite association as Israel's eventual aim were more worrying; this would disclose Israel's true motives and portrait its prior agreement for a limited trade agreement as a deception, of which the Commission was a collaborator.. Therefore, Hallstein and Rey asked the Israelis to ensure that Eshkol's speech was as restrained as possible, in particular avoiding any mention of association as Israel's final goal. Rey reminded the Israelis that he and Hallstein had stood at Israel's side through the long campaign which finally led to the decision to begin negotiations; now it was his turn to ask Israel for a favor. The Israelis, knowing that they must under no circumstances endanger the valuable asset of Commission support, acceded to the request.[12] Meanwhile, the Commission was forced to acquiesce to demands from The Six that the opening ceremony be relocated from the festive Val Duchesse palace— where important international agreements had been signed in the past—to a more modest setting, thereby limiting the media coverage. The Six were very worried about how the Arab states would react and therefore no senior figures represented them at the ceremony.[13]

Although Eshkol's speech was edited to avoid overly embarrassing Commission officials or making any mention of association, the Israeli Finance Minister did not intend to relinquish his basic demand for a comprehensive arrangement, anchoring it in the moral debt that Europe owed Israel. His first words reminded the Europeans that the Jews had obtained special rights in Europe over the course of centuries:

> For two thousand years, the history of our nation has been interwoven with the history of Europe . . . Europe's Jews offered a great contribution to the continent's spiritual life in all fields of science, art and thought, and the most remarkable figures among them became incontrovertible assets in Western culture and tradition.

He then ensured that his listeners recalled the terrible price the Jews and State of Israel paid following the Holocaust:

> The atrocities committed by Hitler against our people were intolerable. The European Jewish community, numbering many millions, was annihilated. A tremendous treasure trove of knowledge, talent, wisdom and understanding, hope and daring, faith and love were lost forever in the crematoria and killing pits. Only after the end of the war would we, the surviving orphans, gather up the remaining remnant from the edges of the continent and bring them safely to their homeland.[14]

Following this, Eskhol proceeded to describe Israel's economic difficulties. His message was clear: there was a direct connection between Europe's past wrongs and the challenges Israel was facing in the present day. In the first session of the negotiations, which opened in Brussels on December 26, 1962, Eshkol expressed Israel's desire for a comprehensive and dynamic arrangement that could adjust to changing circumstances. At the same time, he noted the need to examine all possible *forms* of arrangement, focusing on practical solutions rather than formal definitions.[15]

The Israelis anticipated from the outset how the negotiations would unfold and prepared accordingly. They knew that the GATT agreement forbade preferential trade benefits between countries not part of a free trade area or customs union. Although suggesting the solution of a full or partial customs union, the Israelis understood that the Europeans were not interested in this.[16] Instead the Israelis proposed an alternative plan: the EEC would grant privileges only to countries meeting a series of ostensibly objective criteria agreed upon during the negotiations. These criteria, carefully designed so as to suit Israel specifically, included the following: that the country's export products were especially sensitive to the establishment of the EEC; that exports accounted for a significant portion of the country's economy; that the country constituted the main supplier to the EEC with regard to a very small number of products; that the country suffered from a severe lack of equilibrium in its balance of payments;, and finally that the country was geographically close to Europe while alternative markets for its products were very distant.[17]

This was a creative idea: by adopting these criteria as conditions for granting privileges to external countries, the EEC would reduce the number of candidates to receive them, in turn diminishing the danger that a flood of similar requests from other non-European states would ensue. This would prevent the economic damage which The Six anticipated following a comprehensive agreement with Israel. In addition, the consolidation of seemingly objective criteria could serve The Six as a justification in the face of expected criticism from the Arab states. The solution was not completely unproblematic, however. While the criteria were governed by economic logic and therefore could be justified theoretically, their implementation was liable to expose the EEC to various types of legal censure from various sources. Furthermore, if the principle of criteria was accepted, other countries would likely claim that their cases, too, demanded special consideration.[18] The EEC was not prepared to take such risks for Israel's sake.[19]

In response to these objections, the Israelis asked how the EEC was prepared to help Israel face the challenges posed by the establishment of the Common Market. They highlighted the damage which the process of customs unification and the Common Agricultural Policy had already caused Israeli exports. For example, in 1961, eggs constituted Israel's second largest export product. More than 70% of egg exports were dispatched to the EEC, a substantial proportion of this to the Italian market.[20] However, since the implementation of the Common Agricultural Policy in summer 1962, Israel had not sold a single egg to the EEC.[21] The fate of exported poultry was similar. At the time, 100 tons of Israeli poultry were stored in cooling warehouses at the port of Hamburg, as new EEC regulations prohibited entry of the goods into the Common Market.[22] The Israelis viewed their egg and poultry exports to The Six as an important economic interest and sought to persuade the EEC to find an arrangement that would enable them to continue. Indeed, the quantity of eggs Israel dispatched to Western Europe was negligible (a few million each month) compared to the hundreds of millions of eggs consumed by Europeans every day.

However, the Europeans viewed the issue from a completely different perspective. Since the summer of 1962, the EEC had been engaged in a bitter struggle with the US government concerning European poultry imports. Before the implementation of the Common Agricultural Policy, the US had exported poultry to Germany and paid customs at a rate of 4.5%. However, following the introduction of the CAP, customs had risen to 13.5%, resulting in trade diversion. German consumption of American poultry had dropped sharply because the German consumers preferred to purchase cheaper French products.[23] This development had aroused agitation among US farmers, and the government in Washington was exerting heavy pressure on Community institutions to solve the problem. The Six, however, were not willing to compromise on this issue. The episode, known as "the Chicken War," also affected the EEC's agricultural trade policy toward other countries.[24] In these circumstances, it was impossible to cede to Israeli pressure on the eggs issue: it would provide the US with additional ammunition in their battle against the EEC.

In addition to egg exports, other Israeli sectors also suffered; and according to projections, the negative impact would increase significantly in the future. The Israelis were especially sensitive concerning products they produced using raw materials imported from EEC countries or using European machinery, for example textile products (bathing suits, nylon socks), metal products (pipes), and plywood.[25] Israel argued that the customs it pays on its exports to European markets, constitute double taxation. According to Israel, its exports often included inputs originating in EEC member states, which should be exempted from the calculation of the amount of customs it is required to pay. Israelis felt that this issue, which they referred to as the "European product," justified special consideration by the EEC, with the customs rate calculated only according to the added value.[26] Although the Israeli request that the Europeans accord special treatment to the "European product" was to some degree justified, the Europeans feared it no less than the idea of criteria. One reason for this was the technical complexity involved in implementing this solution. However, more worrying was its inherent economic threat. Granting Israel tariff relief based on this principle would lead to similar demands from other countries. Certain nations, such as Hong Kong and Japan, which because of their physical size had limited natural resources, tended mainly to produce goods made from imported raw materials; granting them preferences on this basis would give their products, already highly competitive, an even greater advantage.

At this stage it became clear to the Israelis that the EEC was prepared to do almost nothing to respond to their requests. The Europeans were very surprised by the extent of the Israeli demands, as well as the energy and resourcefulness which the delegation revealed in its search for a creative formula to meet their aims.[27] Thus, the Europeans sought to cool Israeli enthusiasm and bring them to reality. At the sixth meeting, the Commission representative presented the very meager outline of concessions around which the EEC member states had managed to reach a consensus. First, the EEC would be willing to give special consideration in the coming round of negotiations with the US (the Kennedy Round) to the products that interested Israel; any concession to the US would automatically apply to other GATT members and therefore Israel would benefit from the results of these talks. Second, the EEC was prepared to accelerate the process of tariffs convergence towards common external tariffs for certain products, which were significant for Israel. Third, the EEC suggested increasing the customs quotas for a number of products.[28] The Israelis regarded these suggestions as a mockery. In the best-case scenario, the Kennedy Round would touch upon 3% of Israel's export products, and implementing any results would be a lengthy process. Customs convergence would mainly harm Israeli exports. Cancelling customs quotas was essentially an empty gesture, as Israel had almost completely solved this problem in mutual talks with each one of The Six individually. These proposals did nothing to respond even in part to the other serious challenges— the high common external tariff rate, CAP restrictions, the double taxation of the "European product"—which Israeli exports encountered.[29]

The Israelis returned from the first round of talks disappointed. Even those who had suspected that the Council of Ministers would be unwilling to grant Israel serious concessions—mainly among the ranks of the Ministry of Foreign Affairs—had never imagined that the EEC officials would be reluctant to endow the Council's decision with any real content. It was now obvious that the Europeans regarded the negotiations themselves as the heart of the gesture. The Israeli Ministry of Foreign Affairs deemed Israel's situation hopeless and decided that the situation required an urgent re-assessment.

Therefore, at the end of December, a conference of diplomatic representatives serving in The Six was held at the King David Hotel in Jerusalem, along with representatives from other ministries with an interest in the negotiations. Most agreed that the Community's proposal offered Israel almost no benefit and that the outline of this arrangement could not serve as a basis for negotiating. Yet, despite feelings of intense disappointment, most of the participants believed that Israel should not assume a position that was too uncooperative. Continued Israeli insistence on a comprehensive agreement would give the Europeans an opportunity to stop the negotiations due to "insurmountable differences." The bureaucrats still believed that the key to success lay in correct tactical behavior: exploiting the existing framework to expand the arrangement, with the help of supportive EEC parties, such as the Benelux nations and the Commission. They were convinced that the main threat to the future of the arrangement with the EEC was not the minimalist stance of the Community's negotiating delegation, but rather the overambitious positions of Eshkol, Meir, Sapir and Dayan, who were encouraged by vigorous public opinion. Most of the officials believed that if the campaign were still in their hands, it would be possible to reap substantial gains. However, they feared that Israeli decision makers would behave intransigently in the face of the EEC's diffident stance, giving those opposed to an arrangement with Israel a perfect excuse to nip the negotiations in the bud. Thus, in their report, the conference participants sought to minimize the negative ramifications of the negotiations and furnish the ministers with cause for hope:

> Before the delegation set out for Brussels it was clear to everyone that our demand for a comprehensive arrangement would be rejected . . . therefore we should not see the minimal results of the negotiations as a failure but rather as the beginning of a difficult struggle. We can even say that some of the proposals made by the EEC delegation can serve as a starting point in the next stage of negotiations . . . our task now must be to act in such a way as to ensure that the joint report by The Six and the Commission will not be negative, meaning it will not conclude that our demands exceed the possibilities they are willing to consider.[30]

To minimize the severity of the EEC's reaction, conference participants informed the press that although the talks had encountered some difficulties, "we must not talk about a crisis and any attempt to depict the present situation as a crisis is not an accurate reflection of the facts."[31]

However, not all participants agreed that the Israelis should continue this game with the Community institutions. Among them was Moshe Bartur, who adamantly argued that there was no reason to proceed with the existing talks following such a meager European proposal. He firmly believed that the pragmatic tactics advised by Israeli bureaucrats were mistaken in their very foundations. Israel should not continue along the path of compromise, expressed in its repeated willingness to reduce the content of the arrangement, but should instead adhere to maximum demands—that is, full association. While in the short term this could cause a crisis in the talks and lead to their suspension, Bartur was certain that if Israel persisted with the political campaign, it could in the long term achieve the country's goals. Bartur's lone opinion, however, was not included in the recommendations presented to the financial cabinet; rather it was appended as a draft at the end of the document, signed with the comment "this proposal was not supported in further consultations."[32] The conference feared that Bartur's intransigence would resonate with the decision makers, who tended toward more ambitious aims—a comprehensive or at least "respectable" agreement. Bartur, feeling that he had been silenced, found other channels through which to voice his arguments. At a conference of Israeli exporters in Tel Aviv, he stated, "[W]e must fight for full association and an organic connection with the Common Market and to obtain a custom union with the Market countries, because only this arrangement is likely to ensure our economic aims"; these comments were published in the press.[33] A few days later, he sent a long letter to the Foreign Minister arguing that, following the first round of talks, the Europeans were evidently unwilling to sign an agreement which would satisfy Israel. Efforts to widen the framework of the agreement were "barren and without chances of success." Such endeavors were harmful rather than effective, halting the momentum of Israel's search for a comprehensive solution.[34]

As Israeli officials had feared, the political echelon appeared less willing to restrain itself in the face of what it viewed as a humiliating blow from the EEC. When the Cabinet for Economic Affairs met, the four ministers agreed to demand a comprehensive solution for Israel's problems, even if it would only be implemented gradually. They ordered the Israeli representatives serving in The Six to initiate a campaign among Israel's friends pressuring the Council of Ministers to broaden the mandate for the negotiations.[35] This stance met a chilly response from various EEC actors, mainly those who indeed sought to facilitate a more comprehensive arrangement in the future, among them senior Commission figures. They believed that the Israeli government's stubborn position played into the hands of those searching for a reason to end the negotiations—first and foremost the Italians.

In the days following the failed talks, Commission personnel shifted to an apologetic tone in attempts to justify the European delegation's intractable position. They tried to calm the Israelis, minimizing the negative significance of the latest developments and even painting them as positive from Israel's perspective. In a conversation with Nirgad, Seeliger argued that the passive stance adopted by the Commission during the negotiations was a tactical move: the situation would become so absurd that the Council of Ministers would be left with no option but to broaden the Commission's authority in managing the negotiations.[36] In his conversation with Najar, Rey claimed that he had expected from the outset that the first round of talks would end in stalemate; he was not surprised by this development at all, as this pattern had recurred also in the talks with Greece and Turkey. He predicted that a breakthrough would not occur until the third round of talks. Rey explained that the EEC's fundamental agreement to establish a committee to implement the agreement (follow-up committee), which included permanent Israeli and European representatives, should be regarded as the most important step. He reminded Najar that he himself had expressed this idea as a means to widen the arrangement with Israel "through the back door."[37] Rey, finding himself in a defensive position, and probably feeling a certain degree of responsibility for the Israelis' disappointment, agreed to consider a visit to Israel at the head of a delegation of Commission officials—in stark contrast to his former rejections of Israeli invitations.[38]

Both Seeliger and Rey thus pleaded with their Israeli counterparts to refrain from behaving too stubbornly and avoid demanding once again that the negotiations consider a comprehensive arrangement, actions that were liable to endanger the talks needlessly. At the end of January, Hallstein joined this choir, informing his friend Nachum Goldman that Israel must be satisfied with what it could obtain at present as a tactical step—"keeping a toe in the door"—toward achieving its future desires. Hallstein criticized the moderate Israeli campaign in the capitals of The Six and especially Germany, divulging to Goldman in secret that although the Germans gave the impression of acting energetically on Israel's behalf, this was not in fact the case. He asked Goldman to impart this message to the Israelis so that they could act upon it.[39]

These testimonies demonstrate quite clearly that the highest ranks of the Commission were interested in continuing the talks and sought to ensure that the Israelis would adopt a position enabling this. They viewed the talks as leverage to strengthen the process of integration among EEC members and guarantee a more central role for the Commission as a body (and for themselves as its leaders). They were not pleased by the incursion of representatives appointed by the Council of Ministers into their domain, disinheriting them from the role of managing the talks with Israel. Rey was similarly angered by the behavior of Commission representatives in the joint negotiating delegation: instead of leading, they followed the line dictated by the representatives of The Six. He rebuked Seeliger in a letter a few days after the end of the first round of talks, stating that "the role of the Commission is not to wait for instructions from the Council but rather to mold policy," and added, "We have here a clear example of the character which the negotiations assume when the Commission is not leading them".[40] Seeliger himself was concerned about the negative effects of failed negotiations with Israel on the EEC's relations with the world; other countries might see it as proof of the EEC's bad faith.[41]

Whereas Rey wanted to advance the arrangement with Israel, he was not prepared to listen to repeated requests from Israeli diplomats that the content of the talks be widened. Such a step would set the Commission on a path to collision with the Council of Ministers, the latter having made it abundantly clear that a comprehensive or preferential agreement was out of the question.

Rey sought to give the Commission a central role in leading the negotiations, and to do so it was vital to regain the trust of the Council of Ministers and dissipate the skepticism resulting from Israel's intractable position, in contrast to earlier Commission assessments.[42] He felt it important to give the impression that the Commission was in full agreement with the Council of Ministers regarding the outline of the future agreement with Israel. This angered the Israelis.[43] Spaak also criticized Hallstein and Rey, bemoaning their lack of initiative and that they avoided voicing their real opinions in public in a conversation with Najar.[44] Rey was only willing to exceed the hesitant approach of the EEC's delegation on one specific matter. Although he believed that the ideas the Israelis presented to the Europeans in the first round of talks were unrealistic, the concept of the "European product" caught his attention. In bilateral trade agreements, it was accepted that country A was entitled to custom benefits from country B if the product produced by country A was based on raw materials imported from country B. The Israeli proposal of the "European product" was based on the assumption that the Common Market should be viewed as one unit. Therefore, if France sold aluminum to Israel, which the latter then made into pipes, Israel could demand a reduction when selling these pipes to any one of The Six.

Adopting this principle would constitute an extensive step in terms of integration and involved many technical problems. Nevertheless, Rey viewed positively actions advancing the EEC's economic integration and therefore decided to exploit the Israeli request in attempt to advance it, albeit gradually. Thus unsurprisingly, in the Commission's communication to the Council of Ministers, which was submitted at the end of January, the idea of the "European product" was the only concrete Israeli idea to receive positive endorsement. Once again, it is evident that the Commission was willing to cooperate with Israel when such cooperation served its own agenda. This issue, which deals with rules of origin— rules and regulations defining the origin of the product—formed a cornerstone of the consolidation and deepening of European integration through its relations with third-party countries. Moreover, the issue of rules of origin would accompany the relations between Israel and the EEC over the years.

The Dutch initiative

Another party supportive of Israeli interests and seeking to advance them was angered by the Israeli political echelon's intransigent position, which threatened to halt the negotiations at a very early stage: the Benelux countries, in particular the Netherlands. Since Israel's first contact with the EEC, the Dutch had been the most active proponents of an arrangement with them, for political and economic reasons, as was outlined above. In the final months of 1962, relations between Israeli diplomats and their counterparts at the Finance Ministry in The Hague became much warmer. The Dutch presented suggestions to the Community institutions which they had ostensibly composed but the Israelis had in fact penned—translating them into French to conceal their true origins.[45]

Dutch officials forwarded to the Israelis many confidential documents from Community institutions, including the Commission, enabling the Israelis to plan their course of action more effectively. At the end of 1962, for example, a senior Dutch official in the Commission made contact with Najar's new deputy, Itzhak Minerbi, promising to give him copies of the main diplomatic correspondence and summaries of discussions in the Council of Ministers and Commission. True to his word, the Israeli representation in Brussels regularly received all the relevant material distributed among the Community institutions. This was a true gold mine, divulging to the Israelis the misgivings and disagreements among the EEC members and the Commission, which they could then exploit to their advantage. The Israelis knew in advance what tactics the Europeans were planning to use in the negotiations, and the real red lines which could not be crossed. Indeed, they utilized this information expertly.[46] The Dutch also provided Israel with a continuous and detailed report of what was written in the proceedings in other forums, for example various committees; and Israeli representatives were admitted as observers in the discussions of the Benelux delegation to the negotiations. Various officials in the Community institutions began to sense that the Israelis were receiving details of the different opinions voiced at the meetings; an official at the Belgian Foreign Ministry complained to his superiors that the Israelis appeared to know everything said by the Belgian representatives.[47] On another occasion, a lack of Israeli caution led to the publication of details from the discussion of the COREPER in the press. This angered Seeliger, who demanded action to prevent such leaks.[48]

At this juncture, officials in the Dutch Ministry of Finance, such as Kalshoven and de Waard, warned the Israelis against voicing exaggerated demands: "At least at present there is no real chance of a comprehensive arrangement, whether this is called a customs union, a free trade area or by any other name," de Waard informed the economic advisor at Israel's Embassy in The Hague.[49] The Dutch also highlighted the possibility of widening the arrangement via the accompanying committee which would be established as follow-up to the agreement.[50] Likewise, many voices in the French government called for Israeli moderation. General Catroux, considered one of Israel's greatest friends in the French political sphere, advised the Israeli Ambassador to France to reach an agreement right away, even if limited in content, thereby obtaining a foothold in the EEC as a first step to achieving the country's full aims.[51] Boegner was less friendly but optimally positioned to assess the atmosphere in the Community institutions. He warned Najar that the EEC was in no way ready to reach any kind of comprehensive agreement. "Anyone who gives the Israeli government the hope that at this stage and under the present conditions a global agreement is possible, he reveals a total lack of responsibility." Yet he added that a preliminary agreement was not without meaning. Certainly, such an agreement would constitute the beginning of a connection with the EEC and would be a significant achievement for Israel.[52]

The Israeli diplomats in the European capitals, most of whom were convinced of the need to reduce the demands, found these warnings helpful.

They dispatched recommendations to Jerusalem advising the decision makers to consider drafting more modest aims:

> The content of these paragraphs [which the Europeans proposed] can be an important step, which will give us a serious foot in the Market's door, and likewise an achievement which will make an impression, if explained appropriately, in Israel and abroad. I would not give up on this accomplishment, even though it will clearly give us much less than we wanted. You could say that I am a minimalist, and certainly I know that it is more respectable to be a maximalist like Bartur, but if the available options are little or nothing, I personally prefer the little.[53]

The feeling among Israeli diplomats that it was necessary to be satisfied with what was currently on offer was augmented by another development which occurred at this time. At the end of January 1963, the talks between the EEC and Britain reached a dead end after President de Gaulle vetoed the latter's membership in the EEC, provoking strong opposition among Britain's supporters—mainly the Benelux countries. A serious crisis swept through the EEC; some feared that it was on the verge of collapse. In such an atmosphere, it was difficult to believe that The Six would reconsider and expand the decision they had made the previous September. Israeli diplomats realized that obstinacy in such circumstances would give the countries a perfect excuse to strike at least one nuisance from their agenda. Considering this situation, the economic advisor at the Embassy in Paris recommended a re-examination of the ministers' decision to persevere with the demand for a comprehensive arrangement.[54] Aryeh Levavi, the Director General of the Ministry of Foreign Affairs, agreed with his officials.[55] Nevertheless, he and others in the Ministry knew that changing the minds of the political echelon would be no easy task. They presumed there was no real chance that the economic ministers would authorize an agreement which did not provide a real solution to Israel's trade problems.[56]

The Dutch, concerned by the possible ramifications of Israel's inflexibility over the arrangement with the EEC, suggested in February 1963 a new initiative, intended to salvage the negotiations. They asked the Israelis for a limited list of products which accounted for the most significant portion of the country's exports; the EEC would then reduce the customs on these products by 25% in a non-discriminatory manner toward all countries, even when Israel was not considered the main supplier.[57] Thus, for example, if the customs rate on Shamouti oranges was 16% at that time, it would decrease to 12% for *all countries*. Given the extreme economic ramifications of such a step, this was intended as a temporary measure—for a period of three or four years at most. The Dutch believed that by including a sufficient number of products in this arrangement (a dozen), it would be possible to encompass more than 90% of Israel's total exports. Furthermore, they believed the Israelis would accept such a suggestion because, in the short term, it would prevent damage to Israeli exports and allow breathing space to look for permanent, long-term solutions.

The proposal had significant implications, entailing a change in the EEC's common external tariff policy for the sake of one small country. It sharply deviated from the principle that the EEC would only consider granting tariff relief in the framework of negotiations vis-à-vis a single state when that country constituted the main supplier of a certain product, because the MFN principle would oblige the EEC to extend this privilege to all GATT member states. Even if reducing the custom on a product of interest to Israel would not seriously harm one of the EEC member states, it would "waste ammunition": the EEC would not be able to use these concessions in the planned Kennedy Round. Thus, this plan was daring and the Dutch knew that it would face strong opposition from France and, especially, Italy.

However, when the Dutch presented the plan to the Israelis, asking for a list of the country's most important products, Israel refused to cooperate, fearing that even if the arrangement solved Israel's current export problems, it would not address Israeli exports that were presently limited but seeking to expand, or those future, as yet unknown, export products. They were also concerned that cooperating with this initiative would mark this as the line to which Israel was willing to concede. If the EEC accepted the plan, then Israel would effectively be renouncing its demand for a comprehensive arrangement.

The Dutch were discouraged by their Israeli colleagues' cold response, but presented their proposal independently at the meeting of the COREPER. Acting in the name of the Benelux countries, they justified their proposal, arguing for the need to endow the negotiations with a "logical" foundation which Israel might accept. Alongside the idea of tariff preferences for the main export products, the proposal also suggested offering a guarantee that should the Kennedy Round fail to provide a cure for Israel's most important products, the EEC would find a way to compensate the Israelis. As expected, the main opponent to this plan was Italy.[58] The Italians highlighted that their nation would bear the main economic cost of concessions to Israel,[59] a justified claim. Reducing the EEC's external custom walls for certain products would affect the fragile balance between the economic sacrifices each country among The Six was asked to make for the sake of European integration. Because Israel's exports mainly competed with Italian products, the latter would pay the price: the tentative list which the Benelux countries compiled did not include any products competing with Dutch exports, and only one product in competition with Belgian goods.

However, the Netherlands promoted its initiative energetically. At the meeting of the Council of Ministers held at the end of February, Dutch representative Dirk Spierenburg stipulated a condition: the Netherlands would agree to the tariff concessions for Iran which were needed to advance the negotiations with that country *only* if the Council of Ministers would offer tariff concessions to Israel. The Dutch government was conscious that there was no similarity between the Iranian and Israeli cases, as only two Iranian export products of any importance were negatively affected by the establishment of the customs union: raisins and dried apricots. Iran was the main supplier of these products, and had no competitors among The Six; thus there was no economic difficulty in granting Iran customs benefits. Yet the Netherlands decided to exploit the designs among some of The Six to advance the Iranian channel and force them to give concessions to Israel.

The Netherlands's move was effective: the hesitant Italy reluctantly agreed to examine which Israeli products would be included in the arrangement.[60] In contrast to the past demand for concurrent negotiations with Israel and another Arab nation, in this case linking the Iranian issue to Israel's case was intended to serve the latter. Thus, this can be understood as an additional layer in the EEC's foreign policy towards Israel and the Middle East which consolidated over the years, including an attempt to create symmetry between Israel and the Arab nations, or at least those on the shores of the Mediterranean.

The Dutch proposal was not without value for the Israelis. A study conducted by the Economic Department at the Israeli Ministry of Foreign Affairs estimated that the proposal would include 93% of the volume of Israeli exports to the Common Market by 1962.[61] Whether the Dutch would be able to implement their proposal depended to a great extent on Israel: Israel's cooperation in providing a list of their most vital exports would give the Dutch effective leverage in "marketing" the proposal to their partners. This would enable the Dutch to present the gesture as the price of appeasing Israel, which for four years had incessantly bothered politicians, officials, members of professional commissions, journalists and other influential figures.

The Dutch thus pressured Israel to be satisfied with its proposal. "The time has come for you to forget briefly what you want—we are all aware of this—and act based on the existing options," Kalshoven of the Dutch Ministry of Finance advised the economic advisor at the Israeli Embassy in The Hague.[62] Israeli diplomats in The Six, mainly those serving in the Benelux countries, understood that such a chance would not return. They advised the Ministry of Foreign Affairs to consider acceding to the Dutch proposal.[63]

In Jerusalem, however, the same diplomats insisted that this proposal could form the basis of an agreement only in addition to the two suggestions which Israel had already submitted: the "European product" and the system of criteria.[64] Israel's resistance to the Dutch proposal ruined its chances of success: none of The Six wanted to pay the price of a gesture toward Israel if this did not guarantee the latter's satisfaction.[65] When the Council of Ministers' Committee for Trade Affairs discussed the various products on the list, each one of the states expressed doubts about certain items, finally reducing the list to three: grapefruit, bathing suits, and fertilizers.[66] These constituted no more than 7% of Israeli exports to the EEC, and the amount of the total tariff exemption they granted to Israel in customs was no more than $72,000.[67] The Dutch were now forced to withdraw their opposition to customs benefits for Iran, thus losing the most effective leverage available to pressure those countries hesitant towards Israel.[68]

At the same time, the Israelis were unsuccessful in forcing the EEC to accept the solutions they desired. At the meeting of the Permanent Representatives on March 25 and the meeting of the Council of Ministers one week later, The Six agreed to renew the negotiations with Israel, although adhering to the content suggested by the joint committee in the first round (aside from the reduction of customs on the three items noted above). Even the Commission's efforts to advance the idea of the "European product" were unsuccessful. The Council determined that "the issue creates sensitive and complex problems which require further study" and therefore "it should be rejected at present." The Council, however, agreed to accept the Commission's recommendation for the establishment of a follow-up committee to implement the trade agreement with Israel, upon the eventual signing of an agreement. However, it decided explicitly that "the committee will in no way be authorized to manage negotiations concerning change or renewal of the trade agreement without the approval of both sides." Likewise, the Council decided that its representatives would participate in this committee, alongside Commission officials.[69] This indicates that the Council was conscious of the Commission's plan to use this committee as a means to take control of the negotiations and widen their content. Indeed, it intentionally erected these fences so that Rey would find it difficult to transform his covert promises to the Israelis into reality.

The negotiations hit rock bottom

The Council's decision to offer Israel a temporary customs reduction on three items alone was the lowest point in the story of Israel-EEC relations. It seems that with this humiliating proposal, those opposed to continuing the negotiations tried to remove Israel from the EEC's doorway once and for all. An Israeli decision to end the talks would provide the EEC with a convenient way out. The Israelis indeed reacted severely, referring to the proposal as a "mockery," a "bad joke," and a "humiliation." Minister Sapir noted bitterly that in economic terms the European concession totaled $72,000 per annum, an amount that would not even cover the costs of the Israeli negotiating delegation.[70] When Emile Rouche, one of the leaders of the Radical Party in France, visited Israel at the end of April, Levi Eshkol informed him sharply that the European proposal had no meaning whatsoever and was an affront to the State of Israel.[71] Many began to believe that the only way for Israel to retain its dignity was to slam the door in the EEC's face, leaving the negotiations. The Israeli press was replete with such calls, seeming to echo the opinions of a wide sector among the Israeli public.[72] Indeed, it also appeared that officials at the economic ministries shared these feelings; even among the political echelon, some began to question whether Israel should declare a crisis and stop the talks. In a meeting of the inter-ministerial echelon, Israel Gal-Ed and David Golan demanded the talks continue only with the EEC's agreement to a number of preliminary terms.

By contrast, officials at the Ministry of Foreign Affairs sought to persist with the talks at any price. Aware that stipulating terms would cause the talks to collapse, they ignored the suggestions of officials from other ministries and even stopped inviting them to advisory meetings, leading to a confrontation. At the beginning of May, the Director General of the Ministry of Trade and Industry, Michael Tsur, sent letters protesting at what he called an intentional attempt to exclude his officials from managing the talks with the EEC.[73] This disagreement between the Israeli ministries derived from their different perspectives. In the view of the economic ministries (Finance Ministry, Ministry of Trade and Industry, Ministry of Agriculture), the uncompromising position adopted by the Council of Ministers meant that the negotiations would not satisfy any of the Israeli economy's needs, thus it was logical to generate a crisis which could be exploited to renew the talks on better terms in the future. The Israeli Ministry of Foreign Affairs, by contrast, regarded the talks through the prism of political interests: the very willingness of the EEC to engage in negotiations with Israel was a meaningful achievement. Stopping the negotiations would not only annul this achievement but also represent a blow to Israel's prestige and a step backward in international status.

Among the ministers there was greater consensus that Israel should stay at the negotiating table. At a meeting on May 12, the four ministers involved agreed that it was necessary to continue the talks with the EEC, but at the same time to refuse outright the arrangement it had proposed. They ordered the negotiating delegation to initiate a stalemate in the negotiations; the matter would then be returned to the Council of Ministers, which would hopefully decide to widen the content of the arrangement. To prepare the ground for this, the ministers decided to employ the same tactics that had so far yielded such meager results: pressuring the political echelon in the capitals of The Six to broaden the content of the negotiations, relying on moral justifications, and using apocalyptic language in describing the effect that failure to reach an agreement would have on Israel's economy. Yet using powerful allies in the EEC—among them trade union leaders, heads of political parties and other influential figures—to pressure the decision makers in The Six had rarely brought the desired results. Surprisingly, even personal support from the most senior statesmen in each of The Six, with the exception of Italy, had not translated into a positive decision in favor of Israel in the Community institutions, apart from the Council's decision to begin the talks, and even this only after significant delay and with great hesitancy. It seemed that a kind of impenetrable border isolated the Community institutions in Brussels from any external influence that was not in the pure interests of the EEC. Yosef Cnaan, *Davar*'s correspondent in Brussels, depicted this perfectly:

> While in Bonn or in Paris they are occupied with policy as they deal with fine art, pretending, in Brussels they "tell it as it is," here they speak only the truth, here it is possible to examine in reality whether the promise given in Bonn or in Paris was serious or was a worn-out coin with no real value. Therefore, many diplomats say—not one of whom has been burned by an overly optimistic report—that Brussels is like a "slaughterhouse": here they cruelly shred illusions.[74]

The Israeli ministers had already learned the truth of this observation. Despite this, they felt that this was the only means at their disposal to battle the EEC's refusal, apart from traditional lobbying. The ministers knew that Israel had no

alternative markets for its merchandise or effective leverages, negative or positive, that could force the EEC to give them greater consideration. The idea of
endeavoring to obtain association with EFTA, even if only for tactical purposes,
had been rejected outright as unrealistic.[75] The hope that the EEC member states
were likely to view Israel as a useful means in economic penetration of Third
World markets had dissipated long ago. Thus, the Israeli fixation was a result of
constraints more than foolishness. The director of the Economic Department
expressed the feeling of Israeli helplessness: "Because we don't have anything to
sell except our poverty, we are crying that we are being harmed. We can do nothing but try to use political means to gain also economic advantages."[76]

Until this point, the Israeli tendency to dramatize had been ineffective in sway-
ing the Europeans. Yet now the Israelis decided to intensify it further; it would be
no exaggeration to call this "hysterical sensitivity." Indeed, a few days after the
meeting of ministers, Eshkol sent a personal letter to each one of The Six's heads
of state outlining Israel's troubles: the relations between Israel and the EEC were
in *a critical situation*. The Council had rejected Israel's requests, on which the
country's economic future rested. The Jewish nation was tied to Europe by strong
historical and cultural bonds and the EEC's refusal to accede to Israel's requests
contradicted this link. Therefore, the addressees were asked to send immediate
instructions to their representatives that they should agree to widen the content
of the negotiations with Israel.[77] In Rome, the Israeli Ambassador informed the
Director General of the Foreign Ministry, Gattani, that Israel understood Italian
economic interests very well, but if Italy desired *Israel's continued existence* it must
show goodwill towards the country's trade links with the EEC.[78]

The Europeans were now repeatedly informed that the Israelis viewed the
stance adopted by the Council of Ministers as equivalent to joining the Arab
boycott, no less.[79] Simultaneously, Israeli diplomats were asked to show their
European contacts new data proving without any doubt the negative impact
which the process of integration would have on Israeli exports to the Common
Market. They were armed with a small file containing enlightening tables written in bold letters which clearly demonstrated the losses Israel had suffered in
the preceding year. They emphasized that the percentage of exports to the EEC
within the country's total exports had decreased from 28.3% in 1961 to 25.4%
in 1962; similarly, the extent of growth in exports to the EEC was only 2.1% in
1962, compared to 12.1% in 1961 and 44.2% in 1960.[80] The Israelis produced
these tables at all meetings with representatives of The Six concerned with EEC
matters. Thus, for example, Couve de Murville was forced to examine them at a
meeting with the Israeli Ambassador.

The French Foreign Minister was highly skeptical concerning the numbers
in the tables—apparently with good reason. The statistics presented in them
were tendentious, doubtful and only reflected a tiny portion of the real numbers.
Studies conducted by other ministries, the results of which were well known to
the people at the Ministry of Foreign Affairs, indicated very different results; for
example, the Ministry of Trade and Industry estimated that the Israeli exports
to the EEC had grown by 10% in 1962, not 2.1%.[81] Indeed, a study conducted a

few years later clearly proved that Israeli exports to the EEC grew impressively in these years. In 1961, Israel exported goods to the EEC totaling $64 million. In 1962, the exports increased, reaching $72 million. In 1963, this number continued to rise even more significantly: the entire exports to the EEC reached $107 million. Thus, Israeli claims of broad damage to their exports were evidently not an accurate reflection of reality.[82]

However, without doubt some products were detrimentally affected. In 1962, the export of bromine and its products to the EEC declined by 80%, a direct result of the Italian government's decision to impose quotas on bromine imports with the aim of supporting the new factory in Sicily. A large percentage of Israeli bromine was exported to Italy and therefore these quotas had a dramatic effect on this sector: in 1961, Israel sent 20% of its bromine products to the EEC member states, yet by 1962 this number had decreased to 8%.[83]

The hysterical battle which the Israelis waged also had certain victories. In April 1963, Sapir visited Geneva and met with the German Finance Minister Ludwig Erhard. Bartur and several other senior German officials also participated in the meeting. During their conversation, the Israeli minister spoke at length about the crucial importance of an arrangement with the EEC for Israel, defining it as "critical." He described the Council of Ministers' proposal as "funny." Erhard agreed with him, adding that in his opinion the term "funny" was insufficient; rather it was "offensive." When German Secretary of State Wistrok and the Director General of his office, Reinhard, tried to explain the difficulty of taking steps that gave preferential discrimination to Israel because of the GATT regulations, Bartur seized the opportunity to embark on a long monologue, arguing that for this precise reason, association was the only possible solution which would both address Israel's problems and accord with the GATT regulations. When he finished, Erhard surprised those present, Israelis and Germans alike, by commenting that Israel seemed to have erred in choosing the route it had followed thus far—the time had come to submit an official application for association. The assistants to the Finance Minister (who became Chancellor a few months later)—dismayed by these statements and knowing only too well what damage they could cause—attempted to persuade Erhard to moderate his declaration.[84] However, he stuck to his opinion.[85] Only a few days later, Erhard reiterated to Bartur his support of association, noting that this is "according to the opinion of the entire German nation."[86] Such a promise from a senior figure in one of the most influential countries among The Six revived in Jerusalem the old hopes for an arrangement far more significant than the narrow trade agreement on the horizon. However, all Israeli efforts to translate this promise into the language of action were in vain. The German bureaucrats ignored repeated Israeli requests to act in the spirit of this promise; some even denied it openly, calling it "hasty and unrealistic."[87] Germany's Foreign Ministry was particularly alarmed by any actions that the Arab states might construe as pro-Israeli. Indeed, the ministry frequently issued warnings that publicity surrounding visits by German personalities in Israel should be kept to a minimum.[88]

The claims of crisis among the Israeli leadership were limited to conversations with external contacts. Domestically, ministers endeavored to broadcast to the public a message of business as usual. Indeed, the stance of the European institutions in Brussels was intransigent, and Israeli exports were liable to sustain a certain amount of damage if a satisfactory solution was not found; however, the negotiations were far from a failure and there was cause for optimism. In a conversation with a journalist from *Davar*, Minister Sapir stated that despite the difficulties, the fact that the Council of Ministers had agreed to the negotiations was a great political achievement, "a kind of Balfour declaration."[89] At a symposium of the Economic Council, Sapir opined that "there is no progress; however, there is also no regression in the matter of the agreement between the Common Market and Israel."[90] The ministers voiced these calming messages in an attempt to pacify the public criticism which found great expression in the press, in turn making the diplomatic campaign even more difficult; indeed it was likely to pressure decision makers to adopt a harsher line than they really desired. Certainly, signs of this were already evident. At the beginning of May, members of the directorship of the Farmers' Federation of Israel demanded insistently that no less a figure than Ben-Gurion lead the negotiating delegation, to prevent the disaster looming over the citrus sector.[91]

If the Israelis hoped that strumming on the heartstrings of the Europeans would encourage old friends to act with increased vigor and at the same time recruit new supporters, it in fact achieved the opposite. The decision by the Council of Ministers to reduce the Dutch proposal to a minimum, combined with its hesitancy regarding both the idea of the "European product" and the accompanying committee, weakened the hand of Israel's two most vocal supporters: the Dutch and the Commission. The Dutch pushed to widen the arrangement with Israel and were willing to employ their institutional power (the right of veto) for this purpose, delaying the negotiations with Iran. In so doing, they succeeded in angering some of the other delegations, who regarded this as uncalled-for extortion. Following their meager success and the lack of gratitude from the Israeli side, they now sought to reduce their profile. In a discussion before the Dutch Parliament, Foreign Minister Luns stated that in view of the difficulties which his attempt to advance the proposal for a temporary reduction of customs had encountered, "I do not see in rosy hues the possibility of pushing the EEC to make additional concessions in the near future."[92] The Israeli Ambassador received the impression that the Dutch

> are no longer willing to break their heads against the wall of opposition created by "the big three" and there is no chance of them renewing their battle without a guarantee that one or more of the ministers from "the big" [three] will stand with them.[93]

The Commission's position also began to alter. The Commission leadership had been harmed by appearing overly amenable toward Israel; indeed, as a result, the Council of Ministers had demanded that the delegation to the negotiations with Israel also include representatives of The Six. This reduced the status and authority of the Commission, which in the past had been solely responsible for the negotiations with Greece and Turkey. Now the Council of Ministers demanded that the model implemented vis-à-vis Israel be applied also in the negotiations with Iran; despite his adamant opposition, Rey was forced to accept this situation. Thus, the Commission began to comprehend that the negotiations with Israel not only failed to advance their agenda and the status of the Commission within the EEC, they were even detrimental to them. Commission officials became convinced that Israel's insistence on a comprehensive agreement, or at least a discriminatory arrangement, had ensured the failure of the negotiations from the outset; in such circumstances, it was preferable to refrain from negotiating. Commission figures did not forget how the Israelis had deceived them into believing that Israel would be satisfied with a limited agreement, only to discover during the negotiations that the Israeli desire for a comprehensive arrangement remained unchanged. Therefore, Israeli diplomats were informed that as a condition for beginning the second round of talks, Israel must promise to avoid requesting anything that exceeded the arrangement favored by the EEC—one that was neither comprehensive nor discriminatory.[94] The Israelis were angered by this demand, which seemed to exceed the authority of the Commission, and threatened to rouse public opinion in Europe against what they saw as the EEC's abuse.[95]

Originally, the Israelis planned to initiate a crisis that would force the EEC's negotiating delegation to return its mandate to the Council of Ministers. Yet the trigger for this could not be the presentation of exaggerated Israeli claims which the EEC had no interest in satisfying. Indeed, this would give the Europeans a convenient excuse to leave the negotiations and blame Israel for the failure. The Israelis wanted the crisis to develop naturally as the lack of congruence between the EEC's proposal and Israel's problems emerged. According to the Israeli plan, in response to the proposals raised by the EEC delegation—the meager content of which was already known to them—the Israeli delegation would submit a long list of questions and clarifications, exposing the suggested solution's lack of real value. In this way, Israel could avoid presenting a counter-proposal that was phrased along the lines which Israel desired (a comprehensive or discriminatory agreement) and would therefore endanger the future of the talks, or one based on the outline dictated by the EEC (a non-discriminatory trade agreement) and thus insufficient from Israel's perspective.[96]

However, when the Israeli delegation arrived at the negotiations, which began again at the start of June, a surprise awaited them. The EEC's delegation was no longer prepared to play games. They explicitly informed the Israelis that if they were unhappy with the EEC's proposal, they must submit a counter-proposal. The EEC delegation disapproved the emphasis which the Israelis placed on the need to search *together* for "additional solutions" beyond those suggested by the EEC. This approach was characteristic of the Israelis, who tended to present their country's problems as an issue for which Europe must find a solution, reflecting the assumption that Europe was morally responsible for Israel's fate and therefore could not evade accountability for the damage to the Israeli economy. Now European delegation members informed the Israelis that, despite their sympathy and feelings of friendship toward Israel, the delegations were involved in trade negotiations and not a business partnership. It was not the EEC's responsibility to search for solutions that the Israelis would find acceptable.

The Israelis had thus arrived at the moment of truth. They could no longer avoid deciding whether to adhere their aims, at the price of torpedoing the negotiations, or to compromise with the outline offered by Europe. The Israeli delegation felt that Israel's interests obliged them to choose the second option, a decision that required the endorsement of the ministerial level.[97] In Jerusalem, following a discussion, the Cabinet for Economic Affairs decided that, in the absence of other options, they would accept the delegation's recommendation. However, the Israeli delegation was asked to impart Israel's resentment orally.

Najar, the head of the delegation, took this instruction seriously, giving an impassioned speech in which he castigated the EEC, expressing the frustration that had built up in the hearts of the Israelis over the past years. He accused the EEC of insensitivity to the economic distress which Israel was suffering due to the establishment of the Common Market, and described the Israelis' feelings of shock upon hearing that while the Europeans were seriously considering the association of African states,[98] there was no similar solution for Israel, which was European in terms of heritage, history and culture: "I think that civilization is defined according to certain values more than an arbitrary geographical division," said Najar, adding that "Israel's location on the Mediterranean coast and its past history do not allow us to accept the European outlook as it is expressed in geographical limitations which, in our opinion, are ephemeral." He accused the EEC member states of aiding the Arab boycott against Israel, thus revealing the hypocrisy of those countries that lauded the principle of non-discrimination. He emphasized the practical approach which Israel had adopted in the past year, withdrawing the request for association, and expressed sadness that the EEC had not reciprocated this gesture. Despite this, he stated:

> We are prepared to renew our efforts to search for a pragmatic solution and in this spirit we will present our proposals. They do not reflect our final hopes, however they are intended to bring about a solution to our realistic problems, to ensure the vital development of our exports to the EEC countries. This is our obligation, but also, to a certain extent, yours.[99]

At this point, the Israeli delegation presented a list of 37 products, requesting for them various arrangements that the EEC had been willing to adopt in the past: temporary reductions (in the format of the Dutch proposal), canceling quotas, accelerating the common external tariff, and the obligation that products of importance to Israel would be included in the coming Kennedy Round. Two requests exceeded the limits suggested by the Europeans: tariffs imposed on the added value of goods (the "European product") and a special request to consider two agricultural products—oranges and eggs. The Israelis asked Rey to ensure that the Israeli proposal would be deliberated in its entirety and would not be broken down and thus emptied of content. Rey, who was very pleased by the change in the Israeli line, promised repeatedly that he would do so.[100]

In the winter of 1962, as was noted, Israel had abandoned its demand for an association agreement with Europe. Now, eighteen months later, Israel also relinquished its goal of achieving a comprehensive or discriminatory agreement. To internal audiences, the Israeli retreat was presented as the result of a sudden change in the approach of the EEC's delegation toward the arrangement.[101] In reality, there was no such change; this was a public relations attempt to conceal the Israeli government's decision to compromise on a matter it had consistently portrayed as fundamental.

The difficult choice made by Israeli decision makers and officials, who had been occupied for so long with the negotiations, requires further explanation. An important factor motivating the compromise was the continued failure to change the rejectionist European stance despite exerting continuous pressure on the political echelon in the capitals of The Six. To the surprise of the Israelis, the bureaucrats staffing the COREPER revealed impressive ability to withstand this pressure, although the Israelis succeeded in recruiting influential figures in the member states and Community institutions (the European Parliament, the Commission leadership). When the Israelis discerned this, they exerted yet more pressure, believing that the opposition would eventually collapse. However, this was not the case, and the Israelis discovered that the officials in Brussels had no qualms about reneging upon agreements reached with key people within the EEC during private conversations. Israeli attempts to achieve their goals using cunning also failed. For example, their endeavors to exploit the trade agreement as cover for a comprehensive agreement were halted by the Commission, and the European delegation rejected the creative ideas which would facilitate a preferential agreement without contradicting the GATT regulations.

However, Israeli despair at the chances of reaching a better agreement was not the only motivating factor. No less important was the growing panic among Israelis with respect to future orange exports to the Common Market. Until 1963, this threat had seemed distant. However, the situation altered completely when, in 1963, the EEC began to conduct talks with the Maghreb states regarding association, similar to the status accorded to the countries in sub-Saharan Africa. These countries together exported to the EEC more than 20% of its orange consumption—three times the amount exported by Israel. Even more worrying, in 1962 Spain, whose orange exports to the EEC countries accounted for 50% of the market, had submitted a request for a comprehensive trade agreement: for example, association. Spain received strong backing from Germany and France, although other countries such as the Netherlands and Belgium were firmly opposed to association with Franco's dictatorial regime. However, it was reasonable to presume that this opposition would gradually dissolve and that over time it would be difficult to continue refusing such a request from a clearly European country. Once oranges from Spain and the Maghreb countries gained free access to the EEC markets, whereas the Israeli orange remained subject to customs levies, the conditions of competition would become unbearable. It was vital to avoid this scenario at all costs; thus, the Israelis were willing to sign a depleted agreement if this would guarantee Israel's portion of orange exports to the EEC.

Notes

1 See, for example, the following newspaper articles: *Ma'ariv*, "Difficult Negotiations Ahead with the Market," *Ma'ariv*, September 25, 1962; *Davar*, "Negotiations with the Market to Begin Next Month," *Davar*, September 25, 1962.
2 Najar to Levavi, ISA, FM, file 1959/6, October 9, 1962; Ministry of Agriculture Memorandum: "Preparing for Negotiations with the Common Market," ISA, MA, file 2424/3, October 12, 1962.
3 Shortened minutes of the meetings concerning the EEC, ISA, FM, file 1959/6, October 10, 28, 1962.
4 Kitron to Levavi, ISA, FM, file 1959/8, November 20, 1962.
5 ISA, FM, file 1045/24, November 13 and 16, 1962. Such contacts demonstrate the particularly intimate relationship between Israel and Germany at this time, three years before official diplomatic relations were established between the two nations.
6 Najar to Levavi, ISA, FM, 1959/6, September 9, 1962.
7 Najar to Levavi, ISA, FM, file 1959/6, October 2, 1962.
8 MAE, Projet d'accord commercial entre les six et Israël, CE-Is-1467, October 20, 1962.
9 Segreteria Generale-Archivio Storico, "Accordo Commerciale Israele-CEE," Direzione Generale Affari Politici III, 1959–1962, file 277, October 17, 1962.
10 See: Confidential summary of the conversations given to the Israeli Ministry of Foreign Affairs: ISA, FM, file 1959/6, November 9, 1962. In addition see the Commission's report: Prochaines négociations avec Israël, AUE, BAC3/1978-323, November 12, 1962.
11 ISA, FM, file 1959/8, November 16, 1962.
12 Najar to the Ministry of Foreign Affairs, ISA, FM, file 1959/8, November 16 and 19–20, 1962
13 Négociations avec Israël, AMAECEB, file 6.110/VI, November 4, 1962.
14 Eshkol's speech, ISA, MF, file 19785/7, November 1962.
15 Séance d'ouverture, AUE, BAC 3/1978-323, November 26, 1962.
16 Israel proposed that the customs union be implemented regarding only twelve groups of products, which together constituted more than 50% of Israeli exports to the EEC countries. However, the European delegation rejected this suggestion. See: Quatrième séance de négociation, AUE, BAC 3/1978-323, November 28, 1962.
17 Cinquième séance de négociation, AUE, BAC 3/1978-323, December 29, 1962.
18 Delegation in Brussels to the Ministry of Foreign Affairs, ISA, FM, 1045/24, December 6, 1962.
19 The Italian Prime Minister summed up this stance, admitting to the Israelis that although "the solution of criteria" was *possible*, there was a difference between possibilities and *the desire* to implement them. See: Economic Department to the Israeli embassies in Paris and Rome, ISA, FM, file 1959/8, December 4, 1962.
20 Egg exports to the Common Market in 1961 amounted to $7,104,300 out of $9,135,000 of its total exports of eggs (see "Israel's Agricultural Exports in 1961," ISA, FM, file 1959/8, December 25, 1962. The EEC countries received 85% of the eggs for consumption which Israel exported, 90% of meat and poultry exports, and 99% of egg incubation exports (see David Gilboa, "Agriculture and the Common Market," *Davar*, August 3, 1962).

21 In the talks, Israel asked the EEC to guarantee the import of 400 million eggs annually. This request was resoundingly rejected. See: Deuxième séance de négociation, AUE, BAC 3/1978-323, November 28, 1962.

22 Ma'ariv, "Israel's Egg Exports Harmed by Common Market Restrictions," *Ma'ariv*, October 29, 1962.

23 Desmond Dinan, *Europe Recast: A History of European Union* (Basingstoke: Palgrave Macmillan, 2004), 97.

24 Robert E. Hudec, "Legal Issues in US-EC Trade Policy: Gatt Litigation 1960–1985," in *Issues in US-EC Trade Relations*, eds. Robert E. Baldwin, Carl B. Hamilton and Andre Sapir (Chicago: University of Chicago Press, 2009).

25 For example, in 1961 Israel imported $800,000 worth of aluminum from France and exported to the EEC aluminum products worth $200,000. The need to pay full customs on these products was viewed as unjust. See: Ministry of Trade and Industry Memorandum, ISA, FM, file 1960/9, January 1, 1963.

26 Réunion d'experts pour les produits industrieles, AUE, BAC 3/1978-323, November 27, 1962.

27 Najar to the Ministry of Foreign Affairs, ISA, FM, file 1045/24, December 12, 1962.

28 DDF, 1962, tome II, doc. 178, December 3, 1962.

29 Cohen to the Head of the Economic Department, ISA, FM, file 1959/8, December 6, 1962.

30 "Summary of Suggestions for Action," ISA, FM, 1959/8, December 27, 1962.

31 *Davar*, "Israel Will Demand the Expansion of EEC's Delegation Authority," *Davar*, December 30, 1962.

32 "Summary of Deliberations Regarding Further Negotiations between the EEC and Israel," ISA, FM, file 1959/8, December 22–23, 27, 1962.

33 *Davar*, "Ambassadors' Consultation on the Market Issue Arrive at Conclusion," *Davar*, December 28, 1962. On other occasions too, Bartur used the press to publicize his opinions (see, for example, Moshe Bartur, "Tariff Reduction Would Expand Israeli Commerce," *Davar*, August 23, 1963; Moshe Bartur, "The Negotiations with the Common Market Will Not End Well," *Davar*, September 4, 1963). He believed that the Ministry of Foreign Affairs was trying to silence him and therefore he was at liberty to use alternative channels to reach decision makers. This angered his colleagues in Jerusalem, who viewed his acts as outside the norms and rules governing the behavior of government officials. See: Amir to Levavi, ISA, FM, file September 4, 1963.

34 Bartur to Meir, ISA, FM, file 1959/7, January 8, 1963.

35 Levavi to Israeli representations in the capitals of The Six, ISA, FM, file 1959/7, January 18, 1963.

36 Nirgad to Alon, ISA, FM, file 1959/8, December 14, 1962.

37 Najar to Levavi, ISA, FM, file 1960/9, December 21, 1962.

38 Najar to Alon, ISA, FM, file 1959/7, January 12, 1963.

39 Israeli Embassy in London to the Ministry of Foreign Affairs, ISA, FM, file 1959/7, January 30, 1963.

40 Note pour M. Seeliger, BAC 3/1978-323, December 18, 1962.

41 FFOPA, box. 39, file 2/401-88, January 15, 1963.

42 A memorandum composed by the Italian Foreign Ministry (February 15), which reached the Israelis, noted that "It has become clear that the Israelis are still not willing to renounce their initial, far-reaching position regarding a comprehensive agreement and there exists a great disparity between the positions. *It is not impossible that a number of delegations are encouraging the Israelis in this regard*" (original emphasis). See: Elron to Alon, ISA, FM, file 1960/9, April 8, 1963.

43 Najar to Levavi, ISA, FM, file 1959/7, February 8, 1963. Rey promised to reconsider the recommendations to the Council and correct them if he would find the

phrasing too minimalist. However, he did not battle the diffidence of the Council of Ministers with direct confrontation but under the surface, by establishing the committee managed by the Commission.

44 Najar to Levavi, ISA, FM, file 1960/9, March 5, 1963.
45 Kitron to the Economic Department, ISA, FM, file 1959/7, January 15, 1963.
46 Gadi Heimann, "Interview With Itzhak Minerbi," April 2016.
47 Note pour M. l'Administrateur Directeur Géneral, MAECEB, 6405/B, November 23, 1963.
48 Négociation avec Israël: fuites, AUE, BAC3/1978-323, November 9, 1962.
49 Kitron to Levavi, ISA, FM, file 1959/7, January 8, 1963.
50 Kitron to Levavi, ISA, FM, file 1959/7, February 4, 1963.
51 Eytan to the Ministry of Foreign Affairs, ISA, FM, file 1959/7, January 19, 1963.
52 Najar to Levavi, ISA, FM, January 22, 1963.
53 Eytan to Levavi, ISA, FM, file 1959/7, January 24, 1963.
54 Boaz to Alon, ISA, FM, file 1959/7, February 7, 1963.
55 For example, his comments to Bartur that "in these circumstances there is nothing easier than to lose out both ways; many and strong [European counterparts] will be pleased to place us among the anonymous category of the masses of third [world] countries." See: Levavi to the Representation in Geneva, ISA, FM, file 1959/7, February 4, 1963.
56 Alon to Boaz, ISA, FM, file 1960/9, February 18, 1963.
57 On the components of the Dutch proposal see: Note pour M. l'Administrateur Directeur Géneral, MAECEB, 6405/B, February 11, 1963.
58 See: SGAS, Direzione Generale Affari Politici III, 1963–64. file 22, 26/02/1963.
59 Note d'Information, Négociation avec Israel, BAC 3/1978-324, February 15, 1963.
60 EUA, CM2/1963-12, February 25–26, 1963.
61 Memorandum of the Economic Department, ISA, FM,1960/9, March 19, 1963.
62 Kitron to the Economic Department, ISA, FM, file 1960/9, March 12, 1963.
63 Cidor to the Economic Department, ISA, FM, file 1960/9, February 16, 1963; Cohen to Alon, ISA, FM, file 1960/9, March 12, 1963; Kitron to the Economic Department , ISA, FM, file 1960/9, March 12, 1963.
64 Economic Department to the Representations in the Capitals of the Six, ISA, FM, file 1960/9, March 14, 1963.
65 A meeting of the committee for trade matters decided that a positive decision regarding reducing customs on Israeli products would be conditional on Israel's guarantee that these concessions constituted a "real interest" for the country. See: Rapport sur les tarvaux effectues par le groupe des questions commerciales, EUA, BAC 38/1984-74, March 22, 1963.
66 It is no coincidence that the EEC member states did not produce these products themselves and therefore were willing to grant Israel benefits. Italy opposed including grapefruit, finally conceding only after being promised that oranges would be removed from the list. Even the Netherlands, which was generally supportive of Israel's request, demanded that eggs be omitted from the list because the two countries were competitors in exporting eggs to Italy. This illustrates that The Six tended to be generous concerning products which they did not export but not when they would have to pay the price.
67 This amount should be compared to the total customs which Israeli exporters paid to the Market countries. In 1961, this amount reached $1,400,000 (see: *Davar*, "It's Indeed Another Border, but at Any Rate Europe," *Davar*, March 8, 1962). Thus, the Europeans were offering a customs reduction of around 5% at most.
68 EUA, CM2/1963-17, April 1–2, 1963.
69 Note d'Information, négociations avec Israël, EUA, BAC 3/1978-324, March 25, 1963.

70 Testimony of Sapir to the Knesset Foreign Affairs and Defense Committee, ISA, Knesset, file 8160/1, July 16, 1963.
71 Editorial, *Davar*, April 3, 1963.
72 Editorial, *Davar*, April 3, 1963
73 Tsur to Levavi ISA, FM, file 1960/6, May 1, 1963; Levavi to Tsur, ISA, FM, 1960/6, May 2, 1963.
74 Yosef Cnaan, "At This Stage, Only a Limited Trade Agreement May Be Achieved," *Davar*, June 7, 1963.
75 Avner to Alon, ISA, FM, file 1959/7, February 4, 1963; Gal-Ed to Alon, ISA, FM, file 1959/7, February 5, 1963.
76 Alon to the Knesset Foreign Affairs and Defense Committee, ISA, Knesset, file 8160/1, December 22, 1964.
77 See, for example, Eshkol to Erhard, ISA, FM, file 1045/25, May 14, 1963.
78 Fischer to the Ministry of Foreign Affairs, ISA, FM, file 1960/6, May 13, 1963.
79 Thus, for example, Fischer noted to the Italian Foreign Minister. See: ISA, FM, file 1045/25, May 13, 1963.
80 Alon to the Israeli Representations in the capitals of The Six, ISA, FM, file 1960/6, May 17, 1963.
81 "Israeli Exports to the European Community in 1962 and Their Problems," ISA, FM, 1960/9, December 1962. Another report composed by the Ministry of Industry and Trade revealed that the extent of exports to the EEC had declined to a certain extent, but not in the significant fashion indicated by the tables which the Ministry of Foreign Affairs prepared: from 27.4% of total exports in 1961 to 26.3% in 1962. See: Government Yearbook, Report of the Ministry of Trade and Industry, 1963/1964.
82 Israël et la CEE, ISA, FM, file 3154/5, October 1966.
83 Ibid., The export of citrus fruits to EEC member states not only had failed to decline but even increased substantially. The reason for this was a frost wave in Europe, which severely damaged Spanish and Italian oranges. In Israel, by contrast, the 1962/63 season was the best since the foundation of the state. The yield rose by 41% compared to that of the previous year. Therefore, the Israeli fruits were welcomed in Europe's markets. However, the Israelis held no illusions that this convenient constellation would persist. See: State of Israel, "Government Yearbook 1963/1964," (Jerusalem: Prime Minister's Office, 1964).
84 A memorandum sent by the Secretary of State to the Chancellor's office reveals the extent to which the German Foreign Ministry was displeased by the positive stance which German leaders adopted toward a comprehensive agreement with Israel. In the memorandum, the Secretary listed the reasons why such an agreement was dangerous. See: FFOPA, box 39, November 14, 1963.
85 A protocol of the conversation can be found in a Ministry of Foreign Affairs memorandum, ISA, FM, file 3154/2, January 1965.
86 Bartur to Sapir, ISA, FM, file 1045/25, no date.
87 See, for example, Nirgad to the Ministry of Foreign Affairs, ISA, FM, file 1960/5, July 24, 1963; Passweg to the Ministry of Foreign Affairs, ISA, FM, file 1960/5, July 26, 1963.
88 FFOPA, box 39, file 2-80.02-82.19, no date.
89 *Davar*, "The Decline in the Pace of Exports to the Common Market," *Davar*, July 5, 1963.
90 *Davar*, "Israel Will Continue Its Struggle for an Agreement with the Common Market," *Davar*, May 10, 1963.
91 *Davar*, May 3, 1963
92 Yinon to Levavi, ISA, FM, file 1960/6, May 6, 1963.
93 Cidor to the Ministry of Foreign Affairs, ISA, FM, 1960/6, May 3, 1963.
94 Najar to the Ministry of Foreign Affairs, ISA, FM, 1960/9, April 4, 1963; Najar to the Ministry of Foreign Affairs, ISA, FM, file 1960/6, May 21, 1963.
95 The Economic Department to the Embassy in Brussels, ISA, FM, file 1960/9, April 26, 1963.

96 "Lines for Renewing the Negotiations with the Market," ISA, FM, file 1960/6, May 20, 1963.
97 Delegation in The Hague to the Ministry of Foreign Affairs, ISA, FM, file 1045/25, June 19, 1963.
98 During this period, the EEC and 18 African states, former colonies of The Six (some even former British colonies) conducted negotiations concerning association. In July 1963, this matured into the Yaoundé Convention. At the very same time, the negotiations with Turkey ripened into an association agreement; in the first stage, the Turks received a preferential agreement for their main export products and aid totaling $175 million. See DDF, 1963, tome II, doc. 56, August 10, 1963.
99 Stenograph of the Ambassador's speech, ISA, FM, file 1960/8, June 12, 1963.
100 "The Second Stage in the Negotiations between Israel and the EEC," ISA, FM, file 1960/8, June 14, 1963.
101 *Davar*, "An Unexpected Turning Point in the Negotiations with 'the Common Market'," *Davar*, June 11, 1963.

References

Bartur, Moshe. "The Negotiations with the Common Market Will Not End Well." *Davar*, September 4, 1963.

———. "Tariff Reduction Would Expand Israeli Commerce," *Davar*, August 23, 1963

Cnaan, Yosef. "At This Stage, Only a Limited Trade Agreement May Be Achieved." *Davar*, June 7, 1963.

Davar. "Ambassadors' Consultation on the Market Issue Arrive at Conclusion." *Davar*, December 28, 1962.

———. "The Decline in the Pace of Exports to the Common Market." *Davar*, July 5, 1963.

———. "Israel Will Continue Its Struggle for an Agreement with the Common Market." *Davar*, May 10, 1963.

———. "Israel Will Demand the Expansion of EEC's Delegation Authority"." *Davar*, December 30, 1962.

———. "It's Indeed Another Border, but at Any Rate Europe." *Davar*, March 8, 1962.

———. "Negotiations with the Market to Begin Next Month." *Davar*, September 25, 1962.

———. "An Unexpected Turning Point in the Negotiations with 'the Common Market'." *Davar*, June 11, 1963.

Dinan, Desmond. *Europe Recast: A History of European Union*. Basingstoke: Palgrave Macmillan, 2004.

Gilboa, David. "Agriculture and the Common Market." *Davar*, August 3, 1962.

Heimann, Gadi. "Interview with Ambassador Itzhak Minerbi." April 2016.

Hudec, Robert E. "Legal Issues in US-EC Trade Policy: Gatt Litigation 1960–1985." Chap. 2 In *Issues in US-EC Trade Relations*, edited by Robert E. Baldwin, Carl B. Hamilton and Andre Sapir, 17–66. Chicago: University of Chicago Press, 2009.

Ma'ariv. "Difficult Negotiations Ahead with the Market." *Ma'ariv*, September 25, 1962.

———. "Israel's Egg Exports Harmed by Common Market Restrictions." *Ma'ariv*, October 29, 1962.

State of Israel. "Government Yearbook 1963/1964." Jerusalem: Prime Minister's Office, 1964.

8 A non-preferential agreement

In the summer of 1963, there was a predominant feeling in Jerusalem that Israel could not make any further concessions. The list of products had been reduced to only 37 items (a year earlier it had numbered more than a hundred) and the form of the desired arrangement accorded with the solutions that the Europeans had suggested. Thus, officials at the Israeli Ministry of Foreign Affairs believed that the EEC's negotiating delegation could no longer justify a lack of progress towards an agreement. Indeed, there were numerous signs that the Israeli proposal had been received with satisfaction in the capitals of The Six. Two French officials, Wörmser and Boegner—who were considered particularly uncooperative in the negotiations with Israel—informed Israeli diplomats of their satisfaction with the new Israeli line and optimism that they would shortly reach an arrangement.[1] Rey, who took pleasure in Israel's change of approach, believed that a real basis for an agreement now existed. He therefore promised the Israelis that the Commission would discuss their proposal as one bloc and not break it down into fragments, as had happened in the case of the Dutch proposal. In his speech to the European Parliament on June 28, Rey stated that the new Israeli proposal obligated the governments of The Six to alter their outlook. Seeking to impel the Europeans to accept their requests, the Israelis threatened that if their proposal was not adopted as one bloc, they would have no choice but to return to their previous demand for a preferential and comprehensive agreement.[2]

However, the Israelis did not trust that these developments were sufficient to secure success. They planned a new diplomatic campaign in the capitals of The Six.[3] This time, however, they decided to employ a different tactic. Formerly, they had directed their lobbying campaigns toward the political echelon, presuming that this circle was especially amenable to accepting Israel's arguments. Indeed, the Israelis believed that while the technical experts in the Foreign Ministries and Community institutions viewed an arrangement with Israel through a narrow economic prism, the statesmen considered broader political implications, such as their desire to ensure Israel's security. The Israelis also had at their disposal more effective leverage to use among the statesmen: as politicians, they were exposed to the demands of pressure groups and sensitive to electoral considerations. Finally, these were the ultimate decision makers. Therefore, it was only natural to presume that effective persuasion would lead them to instruct their officials accordingly; the latter would have no choice but to follow their orders.

However, in considering the EEC's repeated rejections of Israel's requests, the Israelis understood that this assessment was based on erroneous foundations. Five years of lobbying among the political echelon in each of the capitals of The Six had yielded seemingly impressive results. Many of Europe's highest-ranking decision makers expressed support for Israel: de Gaulle, Debre, Pompidou and, to a certain extent, Couve de Murville in France; Adenauer, Laher and Erhard in Germany; Spaak in Belgium; Luns in the Netherlands; Shaous in Luxembourg, and Colombo in Italy. However, this underlying support, sometimes accompanied by explicit promises that they would instruct their officials in Brussels to back Israel, had failed to influence the final result. The representatives of The Six in the Community institutions viewed themselves as free to act as they deemed fit. One reason for this was that the official bureaucrats in the financial ministries of each of The Six (apart from the Netherlands) advised their representatives to adopt a cautious line, even upon receiving a fundamental instruction from above to support Israel's request. They were able to do so because of the complex technical problems involved in the issue; these officials, experts in these matters, enjoyed great independence in adapting the basic political instruction to suit practical economic-legal language.

Israeli diplomats in the capitals of The Six had been aware for some time that professional bureaucrats were highly influential in molding the position of their representatives in the Community institutions. On more than one occasion, they had preached that it was necessary to win over these ranks. Despite this, decision makers continued to view the political echelon as Israel's target. In light of the repeated failures, however, they also began to understand the need to transfer their efforts to the professional bureaucrats. The Israelis decided to dispatch to Europe a delegation of experts from ministries concerned with financial matters, where they would meet with their counterparts in each of the capitals of The Six to discuss the issues currently shrouded in disagreement—in this way finding solutions for the problems and doubts even before the negotiating delegations convened.[4] Three targets were highlighted as of particular importance—Italy, Germany and France—where officials were known to be most hesitant towards an arrangement with Israel.[5]

New proposals in Rome and Bonn

Softening the Italian stance remained the most difficult challenge in Jerusalem's view. The Italians constituted the stumbling block to achieving tariff benefits for two of Israel's main exports to the EEC: oranges and bromine. In September 1963, two Israeli experts—Gal-Ed, Deputy Director General of the Ministry of Trade and Industry, and Nitzani, Deputy Director of Dead Sea Bromine Company—arrived in Italy with the aim of reaching an agreement with the Italian administration, once and for all, regarding these problems. In the past, Israel had tried to overcome the Italian government's opposition by offering

Israeli technical aid in the form of joint agricultural projects and proposing to divide the citrus market between Israel and Italy.[6] Since 1961, covert talks regarding a suitable arrangement had been under way between the Israeli Agricultural Ministry and its Italian counterpart;[7] these, however, yielded no results.

The central problem remained the great pressure which Italian citrus growers, most of them Sicilian, exerted on the Italian government. These citrus growers feared what the Italian media frequently referred to as the "Israeli miracle"—the meteoric development of Israeli agriculture—which was the ostensible product of Israel's innovative thinking, as they employed new, sophisticated growing techniques using advanced technology. Visits to Israel by a delegation of Sicilian citrus growers had not only failed to dispel these concerns, but intensified them. The Israelis' great success in impressing their Italian guests with their organization of the sector, product improvements and marketing tactics led the latter to feel completely incapable of confronting the trade threat posed by the Israeli orange.[8]

In fact, this threat was exaggerated. Italian orange groves enjoyed considerable advantages, placing the Jaffa orange in a constant position of inferiority. The Italian orange was geographically closer to its markets than the Israeli fruit; it was transported by railway and did not require packaging, while the Israelis needed to pack their fruit. In addition, Italian citrus required only a third of the amount of water which Israeli fruits needed, due to Italy's more agreeable climate conditions and soil type. Indeed, any difficulties the Italian fruit faced in external competition resulted from two main factors: first, the Italian orange was relatively small, contained many pips and its taste was less rich than its Israeli or Spanish counterpart. Second, inefficient cultivation, marketing and dispatching practices increased its price, making it more expensive than its competitors, despite any structural advantages.[9] In order to remain competitive, special regulations protected the Italian orange. Thus, for example, the Italians attempted to establish a minimum reference price, aiming to forbid the sale of oranges in the markets of the EEC at a lower price, thus impairing the ability of more efficient exporters to compete with the Italian product.

Italy also stood at the forefront of the battle to prohibit the use of diphenyl in the citrus sector. The packing paper that lined the crates for transporting Israeli oranges were soaked in this chemical to preserve their freshness during the long sea voyage. Indeed, the Israeli orange endured many hardships before reaching the fruit stalls in the markets of Western Europe: it crossed the Mediterranean on ships, exposing it to extreme changes in temperature; it was then loaded onto trucks for long journeys, and damaged by the humidity of Europe's rainy marketing season.[10] Without a preservative chemical such as diphenyl, the Jaffa orange would be extremely unattractive by the time it reached European fruit sellers. In 1959, the Citrus Marketing Board conducted an experiment, sending oranges that had undergone only washing without chemical spraying. By the time they arrived, most of the oranges were nearly rotten.[11] Clearly, if Israel wanted to continue selling citrus fruits to Europe, it was necessary to use pesticides.

Although a number of Israeli-initiated studies in various European institutes, for example in Utrecht and Munich, had established that low levels of diphenyl were not harmful, its use remained controversial. Some lobbied for its prohibition, mainly because of its unpleasant smell, and the Italian Ministry of Agriculture joined these voices. This Italian involvement in the campaign against diphenyl especially angered the Israelis; considering that Italy did not import Israeli oranges, it was clear that their opposition was motivated by selfish trade considerations. The campaign against diphenyl was successful in Germany, where wholesalers and retailers of citrus fruits were required to clearly note on the packaging that the fruit was dipped in diphenyl. The Germans, despite being enthusiastic consumers of Jaffa oranges, were unwilling to endanger their health, and so this regulation led to a decline in sales of the Israeli fruit. The Citrus Marketing Board financed a comprehensive advertising campaign on German television assuring viewers that diphenyl did not pose a health threat, but it proved only partially effective.[12]

Among the problems in reaching an arrangement with the Italian government on the orange issue was the status of Sicily, an autonomous Italian region with its own Ministry of Agriculture. This necessitated that Israel conduct talks simultaneously with the Ministry of Agriculture in Rome and that in Palermo. Moreover, even after concluding agreements with these two bodies, it was still necessary to placate the citrus growers. The Israeli Ministry of Agriculture and the Ministry of Foreign Affairs tried to talk directly with the growers. However, efficient negotiations required dialogue with a union representing all the growers; and no such union existed in Sicily. The Sicilian government's attempt to establish a union to represent the hundreds of growers had failed, because the Sicilian citrus growers zealously guarded their independence.[13] Consequently, Israeli actions to calm Sicilian fears—for example, inviting a delegation of citrus growers to a guided tour in Israel or a visit by the Citrus Marketing Board to Sicily in October—had only limited success.[14]

Recognizing the many obstacles on the path to reaching an agreement with Italy regarding citrus fruits, the Israelis reduced their expectations. The experts sent to Rome were instructed to focus on persuading their Italian counterparts to support including within the expected agreement a declaration, according to which the EEC would guarantee to grant Israel any benefit in the citrus sector accorded to a third-party country that, as yet, had not signed an agreement with the EEC.[15] At the very least, this cautionary measure would ensure no additional damage to Israel. However, it soon became clear to the Israelis that the political echelon in Italy—which, as was noted above, was under tremendous pressure, in particular the Minister of Agriculture, a native of Sicily—were not prepared to compromise in any way on citrus fruits. The most the Italians were prepared to offer was a gentlemanly promise that efforts would be made to prevent new citrus exporters from attaining privileges within the Common Market.[16]

Regarding bromine, there was a broader basis for cooperation between the two countries. Italy had for years imported large quantities of bromine from Israel. The development of the Italian bromine industry had motivated the country to implement defensive measures which, as was discussed above, led to a significant reduction in the purchase of Israeli bromine. However, the Italian companies could not supply the entire quantity of the substance required by the country; for example, they did not produce bromides for the improvement of agricultural crops—a new technology then in the developmental stage and revealing impressive results. Likewise, Italian companies imported ethylene dibromide from the Dead Sea—a substance used for disinfection of soil (before its detrimental environmental effects were discovered)—then processed it, and exported it to other countries. The Italians thus had no reason to refuse a tariff reduction and increase import quotas on these products.

Israeli experts focused on these topics in their talks with officials in Rome. The Italians accepted their suggestions positively and even proposed plans of their own to widen cooperation. In a conversation with Nitzani, a senior Italian official noted that his government was interested in the Dead Sea Factories purchasing one of the Italian bromine companies, a step which would propel the Italian bromine industry forward. In return, the official promised that Italy would change its tariff policy toward bromine.[17] In further investigations of this offer, the Israeli Ministry of Foreign Affairs approached the Dead Sea Factories, asking whether the company would be interested in investing in the Italian sector. A delegation of senior company directors, including the Director General (retired Lieutenant General Chaim Maklef), traveled to in Italy to investigate the deal's profitability. They visited two factories belonging to the Italian company, as well as the head offices in Bologna. The Italians, hopeful that the Israeli company would acquire their business, showed the delegation the entire production process, as well as the company balance sheets, both public and confidential. The Israelis concluded that the company was well-established; purchasing it would certainly yield a good profit, enabling the penetration of markets presently closed to them.[18] However, the main point in favor of purchasing this Italian factory was ensuring that the Italians would reduce import restrictions on Israeli bromine. Maklef discussed this matter with the Director General of the Italian Ministry for Foreign Trade and they reached an understanding.[19]

Concurrently, an Israeli delegation arrived in Germany for talks with the local bureaucrats. There was a significant disparity between the support Israel received among the German political echelon and the negative stance of the country's experts, as was evidenced by the representatives in the negotiating delegation and the COREPER. The Israeli delegation sought to reduce this disparity. In talks with German statesmen, the Israelis requested that the German government supervise more closely to ensure that the professional ranks implemented its positive approach.[20] However, following the new line in Jerusalem, the delegation was not satisfied with these measures but also conducted a marathon series of meetings with officials at the Economic Ministry, the Treasury, the Ministry of Agriculture and the Foreign Ministry in Bonn.[21]

German experts were concerned especially by Israel's request for a substantial expansion of the list of products which would enjoy temporary tariff benefits (beyond the three products in the basic agreement of Council of Ministers from

April 1963). How could this be achieved without exposing the EEC to a flood of similar merchandise from other countries? In intense meetings with German officials, the Israeli officials devised a new formula to resolve this problem.[22] By redefining the classification of various industrial products through their division into subcategories, it would be possible to isolate a specific product, of which Israel was the main supplier: this would enable the EEC to grant Israel significant tariff relief, as in the case of Iran. For example, Israel provided only a tiny volume of juice imports compared to the US giant; however, Israel's share in natural juices was much larger. With regard to textile products, Israel was a small supplier, yet it accounted for a substantial portion of the children's clothing market. Therefore, if these products were classified as separate categories, the EEC would find it easier to grant concessions.[23] Israeli officials, who viewed this new idea as an opportunity to overcome one of the central obstacles preventing an agreement, quickly composed a list of 15 products of which Israel was arguably the major supplier, among them avocados, dried vegetables, fresh citrus juices, plywood and children's clothing.[24] The Germans approved most of this list, as did the Benelux countries.

However, the solution which the Germans and Israelis concocted was not without problems. It contradicted the EEC's common customs policy, which espoused limiting tariff categories as far as possible in order to prevent corruption and complications. It also threatened to problematize the concept of a "main supplier." The EEC was willing to grant tariff reductions to a state that supplied the decisive share of a certain product because, in fact, this situation occurred relatively infrequently. However, in the wake of the Israeli precedent, many countries would seek similar arrangements, leading to a multiplication of main suppliers. To limit the damage involved, the German experts suggested that Israel be accorded trade benefits not within a bilateral trade agreement between the EEC and Israel, but rather as a one-sided European gesture.[25] This would make it difficult for other countries to obtain comparable privileges.[26]

This was not the first time that such an idea had been raised. A few months earlier, in March 1963, Italy and France had proposed that the arrangements with both Israel and Iran take the form of unilateral gestures, without the framework of a trade agreement.[27] This proposal was motivated by the third section of article 111: upon completion of the second stage in the process of establishing the Common Market (expected to be 1966), decisions concerning negotiations with external parties would no longer be made by unanimous vote but rather according to a majority. However, this did not apply to unilateral gestures; in this case, the principle of unanimous vote remained in place. France and Italy feared that losing their right to veto would harm their vital economic interests. Israel, for example, was likely to exploit the support of the Benelux countries and Germany in order to widen the content of any agreement. So too, the fear of setting a precedent once again played a role. Other countries, for example India and Pakistan, had begun approaching the EEC, asking to begin trade negotiations.[28] Trade concessions to countries with such enormous domestic markets could potentially cause immense economic damage. Thus, retaining the right to veto was perceived as a vital safeguard against negative developments. The price involved in such a step—relinquishing the mutual trade benefits given by the other party in a bilateral trade agreement—was negligible compared to the advantages France and Italy could reap by granting unilateral gestures. Indubitably, the arrangement with Israel had always been a political and moral gesture rather than an economic interest; Israel's potential concessions were not accorded any great significance. Likewise, unilateral gestures were more comfortable politically. They avoided a formal agreement between the EEC and the State of Israel, thus enabling the Arab countries to accept the arrangement with less protest. However, France and Italy had failed to persuade their partners in the Council of Ministers and the Commission to support them on this issue and therefore the option had been abandoned.

In October 1963, however, an additional consideration pushed the German experts towards the solution of unilateral gestures. Germany was under constant pressure from the Arab countries to eschew a trade agreement with Israel. For example, in May 1963, Iraq dispatched an unambiguous warning to Bonn, stating that the Arabs would regard a trade agreement between the EEC and Israel as a hostile step. German companies received warning letters, threatening to include them in the Arab boycott list; indeed, in November 1963, a number of new German companies were added to the list.[29]

The Israeli Ministry of Foreign Affairs was vehemently opposed to this new German initiative, largely because unilateral benefits would negate the need for a follow-up committee, which was an obligatory part of a trade agreement. Indeed, the establishment of such a committee was one of the central assets which the Israelis hoped to obtain in a trade agreement with the EEC. They had reconciled themselves to accepting an agreement severely limited in terms of content, but the establishment of the committee would provide an opportunity to widen it in the future. Surrendering this asset would mean settling for the marginal economic benefits presently on offer.[30] From the Israeli perspective, such a step would drastically reduce the importance of the arrangement and render their five-year campaign a complete failure. The Israelis pressured Bonn to give up this initiative. However, the Germans steadfastly claimed that it constituted the optimal solution and would not harm their interests in any way.[31] It therefore seemed that the Council of Ministers could very well accept this initiative. France and Italy had supported it previously; with the addition of Germany's endorsement, the united strength of The Big Three was likely to be decisive.

At this critical juncture, the Commission became Israel's faithful ally in the battle against this plan. On November 16, Najar spoke with Rey. "His response to the German proposal was sharp and absolutely negative," the Israeli diplomat stated in a telegram to his office. Rey warned Najar that Israel should not follow this path, emphasizing the meager advantages it would offer.[32] Rey opposed the German plan because it clearly threatened the Commission's authority. As head of the directorate responsible for the EEC's foreign relations, Rey was especially interested in cultivating this common foreign trade policy. Moreover, senior Commission figures supported the negotiations with Israel as part of a more general battle to restrict the individual member countries' authority in reaching bilateral trade agreements, transferring this instead to the Community level, with a key role reserved for the Commission. By contrast, granting unilateral trade benefits in the framework of article 28 threatened to damage the common trade policy and was akin to a step backwards in the process of integration; it would also deprive the Commission of the role accorded to it by article 111. Unsurprisingly, when France and Italy had first proposed this route in the previous April, the Commission argued against it.[33] At this juncture, Rey sought Israel's cooperation in battling the new German initiative, exerting all his influence on the government in Bonn so that the latter would retract the plan.[34] For his part, Rey promised that he would advance the proposal which Israel had submitted the previous June as one bloc and act independently to prevent the EEC's negotiating delegation from delaying or even dissolving the agreement with Israel.[35]

Rey assumes the reins

Rey's promise to Sapir suited the interests of the Commission and the Israelis alike. The Commission had previously been forced to yield to include EEC member states' representatives in the negotiating delegation, at the behest of the Council of Ministers (as was noted, Rey wanted these representatives to act as mere observers). Rey's expectations that they would delay the progress of the negotiations had proved correct. Their cautious and at times hesitant stance also influenced the Commission's bureaucrats, leading them to adopt an overcautious, passive position.[36] This angered Hallstein, Rey and Mansholt, who wanted the Commission to take the initiative and lead the negotiations. Therefore, immediately following the conclusion of the first round of talks in June, Hallstein and Rey promised that they would pressure their officials to devise a proposed trade agreement with Israel within a short time.[37] The bureaucrats, however, were not pleased by these explicit instructions.[38] At the end of August, the officials phrased a minimalist document accepting almost none of the Israeli requests; consequently, Rey and Mansholt pressured them to compose a new document containing more real content.[39] In this document, which eventually formed the basis for the trade agreement between the EEC and Israel, the Commission revealed a great deal of creativity. It borrowed the German idea of tariff sub-categories to enable the focused reduction of tariffs for the products Israel considered most important—a suggestion which most other countries deemed overly generous—limiting it to industrial products made of raw materials imported from EEC countries—those products known as the "European product." This was expected to solve, at least temporarily, one of the most complex problems between the EEC and Israel, and an issue that had elicited much ill feeling. Regarding what Israel viewed as the other most serious problem—that is, oranges—the Commission recommended drafting an EEC declaration promising that the relative volume which Israeli exporters enjoyed at present would remain unaffected by any agreement with another large citrus exporter (for example, the Maghreb countries or Spain). This arrangement would maintain the status quo, guaranteeing that Israel—which provided 7% of the oranges consumed in The Six—would maintain this portion even if a large competitor received new benefits following association with the EEC. Beyond these two new solutions, the Commission proposal contained additional gestures that had been offered to Israel in the past: reducing tariff restrictions (liberalization), accelerated convergence to the Community's common external tariff in cases which would benefit Israel, and consideration of Israel's needs in the coming Kennedy Trade Round.

Rey planned to present the Commission's proposal directly to the Council of Ministers. However, the representatives of The Six in the negotiating delegation demanded insistently that they first peruse and authorize the document.[40] When the document was brought before the delegation on October 23, the representatives of The Six again requested an additional postponement to study it.[41] Rey, who was losing patience, together with Mansholt and other members of the Commission leadership, decided that if no clear decisions with real content were reached at the next planned meeting of the delegation (scheduled for November 11), he would prepare his own proposal and submit it directly to the Council of Ministers as a basis for discussion.[42] Likewise, the new German initiative to detach the agreement from the EEC framework drove Rey to prefer independent action over cooperation with the representatives of The Six. He knew that the interests of the Commission and Israel dovetailed completely on this point.

Sapir found Rey's proposal acceptable: "We accept Rey's opinion that the minimum we must demand is that the negotiations are conducted according to paragraphs 111–116 [sic]," he stated, adding, "I personally asked Rey to ensure that in the next discussion in the [Common] Market delegation they would agree on a position without any further foot-dragging, even if this requires his personal intervention in the delegation's debates."[43] On the same day, Sapir fulfilled his part of the agreement and sent a letter to the Israeli representation in Cologne, instructing them to pressure the German government to withdraw its proposal: "If their desire to help us is honest, then they will support our proposal without asking for additional [favors]," he wrote.[44] The unambiguous Israeli opposition was effective: Bonn ordered its representatives in the joint delegation to declare that a misunderstanding had arisen and remove their proposal from the agenda.

The independence that Rey and his colleagues in the Commission leadership revealed vis-à-vis the representatives of The Six was not restricted to the matter of retracting the German proposal. A number of weeks previously, the Commission had authorized Israel's request to join an EEC technical aid program in Africa. During 1962, the Europeans had consolidated a program of technical aid for 18 African states. In March 1963, the Commission announced that third-party countries with special ties to both the EEC and African states could integrate into this program. Israel already provided technical aid of various kinds to some of the states included in the program and feared that the European initiative would push it aside. Likewise, considering that only African and European countries could participate in these programs, Israel's inclusion would signify its unique position vis-à-vis the EEC. Accordingly, the Israelis informed the Commission of their desire to participate in the program: African students would continue studying in Israel, with EEC funding.[45] The Commission examined the Israeli request and, at the end of September, informed the Council of Ministers of its positive decision. The Permanent Representatives of The Six, unhappy with the freedom exercised by the Commission in this matter, demanded that it refrain from sending any response to Israel before discussed deliberation in the Council of Ministers.[46] Yet the Commission ignored this demand and, at the beginning of October, President Hallstein sent the Israeli representation in Brussels an official acceptance letter.[47] A few weeks later, the European Overseas Development Commissioner, Henri Rochereau, visited Israel together with his assistants, investigating possibilities for Israeli cooperation in development plans in African countries associated with the EEC using funding from the Community development fund. He also examined the idea of utilizing scholarships paid for by the EEC for the training of Africans in Israel. During his visit, Deputy Prime Minister Abba Eban reached a basic agreement with Rochereau concerning arrangements to execute the Commission's decision—for example, agreeing in principle that Israel would be included in tenders for development factories in Africa.[48] At the end of October, a meeting of the Council of Ministers allocated scholarships for African students in the year 1964. Some of the Permanent Representatives (mainly the Italian and French), fearing that in acceding to the Israeli request the Commission had exceeded the bounds of its mandate, harshly rebuked the Commission representatives present at the meeting. Despite this censure, the Commission succeeded in reserving a number of places for Israel.[49] Indeed, within a few months, the Israelis began to ask the EEC to contribute towards the funding of Israeli projects in Africa, among them the Solel Boneh Company's contract for building housing cooperatives on the Ivory Coast and the development of water sources in Niger. The latter was a joint project run by the Israeli company Vered and the government of Niger, and Israel attributed great importance to this endeavor in a Muslim country.[50]

Following three successive postponements, the EEC's negotiating delegation met in December 1963 to consider the Commission's proposal for the third round of talks with Israel. As Rey had expected from the outset, the representatives of The Six rejected almost all the Commission's proposals, including the idea of the "European product," fearing that it would create a precedent which countries skilled in improving and upgrading products—such as Hong Kong, Japan and India—would rush to exploit. Additional tariff reductions were ruled out for two reasons. First, they would give Israel only meager benefits while mainly serving the interests of other exporters. Second, these tariff reductions would improve Israeli competitiveness vis-à-vis Europe. The Commission's proposed declaration regarding oranges was dismissed outright by the Italian delegation, concerned about the ability of its fruit to compete with the Israeli produce. It was clear to the representatives of The Six that the Israelis would never accept what remained of the Commission's proposal as a basis for negotiations. Therefore, in their concluding recommendation they advised:

it seems that before returning to the talks it would be best to update the Israelis regarding the limited mandate of our negotiators, so that it will be their decision whether they prefer to delay the negotiations until more positive circumstances have emerged.[51]

In this way, the experts once again tried to divest the EEC of the Israeli problem. They apparently sought to force Israel, due to both economic reasons and feelings of wounded national pride, to reject the basis for negotiations.

Upon discovering the outcome of this meeting, Rey decided that he could no longer play by the rules of the game dictated by The Six. He instructed that the Commission's proposal should be submitted directly to the Council of Ministers, over the heads of the EEC delegation.[52] To a certain degree, this was a rebellion against the bureaucratic echelon of The Six. Such an unconventional step required the approval of the Commission leadership and therefore Rey placed the matter on the agenda of the next meeting. A number of factors provoked Rey's act of defiance. First, he was concerned that the failure of the negotiations between the EEC and Israel after such an extended period would have detrimental ramifications. In the wake of the crisis surrounding the UK's entry into the EEC and the obstacles encountered in implementing the Common Agricultural Policy, a failure in the Community's common foreign trade policy seemed like a further blow. Second, Rey saw this as an opportunity to restore the power equilibrium between the Commission and the representatives of The Six in the negotiating delegation. The representatives of The Six, supposedly observers appointed by the Council, had seized control of the negotiations, a fact that the Commission did not view favorably. The delegation's continued failure to consolidate a reasonable proposal proved its ineffectiveness, providing Rey with a comfortable excuse to return the reins to the Commission. Concurrently, the Commission was enjoying renewed prestige due its role in solving the agricultural crisis besetting the EEC, adding to Rey's self-confidence.[53] It is likely that Rey also felt personal responsibility towards the Israelis: he had repeatedly expressed optimism that an agreement would be possible if the Israelis sagely reduced their demands to a reasonable level. Following the second round of talks, Rey had explicitly informed them that the new Israeli position offered a real basis for an arrangement. The present decision by the EEC's negotiating delegation made a mockery of his words.

As part of his battle against the joint committee, the Belgian commissioner declared his intention to visit Israel at the end of December 1963. As was noted, the Israelis viewed visits by statesmen and high-ranking foreigners not only as a propaganda tool to be used vis-à-vis external audiences, but also as an opportunity to win over their guests. As early as 1960, they had invited Rey and Hallstein to visit Israel, but the two had rejected the invitation in an effort to avoid embroiling the EEC in complications with the Arab states, promising to visit in the future. Rey now resolved that the time had come to fulfill his promise and intended, during his visit, to persuade the Israelis to accept the Commission's proposed outline, which was modest in relation to their aspirations. However, this visit was no less a signal that the Commission had taken up the reins and was obligated to concluding the exhausting negotiations which, though under way for a year, still showed no evident progress. Directly after landing in Israel, in a speech at the airport, Rey declared with certainty that an agreement would be signed within six months at the most, repeating this promise again moments before his departure.[54] During his week-long stay in Israel, he was taken to visit factories, kibbutzim, agricultural fields and every economic sector threatened by the establishment of the Common Market—with the Israelis especially empha-sizing the citrus grove sector. It seems that this campaign of Israeli persuasion was effective. Indeed, Rey announced:

> During my visit to Israel I discovered for the first time with what urgency Israel views the link with the Common Market, a feeling which was not suf-ficiently known in Brussels—until now it was assumed that the Israeli econ-omy is blooming and the problem is not so pressing. However, now I know that the issue is especially important to those institutions in Israel responsi-ble for long-term economic planning, for whom the question of Israel's ties with the Common Market is of the greatest urgency.[55]

At a lunch hosted in his honor by the Israeli Liberal Party (indeed Rey himself had previously been a leading liberal in Western Europe) he stated, "[My] visit to Israel reinforced the feeling of urgency with respect to arranging the relations between Israel and the Common Market."[56] It is doubtful that Rey's public expres-sions were the result of sudden enlightenment. The Europeans indeed tended to minimize the negative effects which the defensive measures implemented by the EEC had on the Israeli economy, just as the Israelis were inclined to exaggerate them. However, even if Rey was impressed by the statistics which the Israelis showered upon him during his visit to prove that the Israeli economy was under a serious threat, his willingness to announce, publicly and so unequivocally, the need to finalize the agreement as soon as possible was intended for the ears of the Europeans, principally to prepare the ground for the Council of Ministers to adopt the Commission's proposal.

However, Rey was not satisfied with mere declarations. During his visit, he witnessed the distress of the kibbutzim on the periphery, which relied heav-ily on egg exports. The gates of The Six had been closed to their eggs upon the implementation of threshold prices, commonly known as minimum import prices, in this sector. The threshold price was a protective measure to supple-ment tariff protectionism. It forced exporters to sell their product at a price significantly higher than the local product, permanently ruling out the pos-sibility that external suppliers would be able to compete with EEC products.[57] Consequently, a sharp decline in Israel's egg exports to the EEC ensued. At the end of the 1950s, Israel exported $8,000,000 worth of eggs to The Six (90% of them to the Italian market); in 1962, following the first stroke of the Common Agricultural Policy, this figure decreased to $6,213,000, further declining to $4,488,000 in 1963.[58] Rey's hosts pressured him heavily to act in this regard and the Belgian acquiesced, reaching a covert agreement with the Israelis that would enable Israeli exporters to sell their eggs at a price 10–15% lower than the threshold without incurring sanctions. This was a noteworthy gesture, giving Israeli eggs privileges not granted to any other country.[59]

Officials in Brussels were not pleased by Rey's endeavors to reach an agreement with Israel. Although the Commission had defined his trip to Israel as a "courtesy visit," thus seeking to avoid censure from the Arab countries, Rey's declarations did not fit with this claim. When the German paper *Die Welt* published an article claiming that the aim of Rey's visit was in fact to advance the talks with Israel, the German representative in the COREPER hastily denied this, claiming that although Rey's hosts repeatedly attempted to discuss Israel's relationship with the EEC, the Commissioner politely avoided the topic.[60] Upon his return to Brussels, Rey participated in a meeting of the Commission leadership during which he pressured the other Commissioners to approve the Commission's proposal and submit it directly to the Council of Ministers.[61] This meeting reached a positive decision. On January 30, 1964, the Commission's proposal was presented to the meeting of the Permanent Representatives in the Council, together with a diffident document penned by the EEC's negotiating delegation. The Permanent Representatives, despite expressing their appreciation of the Commission's efforts to find constructive solutions, only approved those same meager benefits regarding which the delegation had reached a consensus. Most of the representatives, first and foremost the Dutch representative, demanded further action, in particular advising the Council of Ministers, which was due to meet a few days later, to adopt at least part of the Commission's program (the Dutch representative in fact demanded that it be adopted in full). However, the Italian representative withstood this pressure and dismissed anything beyond the delegation's meager recommendations. The French representative, seeking to bridge between the various positions, suggested a version of the "orange declaration" that was less binding than the Commission's proposal, omitting the promise to maintain the status quo among citrus-fruit exporters to the market and instead adopting a more intangible and less binding formula: "[I]n the case of association with a large orange producer, the follow-up committee will be authorized to study the problem of Israeli exports." Despite these efforts, the Italian representative remained firm in his refusal. Therefore, the recommendations which the Permanent Representatives imparted to the Council of Ministers were ambiguous; alongside a presentation of the various positions, as was required by the EEC's constitution, the supporters of the Commission's plan inserted a paragraph highlighting that a failure to decide in favor of additional concessions to Israel, beyond those on which a consensus already had been reached, would seriously endanger the possibility of concluding an agreement.[62] The decision now rested with the Council of Ministers.

Rey understood that the defining moment had arrived and was determined to receive approval for the Commission's proposal. At the beginning of the meeting, he spoke decisively, without embellishment, in contrast to the Commission's usual behavior (at least when the topic of Israel was under discussion). He stated the Israelis had for a long time clung to their desire for a comprehensive agreement, yet had finally agreed to be satisfied with a limited arrangement. The European Parliament had resolved in favor of a trade agreement with Israel. During his visit to Israel, Rey had taken upon himself the task of persuading the Israeli authorities to be satisfied, at least at the first stage, with a limited agreement. Now the Council of Ministers must offer something with real content as a basis for reaching an agreement. Rey reminded the Council of the political importance of the problem and the severe ramifications of a failure for the EEC's common trade policy. He highlighted the three points which remained obstacles to an agreement: bromine, oranges and the "European product." He did not hesitate to note explicitly that the central obstacle to any reasonable agreement was the stubborn position of the Italian government. "Of course, the other countries must reveal the utmost consideration of Italy's concerns," noted Rey, "but he [i.e. Rey] cannot but be surprised by the *intransigence* which Italy is exhibiting on these matters" (emphasis added).[63]

The French Foreign Minister, who spoke directly after Rey, offered the Commissioner his complete endorsement: "I believe that the agreement with Israel is not only most desirable but also does not constitute an insurmountable obstacle," he pronounced. Cattani, representing Italy at the meeting, found himself isolated and was forced into a defensive position. He noted that, "regarding bromine, the Commission's suggestion for a general reduction of tariffs on this product goes beyond what Israel itself is asking for," hinting at the gentlemanly agreement Israel and Italy had reached on the matter. He attacked the other states, maintaining that they were not sufficiently sensitive to the needs of such an impoverished region as Sicily. Even worse: the EEC countries were not adequately aware of the direct correlation between the stability of the deprived regions in Italy and the solidity of the Community in general—a hint that satisfying the Sicilians was not merely the Italian government's problem but also a general European concern.[64]

The Dutch representative, Spierenburg, rejected the Italian's explanations: if, after two rounds of negotiations with Israel and such extended deliberations within The Six, the EEC was unable to reach agreement, the situation was extremely grave. He was skeptical concerning the validity of Cattani's arguments that citrus growers in Sicily would suffer; indeed, the EEC had no intention of granting Israeli oranges the same preferential treatment as the Italian orange enjoyed. "In fact, our proposal is so limited that I am not at all sure that the Israelis will find it reasonable," he added. The representatives of other countries in turn each expressed their support of the Commission's proposal. However, Cattani would not withdraw his opposition and the issue was returned to the Permanent Representatives for the drafting of new proposals, which the Council of Ministers would consider at its coming meeting in February.

Even before the meeting of the Council of Ministers, the Israelis had concluded that a dramatic final effort was necessary to overcome what were perceived as the two greatest obstacles to an agreement with the EEC: France and Italy. At the beginning of February 1964, the Israeli Foreign Minister flew to Paris and

Rome to persuade her counterparts there to withdraw their opposition to the Commission's proposal.[65] Meir soon discovered that her efforts were unnecessary in Paris and the journey had apparently been superfluous; indeed, the Quai d'Orsay had concluded that it was necessary to reach an agreement with Israel and any additional delay was likely to harm French interests. This change was a result, among other things, of threats made by Israeli diplomats, warning that a lack of French support for Israel's interests in the EEC would lead to a re-appraisal of the preference, which Israel granted to French products.[66] In November 1963, the Economic Department at the Quai d'Orsay submitted a recommendation to the Foreign Minister advising that it would be best to strive for acceptance of the Commission's proposal.[67]

Indeed, the French suddenly became the most active proponents of the deal with Israel among The Six, apart from the Dutch perhaps. They were the only party willing to adopt a general solution of the "European product" along the lines Israel requested. They also assumed the task of finding a compromise formula for the "orange declaration," one which Italy would deem acceptable. In March, the Economic Department instructed Boegner to abandon French doubts regarding four of the products on the Israeli list (of 37 in total), and thereby avoid ruining the consolidating agreement:

> If we will continue to cling to our position we are likely to be responsible for the failure of the negotiations . . . to prevent this development, which is intolerable from the political perspective, you must endorse any formula acceptable to The Six.[68]

This new line in Paris surprised the Israelis: "Over the past two years we tended to see France as one of the main bad guys in the Market drama —maybe the main bad guy, with a capital 'The'—and now, in this respect, we must note a change," commented the economic attaché at the Embassy in Paris.[69]

If the Foreign Minister's lobbying was very easy in Paris, a tough challenge awaited her in Rome. In December 1963, a new center-left government had risen to power in the Italian capital, with members from the Christian Democratic, Socialist, Social Democratic and Republican parties. This government faced difficult challenges, mainly in the economic realm. The growth of the Italian economy, which had reached astonishing rates in the years 1959–61,[70] had dropped to the rate of 4.8% in 1963 and was predicted to fall to even 3% in the years 1964–65.[71] The trade deficit rose, reaching $2.5 billion.[72] Inflation increased at a higher rate than the economy's growth. Despite the size of the agricultural sector in Italy—around 30% of the country's population was employed in agriculture—its part in the national product remained small—less than 20%. Due to the frailty and sensitivity of Italian agriculture, any government decision which threatened to damage it was exceedingly problematic. In addition, the agricultural sector's fragile economic state did not accord with its political power. In fact, the farmers enjoyed great influence and constituted a serious pressure group in Italy. Sicilian farmers possessed particular power due to the island's unique status and because the Minister for Foreign Trade, whose position gave him the greatest degree of influence on Italy's position in the EEC, was Sicilian. Furthermore, a wave of strikes erupted in Italy at this time: 1.5 million workers joined these protests, including civil servants.

Thus, the Italian government was subject to extensive internal pressure and this was not an opportune time to complicate the country's situation even further by granting benefits to Israel. In an attempt to overcome this unamenable constellation, the Israelis decided to activate Israel's many friends in the Italian government: Foreign Minister Saragat, Agricultural Minister Aggradi and the Socialist Deputy Prime Minister Nenni. However, the Israeli Foreign Minister's talks with these supporters revealed the difficulty she faced. They promised to try to soften their government's position, but remained skeptical regarding the possibility of success.[73]

It was legally impossible to renew the talks with Israel in the face of Italian opposition. However, Italy's isolated stance caused the country discomfort. Throughout the long negotiations with Israel, even before they became official, it was almost always possible for the opposing countries to rely on the support of at least one other party. On the few occasions when a country found itself isolated, it eventually withdrew its opposition. This had been the case at the end of September 1962, when Italy finally agreed to begin negotiations with Israel, and it occurred again at this juncture. This illustrates the complexity of consensual decision making and the double-edged sword of the veto, in decision making by consensus or qualified majority voting. When a consensus is required, over time the majority states are pressured to consider the needs of the country in the minority position. Decisions in consensus voting are pushed to converge around the lowest common denominator.[74] However, in qualified majority voting, a state can maintain its opposition symbolically without blocking the EEC decision-making process. Consensual decision making, as exemplified in the Italian case, can also lead to a further result: it can weaken a country's power to oppose the majority's position, especially if this country (in this case, Italy) remains the only country against the decision. When this country succumbs to the majority position, it must adhere to the consensus, thereby losing its ability to carry out symbolic resistance which is useful in sending out a positive message to its domestic audience.

On February 24, the Israeli matter was once again included on the agenda of the Council of Ministers, after the Permanent Representatives had completed their work. The problem of oranges remained the only obstacle to renewing the talks. Italy, refusing to accept France's version of the declaration, was forced to suggest an alternative that further diluted the obligation to Israel. The ensuing long argument over the drafting details reveals the particular sensitivity with which the Council viewed the matter.[75]

With the way finally open to resume the talks, on March 10, the Council of Ministers, resolved in favor of opening talks with Israel based on the outline of the Commission proposal, minus two products and with a weakened "orange declaration." In certain countries, where the professional echelon continued to insist on removing products from the list, the political ranks issued a clear instruction to withdraw any objections. The French Foreign Ministry informed Boegner that he should not continue to insist on the four products which concerned France, and Belgian Foreign Minister Spaak ordered the Belgian representative to raise no further objections regarding the six products of particular interest to Belgium. The European statesmen were well aware that their instructions often evaporated in the meeting of the COREPER; therefore, the Belgian and Italian Foreign Ministers, whose representatives had acquired a reputation as "trouble makers," attended the meeting to ensure that everything proceeded smoothly.[76] Only one question remained unanswered: would the Israelis agree to such a limited arrangement—one that satisfied almost none of their ambitions?

The Israeli dilemma

Upon accepting the arrangement proposed by the EEC, the Israelis would necessarily relinquish what they viewed as the minimum condition for even a limited trade agreement: a solution for Israeli oranges and the "European product." The tariff reductions offered to Israel were tiny, including only 23 products and accounting for no more than 25% of Israeli exports to The Six. These would give Israel direct tariff savings amounting the ridiculous sum of around $625,000. In any event, these reductions would soon be granted to all countries as part of the coming Kennedy Round, and therefore would not accord Israeli exports any advantage in the long term, even over exporters from other countries. This proposal was therefore very far from what the Israelis desired and had battled for over the years. It constituted a severe blow to the prestige of those charged with the negotiations, who had attained so little after cultivating the high hopes of the Israeli public for so long. There was little illusion concerning how the Israeli public would receive the agreement, or the delight the opposition parties would derive from it.

Despite all this, Israeli decision makers tended towards accepting it. For years Israeli bureaucrats had struggled to persuade their superiors to adopt a pragmatic stance in the negotiations with the EEC, advising them to bargain as best they could, but eventually be content with what the Community was willing to give. In other words, they had advised them to stay at the negotiating table. They viewed the agreement with the EEC as a first step toward a more binding arrangement in the future. The political echelon was not easily convinced: indeed, officials had long been instructed to insist on association; when it finally became clear that this was impossible, they were told to strive instead for a comprehensive agreement. This was not a tactical step intended to extricate maximum concessions from the other party, but rather a fundamental perception that the only way to protect Israel's vital economic interests was a comprehensive agreement and therefore the Israelis must settle for nothing less. The fact that Israeli decision makers did not relinquish their ambitious demands, even after the repeated failure to achieve them, serves as proof of this. This led to a significant delay in finding an arrangement for the most critical problems among Israeli exports.

Only in June 1963, when the talks were on the verge of collapse, did the political echelon change its position. "First we will open a small hatch, then a door, and finally maybe [break down] the wall," said the new Finance Minister, Sapir, to the Knesset Foreign Affairs and Defense Committee in July 1963, thus expressing the shift underway among the decision makers in Jerusalem.[77]

The logic was simple, and Sapir outlined it to the committee:

> Sometimes I too agree with those who believe we must say: "Give us association or we will not talk to you." This position intensifies especially when they offer us only three paragraphs, while dragging us along interminably. Yet I want to say that if we will attain association, and I believe that one day we will do so—this can only be via the path of elimination. If it will become clear that the path they want to walk with us is so constrained from all sides—no membership, no association and no comprehensive or preferential agreement—then they will need to conclude that there is no other option. If they don't want to cut off communication, they must return to the path of association.

According to this strategy, Israel would not surrender its ambitious goals but rather achieve them over the long term by means of short-term concessions. This idea was based on exploiting the European desire, for various reasons, to avoid rejecting the Israeli approaches outright and their recognition of Israel's entitlement to special consideration. In so doing, they revealed a point of weakness which the Israelis could exploit to their advantage. Their excuse for not acquiescing to the Israelis was founded on arguments regarding objective difficulties, combined with the claim that intermediate steps could solve Israel's problems without a comprehensive, preferential agreement. By agreeing to a narrow trade arrangement, the Israelis sought to prove indisputably that this gesture would not remedy their troubles, thus forcing the Europeans to broaden the agreement in the future.

However, the Israeli course of action, although sophisticated and cunning, incurred high psychological costs. It demanded a substantial degree of restraint in the face of repeated humiliations; the constant and vigorous wooing of European goodwill, even in the face of stubborn positions or—worse—offensive proposals. At times the Israeli decision makers felt exasperated, unwilling to continue playing the game. Three months after Sapir decisively expressed his support of the gradual approach—which would enable the Israelis to "sneak in"—the Finance Ministry in Jerusalem called an inter-ministerial meeting regarding the EEC. When Sapir discovered that the Community proposal offered tariff reductions of only around $750,000 per annum, he stated that in these circumstances it was preferable to end the negotiations and bring the battle into the public sphere:

> We have withdrawn from the political content of association with the European Market . . . when we gave up on association with the market, all the rest is pragmatics and therefore we need to know to what extent the agreement is advantageous.[78]

Israeli officials—Gal-Ed, Ofer and Golan—tried to persuade him that the benefit to Israeli exports would be much greater because these reductions would allow Israeli products to remain competitive; but Sapir remained unconvinced. Over the course of the coming weeks, he tried, once again, to revive the solution of association. In his conversation with the Italian Minister of Trade and Industry Colombo while in New York, Sapir commented that association according to the model of Greece and Turkey was the logical solution for an arrangement with Israel.[79] He repeated this a number of times over the next few days, at various opportunities.

However, Sapir knew well that this was a dream. Rejecting the little that the EEC was willing to offer would forfeit all the achievements the Israelis had made up to this point. Officials at the Ministry of Foreign Affairs in Jerusalem understood that abandoning the strategy Israel had employed up to this point would be an error:

> The economic content of the agreement which the Community is willing to offer remains, until now, limited. There are three questions before us: 1. Will it be possible to broaden the content of the agreement? 2. Should the limited agreement with the Community be viewed as a worthless piece of paper? 3. Will breaking up the present negotiations advance a comprehensive agreement?[80]

Najar believed that the answer to the last two questions was negative; therefore, the only reasonable alternative was to accept what the EEC offered and focus on broadening the agreement in the future. From Paris, Ambassador Eytan wrote:

> the agreement according to the Commission's proposals will not be sufficient to fulfill our full demands—far from it. However, rejecting it will create a severe and prolonged crisis. I regard signing an agreement which does not satisfy us completely as less of a disaster than creating a crisis.

Understanding the doubts of his superiors, he added:

> Failure to sign the agreement will give us nothing apart from the good feeling that we didn't "surrender" and did not allow the Community to "fool" us. However, we will come out of it with our hands completely empty, without a reasonable chance of success in the future."[81]

The Foreign Minister, similarly to Israeli officials, believed that Israel must stay in the game. More than any other government minister, Meir advocated a pragmatic, gradual approach. When Knesset Member Eliezer Rimlet of the General Zionist Party censured the meager content of the proposed agreement, she replied sharply:

I want to tell you, MK Rimlet, it is not important if the amounts are small . . . we have a choice: to continue and argue with the [Common] Market for years, who knows how long, regarding association or anything else, to rebuke and admonish them—and nothing will happen. None among The Six, not even the Netherlands, has said that it is possible. The second option is to take this route. It is more difficult, but it provides a way in.[82]

Meir did not attribute any importance to the critical discourse using terms such as "wounded pride," "national humiliation," and "self-respect": "I say that if this time it will not succeed—then we must try again. We cannot give up on this."[83] Yet at the same time, there was a decided consensus among Israeli decision makers that the EEC's proposal itself had almost no practical value aside from forming a basis for future expansion. They thought it important, already at this stage, to elucidate their expectations to the Europeans. At a lunch in The Hague attended by the Israeli Finance Minister and the German Secretary of State Neef, Sapir once again emphasized that Israel's aim was full association with the EEC; while Israel agreed to a limited trade agreement at present, understanding the constraints of The Six, it assumed that association would be discussed at a later stage.[84] So too, Prime Minister Levi Eshkol sent a missive to German Chancellor Erhard in which he noted explicitly:

> If, indeed, we will obtain, as we hope, first a *temporary* arrangement which reduces the immediate damage to the Israeli economy, we will necessarily regard it as a preparatory and transitional stage on the way to the full solution which logic requires. [Original emphasis][85]

The Commission, seeking to bring the negotiations with Israel to a successful conclusion, and aware of Israeli deliberations over whether to accept or reject the EEC outline offered, encouraged those in favor of the limited agreement. When the Israeli Foreign Minister visited Brussels at the beginning of March, the Commission leadership lavished attention on her. Mansholt, who was in Washington at the time, returned from the US two days early to speak with Meir. During a festive lunch in her honor, including "French champagne, Italian wine and Israeli orange juice," Hallstein warmly promised that the agreement on the horizon was a first step in Israel's relations with the EEC.[86] Meir received a similar guarantee from Rey and Mansholt.

On March 19, the third round of talks between Israel and the EEC began. At the opening session, Commission representative Herbst, serving as the president of the EEC's negotiating delegation, explained the Community's proposals, noting that although this limited arrangement did not satisfy Israel's expectations, "it offers real content on the economic sphere, and is of psychological and political value, which should not be dismissed lightly."[87] In a private conversation, Herbst warned Najar that Israel should avoid creating a crisis at this time: such a step would not only spoil the atmosphere of goodwill towards Israel within the EEC

but also damage the special status Israel had obtained through the official negotiations. He hinted that Israel would later be able to broaden the agreement.[88]

Herbst's concerns, however, were unnecessary: the Israelis had already
resolved to accept the EEC's proposals, precisely for the reasons that he outlined.
The Israelis' non-obligatory, and seemingly indecisive, attitude when the negotiations began was a mere pretense to extort final gestures from the Europeans.
The Israelis, understanding that at this stage they would not be able to improve
the contents of the agreement in any significant manner, had two aims. The first
was to give the agreement the most general form possible so that it would exceed
the bounds of a standard trade agreement; the second was to include within it
phrasing indicating that it was a first step on the way to a wider arrangement.
They proposed that, in addition to the title "trade agreement," the words "and
economic cooperation" be appended to the agreement, differentiating it from
that signed with Iran. They also pressed to include a sentence in the introduction explicitly noting that agreement was designed "to create a basis for *gradual
broadening* of the trade relations between Israel and the EEC" (original emphasis).
The EEC delegation, however, opposed most of these initiatives and only minor
corrections were made to the Commission's phrasing.[89]

At the end of April, a special consultation was held in Meir's home, attended
by ministers and senior officials with an interest in the agreement. Following
deliberation, those present resolved that despite the miniscule and insufficient content of the proposed agreement, and considering its political value,
the Israeli delegation should be instructed to sign it.[90] At a press conference
in Jerusalem, Minister Sapir announced the government's decision to sign the
agreement. While he agreed that the arrangement was not as far-reaching as
desired, it constituted "a foot in the door": indeed, he noted, Israel viewed it as
the beginning, not the end, of a chapter.[91]

The trade agreement between the EEC and Israel was signed on June 4, 1964,
at a festive event in the beautiful Palais des Congres in Brussels. Representing
Israel were Foreign Minister Golda Meir and Minister of Trade and Industry
Akiva Guvrin, accompanied by Ambassador Amiel Najar, who had toiled cease-
lessly for years to strengthen the ties between Israel and Europe. Although the
EEC Council dispatched Belgian Deputy Foreign Minister Henri Fayat, then
serving as stand-in President of the Council, the Commission's representative
was none other than President Walter Hallstein. In speeches, both Fayat and
Hallstein cited the agreement as further proof that the EEC had no desire for iso-
lationism and internal fortification, but in fact sought to advance international
trade. Meir referred to the signing of the agreement as "a noteworthy event in the
history of our nation." In her speech, she did not forget to thank Rey personally
for the important role he had played in reaching an agreement.[92]

Israelis were divided in their views on the trade agreement of June 1964: some
viewed it as a resounding failure, while others deemed it a substantial achievement. Those who mocked the agreement commented that "the politicians
describe it as an economic success, while the economists view it as a political
achievement."[93] Indeed, the content of the agreement was meager even compared

to the Israeli requests during the second round of talks (June 1963), which themselves were a serious compromise relative to the original demands. It is difficult to describe the outcome as a success, considering the long period of negotiations between the sides and the great investment of effort: dozens of trips by ministers and senior officials to the EEC countries, hundreds of conversations between Israeli representatives in the capitals of The Six and figures concerned with EEC matters, numerous studies clarifying Israel's needs or providing "ammunition" for the negotiators, and special initiatives, such as the endeavors among Sicilian citrus growers or investment in Italian factories, to generate goodwill towards Israel. These Israeli efforts had required not only time and attention, but also the investment of the country's limited material resources. It is no coincidence that Israeli statesmen complained about the expensive costs of the campaign, costs that were immeasurably higher than the economic advantages the arrangement accorded.

Yet it was no small feat that, as a result of Israeli pressure, the EEC's first trade agreement with a third-party country which was neither European nor a former European colony was signed with Israel.[94] Considering the evident lack of desire among various EEC members to conclude *any* agreement with Israel, without reference to its content, the agreement of June 1964 appears a substantial achievement. Moreover, the Israelis viewed the agreement as a way to obtain more ambitious goals: it provided a foothold in the EEC, making it possible to widen the existing arrangement using the institutional tools it granted (meetings of the follow-up committee). It ratified claims that the EEC was morally obliged to consider Israel's problems, providing a basis for demanding additional gestures should the existing agreement fail to offer a satisfactory solution.

No less interesting is the question of what led the EEC to sign the agreement with Israel. In view of its very modest content, it could erroneously be assumed that the agreement did not constitute a major sacrifice for the Europeans. However, few welcomed it. The agreement with Israel offered EEC countries negligible economic benefits while threatening to embroil The Six in political complications with the Arab states. Fear of this scenario was so decisive that a short while later the EEC signed an agreement with Lebanon which was similar in terms of format (although not content) to the arrangement with Israel: in its framework, the EEC was obligated to grant Lebanon technical aid. This move was clearly intended to dissipate somewhat the tumult in the Arab world. Likewise, it was not the first agreement signed with a third-party country designed to limit the damage of acceding to Israel's requests. As was noted, the decision to begin talks with Iran was intended to counter any potential claim that Israel was the first non-European country with which the EEC held such negotiations.

Thus it appears that the Israeli factor had a significant influence, by way of constraint, on the EEC's policy towards non-European countries in the first years of its existence. How can this be explained? The answer is that the Israelis maneuvered the Europeans into a corner and they could no longer dismiss the Israelis empty handed. Israel achieved this, to a certain extent unconsciously, by repeatedly swallowing its dignity and retreating from the red lines its leaders had set. Many European bureaucrats hoped that the EEC's obstinacy would lead the Israelis to leave the negotiating table; indeed, on more than one occasion it seemed that they seriously considered this option. However, this did not come to pass because the Israelis, despite their humiliations, felt it would be foolish to cut the ties established between Israel and the EEC and release the latter from its moral obligation to safeguard Israel's important economic interests.

Notes

1 Najar to the Ministry of Foreign Affairs, ISA, FM, file 1960/8, June 22, 25, 1963.
2 Ministry of Foreign Affairs to Israeli representations in the capitals of the Six, ISA, FM, file 1960/7, September 19, 1963. In an interview with *Davar*, Israel Gal-Ed, Deputy Director General of the Ministry of Trade and Industry, cautioned that Israel would react to the rejection of their proposal in this manner. See. *Davar*, "Interview with Israel Gal-Ed," *Davar*, September 18, 1963.
3 See the protocol of the inter-ministerial meeting concerning the Common Market. ISA, PM, file 6354/5, August 25, 1963.
4 Memorandum concerning the negotiations between Israel and the EEC, ISA, PM, file 6354/5, August 25, 1963.
5 Another reason for focusing efforts on these states was the need to reach an agreement on those trade gestures granted at the sole authority of the states: minimizing quantitative caps and immediate reduction of the national tariff to the level of common external tariff. These were relevant mainly for the Big Three among The Six.
6 See, for example, the conversation between the Israeli Embassy in Rome and Guttadauro, one of the senior Sicilian citrus growers :ISA, FM, file 280/14, June 28, 1961.
7 At the meeting between the Israeli Minister of Agriculture, Moshe Dayan, and his Italian counterpart in November 1961, it was decided that Israel would dispatch an expert to maintain constant contact with the Italian Ministry of Agriculture. See: ISA, FM, file 280/14, November 8, 1961.
8 See a series of articles on this issue in *Giornale di Sicilia*, March–April 1962, ISA, FM, file 286/8, April 1962.
9 In February 1964, the Italian Minister of Agriculture revealed to the Israeli Foreign Minister that enormous quantities of Italian oranges were at that moment left rotting away because there were not enough railway wagons to transport them to the Community countries. The Italian minister took this opportunity to criticize the efficiency of his country's growers. See the testimony of the Foreign Minister to the government: ISA, PM, February 16, 1964. One of the factors contributing to the fruit's high price was the involvement of the Sicilian mafia, which sought to derive profits from this prospering sector. See: Ada Luciani, "Mansholt Plan Attracts Italian Farmers," *Ma'ariv*, December 23, 1963.
10 "Report on the Results of the Shipments", ISA, MA, file 2421/7, August 7, 1958.
11 Protocol no. 573 of the Citrus Marketing Council, ISA, MA, file 2423/10, November 22, 1959.
12 Yosef Cnaan, "We Are Treading Water in the British Citrus Market," *Davar*, June 19, 1963.
13 On these attempts see: Elron to the Economic Department, ISA, FM, file 286/5, May 24, 1963; Fisher to Shinnar, ISA, FM, file 1960/5, July 19, 1963.
14 These visits included a delegation of citrus growers from Sicily and Calabria in March 1962, the visit of the Director General of the Italian Ministry of Agriculture and the Director General of the Italian Ministry for Foreign Trade in April 1962, and the visit of a delegation from the Italian Institute for Foreign Trade in December 1962. Significantly, the Israeli Embassy in Rome believed that the Israeli Ministry of

Agriculture and the Citrus Marketing Council were not acting with sufficient fervor on the matter. See: ISA, FM, file 1960/2, November 28, 1963.

15 The Israeli demand for consultations following any agreement with another orange exporting country was not an innovation but rather constituted accepted procedure. It was included, for example, in the association agreement with Greece (regarding avocado exports).

16 See the Israeli Ministry of Foreign Affairs Memorandum, "Italy and the Negotiations with the Market," ISA, FM, file 3146/5, February 1964.

17 Nitzani to Gal-Ed, ISA, FM, file 1960/3, October 15, 1963.

18 Elron to the Foreign Minister, ISA, FM, file 1960/3, November 12, 1963.

19 Elron to the Ministry of Foreign Affairs, ISA, FM, file 1960/2, November 17, 1963; Gal-Ed to Alon, ISA, FM, 1960/1, December 1963.

20 Shinnar to the Prime Minister, ISA, FM, file 1960/7, September 5, 1963.

21 Shlomo Shafir, *Outstretched Hand: German Social Democrats and Their Attitudes Towards Jews and Israel, 1945–1967* (Tel Aviv: Zemora Bitan, 1987).

22 ISA, FM, file 1960/7, September 12, 1963.

23 *Davar*, "Ambiguity During the Technical Debate with the Market," *Davar*, October 30, 1963.

24 Golan to the Finance Minister, ISA, FM, file 1960/2, September 1963.

25 On this see: Francesca Martines, "Foreign Commercial Policy," in *Italy and EC Membership Evaluated*, ed. Francesco Francioni (New York: St. Martin's, 1992).

26 Passweg to the Ministry of Foreign Affairs, ISA, FM, file 23/12, October 29, 1963. The Germans agreed that Israel could provide them with a list of products relevant to this solution, which they would then present to the remainder of the member states as their proposal.

27 Regarding this idea see the memorandum of the Economic Department at the French Foreign Ministry: AMAE, DE-Ce-1961-1966, file 1469, March 30, 1963.

28 Rajendra M. Abhyankar, "India and the European Union: A Partnership for All Reasons," *India Quarterly* 65, no. 4 (2009); Idesbald Goddeeris, "EU-India Relations" (Leuven: Leuven Centre for Global Governance Studies, 2011).

29 GGOPA, B36-044-01, May, 15, 1963; July 12, 1963; November 25, 1963.

30 Foreign Ministry to Representation in Cologne, ISA, FM, file 1960/3, October 31, 1963.

31 Passweg to the Ministry of Foreign Affairs, ISA, FM, file November 1, 1963; Shinnar to the Ministry of Foreign Affairs, ISA, FM, file 1960/2, November 17, 1963.

32 Najar to the Ministry of Foreign Affairs, ISA, FM, file 1960/2, November 16, 1963.

33 Note a l'attention de M. Gaudet, EUA, BAC 3/1978-324/3, April 4, 1963.

34 Rey was also concerned by another phenomenon: Israel had begun to employ the tactic of discussions and bilateral negotiations with officials in Italy and German instead of discussing and clarifying matters with the joint committee or EEC officials. The Belgian Foreign Ministry, which, along with the other Benelux countries, viewed advancing integration as an important interest, similarly opposed the new Israeli modus operandi (and perhaps the Belgian Rey was able to recruit its support in this matter). See Note pour M. le Secretaire Géneral, Négociations commerciales C.E.E.-Israël, MAECEB, 6405/B, October 4, 1963.

35 Najar to Sapir, ISA, FM, file 1960/2, November 22, 1963.

36 Israeli diplomats too were concerned by this. According to the accepted explanation, the junior Commission officials on the various committees regarded the representatives of The Six as the highest authority and therefore from the outset phrased their proposals to accord with their opinions. Another possible explanation is that these bureaucrats were at the beginning or at most the middle of their careers and expected to return to serve in their home countries; therefore they did not want to create antagonism. See: Najar to Levavi, ISA, FM, file 1960/2, November 19, 1963.

37 Foreign Ministry to Representations in the capitals of The Six, ISA, FM, file 1960/5, July 12, 1963; Najar to the Ministry of Foreign Affairs, ISA, FM, file 1960/5, July 16, 1963. Rey believed that following the reductions in the Israeli demands, there was a realistic framework for progress. This was expressed in his promise that he would relate to the entire Israeli proposal as one bloc in his speech to the European Parliament.

38 Note á l'attention de M. Millet, AUE, BAC 3/1978-325, August 8, 1963.

39 The Israelis, who received a copy of the document covertly, worked to change it. In September Sapir, who had in the meantime been appointed as Finance Minister, met with Rey and rebuked him for the EEC's position. Rey justified himself, blaming The Six: "To our great sorrow, many of the promises that you receive in one capital or another are not reflected in the discussions that take place in the Council of Ministers," he said. "The duplicitous behavior by the governments of The Six is liable to cause the erroneous impression that the Commission is delaying matters and preventing a solution," he added. He revealed to Sapir that at the meeting of the Commission leadership, all the members stated that they had no opposition to a comprehensive agreement with Israel (either association or a customs union), if the Council of Ministers would authorize it. See: Najar to the Ministry of Foreign Affairs, ISA, FM, file 1960/7, September 23, 1963.

40 Roussel to Rey, AUE, BAC 3/1978-325, October 7, 1963.

41 Surprisingly, the Germans pressured to postpone the discussion. Following this, Sapir insisted that Shinnar complain to the authorities in Bonn: "[A]gain we encounter the fact that the words of the people you talk with are one thing and the officials act in a completely different manner . . . it is not possible that the German delegation appears in Brussels without clear instructions coordinated between the German financial ministries" (Sapir to Shinnar, ISA, FM, file 1960/3, October 29, 1963). It seems that the reason for the delay was the Germans' desire to advance their new proposal, as outlined above.

42 Najar heard this from Rey himself. See: Najar to the Ministry of Foreign Affairs, ISA, FM, file 1960/3, October 31, 1963.

43 Sapir to Najar, ISA, FM, file 1960/2, November 22, 1963.

44 Sapir to Shinnar, ISA, FM, file 1960/2, November 21, 1963.

45 Najar to Hallstein, AUE, BAC 17/1969-16, July 16, 1963.

46 Telegram, AMAE, DE-CE-1469, September 27, 1963.

47 Hallstein to Najar, AUE, BAC 17/1969-16, October 1, 1963.

48 Davar, "Principle Agreement for Training African Experts in Israel," October 16, 1963. This publication embarrassed the Commission because, according to accepted practice, only the Council of Ministers was authorized to approve it. Therefore, the Commission was forced to deny that a final agreement had been reached on the matter; a decision had been made only to conduct talks. See: Economic Department to Israel's representatives in the capitals of The Six, ISA, FM, file 23/12, October 20, 1963.

49 Ziv to the Economic Department, ISA, FM, file 23/12, October 20, 1963.

50 Alon's testimony to the Knesset Foreign Affairs and Defense Committee, ISA, Knesset, file 8160/9, December 22, 1964.

51 AUE, BAC 3/1978- 325/2, December 1964.

52 Rey's report to Najar regarding this matter. See: Najar to Levavi, ISA, FM, file 1960/1, December 20, 1963.

53 At least this is how the Israelis interpreted matters. See: Najar to Levavi, ISA, FM, file 1960/1.

54 Davar, "In Six Months the Agreement between Israel and the EEC Will Be Concluded," Davar, December 30, 1963.

55 Davar, "Rey: The Final Stage of the Negotiations with Israel in March," Davar, January 5, 1964.

56 *Davar*, "Rey: My Visit in Israel Strengthened My Conviction of the Urgency of an Agreement with That Country," *Davar*, January 2, 1964.
57 Wyn Grant, "Policy Instruments in the Common Agricultural Policy," *West European Politics* 33, no. 1 (2010).
58 European Parliament Report, BAC 8/1973-12, March 28, 1965.
59 Alon's testimony to the Knesset Foreign Affairs and Defense Committee, ISA, Knesset, file 8160/9, December 22, 1964.
60 Dr. Guenther Harkort to Bonn, FFOPA, file B36 111-02, January 10, 1964.
61 Even before the meeting, he sent a letter to Hallstein requesting amendments in the Commission's proposal on a number of points so that it would accord with Israeli expectations. See the translation of the letter given to the Israeli Ministry of Foreign Affairs, apparently by Rey himself: ISA, FM, file 3146/5, January 15, 1964.
62 Note a l'attention de M. le minister Rey, AUE, BAC 3/1978-325/2, January 31, 1964; Note introductive: Relations entre la Communauté et Israël, February 3, 1964.
63 Relation entre la Communauté et Israël, AUE, CM2-1964-6, February 3–5, 1964.
64 The EEC members were concerned that impoverished and uneducated Italian workers from the south would vote en masse for the Communist Party, a trend that was already in evidence. See: Karl-Heinz Narjes, "Walter Hallstein and the Early Phase of the EEC," in *Walter Hallstein: The Forgotten European?*, eds. Wilfried Loth, William Wallace and Wolfgang Wessels (Springer, 1998).
65 Concurrently Sapir flew to Bonn, to convince the Germans to press their French and Italian partners on the matter. He informed his hosts without embellishments that "more than any other country, we expect Germany to support Israel due to moral considerations." Golan to Levavi, ISA, FM, file 1046/20, February 19, 1964.
66 In 1962, the ratio of export/import between Israel and France was 6:1 in favor of the latter.
67 "Due to the relations between France and Israel, I attribute importance to the success of the negotiations and, at any rate, if they are to fail, the blame should not fall on us. It is necessary to note that Israel is an excellent client for France and you know, of course, the importance of Israeli ship orders for our dockyards. Therefore, I recommend viewing positively the Commission's proposal": Wörmser to the Minister of Industry, AMAE, DE-Ce-1469, November 22, 1963.
68 Note: Israël et le C.E.E, AMAE, DE-CE-1470, March 5, 1964.
69 Maruz to the Head of the West Europe section in the Ministry of Foreign Affairs, ISA, FM, file 3589/6, February 10, 1964.
70 However, this impressive Italian economic growth was no different to that experienced by other European states at the time, a part of the period, lasting until 1973, during which European countries experienced exceptional growth resulting from the rehabilitation of their economies after the Second World War, the Marshall Plan and the success of the Bretton Woods Agreement. See: Nicholas Francis Robert Crafts, "The Golden Age of Economic Growth in Western Europe, 1950–1973," *The Economic History Review* 48, no. 3 (1995); "Long-Term Growth in Europe: What Difference Does the Crisis Make?," *National Institute Economic Review* 224, no. 1 (2013).
71 Walter Laqueur, *Europe since Hitler* (London: Weidenfeld and Nicolson, 1970), 172.
72 Ministry of Foreign Affairs Memorandum, "The Challenge to Center-Left Control in Italy", ISA, FM, file 218/9, July 17, 1964.
73 Embassy in Rome to Levavi, ISA, FM, file 3146/5, February 5, 7 and 10, 1964.
74 Fritz Wilhelm Scharpf, "The Joint-Decision Trap: Lessons from German Federalism and European Integration," *Public Administration* 66 (1988); George Tsebelis, "Decision Making in Political Systems: Veto Players in Presidentialism, Parliamentarism, Multicameralism and Multipartyism," *British Journal of Political Science* 25, no. 3 (1995).
75 AUE, CM2-1964-13, February 24–25, 1964.
76 See Golda Meir's testimony to the government: ISA, PM, March 15, 1964.

77 Protocol of the Knesset Foreign Affairs and Defense Committee: ISA, Knesset, July 16, 1964. On the same occasion, Sapir mocked Knesset Member David Lifshitz and Moshe Bartur for clinging to the "all or nothing" approach, even though he too had followed this line until recently.
78 Protocol of the meeting regarding negotiations with the Common Market, ISA, FM, file 1960/3, October 21, 1963.
79 Manor to Alon, ISA, FM, file 23/12, October 24, 1963.
80 Najar to Levavi, ISA, FM, file 1960/1, December 25, 1963.
81 Eytan to Levavi, ISA, FM, file 3147/3, January 28, 1964.
82 Meir to the Knesset Foreign Affairs and Defense Committee, ISA, Knesset, file 8160/5, March 17, 1964.
83 Meir to the Knesset Foreign Affairs and Defense Committee, ISA, Knesset, file 8160/5, February 18, 1964.
84 Golan to Levavi, ISA, FM, file 3146/5, February 19, 1964.
85 Eshkol to Erhard, PM, file 6354/5, March 15, 1964.
86 *Davar*, "Hallstein to Meir: The Commission Wishes a Solution Which Will Solve Israel's Problems," *Davar*, March 10, 1964.
87 Intervention de M. Hebst, AUE, BAC 3/1978 325/2, March 19, 1964.
88 Najar to Levavi, ISA, FM, file 3147/5, March 20, 1964.
89 Regarding the discussions of these matters, see: Deputy head of the delegation to Alon, ISA, FM, file 3147/6, March 21, 1964; Doron to Levavi, ISA, FM, file 3147/6, April 10, 1964; Doron to Rozen, ISA, FM, file 3147, April 4, 1964.
90 *Davar*, "The Agreement with the EEC Will Be Signed," *Davar*, April 27 1964.
91 *Davar*, "The Agreement Will Be Signed in Brussels on May 6," *Davar*, April 29 1964.
92 Communication à la presse, EA, BAC-326, June 4, 1964
93 *Davar*, Editorial, "Again at the Gates of the Common Market," *Davar*, October 9, 1969.
94 Technically, Iran was the first. However, in this case the agreement was exceedingly limited. Likewise, significantly the agreement with Iran was a direct result of the desire that the first such agreement be concluded with a country other than Israel.

References

Abhyankar, Rajendra M. "India and the European Union: A Partnership for All Reasons." *India Quarterly* 65, no. 4 (2009): 393–404.
Cnaan, Yosef. "We Are Treading Water in the British Citrus Market." *Davar*, June 19, 1963.
Crafts, Nicholas Francis Robert. "The Golden Age of Economic Growth in Western Europe, 1950–1973." *The Economic History Review* 48, no. 3 (1995): 429–47.
———. "Long-Term Growth in Europe: What Difference Does the Crisis Make?". *National Institute Economic Review* 224, no. 1 (2013): R14–R28.
Davar. "The Agreement Will Be Signed in Brussels on May 6." *Davar*, April 29, 1964.
———. "The Agreement with the EEC Will Be Signed." *Davar*, April 27, 1964.
———. "Ambiguity During the Technical Debate with the Market." *Davar*, October 30, 1963.
———. Editorial. "Again at the Gates of the Common Market." *Davar*, October 9, 1969.
———. "Hallstein to Meir: The Commission Wishes a Solution Which Will Solve Israel's Problems." *Davar*, March 10, 1964.
———. "In Six Months the Agreement between Israel and the EEC Will Be Concluded." *Davar*, December 30, 1963.
———. "Interview with Israel Gal-Ed." *Davar*, September 18, 1963.

————. "Principle Agreement for Training African Experts in Israel," October 16, 1963.

————. "Rey: My Visit in Israel Strengthened My Conviction of the Urgency of an Agreement with That Country." *Davar*, January 2, 1964.

————. "Rey: The Final Stage of the Negotiations with Israel in March." *Davar*, January 5, 1964.

Goddeeris, Idesbald. "EU-India Relations." 1–6. Leuven: Leuven Centre for Global Governance Studies, 2011.

Grant, Wyn. "Policy Instruments in the Common Agricultural Policy." *West European Politics* 33, no. 1 (2010): 22–38.

Laqueur, Walter. *Europe since Hitler*. London: Weidenfeld and Nicolson, 1970.

Luciani, Ada. "Mansholt Plan Attracts Italian Farmers." *Ma'ariv*, December 23, 1963.

Martines, Francesca. "Foreign Commercial Policy," in *Italy and EC Membership Evaluated*, edited by Francesco Francioni, 158–75. New York: St. Martin's, 1992.

Narjes, Karl-Heinz. "Walter Hallstein and the Early Phase of the EEC." In *Walter Hallstein: The Forgotten European?*, edited by Wilfried Loth, William Wallace and Wolfgang Wessels, 109–30. Springer, 1998.

Scharpf, Fritz Wilhelm. "The Joint-Decision Trap: Lessons from German Federalism and European Integration." *Public Administration* 66 (1988): 239–78.

Shafir, Shlomo. *Outstretched Hand: German Social Democrats and Their Attitudes Towards Jews and Israel, 1945–1967*. Tel Aviv: Zemora Bitan, 1987.

Tsebelis, George. "Decision Making in Political Systems: Veto Players in Presidentialism, Parliamentarism, Multicameralism and Multipartyism." *British Journal of Political Science* 25, no. 3 (1995): 289–325.

9 Israel's return to association

The signing of the agreement with the EEC in June 1964 did not put an end to the Israeli debate over strategy, although the new reality it created brought about a certain change in its form. Some of the Israelis, such as Foreign Minister Golda Meir and diplomats serving in the EEC countries (first and foremost Najar)—as well as senior officials in other ministries such as Gal-Ed, Deputy Director General of the Ministry of Industry and Trade—were optimistic that the agreement could be broadened by convening the follow-up committee. Others, including Finance Minister and Minister of Trade and Industry Pinchas Sapir and Moshe Bartur, remained skeptical, viewing the agreement mainly as leverage to request association in the future. From their perspective, its main role was to prove beyond any doubt that the agreement was incapable of protecting Israel's exports and therefore a more comprehensive solution was necessary.

Thus unsurprisingly, Israel's policy following the summer of 1964 was of a dual nature. Some Israelis focused all their energy on negotiations with the EEC officials to broaden the content of the agreement in the framework of the follow-up committee, while others were engaged in laying the foundations of the reasoning behind a future Israeli request for association. In the first stage, however, both groups understood that they must do their utmost to exploit Israel's "minimal interests" in the short and intermediate terms: protecting Israel's orange exports and receiving tariff reductions for the "European product." Attempts to obtain these two goals tested the effectiveness of the pragmatic approach, which favored utilizing the possibilities offered by the existing agreement.

Orange exports and the "European product"

The issue of orange exports to the EEC was the most pressing matter. This was and remained Israel's central export sector to the EEC; in the mid-1960s, oranges accounted for around 25% of Israeli exports and approximately 73% of agricultural exports.[1] A detailed analysis reveals that in 1964 Israeli orange exports to The Six declined sharply relative to the preceding year: $12.4 million as opposed to $24.7 million in 1963.[2] However the main, and perhaps sole, reason for this drop in exports was the wave of cold weather that gripped Europe in 1963, severely damaging orange exports from Spain and Italy. This led to a rise in Israeli exports in 1963, filling the vacuum left by the Spanish and Italians, and therefore the decline in 1964 was not indicative of a long-term trend. The Israelis were well aware of this fact, but it did not prevent them from presenting the sharp decline as additional evidence of the agreement's ineffectiveness.

In contrast to how the Israelis presented the issue of orange exports, their true fears concerned the future rather than the present. On January 1, 1965, the second stage of the CAP was scheduled to begin, reducing tariffs on agricultural products within the Community to the level of 50% in 1957 terms (and 30% on industrial products).[3] This stage included fruit and vegetables, according the Italian orange an advantage over its competitors. However, this advantage was not sufficient to close the gap in price and quality with more effective competitors, among them the Israelis' fruit and therefore was not the only protective measure which would be implemented in the framework of the CAP. Indeed, the Italians demanded an additional step—determining minimum threshold prices (reference prices) which would require all orange vendors to sell the fruit above a certain price, set according to that of the Italian product. Anyone selling under this price would incur a special levy at the rate of the difference between the selling price and the threshold price. As a result, orange sellers necessarily priced the fruit according to the cost of the Italian product *and added to this price* the necessary tariff, guaranteeing Italian orange growers an advantage over their competitors.

The levy threatened the profits of third-country exporters selling citrus fruits to the EEC because it would ultimately eliminate between a third and a half of the exporter's profit.[4] Concurrently, negotiations with Israel's main competitors in the field of orange exports to the EEC were progressing: Spain on the one hand, and the Maghreb countries on the other.[5] The Israelis presumed that sooner or later both would be included within the area that enjoyed tariff benefits.[6] It is no coincidence that Spain's association with the EEC, and the likely consequences of this for Israel's orange exports, was one of the central topics raised by Prime Minister Levi Eshkol in talks with Pompidou and Couve de Murville on his visit to Paris in 1964.[7] In March 1965, Golda Meir spoke at length with Couve de Murville concerning this issue, extracting from him a vague promise that in the case of progress in association negotiations with Mediterranean orange-exporting countries, France would acknowledge the severity of Israel's situation.[8]

These difficulties compounded internal complications within the Israeli citrus sector. In the second half of the 1960s, Israeli citrus groves were experiencing distress due to an erosion of income by increased production costs—the price of water, transportation expenses and workers' salaries—while proceeds for every dunam of crop had remained the same for five years.[9] The Citrus Marketing Board was a useful tool for marketing oranges in foreign markets—its annual foreign budget reached 7 million Israeli pounds—yet its involvement in the local market was only marginal because within Israel it encountered numerous mediating elements which raised the price of the fruit and impaired sales.[10] Many citrus growers began to leave the sector, while many others were considering taking this step. The Israeli government was under severe pressure to help the sector, which appeared to be in the process of collapse. Certainly, broadening the export possibilities to Europe appeared a possible solution for the distress.

The second issue on which the Israelis hoped to obtain benefits in the framework of discussions in the follow-up committee was the "European product"—those industrial products based on raw materials or intermediate goods originally imported from EEC countries. The economic value of these products was modest in relation to the issue of orange exports. Israel exported $104 million worth of goods to the EEC during 1964, of which $31 million were industrial products; only $4 million fell into the category of the "European product." However, the Finance Ministry estimated that in coming years the volume of products in this category would grow significantly; according to estimations, by 1967 it would amount to $14 million.[11] Furthermore, the importance of this issue was not restricted to the value of the goods in this category. No less significantly, The Six constituted 30–40% of the market for these products and presumably Israeli exporters would find it difficult to locate alternative markets. Finally, acquiring benefits from the EEC on this issue would indicate that Israel was the first recipient of a preferential arrangement; certainly, no other nation enjoyed a similar privilege. The Israelis viewed such an agreement as the only solution to Israel's trade problems and therefore discerned that it would serve as an important precedent.

Similarly to the orange issue, Italy mounted the greatest opposition to Israel's requests with regard to the "European product". Therefore, in the final months of 1964, the Israelis focused their efforts on changing Italy's position, investing significant resources in their efforts. The Israelis imagined Italy as a fortress: conquering it would ease their entry into the EEC. In conversations with the Israeli Ambassador in Rome in 1964, the Italians complained that Israel continued to demand and request without offering anything in return. The Israelis noted these grievances. For years, the Embassy in Rome had been complaining to its superiors in the Israeli Ministry of Foreign Affairs about the failure to take the initiative and act with the necessary fervor to win over the hearts, or at least the pockets, of those sectors opposing trade gestures towards Israel. However, at this stage, decision makers in Jerusalem became more attentive, deciding to concentrate efforts on increasing purchases from Italy in return for that government's agreement to moderate its opposition in Community institutions. Consequently, regular trade talks were scheduled between representatives of the two nations. Indeed, this was a commonly used framework and Israeli representatives had for many years conducted talks of this kind with France, the Benelux countries, Finland and Norway.

However, the talks with the Italians were exceptional, as is evident from the manner in which the bargaining was managed. During the first round of talks in Jerusalem in December 1964, the Israeli representatives implored their guests to agree to cooperation, promising Italian citrus growers aid "in advertising, distribution, marketing, market analysis, industrial implementations, scientific and technical research, product improvement, reducing production costs and more." To this end, the Israelis proposed, they would establish an Italian-Israeli working group. Likewise, Israel promised that it would endeavor to increase imports from Italy, raising the entire sum of purchases—which then stood at $20 million per annum—to $60–80 million. Finally, the Israelis guaranteed that a project to lay communication cables on the floor of the Mediterranean Sea, a tender for which a number of European companies were bidding, would be given to the Italians.[12] In return, the Israelis asked Italy to soften its position on the issue of the "European product" and agree in principle that Israeli oranges would enjoy the same export conditions in the EEC as fruits from the Maghreb countries or Spain.[13] The Italians were unenthusiastic and unwilling to make promises, although the Israeli representatives concluded that "they did not take the idea so badly."[14]

The Israelis continued to court the Italians in the coming months. In January 1965, Finance Minister Sapir flew to Europe for an additional round of persuasion; it was no coincidence that his first stop was Rome. Sapir met with all the high-ranking officials in the Italian government responsible for EEC matters: the Finance Minister, Foreign Minister, Minister of Trade and Industry and Minister of Agriculture. The main topic of these talks was Israel's willingness to increase purchases from Italy substantially, thus "buying" its vote in Community institutions.[15] In March 1965, an Israeli delegation arrived in Rome to continue the trade negotiations. This time the delegation included representatives of the Citrus Marketing Board, with the aim of advancing a concrete arrangement. The Israelis offered a very generous package: they promised to place their trade, technical and management experience at the disposal of the Italians, facilitating joint activities in citrus production (cultivation systems, orchard planning, irrigation, pest control, reducing production costs, upgrading harvesting processes, treatment of the fruit and its dispatch) and trade (market analysis, cultivating new markets, trade research, cooperation between marketing organizations, coordinated advertising, professional organization, development of factories and treatment of citrus fruits or by-products). In return, the Israelis once again requested that their oranges receive the same benefits in the EEC as those from other countries—that is, Spain and the Maghreb countries. Furthermore, they asked that the Italians withdraw their demand to establish a threshold price for oranges and search instead for a different solution. However, the fat carrots which the Israelis offered failed to elicit the desired response from the Italians: the latter completely rejected the second Israeli request and expressed only loose agreement to the former.[16]

In parallel to using the direct diplomatic channel, the Israelis also sought to apply pressure by recruiting domestic political support in Italy. Representatives of the trade unions were in close contact with representatives of Italian unions, seeking to dispel their opposition to trade gestures in favor of Israel.[17] The Israelis estimated that their attractive proposals had succeeded in bringing about a change in the Italian attitude. When Gal-Ed met with Wörmser in Paris to discuss renewed French support for the "European product," the Israeli bureaucrat revealed that "although the Italians were the ones to block the path to including this in the trade agreement, Israel has good reason to believe that they have recently changed their minds in this regard."[18]

The meeting of the follow-up committee: Israel abandons the pragmatic approach

Israeli optimism concerning ostensible "understandings" between Jerusalem and Rome was highly exaggerated. During the EEC delegation's preliminary discussions prior to the meeting of the follow-up committee, Italian represent-atives demanded insistently that the committee avoid making any promises to Israel or conducting concrete negotiations. The committee was to be sat-isfied with listening to Israel's requests and passing them on the Council of Ministers; only the latter had the right to approve them.[19] Indeed, when the committee first met in mid-April 1965 to discuss the Israeli requests, the EEC delegation was unwilling to negotiate.[20] Even trivial Israeli requests of meager economic significance were rejected outright: for example, the Israeli appeal that tariff reductions given to nylon socks be expanded to include stretch sock leggings—a highly similar product made from the same raw materials.[21] The obstinacy of EEC officials in interpreting the trade agreement ruled out any possibility that Israel would be able to broaden it to suit the development of Israeli industry.

Many Israelis, principally those who had argued that the framework created by the trade agreement could satisfy Israel's needs, were angered by this develop-ment. The frustration was evident when, around two weeks after the conclusion of the talks, Najar complained to Herbst that the EEC delegation had not been granted the necessary authority to conduct effective negotiations, adding that he viewed this as an explicit deviation from the agreement of June 1964. Yet at the same time, as a supporter of the pragmatic approach, Najar wanted to cool tempers in Jerusalem and therefore noted in his report that "according to the concepts of the Community, the discussions conducted in the framework of the follow-up committee are in fact considered much more serious, broad and effective than expected."[22] However, these words did not lessen the serious blow suffered by the pragmatic approach; from this point onwards, the scales began to tip in favor of the proponents of association.

This group was encouraged by a number of concurrent developments: in January 1965, German Finance Minister Kurt Schmücker repeated the declara-tion made by Erhard two years previously, according to which Israel deserved an association agreement and Germany would support such a request. This declaration was made on the background of the decision to establish diplo-matic relations between Germany and Israel, as occurred in May of the same year. At the end of March 1965, the European Parliament passed a resolution recommending to the Council of Ministers that Israel be granted association with the EEC and, until this was realized, that the Council support all steps developing relations with Israel. This was the first time that a Community institution had explicitly and officially ruled in support of Israeli association. It was not especially surprising: for many years, the European Parliament had been the Community institution most supportive of Israel, perhaps because its members enjoyed no real authority and were therefore able to express freely their feelings of support toward the Jewish state. A European parliamentary delegation visited Israel at the beginning of 1965 and submitted an enthusiastic report that served as the basis for the Parliament's decision. The decision was also aided by the visit of a Knesset delegation in March 1965, the members of which garnered support among their European counterparts.[23] The Israelis were under no illusions concerning the practical weight of this decision; indeed, they understood that the institutional power of the Parliament was highly limited. However, they regarded it as a positive sign for the future. The fact that the European Parliament's decision concerned and even worried the officials in the Commission and COREPER perhaps reveals that matters were somewhat complicated. At any rate, the Parliament's decision encouraged and motivated those in Israel who believed that association was a realistic goal.

By contrast, this turn of events placed the supporters of the pragmatic approach in a defensive position, leading Najar to declare that

> we must exploit the existing agreement as though there is no chance of achieving association in the near future and at the same time we must continue our battle for association and utilize the Parliamentary decision without regarding ourselves as limited by the existing trade agreement.[24]

In a special interview with Najar and his deputy Itzhak Minerbi in Davar, the two diplomats fervently defended the agreement of June 1964, arguing that it constituted a historic breakthrough: the beginning of a new age in Israel's relations with the EEC.[25] However, considering the stalemate in the campaign to widen the trade agreement, the belief that limited arrangements were no longer relevant gained weight in Jerusalem and many deemed it necessary to return to the original aim of association, preparing the ground for this change in direction. In the Knesset, Minister Meir was attacked for not persisting with the demand for association. Her apologetic response revealed the waning potency of the political line that had guided Israeli decision makers until now.

However, some remained convinced that the Community institutions could be convinced to accept the minimal Israeli requests within the framework of the existing agreement, and they attempted to persuade others in this regard. In July, Gal-Ed reported on positive progress concerning Israel's interests with various Community institutions, mainly regarding the "European product." In his opinion, should the Council of Ministers eventually accept these arrangements, this would be a significant achievement.[26] A few weeks later, Gal-Ed attempted to persuade Finance Minister Sapir and the new Minister of Industry and Trade Chayim Tzadok that it was still too early to bury the trade agreement:

> The benefits which were given until now and which are currently being offered by the Community institutions remove the danger which was threatening Israeli exports . . . also on the agricultural side we tend, in my view, to exaggerate the extent of the problem, as well as its danger.

However, in the spirit of the period, he also added, "[A]ll this does not contradict the request for a comprehensive agreement with the Market, which will remove at once all the obstacles, with respect to both industry and agriculture."[27]

Yet it was generally concluded that the trial period allocated to the limited agreement had ended in failure. The Deputy Director of the Ministry of Foreign Affairs, Ram Nirgad, who had in the past been an enthusiastic advocate of the pragmatic approach, now adamantly disputed it.[28] Similarly to other former supporters of this path, he began to depict it as a well-planned, crafty stage, preparing the ground for Israel to submit a renewed request for association.[29] Najar also tended to interpret the trade agreement as a tactical step en route to association:

> The main importance of the June 1964 agreement lay in anchoring among many important European circles the idea that Europe is indeed responsible for Israel's economic future, an idea that was strange to the Europeans before it finally put down roots.[30]

In the summer of 1964, many had been pleased to highlight their involvement in concluding the trade agreement, which seemed to constitute a significant achievement; now they divested themselves of it. This was Bartur's moment of grace: from Geneva, he dispatched a series of letters to senior ministers stating that his approach had been vindicated. This was done without the prior knowledge of officials at Ministry of Foreign Affairs and did not earn him favor among his superiors.[31]

Officials, such as Najar and Nirgad—who believed that in signing the agreement in June 1964, the EEC had recognized Israel's future expectations to broaden it and had presumed that this was merely a first stage on the way to a more comprehensive agreement—now felt themselves deceived. The mounting bitterness among Israeli officials was expressed at a meeting of the inter-ministerial committee for Common Market affairs. For the first time, some suggested taking trade measures against EEC countries in retaliation for the damage sustained by Israel. The participants agreed that pleading had proved ineffective and, as the experience of other countries revealed, The Six understood only the language of force. Yet Israel's ability to pressure the EEC countries was limited, making it essential to search for potential allies—within the EEC or outside it.

Surprisingly, France emerged as one of these allies. In November 1964, Minister of Trade and Industry Tzadok flew to Europe as part of the campaign against the oranges levy. In Paris, Foreign Minister Couve de Murville expressed a sympathetic stance, even freeing time for an unplanned conversation during the busy election period. In those same days, a bitter battle was under way between the French government and the European Commission. France viewed the latter as acting of its own accord to speed up the process of integration and in so doing exceeding the bounds of its authority.[32] Since July 1965, France had boycotted the Community institutions in what came to be known as the "empty chair crisis" (see below). The Commission supported—more on principle than for material reasons—Italy's right to force the EEC to adopt the orange levy, and therefore the French government decided to oppose this adamantly. Couve de Murville promised Tzadok that France would do everything in its power to thwart the levy from behind the scenes and guaranteed France's refusal to enforce it. This statement was of meager significance in practical terms for Israel, because the volume of orange exports to France was extremely small, but Tzadok appreciated the symbolic aspect of the gesture.[33]

More serious was the Israeli attempt to establish an alliance between the countries that exported oranges to Europe. This was not the first attempt to coordinate policy with other citrus-exporting countries. In 1950, the Comité de Liaison de l'Agrumiculture Méditerranéenne (CLAM)[34] was established with the aim of coordinating and advancing the export of citrus fruits to Europe from countries in the region. The Arab countries at first participated in this endeavor, but soon left because of Israel's membership. The body established four committees to cover various aspects: a professional agro-technological committee, a trade-economic committee, an industrial committee and a committee for advertising and statistics. These dealt with pesticides, searched for solutions to technical problems and sought to improve new species. The Israeli Tzvi Izakson, who was President of the Farmers' Union in Israel, even served as president of the body and achieved great popularity.[35] At the end of 1965, Israel acted within the framework of this body to consolidate a united front for the battle against the orange levy.

Simultaneously, the Israelis decided to reach out to Spain, whose orange exports would also be harmed by the EEC's protectionist policy, investigating whether a basis for cooperation and coordination between the countries existed in the campaign against the EEC.[36] Spain's request for association with the EEC was at a standstill due to the opposition of the Netherlands and Belgium (for political reasons) and Italy (due to economic considerations).[37] The Spanish and Israeli economies had similar characteristics and the countries were concerned with comparable problems. Spain was at the peak of a process of hastened economic development, but its economy was still developing. As in Israel, agriculture accounted for a significant portion of the Spanish economy (27% in 1962), although this was in steady decline. It suffered from a negative trade balance following the need to import capital, and without its teeming tourist industry—around 15 million tourists visited the country annually—Spain would have been unable to maintain equilibrium in its balance of payments. Likewise, Spain was dependent on the EEC no less than Israel: 38% of its imports and 37% of its exports were with The Six.[38] Finally, the Spanish, like the Israelis, were troubled by the probable ramifications of the orange levy for their future exports to the EEC.

Thus, a possible opportunity for Spanish-Israeli cooperation had emerged. The agricultural advisor at Israel's Embassy in Brussels contacted the Spanish economic advisor, suggesting this possibility. Upon receiving a positive response, Gal-Ed and Shalush met with the director of the section for international institutions at the Spanish Foreign Ministry, who was then attending an OECD conference in Paris. The two discussed an aid plan for orange growers in their nations, as well as the Maghreb countries, and the establishment of a joint information center in Brussels that would register the price of oranges imported to the EEC and alert the various delegations when the threshold price levy was liable to be implemented. The Spanish also promised to invite the Maghreb countries to join this initiative.[39] Indeed, Morocco joined the Israeli-Spanish battle, thus establishing a trade-based alliance between countries with no political relations (Spain because of Franco's regime and the Maghreb due to the Arab–Israeli conflict) which was motivated by the common EEC threat. At the end of 1965, Israeli-Spanish cooperation further intensified, exemplified by the parallel declaration by both governments threatening sanctions in retaliation for a failure to abandon the levy on oranges. Specifically, Israel threatened to cancel a purchasing order for ships from EEC countries' shipyards, whereas Spain threatened to stop purchasing cars made by The Six.[40] The Israeli-Spanish-Moroccan pressure bore fruit: in December 1965, the Commission decided to alter its earlier decision—reached under Italian pressure—and place the threshold levy at the level of $13.10 per ton of produce, instead of $15.50, as had previously been determined, thus significantly reducing the effectiveness of this protectionist measure.[41]

The Israeli-Spanish-Moroccan cooperation was particularly exceptional as an instance of Arab cooperation with Israel, especially considering the Arab boycott and the Arab states' desire to enforce this in Europe. Indeed, this cooperation is indicative of the importance accorded to the battle against the threshold levy, both in terms of its use in the framework of the CAP and its effects on other countries. At the same time, it reveals that the parallel channels Israel used to obtain its goals were at times contradictory. In May 1966, the Spanish Ambassador in Rome warned his Israeli counterpart that Israel's cooperation with citrus growers in Sicily constituted an act of disloyalty towards Spain.[42] Israel's campaign, both with the Spanish and alone, against the regime of orange threshold prices also angered the Italians, who viewed this as insolent and bore a grudge against Israel for the reduction of the levy.[43]

Israel returns to the association solution

In the fall of 1965, a broad consensus had already emerged among decision makers that Israel must once again seek association with the EEC, a goal it had been forced to abandon at the beginning of 1962. The disagreement that had waged for so long—between supporters of the pragmatic approach who preached taking the easiest, albeit very narrow, path, and those who believed that Israel must not deviate from the main route and persist in its demands for association—ended. How was it possible that a line of action which in the past had yielded such complete failure, now suddenly merited a renewal and became broadly accepted policy? The answer is two-fold.

First, it became evident that the Israelis had erred in sacrificing the content of the agreement in the first stage—compromising on what constituted the most important aspects in economic terms—for the sake of an institutional framework which could later be widened. At the time, the Commission leadership had expended a great deal of energy in persuading the Israelis that the follow-up committee monitoring the agreement would facilitate its future expansion, convincing the Israelis that this committee was the agreement's most meaningful achievement. However, the meager accomplishments at the first meeting of the committee revealed that, predictably, it was unable to fulfill the role the Israelis sought to accord it. From the moment that the Council of Ministers decided in principle to establish the follow-up committee (fall 1962), The Six had been on guard to prevent its use as a tool to broaden or deepen the agreement. It was granted very limited authority, making it little more than a conduit to transfer Israel's requests to decision makers, and its recommendations merited almost no consideration. When the committee's suggestions were presented to the Council's working group for trade affairs in September 1965, the latter opposed every item; the only issue it was approved was a 20% reduction on grapefruit segments.[44] Again the Italians played a major part in ensuring the failure of the various proposals. The disappointment at this development had a further ramification: it significantly weakened proponents of the pragmatic route, many of whom now changed track and joined the camp demanding a maximum approach.

An additional factor motivating the return to the association alternative is of vast importance in understanding how a number of decision makers and bureaucrats perceived Israeli strategy. This group attributed a single goal to the trade agreement: its resounding failure. Indeed, such a failure would prepare the ground both within Israel and vis-à-vis the Community institutions for a return to the association option. Members of this faction, as well as large sections of the Israeli public, were captivated by the idea of association: they perceived it not only as the ultimate solution to Israel's economic problems, but also as an important political asset.[45] The political motivation, however, remained concealed; the Israelis never cited it openly in their contacts with The Six. Instead, they justified their request for an association with the argument that only such a framework could protect the Israeli economy from damage by the EEC. The Europeans refused to accept this claim, arguing that the threat to the Israeli economy was not so severe and could be solved within the framework of a regular trade agreement.

However, interestingly, the political echelon of The Six never denied that EEC had an obligation to mitigate any harm which the Common Market might cause to the Israeli economy. Through this equivocal stance, the Europeans placed themselves in an awkward position. Had the Israelis been able to prove beyond any doubt that the trade agreement did not constitute a solution to their problems, this would make the European position uncomfortable. Yet the requirement to provide evidence lay with Israel and, therefore, in the first years of negotiations, the Europeans had easily rejected the Israelis' requests, despite their increasing hysteria. Over time, however, irrefutable proof began to accumulate that, indeed, such damage was occurring, or would so do in the future. The Israelis were highly skilled in collating and organizing the material to emphasize these negative economic impacts. In contrast, the bureaucrats in the Community institutions, who viewed matters from the economic perspective, did not see themselves as obligated in any way to accede to the Israeli requests, which had no legal basis whatsoever. However, by assuming this stance, they contributed to vindicating the Israeli claim that association was necessary. At the end of 1965, many in Israel felt that enough evidence had amassed to refute any argument against the necessity of a comprehensive arrangement. Now was the time to reap the moral capital of the pragmatic policy. Najar summarized matters at the conference of economic attachés held in Brussels in February 1966, at which the Israeli officials resolved to focus their diplomatic efforts on preparing the ground to submit a request for association: "Now we have wiped out all the excuses and no one can say that there is any other path to advance relations, aside from a comprehensive agreement."[46] In April 1966, a "summit meeting" was held in Jerusalem attended by Prime Minister Levi Eshkol, Finance Minister Pinchas Sapir, Foreign Minister Abba Eban, the new Minister of Trade and Industry Chayim Tzadok and Minister of Agriculture Haim Gvati, the Governor of the Bank of Israel, the Directors General of the four financial ministries, and the Israeli Ambassadors in Paris, Bonn, and Brussels; those present decided that Israel would strive for an association agreement, overturning the decision reached four years earlier to abandon this goal in favor of a regular trade agreement.

As a final endeavor before submitting an official request for association, the Israelis focused their full efforts on reinforcing even further the moral capital they had accumulated vis-à-vis The Six and the Community institutions. There are many examples of this, the most obvious being a request for another meeting of the follow-up committee. The Israelis had no illusions about the expected results of such a meeting. Indeed, they had yet to receive an official response to the requests raised at the first meeting, and in the meantime had learned from various sources that the committee's modest proposals had all been rejected, apart from the marginal reduction of 20% on grapefruit segments. Instead of protesting, however, the Israelis were pleased by this development, viewing it as a valuable asset. It proved in an especially tangible way the cessation of the existing trade agreement, adding to the Israeli ammunition in their battle for association. By convening the committee, the Israelis hoped to force the Council officials to reject their requests explicitly, finally signing the death warrant of the trade agreement.[47] The Israelis were no longer worried that their requests would be rejected, but rather were concerned about the opposite: that the committee would suddenly decide to reveal a certain degree of generosity and in so doing detract from the dramatic effect they wished to create. To avoid this, the Israeli delegation to the talks received clear instructions not to reiterate the Israeli requests of the previous year, but rather to limit themselves to complaining that these had yet to be accepted.

A further source of concern for the Israelis was the awkward fact that exports to the EEC continued to rise in 1965. This was even the case with respect to orange exports which, as was mentioned earlier, now encountered new protective measures (threshold price). This rise also negated an important Israeli argument against the EEC: as Eban complained to the inter-ministerial committee on Common Market affairs, "The fact is that the more our cries intensify, so our exports increase," adding, "I fear that our reasoning and our argument until now not only failed to persuade the European countries, but there is a lack of factual evidence."[48] Indeed, throughout the negotiations between Israel and the EEC in the preceding decade, the most difficult challenge facing the Israelis had been to prove that their exports were suffering. Given the current economic climate, at this juncture they considered changing the framework of their arguments: instead of emphasizing the threat to the Israeli economy, they should stress the vital role association with Israel was likely to play in advancing peace with the Arab countries.

However, the Israelis had no real reason to fear a sudden softening in the stance of the European bureaucrats. When the follow-up committee met on June 22, 1966, the Community delegation revealed no greater willingness than before to accede to Israel requests. Instead, the discussion evolved into an argument over the extent of damage to Israeli exports following the consolidation of the Common Market. Indeed, the EEC representatives argued that according to the analysis of a broad period, for example, 1958–65, Israeli exports to the EEC were developing satisfactorily.[49] They noted in particular that the export-to-import ratio between Israel and The Six had improved significantly in the preceding year: in 1964, Israel imported goods worth $240 million, while the country's exports totaled $104 million. By contrast, in 1965, these numbers were $201 million and $122 million respectively.[50] The Israeli delegation denied the significance of these figures in identifying the real damage to the Israeli economy resulting from European integration. Through extensive preparations for the talks, experts had worked to provide a range of updated figures.[51] The Israelis, analyzing the trade development since the signing of the trade agreement, demonstrated that Israeli exports to the EEC countries had remained the same while those to the rest of the world grew. The statistics revealed that whereas in the years 1963–65, Israeli exports to the rest of the world rose by 23%, exports to The Six increased by a more modest rate of 14%. There was even a decline with respect to certain products. The real value of the tariff reductions accorded by the trade agreement was miniscule, totaling $680,000, of which $360,000 was on orange exports to France and an additional $240,000 on grapefruit exports to all The Six. The tariff saving on industrial products was a meager $80,000, out of the sum of $4.5 million that Israeli exporters were required to pay.[52] According to the basic Israeli argument, although the total volume of Israeli exports to the EEC had increased, it would have grown far more without the trade barriers erected by the process of integration. While the EEC delegation accepted at least some of the Israeli arguments concerning the damage to Israel's trade with The Six,[53] the issue of orange exports remained at a stalemate, even outside the follow-up committee. The Israeli delegation was engaged in talks with the EEC delegation regarding oranges in the framework of the Kennedy Round of GATT negotiations, but the parties were unable to reach an agreement.[54]

Israel simultaneously made other efforts to prepare the ground for an association application. For example, the Ministry of Agriculture compiled a five-year plan to harmonize Israeli agriculture with that of the Common Market, determining which agricultural sectors would be expanded and which reduced, or even closed, to accord with the needs of the EEC.[55] Differences of opinion persisted regarding whether the Israeli request should include the word "association"; some preferred the tactic of requesting a comprehensive arrangement, such as a free trade agreement. Israeli diplomats had encountered chilly reactions to the idea of returning to the outline of association among their counterparts in the capitals of The Six, and advised avoiding any explicit use of the term "association" in the official Israeli request.[56] However, the political echelon in Jerusalem decided that the word "association" must appear openly in the letter, making it impossible for the Europeans to evade making a clear decision.[57] They estimated that the cards in Israel's hands were stronger than ever before. Similarly, some proposed a distinction between the industrial and agricultural sectors, limiting the request for association to the first alone. This would allow the Italians "to swallow the pill more easily," because they mainly feared competition with their agricultural exports.[58] Yet this suggestion too was rejected because the severe threat to the Israeli orange sector constituted the most persuasive argument in the case for association; willingness to concede on this matter would significantly erode the logic at the basis of the Israeli request.

The Israeli efforts were not in vain. The moral capital Israel had accumulated following the failure of the trade agreement carried a surprising weight in negotiations with the EEC. The Europeans, no less than in the past, viewed association with Israel as a serious threat, both to relations with the Arab countries and the Community's ability to withstand similar demands from other countries beyond their continent. In conversations between Israeli diplomats and Foreign Ministry officials in France and Germany, the latter tried to dissuade the Israelis from returning to the request for association, arguing there was no chance of success. They indicated that Israel would, instead, be able to achieve a preferential agreement, with preferential discrimination for Israeli products, and such a framework would offer a solution for most Israeli exports.[59] This was a true revolution for bureaucrats who, in the first rounds of negotiations between Israel and the EEC (1962–63), refused outright all Israeli proposals for an agreement of a preferential or discriminatory character (apart from the Dutch officials).[60] Significantly, in contrast to the past, the Germans and French avoided repeating the old mantras concerning the virtues of the non-preferential trade agreement or the absence of any real threat to Israeli exports. It seems that the failure of the talks in the framework of the follow-up committee, and the advanced negotiations underway concurrently with the Maghreb countries, invalidated these excuses.

Officials at the German Foreign Ministry found themselves in a particularly sensitive position, considering the open and explicit support voiced by their head of state, Chancellor Erhard. He had backed Israeli association twice while serving as Finance Minister—first in a conversation with Eshkol in February 1962 and again with Sapir one year later, in March 1963. On Moshe Alon's visit to Bonn in January 1965, German Finance Minister Franz-Josef Strauss promised that Israel would receive the same benefits as those granted to the Maghreb countries.[61] In June 1966, the West German Chancellor once again reiterated to the Israeli Ambassador in Bonn his obligation to endorse Israel's request fully upon its submission. On his visit to Israel, the Director General of the German Ministry of Agriculture told them that most German politicians favored Israel's association with the EEC.[62] However, the German Foreign Ministry persistently maintained that Israeli association was unthinkable; the repeated guarantees of the Chancellor constituted a real problem for them. They used a double-edged approach to deal with this challenge. First, they sought to play down the importance of Erhard's words, hinting that decisions on such matters rested with the professional ranks.[63] "The attitude of the senior officials towards the words of the Chancellor was derogatory and even scornful," complained the economic attaché at the Embassy in Bonn; adding with sadness, "although this is not our business, but rather an internal German matter."[64] Second, seeking to tempt the Israelis with something less than association, German Foreign Ministry officials proposed that Germany would actively support attempts to upgrade the limited trade agreement to a broad preferential agreement, tackling the central problems that worried Israel.[65] An Israeli diplomat, who at the time was touring the EEC countries, summarized the atmosphere:

> Although recently the tone used regarding our affairs in the capitals sounds more positive than ever before, we must remember that in no capital did we receive a clear and explicit promise to support association (apart from the conversation between Erhard and Ben Natan). From the political perspective, not one single country is interested in Israel's association with the Community . . . at the same time each one will carefully avoid head-on opposition or creating a situation in which it can be highlighted as sabotaging the positive solution. The concept of association spreads fear among many in the Community. There is no doubt that an effort will be made to manipulate us to agree to talks concerning broadening the trade agreement; Community members are now ready to give benefits that were unthinkable in the past.[66]

The Commission decides in favor of a preferential agreement

The Commission was extremely receptive to the argument regarding the Community's ostensible moral obligation to Israel. During his visit to EEC countries in February 1965, Sapir met with Hallstein, Mansholt and Rey in Brussels. When the Israeli Finance Minister again commented on the need for a comprehensive agreement, the Commissioners informed him that it was still too early to talk about this, promising that the EEC would do its utmost to exhaust the possibilities of the existing agreement.[67] Now it was clear that these promises had not been kept. When Najar approached the Commission's Directorate General for Foreign Relations in May 1966 to request a further convention of the follow-up committee, Rey and his officials clearly recognized that Israel was trying to cultivate the ground to submit an application for association. Not only did Rey and Axel Herbst, Director General of Rey's Directorate, refrain from dissuading Israel from this intention, they even offered advice on how to improve the country's chances. They advised the Israelis to avoid tying their matter to that of the Maghreb countries or Spain because, in so doing, Israel would lose its relative advantages: the special link between Israel and Europe, and also the fact that it was a small state in terms of area and therefore its agriculture could not expand beyond a certain extent (to calm the Italians). Moreover, they emphasized, factors beyond these differences:

> unique to Israel are the extended negotiations conducted for six years with a combination of obstinacy and restraint. The country's request for association appears today a logical result of its shared experiences with the Community and this provides a serious basis for its demand. Indeed, at the end of the day the decision will be political, but we must not belittle more prosaic considerations which have their own weight.[68]

The views of Rey and Herbst accorded completely with the Israeli line: the EEC had a moral obligation to progress towards association. A few days later, Abba Eban met with Rey in Brussels and once again informed him of Israel's intention to request association. Rey announced that should the Israelis raise this demand in the follow-up committee, the committee would necessarily respond that it lacked the authority to deal with the matter. However, Rey added, the committee was important in creating a "guilty conscience" among the Europeans that they had not done enough for Israel; this factor would prepare the way for an association request.[69]

Rey was not the only Commissioner to endorse verbally Israel's renewed association campaign. In April 1965, the Commissioner for Social Affairs, Lionel Levi-Manderi, visited Israel. The Italian Commissioner was of Jewish descent on his father's side, had served as an officer in Mussolini's army in North Africa and, following the Nazi occupation of Italy, commanded anti-German resistance activities. In his conversations in Israel, he expressed his warm feelings towards the country and, despite his cautious wording, he opined that there was no legal obstacle to Israel's association with the EEC.[70] Mansholt, Commissioner for Agricultural Affairs, offered even more resolute backing. Similarly to his colleagues, the Dutch Commissioner believed this accorded with the Commission's agenda; yet even more than his fellow Commissioners, he was motivated by deep feelings of affection for the Jewish state and a desire to help it. On his visit to Israel in October 1964, in an interview published by the newspaper *Davar*, Mansholt did not hesitate to state explicitly that the EEC's failure to sign an association agreement with Israel had been a mistake; in his view, this was the only solution to the country's problems.[71] In a private conversation with Sapir in September 1966, Mansholt freely told him that the EEC's refusal to sign an association agreement with Israel was its greatest political sin in recent years, explaining it as a resulting of over-sensitivity to the Arab reaction. Following the failure of the second meeting of the follow-up committee, Mansholt encouraged the Israelis to submit their request for association as soon as possible; it was vital to do so before the conclusion of an agreement with the Maghreb states because the latter would be able to leverage their influence to impede a positive decision in the Council.[72] On another occasion, he advised Najar that Israel should stubbornly insist on a full association agreement and not be satisfied with broadening the present trade agreement.[73]

Once Israel submitted an official letter requesting negotiations on association according to article 238 of the Treaty of Rome,[74] Rey, Mansholt and Hallstein together endeavored to pass a decision in the Commission advising the Council to begin preliminary talks with Israel, without any limitation on content. When the Italian and French Commissioners opposed this proposal, Rey and Hallstein pressured Robert Marjoline, who finally acquiesced despite his belief that this would be a mistake.[75] At this juncture, the Permanent Representatives understood that the Commission intended to submit a recommendation to the Council of Ministers in favor of initial talks and consequently tried to impose a preliminary stage to study the problems which the Common Market posed to Israeli exports, arguing that this was the accepted procedure. This angered the Israelis, who rightfully presumed that this step was intended to delay the politically uncomfortable decision to begin negotiations with Israeli concerning association. Rey also perceived the situation thus and, together with the Dutch Deputy Foreign Minister, persuaded the meeting of the Council of Ministers at the end of October 1966 to abandon the intermediate stage and proceed directly to preliminary talks.[76]

Indeed, in December 1966, the Commission succeeded in passing a decision in the Council of Ministers according to which

> the Council invites the Commission to begin preliminary talks with Israel which will enable it to present, as soon as possible, a report to the Council concerning all the problems raised by the Israeli government in its letter of October 4, 1966.

None of the representatives of The Six dared oppose the proposal, even though they unanimously and wholly opposed the possibility of talks regarding an association agreement.[77] Likewise, no one disputed the Commission's management of the talks without the active participation of representatives from the countries: this signaled the end of the joint follow-up committee. Yet the Council of Ministers outlined explicitly that "the decision is not obligatory with regards to the form of a possible agreement with Israel."[78] In addition to the supportive stance of the Commission leadership, Commission officials passed on to the Israelis highly confidential documents such as "Recommendations of the Commission for a Trade Agreement with Spain" and "Report on the Progress of Talks with the Maghreb Countries." These documents improved the Israelis' bargaining position, providing them with advance knowledge about what concessions they could extract from the Europeans.[79]

Why did the Commission so enthusiastically endorse a comprehensive arrangement with Israel? These same officials had, in the past, insisted on a non-preferential agreement. However, they had also repeatedly expressed their confidence that the agreement of June 1964 was none other than a first stage on the way to a more meaningful arrangement that would solve Israel's export problems. Moreover, they had hinted that their central role in the follow-up committee would enable them to widen the agreement. These arguments had exerted a marked influence on Israeli decision makers and constituted one of the principal factors in the decision to accept, in the first stage, an agreement with no content. To a certain degree Hallstein, Rey, Mansholt and others in the Commission leadership accordingly felt a moral obligation to the Israelis. In addition, the unwillingness of the follow-up committee to fulfill even the most minor Israeli requests mocked the Commission's promises, reducing its status within the EEC, at least so the Commission perceived the situation. Therefore, support of the new Israeli request for association was motivated by a combination of factors: on the one hand, the Commission's feeling that its status had been eroded, as evidenced by the Israeli case; and on the other hand, the Commission's willingness to play an active role in advancing a new arrangement as penance for past failures in the name of the EEC.

A further factor was the Commission's increasing confidence that it could establish itself as mandated to manage trade negotiations with third-party countries. Indeed, the Commission was concurrently managing talks both with the Maghreb countries and Spain. In this framework it suggested, among other measures, instituting a new import regime for Maghreb citrus fruits within an association agreement; this would decrease the tariff on Maghreb oranges from 20% (the regular tariff rate on the Israeli orange) to only 8%.[80] For a number of months, preliminary talks with Spain had been under way regarding a trade arrangement. In the fall of 1966, the Commission imparted its recommendations to the Council and these accorded almost exactly with its recommendations concerning Israel: the choice between an association agreement or a preferential agreement (in view of the strong opposition to Spanish association, the EEC eventually decided to sign a comprehensive trade agreement with a preferential character).[81] The Commission leadership recognized that these benefits would in all likelihood impair Israeli agricultural exports to the Common Market, further intensifying the feelings of responsibility towards Israel: it seemed only just to grant Israel the same benefits as those accorded to Spain.[82]

Yet most of Israel's supporters in the Commission believed that an association agreement was not practical, given the evident opposition of The Six; indeed, this was revealed unambiguously in dozens of talks between European diplomats and politicians and their Israeli counterparts during the autumn and winter of 1966–67 and deepened further following the angry Arab reaction to the opening of preliminary talks with Israel.[83] Following the Council's decision in favor of negotiations, the economic council of the Arab League asked Arab states to implement immediate steps to prevent the consolidation of an association agreement with Israel. Consequently, during January–February 1967, most Arab countries dispatched letters to all the EEC countries warning that Israel's association with the EEC would have severe ramifications.[84] The Egyptian Ambassador in Brussels even requested a meeting with the President of the

Commission, at which he personally presented the letter from his government and repeated the warnings again verbally.[85]

The Commission was less sensitive than The Six to the danger of collision with the Arab states. However, it did not intend to force a solution that clearly opposed the will of the member states. This principle guided the activities of the Commission and had been further reinforced by the "empty chair crisis" of June 1965. In an effort to halt the Commission's attempts to advance the supra-national element of the EEC—through instituting the principle of majority decisions and giving the Commission and European Parliament economic independence—French President de Gaulle instructed French representatives in the Council that they should not attend its meetings, thus preventing the proper functioning of Community institutions. Following months of paralysis, de Gaulle was victorious: the Luxembourg Compromise determined that the member states retained the right to veto when the issue on the agenda was of particular importance to their national interests. This prevented the Commission's attempts to speed up the process of integration and grant greater weight to the supra-national element. Likewise, it diminished the dynamism and initiative that had characterized the Commission during the first decade of its existence.[86]

The Commission was thus careful to avoid colluding with Israel, as it had in the past, to advance a solution that opposed the will of The Six. Despite the wish to strengthen its status within the EEC, the Commission leadership preferred the pragmatic approach to an oppositional tactic vis-à-vis the member states; accordingly, the agreement with Israel could not be in the form of association but rather a comprehensive preferential arrangement in the same format as that concurrently consolidating with Spain. The member states were more likely to support an arrangement of this nature; indeed, various European statesmen and officials had expressed a positive approach to this idea on numerous occasions. Therefore, at the opening of the preliminary talks between the Israeli delegation and the Commission at the end of January 1967, Commission officials informed the significant Israeli delegation which arrived in Brussels—including no less than the three Directors General of the Finance Ministry, Ministry of Agriculture, and Ministry of Trade and Industry, as well as senior officials from the Ministry of Foreign Affairs—that it was necessary to examine further possibilities of improving the existing trade agreement, aside from the solution of association. The Israelis were warned that their insistence on association would cause delays. As in June 1963, the Israeli delegation faced a dilemma: should it insist on its demands at the price of a lack of progress? Exactly as then, the Israeli delegation passed the decision on to the political echelon. However, this time the decision makers in Jerusalem were not willing to compromise. Eban's orders were unambiguous: "We must not reveal willingness to discuss any option whatsoever other than association . . . I am convinced with all my heart that we must now reveal singular and fervent devotion to this solution."[87]

Indeed, in the talks between the Israeli delegation and the Commission representatives, the former stipulated that Israel would accept no arrangement other than association. When the Commission representatives suggested finding a solution to Israel's problems using the idea of the "European product"—to avoid breaching the principle of a non-preferential agreement—Najar reacted angrily. In the past, the Israelis would have accepted such a suggestion with open arms, but now, believing that they had a real chance of obtaining an association or at least a preferential agreement, they did not intend to sacrifice such an opportunity. The Israeli delegation outlined explicitly that for many years Israel had been prepared to accept a solution to its problems by means of a non-preferential agreement. However, it was now obvious that this path led to a dead end; therefore the only possible solution was association. The Israelis repeatedly employed arguments regarding the historical affinity between Europe and the Jews and the moral debt Europe owed the Jews following centuries of persecution, especially the horrors of the Holocaust. They rejected the arguments voiced by the chair of the Commission's delegation, Herbst, who weakly claimed that despite the emotional dimension, it was necessary to examine the issue on the basis of dry statistics. The Israelis continually emphasized the dangers threatening their country's economy should they be unable to increase their exports to Europe. The Commission delegation tended to accept this interpretation, while noting that the country's small geographical area and limited market did not sufficiently justify its assimilation into the EEC.[88]

Surprisingly, and in complete contrast to the negotiations conducted in the years 1960–64, the Israeli insistence on association not only failed to wreck the talks, it did not even delay their proceedings. After three days of intensive discussions, officials from Rey's office sent a report in which they defined the talks as "satisfactory" and declared that the preliminary stage should be considered concluded.[89] Consequently, the Commission began drafting its recommendations to the Council of Ministers. These consolidated during the spring of 1967 and were outlined in a long memorandum discussing Israel's problems vis-à-vis the EEC and possible solutions to them. The document noted that "in economic terms there is no doubt that Israel's development will be damaged or at least halted significantly should the country's economy remain isolated." However, it also determined that "in view of the [size] dimensions of the Israeli market . . . the EEC has only a marginal economic and trade interest in signing a preferential agreement with Israel." The document then discussed the existing trade agreement, noting that it apparently failed to answer the needs of the Israeli economy. Although the authors denied the Israeli argument that the establishment of the Common Market had caused real damage to Israeli exports—"it cannot be denied that the trade between Israel and the EEC has generally developed in an acceptable manner"—they highlighted that the benefits given by the trade agreement offered no contribution whatsoever to the development of trade between Israel and the EEC; in fact, the growth in exports occurred in sectors not covered by the agreement. Following an analysis of the talks in the follow-up committee, the authors determined that since the agreement of June 1964, the EEC had not reached any positive decisions on issues of interest to Israel, such as the "European product." They therefore concluded that a continued search for solutions in the framework of a non-preferential agreement such as this "was in fact rejecting the Israeli requests," and would be necessary only if no other solution could be found.

At this stage, the authors of the document investigated the solution of a preferential agreement covering the entire industrial sector and granting Israel agricultural benefits similar to those which Spain would receive. The document determined that such an agreement could assume the form of a customs union or free trade area; there would be no difficulty in tailoring it to be consistent with GATT regulations. Furthermore, it determined that there was no need to base the arrangement with Israel on association but rather on the common trade policy in the spirit of article 111. Thus, there were three possible options—improvement of the existing agreement, a preferential agreement, or an association agreement—and the only difference between the last two options was "cosmetic" in nature. The Commission recommended first and foremost investigating the possibility of association.

The importance of this recommendation should not be diminished. In the summer of 1967, the EEC had not signed a preferential or association agreement with any country outside Europe; even progress with countries in Europe or those connected to the continent remained gradual. In fact, the Commission's recommendation was equivalent to granting Israel the same rights that the EEC intended to accord to Spain. However, Spain, in contrast to Israel, was a European country with a sizeable market, providing the EEC with an economic incentive to cultivate trade relations with it. These factors, together with the fear of complications with the Arab nations and concerns about a flood of similar requests, make this document exceptional. Although a mere recommendation, its practical importance cannot be ignored. It gave Israel an "expert opinion" from the body with the highest authority on this matter that association would constitute the most effective solution to its problems and that this solution was practically and legally feasible. In so doing, it cast doubt on one of the EEC's main justifications for rejecting Israel's requests. It forced the opponents of association—and many of these remained—into a defensive position, pushing them to offer Israel what they considered the lesser evil: a preferential agreement on the basis of article 111, in the form already proposed to Spain; in return, Israel would relinquish the goal of association.

The most surprising aspect of the Commission's memorandum is the *argument* it employed in favor of a preferential trade treatment for Israel. From the outset, the Commission document explicitly stated that the matter was not in the economic interests of the EEC: "In light of the dimensions of the Israeli market . . . the EEC has only a marginal economic and trade interest in signing a preferential agreement with Israel." Therefore, this was evidently a unilateral EEC gesture. Even more surprisingly, throughout the entire document the authors repeatedly denied that the establishment of the Common Market caused Israel any real economic damage: "The Israeli government cannot claim that the country's difficulties were worsened by the development of the Common Market. On the contrary, the opposite is true; indeed, Israel's exports to the EEC have generally developed in a positive manner." Furthermore, the document noted that "the EEC does not take first place as a trade partner for Israel, as it does for many other countries." This point is noteworthy because it negates the Israeli claim that Israel's particular dependence on the EEC made a special agreement essential. Later, the authors concluded that although the Israeli arguments regarding the ineffectiveness of the existing trade agreement were justified, "it cannot be denied that the trade between Israel and the EEC has generally developed in an acceptable manner." Considering this, how did the authors justify their conclusions? The summary of the document noted that:

> Whereas Israel's economic difficulties should in no way be attributed to the development of the EEC, it cannot be denied that the EEC constitutes the only consumer market into which Israel can integrate economically; despite the EEC's relatively modest portion in its foreign trade and Israel's current trade deficit. *Although the situation does not lead to direct responsibility* [on the part of the EEC], *it at any rate bears a certain degree of responsibility.* [Original emphasis]

Therefore, according to the document, Israel should be accorded benefits because the EEC bears a responsibility towards the future of Israeli exports. A reading of the document suggests that the paragraph quoted above was intended to justify to the Council of Ministers the ensuing conclusion: the need to grant Israel a far-reaching solution such as a preferential agreement. The document does not offer any other justification of the ostensible need for this. Yet, reading between the lines, we can discern allusions indicating why the Commission was willing to make such a recommendation. At the beginning of the document, the authors reminded the Council that "Israel was one of the first to appoint a representation to the EEC; since then Israel has unceasingly striven to establish preferential relations with the Community." The significance of this motivation should not be underestimated; it seems that the leadership of the Commission felt a real *obligation* to bring an association agreement with Israel to fruition—the result of a decade-long history of close contacts. It is important to remember that the Commission first encouraged Israel toward the solution of association and that on numerous occasions promised the Israelis that the trade agreement was only a first step toward a comprehensive arrangement. Even if this was due to additional motivations, at this juncture, in view of the more positive approach among The Six towards a preferential agreement with Israel, the conditions were ripe to repay the moral debt of those unfulfilled promises.

At the meeting on June 1, 1967, the Commission leadership approved the report compiled by Rey's officials. Although officially recommending a preferential agreement, Hallstein and his deputy Mansholt personally decided in favor of association, according with Israel's request. It is unclear what led them to take this exceptional step. Had they reached the conclusion that only such a solution could solve Israel's problems? Or was this a protest by the President of the Commission, who at the same time had suffered personal humiliation at the hands of The Six, as the latter sought to replace him (beginning in July 1967)? At any rate, the recommendation to open talks with Israel regarding association now became an official Commission document and was presented to the Council of Ministers on June 6. Israel's chances seemed promising. Over the preceding months, all six member states had recognized the failure of the June 1964 agreement to fulfill its task effectively and were aware that it could not serve as a solution to Israel's problems. Five out of the six—with the exception of Italy—agreed that a "new solution" was required, one necessarily based on a preferential arrangement for Israel's industrial products and at least some of its agricultural crops.

France's approach took the sharpest turn in this respect. In the years 1960–64, as was mentioned, the French had been highly diffident towards Israel's ambition of achieving association and, later, a comprehensive agreement. France's representatives in the COREPER were well known for their stubborn opposition to this and, on more than one occasion, they had succeeded in halting or delaying decisions that would be amenable to Israel, such as those proposed by the Commission or the Dutch delegation. France's hesitancy aided the Italians, ensuring that they were not isolated in their opposition. Indeed, whenever France joined the other four countries, this forced Italy to withdraw its disagreement; this occurred in September 1962 concerning the decision to begin negotiations over a trade agreement, and again at the beginning of 1964, when France's endorsement of the trade agreement forced the Italians to agree.

Now a similar situation arose. A few days after Israel submitted its request for association (October 1966), in a conversation held in New York during the UN General Assembly, the French Foreign Minister informed Abba Eban that the trade agreement had clearly failed, making it necessary to search for a new solution. However, he noted that in his opinion "Israel must insist on the content rather than the form," hinting that it would be wiser to follow the path of a preferential agreement in the framework of article 111 and not ask for association according to article 238 of the Treaty of Rome.[90] On this same occasion, Couve de Murville invited Eban to visit him in Paris after the UN General Assembly, to discuss the matter in detail. Eban accepted and the two met again a few days later. During this conversation, the French Foreign Minister stated, "France has no prejudices and recognizes that the past has proven the need to search for a new solution."[91] Couve de Murville was not the only French politician or official to express himself thus. As was noted above, senior French officials informed their Israeli counterparts that while association was inconceivable, a preferential agreement was a realistic option.

French Prime Minister Pompidou, in a conversation with Ambassador Eytan, voiced a clear and most obliging declaration regarding the country's willingness to support a preferential agreement. Pompidou stated that of the three possible solutions to Israel's problems—widening the existing trade agreement, a preferential agreement, or association—the first was not pragmatic because the agreement had failed to solve Israel's problems; therefore the choice was in fact between the second and third options. He added that France would not respond *a priori* negatively to Israel's request for association, but he was convinced that the second possibility was preferable because "this would be less complicated than managing an arrangement of association in the full meaning of the word." The Israeli Ambassador, understanding the significance of these statements, sought to ensure that there would be no possibility of a retraction. Therefore he asked twice whether France discounted the possibility of extending the existing agreement and obligated itself to one of the other two options. Pompidou responded positively.

Significantly, even the Italians themselves, although unwilling to pursue the path of a preferential agreement, revealed more "generosity" towards Israel than ever before. At the end of October 1966, both the Italian Prime Minister Fanfani and Finance Minister Colombo promised Foreign Minister Eban that they would support the opening of preliminary talks with Israel concerning the possibility of association, yet they did not guarantee their backing for this solution. Indeed, they kept their promise: at the vote in December 1966, the Italian representative voted in favor of preliminary talks—additional evidence that the Italians sought to avoid isolating themselves from the other five.

Notes

1 Report of the Israeli delegation to the GATT Trade Round in Geneva, ISA, MF, file 19785/7, 1966.
2 "Exports to the EEC in 1964," Foreign Currency Section, ISA, FM, file 3148/1, May 1965.
3 Wyn Grant, "Policy Instruments in the Common Agricultural Policy," *West European Politics* 33, no. 1 (2010).
4 *Davar*, "Orange War," *Davar*, December 10, 1965.
5 On February 9, 1964 the Spanish submitted a request to begin negotiations on an association agreement. This request was rejected. However, on June 2, two days before the signing of the agreement with Israel, the Council of Ministers agreed to begin talks and they indeed began that September. In November 1966, the Commission submitted a recommendation to sign a preferential agreement with Spain. Preliminary talks between the EEC and the Maghreb countries began in 1963. At the beginning of 1967, the Commission recommended concluding an association agreement with these countries.
6 One of the solutions to the growing competition was to develop a new type of orange which ripened more quickly than the Shamouti or Valencia so that it could be marketed earlier and thus obtain exclusivity. Indeed, certain efforts were directed toward developing such a species, although without evident success. See: *Ma'ariv*, "Things Are Getting Worse from Year to Year!" *Ma'ariv*, May 30, 1968.
7 DDF, 1964, tome II, doc. 3, July 1, 1964.
8 DDF, 1965, tome I, doc. 124, March 17, 1965.
9 David Lipkin, "The Declining Profitability of the Citrus Sector," *Davar*, August 31, 1966. In 1963, Finance Minister Sapir instituted a policy of "financial stability" which was later known as "recession." This was intended to encourage exports by preventing price increases, which were eroding the advantages of the great currency devaluation in 1962. For this purpose, a special headquarters was established which led the battle to decrease the cost of living, a wage freeze was instituted, and the government waged a media campaign to reduce consumption. See: Speech by Sapir to the 10th Congress of the Workers' Union, ISA, PM, file 6627/8, January 3, 1966. However, this policy led to a slowing of economic activity and many sectors, among them the citrus sector, experienced distress.

10 David Lipkin, "In the Land of Oranges—Consumption of Oranges Is in Decline," *Davar*, October 19, 1966.

11 "The Place of 'The European Product' in General Exports to the Common Market," ISA, FM, file 3148/1, May 26, 1965.

12 Process verbale, EUA, BAC 326, February 21, 1965

13 I. William. Zartman, "North Africa and the EEC Negotiations," *Middle East Journal* 22, no. 1 (1968).

14 Alon at the meeting of the External Affairs and Defense Committee, ISA, Knesset, file 8160/9, December 22, 1964.

15 *Davar*, Editorial: "The Reality of Our Relations with the Market," *Davar*, January 29, 1965.

16 Protocol, ISA, FM, file 3147/10, April 3, 1965.

17 Marcus to Avriel, ISA, FM, file 288/6, February 22, 1966.

18 Note, AMAE, DE-CE-1972, January 1, 1965.

19 Zeiberlich, appointed head of the German delegation in the follow-up committee, informed the Israelis of this development. He resigned after receiving instructions from Bonn to accede to the Italian request "to be satisfied with listening to the Israeli claims without response and without any initiative which could be interpreted as the desire to advance the EEC's relations by giving these or other benefits to Israeli exports." See: Cnaan to the Economic Department, ISA, FM, file 3148/1, May 18, 1965.

20 Information about the content of the talks is available from a range of sources: "Summary of the Meetings of the Joint Committee, April 12–14", Gal-Ed to Sapir, ISA, FM, file 3147/10, April 18, 1965; Telegram, AMAE, DE-CE-1972, April 16, 1965; Summary of the Commission: EUA, BAC 326, April 21, 1965.

21 "Trends and Structure of Israeli Exports to the European Community," ISA, FM, file 3154/6, January 1967.

22 Najar to the Economic Department, ISA, FM, file 3148/1, May 4, 1965.

23 It was no coincidence that the visit of the Knesset delegation was timed to correspond with the European Parliament's discussion of the Israeli matter. The Israeli Ministry of Foreign Affairs acted intentionally to ensure that the visit took place at the most opportune time. On this see: Najar to the Foreign Minister, ISA, FM, file 3147/10, April 4, 1965. Simultaneously, additional Israeli figures worked to create an amenable foundation for Israel's request for association. Thus, for example, Secretary General Aharon Bakar of the Histadrut trade union approached leaders of the unions in EEC countries asking them to support an association agreement and they acquiesced, ISA, FM, file 288/6, October 16, 1966. Indeed, in November, the committee of trade unions in the EEC countries published an announcement expressing enthusiastic support for Israel's association with the EEC (see: Editorial, "Between Israel and the European 'Common Market'," *Davar*, November 16, 1966). Likewise, the Liberal International was recruited to the campaign by representatives of the independent Liberal party in Israel and it too published an announcement expressing support for association (see: "The Liberal International in Favor of Israel's Association with the Market," *Davar*, September 11, 1966). At the seventh meeting of the Socialist parties, held in Berlin in November 1966, association was declared the only conceivable arrangement as far as countries such as Israel and Tunisia were concerned. Following the renewal of talks between Israel and the Commission at the beginning of 1967, various unions sent letters in support of Israel's request to President Hallstein (see: Gabriel Bartal, "Israel, 'the Market' and the Unions," *Davar*, March 15, 1967). Concurrently, the Israeli Workers' Union invited a delegation from the trade unions to visit Israel, with the aim of deepening their commitment to the campaign. (see: Marcus to Avriel, ISA, FM, file 288/6, January 19, 1967).

24 Najar to the Foreign Minister, ISA, FM, file 3147/10, April 4, 1965. It is possible that this comment was a paraphrase of the famous statement made by David Ben-Gurion while serving as chairman of the Jewish Agency, in which he summarized the complex dilemma concerning relations with the British on the background

of the British Mandate in the land of Israel and the Holocaust in Europe: "We will fight the White Book as though there is no war against Hitler, and we will fight Hitler as though there is no White Book."

25 Viktor Tsigelman, "Israel's Status in Brussels," *Davar*, July 9, 1965.

26 Gal-Ed to Minister Tzadok, ISA, FM, file 3148/2, July 9, 1965.

27 Gal-Ed to Ministers Sapir and Tzadok, ISA, FM, file 3148/2, September 14, 1965.

28 Nirgad to the Director General of the Ministry of Foreign Affairs, ISA, FM, file 3148/2, September 8, 1965.

29 Nirgad to Shalush, ISA, FM, file 3154/2, January 2, 1966.

30 Najar to the Foreign Minister, ISA, FM, file 3154/3, July 4, 1966.

31 See, for example, the letter of reproach from the Director General of the Ministry of Foreign Affairs, Aryeh Levavi, to Bartur: Levavi to Bartur, ISA, FM, file 3147/10, May 1965.

32 The French Foreign Minister described in his memoirs how he strongly opposed the Commission's ambition to serve as the implementational authority of an ostensibly sovereign body. See: Maurice Couve De Murville, *Une Politique Étrangère, 1958–1969* (Paris: Plon, 1971), 304–6.

33 A. Dan and K. Grinbaum, "Tzadok to Try to Persuade the French," *Ma'ariv*, November 25, 1965.

34 This body is the most long-standing example of cooperation in this domain. See: Raúl Compés López, José-María García-Álvarez-Coque and Tomás García Azcárate, "EU-Mediterranean Relations in the Field of Agriculture," in *Policy Paper 91* (Paris: Jacques Delors Institute, 2013).

35 Citrus Marketing Council: Protocols of meetings, ISA, Ministry of Agriculture, file 2423/10, November 9, 1959; Yair Dekel, "The Mediterranean Citrus Organization Celebrates Its 10th Birthday," *Herut*, May 3, 1960. Izakson apparently sought to transform the organization into a real cartel. At one of the organization's annual summits, he proposed coordinating the members' planting policies and in this way controlling the supply. However, this step was considered too far-reaching. See: Natan Ben Natan, "The Shadow of the European Common Market," *Davar*, September 30, 1959.

36 Minutes of the inter-ministerial committee, meeting regarding the Market on August 10, 1965, ISA, FM, file 3148/2, no date.

37 DDF, 1964, tome I, doc. 154, March 26, 1964; DDF, 1964, tome II, doc. 180, November 10, 1964.

38 As of 1965. See: Ministry of Finance Memorandum, ISA, MF, file 19785/7, 1967.

39 Rappaport to the Economic Department, ISA, FM, file 3148/2, November 26, 1965.

40 *Davar*, "Tzadok and Gvati Visit the 'Market' Countries to Act against the Increase in Citrus Prices," *Davar*, November 22, 1965.

41 K. Grinbaum, "'Common Market' Discussions About Oranges—Kept Secret," *Ma'ariv*, October 14, 1965.

42 Avriel to the Economic Department, ISA, FM, file 3154/2, May 10, 1966.

43 In this regard see: The Ambassador in Rome to the Department of West Europe, ISA, FM, file 3154/3, June 1, 1966; ISA, FM, 3154/4, August 24, 1966.

44 Note a l'attention de Monsieur Rey, EUA, BAC 326, September 28, 1965.

45 At the time, the Israelis began to express more explicitly than ever the political motivation behind their desire for association. See, for example, Nirgad's words: "Our activity with regard to the European Common Market was motivated by the thinking that Israel must find a way to get as close as possible to Western Europe and even become involved in the movement for European integration, thus removing Israel from its isolation and finding a place for it in the family of European nations, as part of the family of the West." See: Nirgard to Shalush, ISA, FM, file 3154/2, January 2, 1966.

46 Protocol of the meeting of economic advisors, ISA, FM, file 3154/2, February 15, 1966.

47 As Minerbi, deputy head of the delegation, testified: "We decided to demand the convening of the committee mainly in order to prove once again that in the narrow framework of the present agreement it was impossible to find a full solution to Israel's economic problems. For this reason we intentionally avoided submitting any practical suggestions." (See: Minerbi to the Director of the Economic Department). Instructions to the Israeli delegation in the joint committee, ISA, FM, file 3154/3, June 28, 1966.

48 Protocol of the ministerial meeting regarding the Common Market. ISA, PM, April 12, 1966.

49 See, for example, the report of the working group for trade matters to the Council, as background for the discussion in the joint committee: BAC-26 1969-669, June 10, 1966

50 K. Grinbaum, "Israel Asks Again: Affiliation of a Comprehensive Agreement with the 'Market'," *Ma'ariv*, June 23, 1966.

51 See, for example, the special report of the section for foreign trade in the Israel Central Bureau of Statistics: ISA, MF, file 19785/7, 1966.

52 Trends and Structure of Israeli Exports to the European Community, ISA, FM, file 3154/6, January 1967.

53 This was expressed in the summarizing paper written by the EEC delegation, which noted that although a reduction in the negative trade balance between Israel and the EEC was evident, in the past few years there had been a certain freeze in the export of industrial products from Israel to the member states: EUA, BAC-326, June 22–24, 1966.

54 Report of the Israeli delegation to the GATT Round in Geneva, ISA, MF, file 19785/7, 1966.

55 Five Year Plan, updated for 1970/71, in view of trade conditions, towards harmonization with the European Community and increasing the export forecast, ISA, MF, file 19785/7, January 1967.

56 Ozeri to Shalush, ISA, FM, file 3154/2, January 27, 1967; Minerbi to Shalush, ISA, FM, file 3154/4, September 1, 1966.

57 Shalush to Ozeri, ISA, FM, file 3154/4, September 21, 1966.

58 The meeting of economic attachés in July 1966 advised the political echelon to adopt this strategy in order to overcome the Italian opposition to association. See: Shalush to the Economic Administration, ISA, FM, file 3154/3, July 18, 1966.

59 See, for example, Cnaan to the Economic Department, ISA, FM, file 3148/1, May 24, 1965; Cnaan to the Economic Administration, ISA, FM, file 3154/3, June 28, 1966; Ambassador Eytan's conversation with officials at the Quai d'Orsay, Common Market Bulletin, ISA, FM, file 3154/4, June 29, 1966.

60 Even as late as spring 1965, when Foreign Minister Meir visited Paris, the French officials clearly informed her that they could not work to widen the agreement with Israel (see: *Ma'ariv*, "France Is Not Prepared to Help Israel Tighten Relations with the 'Common Market'," *Ma'ariv*, April 5, 1965). However, their approach began to change following the complete failure at the two meetings of the joint committee.

61 *Ma'ariv*, "Sapir—to Brussels for Talks with Bonn's Finance Minister," *Ma'ariv*, October 31, 1965.

62 Har-Gil Shraga, "The Common Market Technocrat," *Ma'ariv*, December 22, 1966.

63 See, for example, Lahr's words to the Ambassador in Cologne: The Ambassador to the Ministry of Foreign Affairs, ISA, FM, file 3154/3, June 27, 1966.

64 Cnaan to the Economic Administration, ISA, FM, file 3154/4, September 6, 1966. The Israelis were very angry that the German officials carelessly annulled an explicit promise made by the German head of state. This reminded them of the repeated failures to translate fundamental support among the political echelon into a clear decision in Community intuitions. The frustration they felt led them to explore ways to inform Erhard regarding his officials' attitude towards him, without of course exposing the

source of this information. See: Shak to the economic advisor in Bonn, ISA, FM, file 3154/4, September 31, 1966.

65 Cnaan to the Economic Administration, ISA, FM, file 3154/4, August 22, 1966.

66 Shalush to the Foreign Minister, ISA, FM, file 4249/4, November 2, 1966.

67 See, for example, comments by Hallstein in a special interview with David Lipkin, an Israeli journalist: David Lipkin, "Israel Is Not Entitled for an Associate Member State Status," *Davar*, March 24, 1965.

68 Najar to the Economic Department, ISA, FM, file 3154/2, May 4, 1966.

69 Najar to the Ministry of Foreign Affairs, ISA, FM, file 3154/2, May 18, 1966.

70 Gil Keisari, "The Only Jew in the 'Market' Leadership," *Ma'ariv*, May 5, 1965.

71 David Lipkin, "Deputy President of the Common Market in an Interview with Davar," *Davar*, October 9, 1964.

72 Najar to the Economic Department, ISA, FM, file 3154/4, September 25, 1966.

73 EEC News, ISA, FM, file 4294/4, October, 1966.

74 The letter noted, among other things, that "the limited content of the trade agreement did not accord with the wishes of the Israeli government, which sought a broad preferential agreement including all the trade in goods and services between the country and the Community. However, *considering the advice of friendly governments*, the Israeli government agreed to adopt what was called the 'pragmatic approach'" (emphasis added). (See: Phrasing of the Letter in Hebrew, ISA, FM, file 3154/7, January 26, 1967).

75 On this see: Embassy in Brussels to the Economic Department, ISA, FM, file 3154/5, October 21, 1966; Najar to the Foreign Minister, ISA, FM, file 3154/5, October 25, 1966. Najar believed: "there is no doubt that the positive stances of the Belgian, Dutch and German Commission members towards preliminary talks, as was expressed in their meeting on October 10 [1966] is intended to push the government and the permanent representatives towards us." See: Najar to the Foreign Minister, ISA, FM, file 3154/5, October 24, 1966.

76 Shalush to the Foreign Minister, ISA, FM, file 4249/4, November 2, 1966.

77 This was made abundantly clear to the Israelis in the days preceding the vote. See: EEC News, ISA, FM, file 4249/4, November 18, 1966.

78 "The EEC," ISA, FM, file 4249/4, December 1966.

79 ISA, MF, file 19785/5, November 23, 1966; January 3, 1967.

80 On these talks see: I. William. Zartman, *Politics of Trade Negotiations between Africa and the European Economic Community: The Weak Confronts the Strong* (Princeton: Princeton University Press, 1971).

81 DDF, 1966, tome II, doc. 174, 418; DDF, 1967, tome I, doc. 299, June 14, 1967.

82 See Mansholt's comments to Najar (Najar to the Economic Department, ISA, FM, file 3154/6, January 5, 1967.

83 See, for example, the series of talks between Eban and the Foreign Ministers of the EEC countries during his visit to New York for the convening of the UN General Assembly. They all recognized that the trade agreement was ineffective, but expressed hesitancy about association: Conversations of the Foreign Ministry regarding Israel's association with the EEC, ISA, FM, file 3154/5, October 24, 1966.

84 EUA, Bac-327, January 20–23, January, 1967.

85 Hallstein, who did not especially favor this approach, noted to the Ambassador: "no decision has yet been made regarding Israeli association. However, the EEC has the right to decide what kind of relations it desires to establish with a third state and in particular those connected to the Community via a trade agreement." Hallstein also added his hope that the Egyptians were not trying to interfere in internal Community matters. The Egyptian Ambassador was not to be outdone. He noted that although the Egyptians did not seek to interfere in EEC matters, association with Israel would be considered no less than taking the Israeli side; this would necessarily cloud the EEC's relations with the Arabs. See: EUA, Bac-327, December 19, 1966.

86 Anthony L. Teasdale, "The Life and Death of the Luxembourg Compromise," *JCMS: Journal of Common Market Studies* 31, no. 4 (1993); William. Nicoll, "The Luxembourg Compromise," *JCMS: Journal of Common Market Studies* 23, no. 1 (1984).
87 Eban to Najar, ISA, FM, file 3154/7, January 25, 1967.
88 Protocol of the preliminary talks, ISA, Ministry of Finance, file 19785/7, January 23–26, 1967.
89 EUA, BAC-327, January 23–26, 1967; Note a l'attention du monsieur le ministre Rey, EUA, BAC-327, February 6, 1967.
90 See Eban's testimony to the government, ISA, PM, October 23, 1966.
91 Eytan to the Head of West Europe Department, ISA, FM, file 3154/8, June 24, 1967; Conversations of the Ministry of Foreign Affairs regarding Israel's association with the EEC, ISA, FM, file 3154/5, October 24, 1966.

References

Bartal, Gabriel. "Israel, 'the Market' and the Unions." *Davar*, March 15, 1967.

Ben Natan, Natan. "The Shadow of the European Common Market." *Davar*, September 30, 1959.

Dan, A, and K. Grinbaum. "Tzadok to Try to Persuade the French." *Ma'ariv*, November 25, 1965.

Davar. "Orange War." *Davar*, December 10, 1965.

———. "Tzadok and Gvati Visit the 'Market' Countries to Act against the Increase in Citrus Prices." *Davar*, November 22, 1965.

Davar, Editorial: "Between Israel and the European 'Common Market." *Davar*, November 16, 1966.

———. "The Liberal International in Favor of Israel's Association with the Market." *Davar*, September 11, 1966.

———. "The Reality of Our Relations with the Market." *Davar*, January 29, 1965.

De Murville, Maurice Couve. *Une Politique Étrangère, 1958–1969*. Paris: Plon, 1971.

Dekel, Yair. "The Mediterranean Citrus Organization Celebrates Its 10th Birthday." *Herut*, May 3, 1960.

Grant, Wyn. "Policy Instruments in the Common Agricultural Policy." *West European Politics* 33, no. 1 (2010): 22–38.

Grinbaum, K. "'Common Market' Discussions About Oranges—Kept Secret." *Ma'ariv*, October 14, 1965.

———. "Israel Asks Again: Affiliation of a Comprehensive Agreement with the 'Market'." *Ma'ariv*, June 23, 1966.

Har-Gil, Shraga. "The Common Market Technocrat." *Ma'ariv*, December 22, 1966.

Keisari, Gil. "The Only Jew in the 'Market' Leadership." *Ma'ariv*, May 5, 1965.

Lipkin, David. "The Declining Profitability of the Citrus Sector." *Davar*, August 31, 1966.

———. "Deputy President of the Common Market in an Interview with Davar." *Davar*, October 9, 1964.

———. "In the Land of Oranges—Consumption of Oranges Is in Decline." *Davar*, October 19 1966.

———. "Israel Is Not Entitled for an Associate Member State Status." *Davar*, March 24, 1965.

———. "Orange War." *Davar*, December 10, 1965.

López, Raúl Compés, José-María García-Álvarez-Coque and Tomás García Azcárate. "EU-Mediterranean Relations in the Field of Agriculture." In *Policy Paper 91*. Paris: Jacques Delors Institute, 2013.

Ma'ariv. "France Is Not Prepared to Help Israel Tighten Relations with the 'Common Market'." *Ma'ariv*, April 5, 1965.

———. "Sapir—to Brussels for Talks with Bonn's Finance Minister." *Ma'ariv*, October 31, 1965.

———. "Things Are Getting Worse from Year to Year!" *Ma'ariv*, May 30, 1968.

Nicoll, William. "The Luxembourg Compromise." *JCMS: Journal of Common Market Studies* 23, no. 1 (1984): 35–43.

Teasdale, Anthony L. "The Life and Death of the Luxembourg Compromise." *JCMS: Journal of Common Market Studies* 31, no. 4 (1993): 567–79.

Tsigelman, Viktor. "Israel's Status in Brussels." *Davar*, July 9, 1965.

Zartman, I William. "North Africa and the EEC Negotiations." *Middle East Journal* 22, no. 1 (1968): 1–16.

———. *Politics of Trade Negotiations between Africa and the European Economic Community: The Weak Confronts the Strong*. Princeton: Princeton University Press, 1971.

10 A preferential agreement

The Six Day War and France's uncooperative stance

In June 1967, the Israelis had excellent reasons for optimism. The Council of Ministers seemed ready to approve the Commission's recommendation and order the opening of talks to investigate the solution of a preferential trade agreement (similar to the form simultaneously being offered to Spain). With all the caution a historian must exercise when trying to estimate the likelihood of events that did not unfold, we can be reasonably certain that had the dramatic developments of June 1967 not ensued, the negotiations between Israel and the Commission would have begun in the summer of 1967 and led, after some time (likely no longer than a few months given that the technical studies were already largely complete), to a comprehensive agreement in the form of a free trade area—the same agreement that was finally reached only in 1975. However, this did not happen.

In mid-May, following the entry of Egyptian troops into Sinai, the evacuation of UN forces and the blocking of the Tiran Straits, a severe crisis erupted in the Middle East. Decision makers and military officials in Jerusalem adamantly refused to accept the new status quo dictated by the Egyptians, preferring a military operation to open the Tiran Straits forcibly. However, fearing the reaction of the Western powers, they were willing to delay the operation and, in the meantime, seek a diplomatic resolution or, alternatively, open the Straits using international forces. As a default, an Israeli diplomatic campaign was initiated, preparing the ground for a future Israeli offensive. The Israelis presumed that France would endorse its actions; for more than a decade, France had served as Israel's armory and on more than one occasion added its political support. For example, in 1957, France announced that it would view an Egyptian blockade of the Tiran Straits as an act of war. Therefore, the Israelis expected de Gaulle's government to stand at Israel's right hand.

However, it soon became apparent that this assumption had been erroneous. De Gaulle adopted a restrained policy towards Israel and pressured the government to refrain from embarking on an offensive. He spoke in favor of finding a solution to the crisis through diplomatic channels, led by the four great powers—the US, the USSR, Britain and France—although he did not promise that the arrangement would recreate the previous situation exactly. On June 2, the French President took a dramatic step and announced an arms embargo on the countries involved in the conflict: it was clear that this would principally affect Israel. De Gaulle's actions were not necessarily motivated by a desire to please the Arabs; more importantly he sought to preserve and advance the political understanding with the Soviets which had begun to emerge in the two years preceding the crisis, in addition to using the crisis to improve France's international standing.[1] De Gaulle considered that a war in the Middle East would impede reaching these two goals and therefore used all the leverage at his disposal to deter Israel from launching an attack (including the embargo). He perceived the Israeli offensive on June 5, 1967 as an irresponsible step and a blow to France's prestige. After the short war, lasting only six days, de Gaulle began to adopt an increasingly hesitant policy toward Israel. This was the result of a combination of factors: his aim to continue the diplomatic alliance with the Soviets, his desire to preserve the new prestige France had obtained among the Arab nations following its opposition during the crisis and the war,[2] and finally his anger towards Israel and his newly consolidating perception of Israel as an imperialist country seeking to widen its borders at the expense of its neighbors, seizing the May crisis to do achieve this end. Following the war, the French government became unwilling to accede to Israel's requests in almost any respect. This policy line was dictated by de Gaulle himself and was imposed on the ranks below him, although not all believed that the rift with Israel was justified or advisable.

This negative attitude toward Israel certainly influenced France's stance concerning an arrangement between Israel and the EEC. There was a significant, sharp deterioration in the French approach to a preferential agreement from mid-June 1967 onwards. In the first days following the war, the French government presumed that relations with Israel would soon be restored, explaining Pompidou's promise to Ambassador Eytan that France would support association or a preferential agreement at the coming meeting of the Council of Ministers.[3] However, near the end of June, the Quai d'Orsay received instructions to adopt an uncooperative stance. In the COREPER, Boegner besmirched the Commission's report, claiming that its analysis was inadequate and demanding the establishment of a working group tasked with completing the gaps. Although it was clear to everyone that the new French demand was driven by political considerations, there was no alternative but to acquiesce.

The working group began its discussions in mid-July, and it became evident at the very outset that the war had completely altered the balance of powers between The Six regarding an arrangement with Israel. Italy, which had for some time been isolated in its opposition, was now joined by France and Belgium. The French representatives in the working group, on orders from above, stubbornly opposed any additional gesture towards Israel beyond slight improvements to the existing trade agreement. They claimed that the Commission had been negligent in its work, failing to conduct sufficiently comprehensive research to prove that a preferential agreement was necessary to counter Israel's negative trade

balance. In their view, a similar result could be obtained through general negotiations in the framework of the GATT (the Kennedy Round). Interestingly,
the French chose to base their opposition to the Commission report not on a
political excuse, but rather on pure economic logic. Indeed, no one doubted that
it was motivated by political factors: the desire to establish firmly France's new-
found prestige among the Arab countries.[4] It was thus only natural to expect that
this would constitute a central component of the French argument; certainly,
French statesmen did not hesitate to highlight the political factors behind their
opposition in informal settings.[5]

Yet France's line of argument is also surprising because, at this juncture,
political reasoning would probably have proven more effective than economic
arguments. Following the war, the rift between the Arab nations and Israel widened. The Arab–Israeli conflict became a central layer in the considerations of
the Arab states, even more so than in the past. All the EEC countries, without
exception, were concerned by how the Arab states would react to negotiations
with Israel in the current climate. A number of German officials articulated
strong doubts about honoring their promises to support Israel and sought to
re-examine the policy.[6] Von Stempel, the German Deputy Foreign Minister,
who in the past had expressed unrestrained support for the idea of a preferential
agreement with Israel, argued during a conversation with an Israeli diplomat
that "Germany too has Middle Eastern considerations and it also thinks it would
be best not to force the issue regarding Israel now, to avoid arousing the anger of
the Arabs." Despite this, he reassured his Israeli colleague that they would not
sacrifice Israel's interests, adding, "However, it is questionable whether the time
is right to take an obvious initiative to speed up the discussions in Brussels."[7] The
Commission likewise felt that, while its conclusions remained valid, the new
political situation in the wake of the war justified a re-examination of the advisability of its recommendations.[8] Although the Commission was mainly occupied
with economic issues—indeed, the initial moves toward European integration
were economic in essence—it was not blind to the relevance of political considerations in molding the EEC's position vis-à-vis a third-party country, even
when the matter on the agenda concerned trade relations.

Yet despite the severity of the political considerations, the French based
their opposition to the Israeli arrangement on economic foundations. This
forced the Commission into a defensive position, casting doubt on its professional expertise or, even worse, the purity of its motives (the French always
suspected that the Commission was in collusion with Israel). Therefore, the
Commission's only alternative was to maintain stubbornly the conclusions of
its report—that Israel expected to experience economic damage due to the
establishment of the Common Market—and refute completely the French
arguments.[9] Moreover, the French insistence on citing economic arguments
provided the Israelis with a convenient pressure point at which to strike. The
Israelis reminded the French of Pompidou's statements to Eytan: proof that
Paris recognized the economic necessity of a preferential agreement for Israel.
This placed the French in an uncomfortable situation and, following a direct

instruction from de Gaulle, Pompidou was forced to deny his comments, claiming that this was a case of misunderstanding.[10]

Interestingly, the French government chose to cling to this version—even though it was abundantly clear that it did not accord with the truth—rather than using the simpler and more reliable alternative of admitting that these statements were indeed made but that the new circumstances in the Middle East had forced a reconsideration of the Prime Minister's promise. However, such an admission would cast doubt on the validity of France's economic argument. The Israelis endeavored to exploit this pressure point; by proving the invalidity of these arguments, Israel could isolate France from the remainder of the EEC members. As the Deputy Director of the Economic Department advised Israeli politicians:

> It is of the utmost importance that France's ostensible economic arguments not receive the support of any other Community member. This will not only make work difficult for the French but, first and foremost, ensure the consolidation of a clear and unambiguous stance in favor of the preferential agreement among the five other members, in addition to the recommendation of the Commission.[11]

Indeed, even if the Commission's firm stance in the face of the attacks on its conclusions and the statistics the Israelis supplied were unable to contradict the French claims or cause the latter to withdraw their opposition, it heightened the pressure on them, gradually leaving them isolated.

Considering all these arguments, why did the French refuse to justify their opposition with formal political considerations and instead cling to economic logic? The answer is linked to the understandings among The Six concerning the nature of a legitimate or appropriate argument. Since Israel had begun feeling its way into the EEC, concern over the reaction of the Arab states had played a central role in rejecting its requests. In closed discussions and internal memoranda written by EEC officials, the "political" consideration was at times mentioned, but always in passing, without explanation or details. It was, of course, never voiced to the Israelis formally, because justifying the rejection in such a manner would be viewed as offensive and likely to generate antagonism among the general public in the EEC states; it would be considered equivalent to surrendering to the Arab boycott, which was viewed negatively in the West. The rejection of Israeli requests could be easily justified using economic and legal arguments (some of which were indeed authentic), thus avoiding any exposure of the political motivation. This forced the Israelis, in turn, to focus their efforts on economic-legal technical channels. During the decade of negotiations, the dialogue between the EEC and Israel assumed a clearly economic-legal character, centering on issues such as the extent of damage to the Israeli economy (in the present or future), or the degree to which The Six could grant benefits to Israel that accorded with the GATT agreement. The question of Israel's association with the EEC was thus framed as an economic rather than a political issue. French adoption of the political argument (which was, without a doubt, more morally acceptable following the Arab defeat in the war and Israel's arrogant position on the issue of the Occupied Territories) would paint the EEC's position as hypocritical, hinting at the existence of hidden motivations throughout the years of the negotiations with Israel, consequently embarrassing the EEC countries and almost certainly arousing internal criticism. At a Cabinet for Economic Affairs meeting, recognizing the Europeans' sensitivity to accusations that their position stemmed from the Arab consideration, Foreign Minister Eban advised:

> We need to reveal the trickery of the [French] economic justifications; although we know that their excuses are artificial, we must prove to everyone concerned that they have no basis . . . afterwards I presume that it is necessary to place constant pressure on European public opinion. I assume that we must argue or cause others to argue that this is a political act, that this delaying or refusing is the fruit of a specific policy and is not justified by the economic situation.[12]

However, the French officials in the working group and the COREPER were unable to convince their colleagues through economic reasoning that the solution of preferential agreement should be abandoned. Among the EEC, a significant consensus had already coalesced regarding the ineffectiveness of the non-preferential trade agreement. The Commission once again argued that the preferential agreement was the only framework that could advance the Israeli economy and attract investments. The French, finding themselves in a defensive position and remaining unwilling to admit the political motivation behind their position, now employed a new line of argument: they cast doubt on the EEC's obligation to help Israel develop its economy, all the more so when at the expense of the member states' interests. For the first time since the negotiations with Israel began, someone dared to explicitly ask a question that had never been broached: in what way was Israel different to other countries? Why did the countries of the EEC need to conduct lengthy discussions clarifying which solutions would be best for the Israeli economy? Israeli alarm at this new line of argument indicates the relevance of the question. They defined it as "extremely dangerous," understanding that it shook the deepest foundations of their request. The many years engaged in persuading the Europeans that the Israeli economy had been damaged by the establishment of the Common Market would have been for naught if the Europeans did not recognize the EEC's basic obligation to minimize this damage. Acceptance of this argument would make any further negotiations irrelevant.

However, the Israeli fears were unwarranted. The French argument, which would have been acceptable on its own, had no chance of gaining support among EEC members; not even those, such as the Italians, who did not welcome a comprehensive agreement with Israel. At the outset of negotiations, when their "guidelines" were laid out, the Europeans felt uncomfortable challenging the Israeli assumption that Europe could not stand on the sidelines as the country's economy was threatened. At that early stage, the Europeans' arsenal was stocked with different arguments, less emotionally loaded and highly effective; they were sufficient to delay a meaningful agreement with Israel for an entire decade. Yet now that the pressure to sign a preferential agreement with Israel had increased—following the failure of the trade agreement and the progress in negotiations with Spain and the Maghreb—it was impossible to return to the argument that Europe was not responsible for Israel's economic well-being without this seeming like a cynical act of vast proportions. The question of Israel's entitlement to preferential status had become incontestable.

The change in the German position and the French capitulation

As the months passed, France's isolation within the Council intensified. The representatives from Germany, the Netherlands and Luxembourg fully supported, albeit unenthusiastically, implementing the Commission's report.[13] When Germany joined the camp of Israel's supporters, this constituted the most significant development in the balance of powers between the EEC's members since the negotiations with Israel had begun. As was noted, in the first years of the negotiations, the German bureaucrats in the Community institutions revealed little support for Israel and at times joined Italy and France in their uncooperative stance, in contrast to the backing promised by the political echelon in Bonn; indeed, the Israelis complained continually about the ostensible "disparity" between Bonn and Brussels. This rift, which also characterized other states among The Six, such as France, served the European statesmen who, on the one hand, did not want to dismiss Israel empty-handed yet, on the other hand, feared the political and economic price their countries would pay upon the realization of their promises. They were thus content to let their officials in Brussels state their reservations and make difficulties, delaying indefinitely the implementation of a policy ostensibly dictated from above. When the statesmen really and truly wanted their policy to be carried out, they knew very well how to enforce their authority. This was especially true with regard to Germany, wherein the subjugation of the bureaucrats to the political echelon was particularly evident; the officials adopted an independent line only when lacking clear instructions from above.[14] This explains the turning point in Germany's practical position regarding Israeli requests that occurred in 1965, which was closely connected to the emerging crisis in relations between Germany and the Arab nations.

As was mentioned, the Hallstein doctrine prevented Germany from establishing diplomatic relations with Israel. Israel continuously pressured Bonn to change this policy, and on more than one occasion Adenauer and Erhard promised Israeli politicians and diplomats that they intended to normalize the relations between the two countries.[15] However, due to fear of the reaction among the Arab nations, they reneged on their promise. In February 1965, East Germany's Head of State, Walter Ulbricht, was invited to make an official visit to Cairo. Although in issuing this invitation Egypt did not explicitly breach the prohibition imposed by Bonn in the framework of the Hallstein doctrine (Egypt did not officially recognize East Germany), the West German government considered this de facto recognition of the country's Eastern neighbor and reacted severely. Erhard announced the cancellation of a development loan that West Germany had granted to Egypt, as well as West Germany's intention to establish diplomatic relations with Israel. The German officials in the Community institutions became, alongside the Dutch, Israel's most consistent proponents. "We see that the German support is warming up and becoming hotter, I would say," testified Shalush to the Cabinet for Economic Affairs, adding:

> we are in a situation that Germany has adopted for itself the Israeli thesis without restrictions and agreed to be the best man at Israel's request for association with the Market . . . for the first time we can say with certainty that not only is what they are saying in Bonn correct, but the instructions from Bonn to the German representatives in Brussels are in this same spirit, and they are likewise being implemented accordingly.[16]

One expression of this was the German willingness to consult with Israel regarding their stance in negotiations with the Maghreb countries. The Germans asked Israel what kind of arrangement it would consider least detrimental and promised to do their utmost to consider Israel's needs.[17] The Israelis consequently viewed Germany as a positive factor, as is evidenced by the importance they attributed to raising the matter of association in the Council of Ministers prior to January 1, 1968, at which point Germany would cease to serve as rotating President of the EEC. And indeed, the Germans guaranteed that as long as they were at the head of the Community institutions (i.e. the rotating presidency), they would not allow France and Italy to veto negotiations with Israel (as they had done in the case of talks with Britain). The Israelis were worried by such a scenario, fearing that it was likely to cause a deadlock for the foreseeable future.[18]

In an opposing trend, from June 1967 onward, the Belgian government's position on an arrangement with Israel became increasingly chilly, mainly due to French influence. In December 1967, the Belgian Foreign Ministry recommended that its government freeze, at least temporarily, the principle of a preferential agreement—which Belgium had previously supported—largely for political reasons. However, the Belgian Foreign Minister Pierre Harmel decided not to deviate from the line adopted by the other Benelux countries and Germany, all of which supported a preferential agreement.[19] Belgium's weight was at any rate not the same as that of the Big Three.

In this situation, Italy would tip the balance: would the Italians exploit France's position to assume, once again, an uncompromising stance? Initially, it seemed that the government in Rome had indeed decided to act in this manner. In the working group on the Israeli matter, Italian bureaucrats voiced a new argument: the existing trade agreement was ineffective due to the structural problems of the Israeli economy; as long as these remained uncorrected, no trade gesture towards Israel would be of any use.[20] They argued that the Israeli government needed to take charge of production planning and limit Israeli industry to a restricted number of products, with regard to which it would be possible to achieve a comparative advantage vis-à-vis the EEC. However, towards the end of 1967, the Italian stance underwent a certain change: the Italian representatives in the Council agreed to negotiations with Israel on a preferential agreement that would accord Israel tariff reductions at a rate of 25% on most of their industrial products, apart from a number of items that The Six deemed especially sensitive. The Italian proposal was very modest compared to that of the Commission's proposal (a reduction of the tariff rate by 100% on all Israel's industrial products).

Once again decision makers and officials in Jerusalem faced a dilemma: in the current circumstances, should they once more adopt a pragmatic stance and support this proposal? Indeed, the proposal contained tempting components; accepting the Italian proposal as a basis for negotiations would leave France completely isolated from the other five members, who agreed in principle to an agreement on a preferential basis. Likewise, it would be possible to try, over the course of negotiations, to increase the reductions. Finally, the first preferential agreement was likely to serve as a prelude to a comprehensive agreement, such as a customs union or a free trade area. It was of the utmost importance to determine once and for all that Israel was entitled to preferential treatment. In his parting conversation before leaving his position, Herbst advised Israel to accept the Italian proposal as a first step toward a more meaningful preferential agreement in the future[21]—a line that accorded with the thinking of many Israeli officials.[22] However, France's uncompromising stance, negating any arrangement whatsoever on a preferential basis, again made Israel's dilemma theoretical. Foreign Minister Eban expressed his opinion in the meeting of the Cabinet for Economic Affairs and received the full support of Finance Minister Sapir:

> It seems to me that if there is no defining economic reason against, I would favor preserving the demand in its entirety, even if they tell us that it is a dead end . . . if we make a few concessions or small reductions, I am not sure that we will ever be able to raise the demand for association again.[23]

In an effort to break the complete stalemate, the Commission proposed conducting a detailed study on the basis of the Italian proposal, although its officials noted that a broad preferential agreement continued to represent the most suitable solution to Israel's trade problems. At the beginning of December 1968, the COREPER ordered the Commission to conduct such a report. However, the Israelis refused to cooperate with this initiative while France continued to reject the principle of a preferential arrangement. The Economic Department at the Foreign Ministry explicitly ordered its representatives in the capitals of The Six not to initiate any conversations about the report, instructing them to emphasize in all encounters with their European counterparts that the Israeli government was insisting on its original request for a comprehensive agreement.[24] The Israeli opposition made the report valueless and the Commission did not hurry to start its work; this situation of treading water continued in the first months of 1969.

However, in the spring of that year, the stalemate which had been in place for almost two years began to crack. The completion of association agreements with Morocco and Tunisia (signed at the end of March 1969)[25] spurred Israel's friends in the Community to demand progress even more vehemently. The Dutch did not dare to make the signing of the agreements with Morocco and Tunisia conditional on a positive decision regarding Israel, but declared that they would be prepared to do so in the future concerning the negotiations with Spain and Algeria. Seeking a compromise between the Italians, who were prepared to grant only limited tariff reductions, and the Israelis, who still dreamed of an arrangement as outlined by the Commission, the Dutch now placed on the table of the Permanent Representatives a proposal to grant tariff reductions at a rate of 60% on most Israeli industrial products. To justify their proposal, the Dutch reiterated the same reasons that had appeared in the Commission's memorandum: "Israel was one of the first countries which, following the establishment of the Common Market, tried to form closer connections with it." Israel had agreed to compromise on a non-preferential trade agreement:

> but it became clear in a short time that this did not accord with the hopes placed in it . . . Distortion of the trade relations in the Mediterranean region to Israel's detriment, a necessary result of the preferential status that the EEC will grant to other countries in the region [Spain, the Maghreb] will create a situation of discrimination, which we must not accept under any terms.[26]

The Dutch proposal was much more generous than that of the Italians, and the Israelis received it with enthusiasm.[27] The Deputy Director General of the Foreign Ministry was sent on a journey of persuasion among all the EEC countries apart from France, with the aim of amassing support for the Dutch proposal. The responses he received everywhere were positive, including the Italians, who noted that the modest reductions they had suggested (25%) were a mere starting point; it would certainly be possible to discuss the final rate. The Germans even agreed to a complete cancelation of tariff on industrial products.[28] The only ones to hesitate were the Belgians, who feared a direct conflict between the Five and France, which could have destructive results.[29]

The pressure on the French to accept the principle of a preferential agreement at this stage became more intense than ever before. In a conversation between German Foreign Minister Willy Brandt and his French counterpart Michel Debre, the former said that the time had come to find a solution to Israel's problems.[30] At the same juncture, a dramatic development in France made the authorities in Paris less immune to pressure than previously. In April 1969, de Gaulle resigned as President of the Republic and withdrew from public life following the internal unrest sparked by student demonstrations in the preceding year. During the eleven years of his rule, the general had molded French foreign policy in an almost completely singular fashion; among his other accomplishments, he was the architect of the revolution in France's Middle Eastern policy since June 1967. France's uncompromising refusal to award Israel a "prize" for its aggression, including a preferential agreement with the EEC, was the fruit of de Gaulle's personal decision. No pressure from Israel, the Commission and other EEC members could move him from this decision.

His successors—the new President Pompidou, Prime Minister Couve de Murville, Foreign Minister Debre (and Maurice Schuman)—remained ostensibly faithful to this line. However, none of them shared de Gaulle's indifference to the opinions of others and his tendency to entrench himself in a fundamental stance, especially in the face of increasing pressure. Likewise, Debre and Schuman had always been obvious supporters of Israel and in the past had even attempted to promote Israel's association with the EEC (the first as Prime Minister and the second as chair of the Foreign Affairs committee in the legislature). They were now destined to confront the united position of the five other EEC members together with the Commission, calling them to withdraw their objections. At the meeting of the Council of Ministers on May 12, 1969, the new Foreign Minister Debre found himself completely isolated. He was forced to cite the claim that the situation in the Middle East was not suited to progress on Israel's matter, although it was evident that he felt great personal discomfort at the situation.[31] His replacement, Schuman, was subject to the same unceasing pressure and eventually surrendered to it. The five other members in the meantime succeeded in reaching an agreement that Israel would receive a reduction at the rate of 45%, midway between the Italian and Dutch proposals.

For the first time, the Five reached a full consensus. At the meeting of the ministers on July 22, 1969, Schuman asked to read out an announcement. This began with a declaration that France maintained steadfastly that Israel did not require a preferential agreement and its problems could be solved by widening the existing agreement. Moreover, a preferential agreement would have political consequences: it would seem to favor Israel over the Arab states. Yet, because France's colleagues in the EEC supported the preferential agreement, France would not oppose it, on the condition that the Council of Ministers was prepared to sign similar preferential agreements with Arab states, should the latter request them.[32] This final stipulation was merely a convenient ladder, enabling the French to climb down from the tree.

In January 1969, the Economic Council of the Arab League had decided to remove the sweeping prohibition on cooperation between Arab states and the EEC. In the coming months, the Arab states, led by Egypt, expressed in unison the desire to initiate contacts with the EEC. This gave Schuman a golden opportunity to reduce somewhat the political significance of a preferential agreement with Israel.[33] The Israelis were not at all concerned about the equivalence the French demanded between them and the Arabs; they only feared that the French condition was another exercise to delay a positive decision.

The Germans, by contrast, had more serious concerns. West Germany's relations with most Arab countries were at a nadir; diplomatic relations had even been severed with some of them following recognition of East Germany. The fundamental obligation to accept their requests for a preferential agreement with the EEC was politically problematic for Germany, even though the Hallstein doctrine had already lost much of its validity and was soon to disappear altogether. The Israelis viewed the French withdrawal of their fundamental opposition as a great opportunity, to be exploited at any price, and therefore exerted heavy pressure on the Germans to agree to the French condition, which in turn could mean closer relations between the EEC and the Arab states—without doubt another ironic outcome of international politics. The Germans felt that they could not place a new obstacle on the way to an agreement with Israel and accordingly withdrew their opposition.

In September 1969, the Council of Ministers passed a decision to begin negotiations with Israel on a preferential agreement. The talks began in November 1969 and included four short rounds that concluded in February 1970 and led to the signing of an agreement in record time—only six months passed from the opening of the talks to the official signing of the agreement. This was possible because the outlines of the agreement were already clear to both sides, which had for twelve years been involved in trade talks in one way or another; there remained little to discuss, aside from some minor matters. The EEC delegation suggested reductions at the rate of 45% on most Israeli industrial products; the Israelis asked for an additional 5% and this was granted. By contrast, the EEC delegation refused the Israeli request that after five years the arrangement would become a full free trade agreement; instead it was agreed that after three-and-a-half years, new negotiations would begin. The real saving for Israeli exports in tariff payments was estimated at no more than 15 million Israeli pounds (around $5 million). Yet the real value of the agreement was that Israeli industries became competitive in European markets, making the country attractive to investors.

Yet the importance of the agreement was political no less than economic. In assessing the value of the agreement, an Israeli diplomat stated:

> This is a blow to the Arab boycott, the basic aim of which, as is known, is to isolate us economically. The fact is that an organization which contains 175 million consumers has signed a preferential agreement with Israel and the tariff reductions which we received were given solely to Israel.

The Deputy Director General of the Ministry of Foreign Affairs described it as a "political landmark,"[34] while the newspaper *Ma'ariv* defined the arrangement as "extremely significant progress from the stalemate which Israel had encountered in contacts with the Market."[35] The odyssey had come to an end.

Notes

1 See: Gadi Heimann, *Franco-Israeli Relations, 1958–1967*, vol. 36 (Oxford: Routledge, 2017).
2 Edward A. Kolodziej, *French International Policy under De Gaulle and Pompidou: The Politics of Grandeur* (Ithaca: Cornell University Press, 1974).
3 Substantial evidence indicates that the French government did not at first understand de Gaulle's new Middle Eastern policy. At the beginning of July, the French Embassy

in Tel Aviv approached the Foreign Ministry in Paris requesting its help to refute rumors concerning the uncooperative stance France had ostensibly adopted at the last meeting of the Council of Ministers. The Embassy was unaware that, over the previous weeks, France's policy on this matter had changed completely. See: DDF, 1967, tome II, doc. 25, July 12, 1967.

4 There is a great deal of evidence indicating this. First, the unambiguous appraisal by various European statesmen and officials concerning France's motives (see, for example, Cnaan to the Economic Department, ISA, FM, file 3154/8, June 26, 1967 and August 29, 1967; Cnaan to the Economic Department, ISA, FM, file 3155/2, September 8, 1967. Second, the French position underwent a sharp and dramatic change following the war, yet the economic statistics had not altered at all. Third, the French were prepared to admit this directly, as in Couve de Murville's comments to Ambassador Eytan: "I always said that the trade agreement did not and would not give enough, but now there exists a certain political background which makes it difficult to conclude a preferential agreement": Eytan to the Economic Department, ISA, FM, file 3155/2, October 25, 1967.

5 See the comments by Michel Debre, the new French Foreign Minister, to the West German Chancellor Willy Brandt (Ma'ariv, "The French Foreign Minister: We Will Foil Any Israeli Attempt to Penetrate the 'Market'," Ma'ariv, March 16, 1969).

6 Cnaan to the Economic Department, ISA, FM, file 3154/8, July 17, 1967.

7 Cnaan to the Economic Department, ISA, FM, file 3155/2, September 8, 1967.

8 This was explicitly stated in a memorandum composed by the Commission's department for Foreign Relations. See: Relations entre la Communauté et Israël, EUA, BAC 327, September 27, 1967.

9 This argument between the Commission and France recurred at all meetings of the working group established to discuss the arrangement with Israel and in the Council of Permanent Representatives and the Council of Ministers. It has not been possible to locate protocols of the working group in the EEC Archive, but translations of memoranda written by the Commission are found in the Israel State Archive in Jerusalem. See: Memorandum regarding the "Israel" working group (translation), ISA, FM, file 3155/2, August 2, 1967; Deputy Director General of the Economic Department (Elron) to the Director General of the Finance Ministry, ISA, FM, file 3155/2, October 29, 1967; EEC News, ISA, FM, file 3155/4, December 15, 1967.

10 The French government claimed that the Prime Minister's intention had only been to present the possible options, without preferring one or another. In a private conversation with an Israeli diplomat, Pompidou admitted making the statements in his conversation with the Ambassador but added that "as long as the present tension in the region continues, the General will not allow any action in the entirety of Israel's relations with the Market." See: Maroz to The Head of West Europe Department, ISA, FM, file 3155/2, November 1, 1967.

11 Elron to the Economic Administration, ISA, FM, file 3155/2, November 1, 1967.

12 Protocol of the meeting of the ministerial committee regarding market matters, ISA, FM, file 4249/4, December 4, 1967.

13 The Israelis received particular support from recently retired German politicians. During Adenauer's visit to Israel in 1966, he personally promised Levi Eshkol to help Israel attain association (see: Uri Dan, "Eshkol and Israeli Ambassadors in Western Europe," Ma'ariv, May 29, 1966). In May 1968, Erhard, who had also in the meantime left his position, published an opinion piece arguing, "[I]f only the Common Market would recognize that Israel is economically and culturally part of the European area, Israel could offer a very valuable contribution to Europe . . . Israel could become a rich country if only the Europeans would gather the courage to stand at the right hand of this nation and its people": A. Deutshkro, "Erhard Calls for Europe to Stand at Israel's Right Hand Side," Ma'ariv, May 1, 1968.

14 Joachim Krause and Lothar Wilker, "Bureaucracy and Foreign Policy in the Federal Republic of Germany," in *The Foreign Policy of West Germany: Formation and Contents*, eds. Ekkehart Krippendorff and Volker Rittberger (London: Sage, 1980), 136–7.

15 See: Felix Eliezer Shinnar, *Between Needs and Feelings: Israel-German Relations, 1951–1966* (Jerusalem: Shocken, 1967).

16 Protocol of the meeting of the ministerial committee regarding market matters, ISA, FM, file 4249/4, December 4, 1967.

17 "Preferential Treatment for Maghreb Oranges," ISA, MF, file 19875/7, March 30, 1967.

18 Deputy Director General of the Economic Department to the Economic Administration, ISA, FM, file 3133/3, November 23, 1967.

19 Relations entre la C.E.E. et Israël, Archives generals du Royaume Belgique [AGRB], Fond Pierre Harmel [FH], file 665, January 23, 1969.

20 Relations entre la Communauté et Israël, EUA, BAC 327, September 27, 1967.

21 Elron to the Economic Department, ISA, FM, file 3176/4, November 18, 1968.

22 See, for example, Economic Department to Shalush, ISA, FM, file 3176/1, August 18, 1968.

23 Protocol of the Ministerial Committee for Common Market Matters, ISA, FM, file 3295/9, March 18, 1968.

24 EEC News, ISA, FM, file 3176/1, December 13, 1968.

25 In their framework, Morocco and Tunisia received significant tariff benefits on around 55% of their agricultural exports to the Community. Regarding these agreements see: *Troisième Rapport general sur l'activité de la Communauté*, 1969, p. 370, and also I William. Zartman, *Politics of Trade Negotiations between Africa and the European Economic Community: The Weak Confronts the Strong* (Princeton: Princeton University Press, 1971), 116–48.

26 Memorandum de gouvernment néerlandais concernant la demand d'association á la Communauté Economique Européenne, AGRB, FH, file 665, January 1, 1969.

27 See, for example. the discussion of his question at the meeting of the directors general of the economic ministries: Protocol of the meeting of directors general, ISA, FM, file 3176/2, March 10, 1969.

28 Embassy in Brussels to the Ministry of Foreign Affairs, ISA, MIT, file 6635/20, April 24, 1969.

29 Haran to Tzipori, ISA, FM, file 3176/2, April 11, 1969.

30 ISA, MIT, file 6635/20, March 23, 1969.

31 Elron to the Ministry of Foreign Affairs, ISA, MIT, file 6635/20, May 12, 1969.

32 Representation Permanente de la Belgique près les Communautés Européennes, AGRB, FH, session du conseil CEE, file 669, July 22–23, 1969.

33 Schuman admitted to Ambassador Eytan that the stipulation in the French announcement was an excuse to make the gesture to Israel politically acceptable (he took credit for the idea). See: Eytan to the Economic Department, ISA, FM, file 1706/8, August 4, 1969.

34 Memorandum, Yaakov Cohen to the Director General of the Ministry of Foreign Affairs ISA, FM, file 3214/1, June 20, 1970; Memorandum, Shalush to the Foreign Minister, ISA, FM file 5254/1, June 14, 1970.

35 *Ma'ariv*, Editorial, "A Crack in the Wall of the 'Common Market'," *Ma'ariv*, October 19, 1969.

References

Dan, Uri. "Eshkol and Israeli Ambassadors in Western Europe." *Ma'ariv*, May 29, 1966.

Deutshkro, A. "Erhard Calls for Europe to Stand at Israel's Right Hand Side." *Ma'ariv*, May 1, 1968.

Ma'ariv. Editorial. "A Crack in the Wall of the 'Common Market'." *Ma'ariv*, October 19, 1969.

Heimann, Gadi. *Franco-Israeli Relations, 1958–1967*. Vol. 36, Oxford: Routledge, 2017.

Kolodziej, Edward A. *French International Policy under De Gaulle and Pompidou: The Politics of Grandeur*. Ithaca: Cornell University Press, 1974.

Krause, Joachim, and Lothar Wilker. "Bureaucracy and Foreign Policy in the Federal Republic of Germany." In *The Foreign Policy of West Germany: Formation and Contents*, edited by Ekkehart Krippendorff and Volker Rittberger. London: Sage, 1980.

Ma'ariv. "The French Foreign Minister: We Will Foil Any Israeli Attempt to Penetrate the 'Market'." *Ma'ariv*, March 16, 1969.

Shinnar, Felix Eliezer. *Between Needs and Feelings: Israel-German Relations, 1951–1966*. Jerusalem: Shocken, 1967.

Zartman, I. William. *Politics of Trade Negotiations between Africa and the European Economic Community: The Weak Confronts the Strong*. Princeton: Princeton University Press, 1971.

Conclusions

The prolonged, one could even say exhausting, negotiations between Israel and the EEC, which lasted for more than a decade, offer insights the importance of which exceeds the historical episode at the heart of this book. Indeed, the tale of these negotiations exposes several conclusions concerning international negotiations, the European Union and its internal relations and power structure during its earliest years, and the relations between the EEC, Israel and the Mediterranean countries. These insights are not necessarily interrelated but are all significant, fascinating and theoretically relevant.

The first insight concerns factors affecting negotiations in international politics and their outcomes, particularly the role of normative arguments. Israel's achievements in the negotiations with the EEC do not accord with standard models explaining conflicts and negotiations which emphasize variables, such as relative bargaining power, common interests shared by the negotiating parties and the availability of alternatives, as well as skills and tactics in explaining the results of negotiations between countries. These factors fail to explain why, in 1970, the EEC agreed to sign a preferential trade agreement with Israel even though The Six had no material interest in so doing and such a step was even imbued with danger. As was demonstrated, this was the result of Israel's success in effectively arguing the country was liable to suffer damage as a result of the establishment of the Common Market, thus forcing The Six to take steps towards Israel. Indeed, it seems that the Israelis succeeded in forcing the Europeans to grant them a preferential agreement by bringing about a situation in which the Europeans had no further excuses at their disposal to refuse. The story of the long negotiations between Israel and the EEC therefore reveals a fascinating phenomenon. A negotiating party with almost no bargaining power, engaged in talks of a purely trade character, can compensate for its weakness through the use of moral arguments.

Why do negotiating parties, in particular that which finds itself in the inferior bargaining position, employ normative arguments?[1] What role do these kinds of arguments play in the framework of negotiations? How do they advance the negotiating party's aims?

The first benefit of utilizing normative arguments is the ability to conceal those selfish motives which are liable to create antagonism among the other party and ruin any chances of reaching an agreement. Fundamentally, revealing the true selfish interest at the foundation of his arguments is likely to give the negotiator an advantage: the other party will have fewer possibilities to force him to accept anything less than his original objectives. Indeed, if a party agrees to enter negotiations based on these selfish motives, it must propose an arrangement that will respond to the first player's selfish desires. However, despite this advantage, negotiators rarely use such arguments because they broadcast a lack of sensitivity and even complete antipathy towards the interests and rights of the other party, thus generating antagonism. Selfish arguments constitute a crude declaration of one party's superiority; indeed, only the strong can allow themselves to present the naked truth, presuming that the weaker party at any rate has no alternative but to acquiesce.[2] They intensify the importance of emotional elements accompanying the negotiations, such as the desire to maintain respect and honor, as well as a positive self-image, and avoid public humiliation.[3] Psychological studies indicate that parties tend to be less cooperative if they believe that the other side in the negotiations regards itself as inferior.[4] For this reason, it is best for the negotiator to choose arguments that will speak to the heart of the other side, providing that he is convinced that he can defend them suitably and persuade the other side of their validity.

As was noted, the Israelis sought much more than a banal trade agreement: they wanted association, largely due to political motivations. However, the need to develop an effective argument, one that would win over the Europeans and could be defended factually, forced them to focus on the economic damage which Israel was likely to sustain as a result of the establishment of the Common Market. In so doing, they provided the Europeans with an opportunity to suggest solutions which offered less than association and which the Israelis were forced to accept, as a tactical step hoping their ineffectiveness would later become evident, forcing The Six to propose a better offer. Choosing from the very beginning to emphasize the political profit which they sought to gain from association, would have significantly restricted the Europeans in offering different alternatives. However, at the same time it would have severely damaged the chances that the Europeans would agree to enter talks based on this argument; therefore, their gain would in fact have resulted in a loss. Throughout the negotiations, both Israel and the EEC suspected that the other party's arguments were instrumental, constituting nothing more than a comfortable excuse. The Six were sure that Israel's desire for political profit by far exceeded concerns about economic damage. The Israelis, for their part, viewed European arguments regarding the legal and trade complexities involved in acceding to Israel as an excuse to cover their unwillingness to harm their relations with the Arab nations. However, both sides almost consistently avoided voicing these suspicions to the other side; if they deviated from this avoidance behavior, they did so in personal conversations with figures of whose support they were assured. In fact, the two sides pretended that they believed one another because they suspected that accusing the other party of hypocrisy would hinder any willingness to reach a compromise and only entrench its position further. Instead, they preferred to tackle the other party's excuses, seeking to destroy the foundations of these arguments. Eventually, the Israelis were more successful at this game.

A second benefit of normative arguments is that they generate an obligation to the parameters of the solution which the party desires, with the aim of extorting concessions from the other side.[5] Declaring that a certain solution is vital for reasons of morality or justice raises the price of compromise and in so doing increases the negotiating party's credibility as unwilling to compromise beyond a certain point. Indeed, it is important to bear in mind that the conclusion of negotiations almost always have emotional ramifications such as gain or loss of honor, prestige and reputation.[6] This obligation becomes even more firmly entrenched when the arguments are made public, because the negotiator is liable to pay a political price in the case of compromises.[7] To anchor this obligation even further, the public at home must be informed of norm-oriented arguments; therefore there is a tendency to publicize them.[8] In this context, negotiations conducted behind closed doors endow the negotiators with more room for maneuver.[9] Naturally, the weaker negotiating party has a greater need to create an obligation artificially, because his weakness leads to uncertainty regarding the ability to maintain his position.

The Israelis often anchored their request for association, or at least a comprehensive agreement, by using arguments based on justice reasoning, explicitly stating that they would not agree to an arrangement which was not fair. When the Europeans offered proposals with little content, the Israelis tended to externalize the resulting negative feelings using terms such as "insult," "humiliation," "mockery," "an offensive handout" and so on. Even if in so doing they expressed their authentic feelings, the instrumental function that these expressions fulfilled in the negotiations must not be ignored: they sought to signal that the Israeli government would not be able to reconcile itself to proposals that did not fulfill a substantial portion of their demands. Sometimes, they intentionally incited Israeli public opinion in order to generate additional pressure in this manner, as after the proposal for tariff reductions totaling $72,000. At the same time, in the case of these negotiations, employing arguments of morality and justice was even more effective for a very simple reason: the common area of interest in the negotiations between Israel and the EEC was extremely limited and perhaps even non-existent. The Europeans were not interested in an arrangement and therefore Israel's threat to leave the talks was ineffective. The Europeans would have been happy for the Israelis to end the negotiations and depart from Brussels in anger. At the end of the day, the Israeli leaders were forced to recognize their mistake and calm Israeli public opinion, as the latter called for Israel to leave the talks immediately and show the Europeans the true meaning of Jewish pride.

The third benefit of normative arguments is that they force the other party to confront and respond to these arguments, thus enabling the negotiator to improve his bargaining position in the negotiations, if he is indeed the winning party. This is accomplished by persuading the other side that his arguments are valid—that the suggested solution is just, moral and accords in the clearest fashion with accepted norms. On occasion, the process of the argument is likely to lead to authentic persuasion of the other party. However, this does not occur often, because on many occasions, the sides view themselves as in a bargaining situation and interpret the arguments of the other side mainly as a tool in the framework of the argument between them. Therefore, the question arises: if the losing side is not persuaded of the authenticity of the other party's argument, what leads them to accept its constraints? Scholars suggest two possible explanations. First, if the argument between the two sides is in the public sphere and has gained the attention of an interested audience, the losing side will feel forced to accept certain constraints, otherwise they will be publicly condemned and humiliated.[10] This interested audience can be a broker, such as another country, the public in the country with which the negotiations are under way and international public opinion in the form of non-governmental organizations concerned with the issue under discussion or other countries with an interest in it.[11] This situation is relevant when the negotiations are conducted in a context of a community which shares values and norms.

Negotiators' desire to maintain their reputation explains why normative arguments can be successful even without the presence of an audience or when the negotiators are not sensitive to audience pressures. Since interactions with the winning side will continue in the future, the losing side has an interest in accepting the outcome. Assenting to the winning argument is thus an act of reciprocity.[12] Just as players hesitate to breach an agreement even when it does not reward them, because they are concerned that this may affect the willingness of other parties to negotiate with them in the future, so it is in their interest not to retreat after losing. There is also another aspect to this explanation: the possibility of using an argument as an effective tool in the framework of negotiations constitutes collective capital shared by community members. These have an interest in preserving normative argumentation because it offers the side in an inferior position a chance to receive a larger chunk than the leverage of influence at its disposal should allow. This is relevant to all members of the community, because the party which has the upper hand today may find itself in an inferior position tomorrow. However, the existence of these public goods depends on the willingness of the parties, including those holding the better cards, to acquiesce, even if only partially, as soon as they lose the argument. Thus naturally, the weaker party tends to use normative arguments, mainly in the early stages of negotiations. However, so too parties with equal bargaining power that have reached an impasse are likely to find in normative claims a possibility to break the stalemate.[13] This accords with March and Olsen's distinction that negotiators who have reached a stalemate usually replace consequential logic with appropriateness logic.[14]

The negotiations saga between Israel and the EEC reveals the weight of the norm according to which the losing side must accede to the will of the victor in some way, irrespective of their bargaining power. It also demonstrates that a target audience is not necessary for normative arguments to be effective. As was noted, public pressure played a relatively minor role in the case study discussed herein. Yet, when it became evident that they could no longer discard the Israelis' requests, The Six felt forced to offer them some kind of gesture. The Europeans' initial negotiation mistake was their hasty agreement to the basic principle that they were obliged to ensure that no harm would come to the Israeli economy following the establishment of the Common Market. Although in the first stages they could have easily disposed of the Israelis, informing them that Israel had no right to special treatment from the EEC—as indeed they did, in their response to the Israeli letter of November 1958—they eventually agreed to take a seat at the negotiation table. This was certainly not due to any belief that they would gain advantages from a special arrangement with Israel. By contrast, they were well aware of the costs that such a step would entail. The answer to this mystery is a combination of two factors. First, many Europeans in key positions felt uncomfortable sending the Israelis away empty-handed. Figures such as Debre, Luns, Erhard and Spaak personally supported Israel. They were influenced by the argument, which the Israelis did not hesitate to use, that Europe owed the state of the Jewish people a moral debt. Some of these figures were even under internal political pressure to accede to Israel. At a certain stage, they themselves presented a proposal for a limited trade agreement, seeking to persuade the Israelis to abandon the sweeping solution of association. The second factor enters at this stage: the assumption—which in hindsight proved erroneous—that Israel would be willing to accept even the most modest arrangement and that at any rate the EEC possessed ample reasons to justify not granting Israel anything beyond what it was willing to give. It was on this basis that the Europeans agreed to enter negotiations in the fall of 1962. However, shocked to discover that the Israelis had not withdrawn in any way from their ambitious aims, the Europeans sought to cause the Israeli delegation to leave the negotiating table—an attempt which failed. Although many Israelis demanded that the negotiators should "slam the door in the Community's face," Eshkol, Sapir and Meir sagely understood that Israel's only chance to obtain its ends lay in continuing the negotiations, come what may. Their willingness to sign the agreement in 1964 gave Israel advantages, painting it as the compromising party and providing it with a golden opportunity to prove to the Europeans the accuracy of the Israeli argument that this solution did not tackle Israel's problems. The Europeans, who remained unenthusiastic about acquiescing to the Israeli requests, understood at this stage that they had been forced into a corner: they had entered the game aware of the rules and now felt forced to abide by the outcome. When the French tried to "break the rules" by arguing at a late stage that Israel really had no special rights vis-à-vis the EEC, they failed to recruit any support for this position among their colleagues and swiftly retreated from this line of argument. This indicates that negotiators avoid denying a line of argument which they adopted throughout the negotiations, even when it collapses. They feel obligated, within certain boundaries, to respond to the dictates of the winning argument, even when it opposes their own interests.

*

The second insight provided by this study concerns certain characteristics of Israeli foreign policy which are particularly evident in this case study. One of these characteristics is the somewhat obsessive Israeli yearning for international recognition. The importance which the Israelis accorded to the type of agreement and the title crowning it, far exceeded narrow economic-legal considerations. The political and psychological benefits which the Israelis sought to obtain via a special status vis-à-vis Europe should be understood on the basis of what can be termed as Israel's "policy of recognition," which guided decision makers in the first two decades of the state's existence. According to this policy, significant resources and efforts were invested—and political prices paid—in the efforts to bring countries and other international players to embrace the nascent state, end its regional isolation, grant it approval as a legitimate member of the family of nations and confirm its good reputation in the global community. This policy was expressed in the ceaseless Israeli efforts to extract from the French open expressions of friendship and public support in the period following the solution of the Algerian problem (1962). This policy did more harm than good to the relations between the two nations. A further example of this policy was Israeli economic aid enterprise in Africa at the end of the 1950s and beginning of the 1960s. One of the aims of the aid campaign was to obtain goodwill among the newly emerged African states. The "policy of recognition" was nourished by a deep existential fear, a feeling of severe frustration at the regional and international isolation forced upon Israel for no reason, and the strong ambition to bring about the collapse of the Arab boycott. In some respects, striving for association was an additional aspect of this policy of recognition, explaining the importance which the Israelis attributed to this goal. Even after so many years, beyond the period discussed in this book, it is possible to say that the policy of recognition continues to function as an important element in Israeli policy. Although many of Israel's political and material circumstances have changed—Israel has become an economically developed country, a member of many international organizations and possesses a dense network of relations with the European Union—the feeling of psychological distress and the fear of regional and international isolation motivate the country's attempts to receive recognition, support and demonstrations of friendship from the global community. Acknowledgment of this distress and its ramifications for Israeli society today nurture the civil BDS movement,[15] as in the past they fed the boycott led by the Arab nations.

However, more than the political-psychological motive expressed in the obsession with an association agreement, this book reflects another aspect of Israeli foreign policy: its highly pragmatic character. From the moment that they were forced to abandon the dream of association, Israeli statesmen and bureaucrats demonstrated exceptional flexibility. Understanding that The Six were not interested in any agreement with Israel, the Israelis adamantly avoided giving the Europeans any reason to block the progress of the negotiations. Indeed, the Israelis believed that they must maintain at any price the close contact with the Community institutions and persevere with the talks, while being ready to accept very little in the early stages. Although they often complained about the never-ending foot dragging in the Community institutions, the broken promises and the deadlines not honored, the Israelis repeatedly accepted the outcome with gritted teeth. The principle of not leaving the negotiations and slamming the door behind them guided the Israelis throughout the talks, although they incurred stark criticism at home as a result, from experts in the various economic ministries, journalists, politicians (mainly, but not only, from the opposition) and the general public who viewed the Israeli capitulation as dishonorable and unwise. It is difficult to determine to what extent this pragmatism was effective at the end of the day. Some claimed that Israel would have achieved more in a much shorter time by remaining faithful to the original ambitious aims and using threats, not only lobbying. However, in truth, the balance of power regarding this matter was based almost entirely on material and institutional elements, and tended clearly to the Israelis' detriment. It is difficult to believe that the Israelis had the power to force the EEC to accede to their requests. It would not be far-fetched to assume that through this pure pragmatism, often described as disrespectable, Israel succeeded in winning an exceptional achievement, much greater than its bargaining power would have predicted.

*

The insights suggested by this case study extend also to our understanding of the internal European power structure and its influence on the consolidation of a common European foreign policy broadly, as well as specifically vis-à-vis Israel and Mediterranean Countries. The development of a common European foreign (and defense) policy is considered secondary in the process of European integration. Instead, the establishment of the Common Market and consolidation of economic, monetary and financial policies, were at the heart of the integration process and among the central forces driving it. Therefore, unsurprisingly when foreign policy and related issues where concerned, EEC member states sought to maintain their decision-making powers and sovereignty, while leaving the Commission restricted room for action where it could advance the process of economic integration. For this reason, the Commission was accorded the important role of managing international relations with third countries. However, in the view of the member states, this role was to be confined to managing EEC trade policy, as part of constructing the Common Market, not as a means to advance the EEC's foreign policy or build its international political status. Foreign policy issues, including those concerning trade matters, remained in the bailiwick of The Six.[16]

This does not mean that the member states did not have an interest in coordinating their foreign policies and bringing them closer. Indeed, quite the opposite: they desired and attempted over the years to make significant advances towards foreign policy cooperation. Together with the US, The Six attempted to join forces on foreign and defense policies even before the establishment of the EEC. However, they failed to establish a European Defense Community, the heart of which was to be a joint army.[17] An additional failure occurred in 1961 following the member states' rejection of the Fouchet Report which called for the establishment of a union of states with a common foreign and defense policy.[18] The turning point in institutional terms took place in 1970, when The Six decided upon the establishment of European Political Cooperation, according to which they obligated to coordinate their foreign policies when key issues were concerned. This political cooperation maintained an inter-governmental and non-obligatory character; consultations with the Commission were required only when the coordination between the foreign ministers was likely to affect the activities of the European Community itself.[19] The Maastricht Treaty of 1993 transformed the European Community into the European Union and created a Common Foreign and Security Policy mechanism, delegating more powers to European institutions in molding a common, albeit not uniform foreign policy. The Lisbon Treaty of 2009 deepened the supra-national foundations of the common foreign policy by establishing a European External Action Service and introducing High Representative of the Union for Foreign Affairs and Security Policy, a position equivalent to a European Foreign Minister. Nevertheless, despite all these developments, until today European foreign policy remains intergovernmental in character and the member states continue to hold the reins. This intergovernmental character of European foreign policy was especially true during the first decades up to 1993, during which not only was there precarious coordination in foreign policy but attempts to tighten cooperation failed repeatedly due to countries' fears that strengthening supra-national cooperation will make them lose control.[20]

For this reason, the story of the trade negotiations between the EEC and Israel becomes essential for developing a profound and more precise understanding of the way in which the European Community operated in the first decades of its existence. This case study testifies to the development of foreign policy via what can be termed as stealth and reaction. The idea of foreign policy making via stealth and reaction represents a situation in which foreign policy is created or forced upon the decision makers without their intention; forces and interests from within and without influencing the decision makers—with or without coordination—and thus forcing them to respond and act. Response is likely to have broad ramifications beyond a specific case or situation; it is liable to dictate or shape the future foreign policy line. In this case study, foreign policy making via stealth and reaction was the result of a combination of factors: on the one hand, the Commission's attempts to establish its own power within the EEC's power structure, as well as to advance the external status of the EEC by stealthily moving from trade policy to foreign policy. On the other hand were the actions of the Permanent Representatives vis-à-vis the member states and the Commission, and the need to respond to Israel's attempts to gain political achievements through the trade channel. These forces acted at times in opposing directions and sometimes in parallel.

In hindsight, there was a great deal of logic in Europe's response to the Israeli approaches. From the perspective of The Six, there was no real political reason to advance an association agreement with a small, non-European state such as Israel at such an early stage of the EEC's existence. Moreover, The Six were subject to pressures from the Arab states, the latter threatening to implement boycotts against them. Therefore, the limited response to the Israeli demands in the framework of restricted negotiations which could be framed as compensation for the economic damage caused to Israel following the establishment of the Common Market, can be interpreted as a legitimate and reasonable step. It is thus reasonable to presume that the European reaction would have succeeded, had they been confronted only by a stubborn country such as Israel, acting alone. However, the Israeli dream accorded with the European Commission's ambition to establish its status in developing and directing European foreign policy and strengthening the status of EEC with respect to international trade.

From the outset, the Commission supported Israeli ambitions both expressly and covertly. At various junctures throughout the long negotiations, Commission figures actively cooperated with Israel behind the Council's back, sometimes in opposition to direct instructions. At first, these contacts encouraged the Israelis to take the initiative and set ambitious goals; throughout the negotiations, Commission officials passed on to the Israelis information and copies of classified documents; they advised them on how to act vis-à-vis the Council, and suggested how the French and Italian opposition could be overcome; likewise, they did not hesitate to criticize the behavior of the Council or one of the member states to the Israelis openly. As early as 1958, Hallstein and Rey suggested that Israel establish an official Israeli diplomatic representation to the EEC. They planted the dream of association with the EEC in the hearts of the Israelis—the ambition to obtain national and political benefit—and together with Mansholt awakened in the Israelis the belief that this was possible and that The Six would eventually view the matter positively. After the signing of the agreement in 1964, it was the Commission that helped Israel to revive the idea of association, encouraged the view that Europe was morally obligated to sign an association agreement with Israel, and exerted pressure on various figures to withdraw their countries' opposition to the Israeli request (as in the case of the Italian and French commissioners). Throughout the process, the Commission leadership acted in a manner that can be viewed as collusion with the Israelis: they passed on confidential information, advised the Israelis how to act in negotiations with the countries, coordinated positions and secretly acted together and took initiatives within and beyond the borders of the authority granted to it the Treaty of Rome. This behavior sometimes came at the price of conflict with the Council of Ministers.

How can we explain such behavior, which ostensibly constitutes a betrayal of the European interest and the responsibility placed on the shoulders of the Commission? In fact, the opposite is true. This cooperation stemmed in fact from an excessive loyalty to the European integration vision and the establishment of the EEC and fortifying its status. This was at least the way perceived by leaders of the Commission, in particular Hallstein, Rey and Mansholt. These figures viewed their roles as decisive in shaping European integration. Their loyalty was first and foremost to the vision of the EEC and they viewed the Commission as a driving force for the process of integration, even if the body was not always entrusted with the official authority for this, as in the domain of foreign policy.[21] According to their method, constructing Europe was not limited to the internal work of creating the Common Market but also involved strengthening its status in the global sphere. They saw the Commission as the engine pulling European integration, and therefore they needed to strengthen the power of this engine at home, within the web of internal EEC relations, and externally by advancing relations with countries that were not members of the EEC. Rey summarized this perfectly when he said that "The role of the Commission is not to wait for instructions from the Council but rather to shape policy."[22] The establishment of direct diplomatic relations with Israel, as with other nations, served this goal and endowed the EEC with a seal of sovereignty; this was especially important in its early days, considering the competition from EFTA. The establishment of such links also signified that the Commission represented the EEC in its foreign relations.

However, there is another explanation for the Commission's positive approach towards a trade arrangement with Israel which is not ideological. The Commission had a selfish motive in ensuring that the talks with Israel proceeded: as with all bureaucratic institutions, the Commission sought to bolster its status and influence within the EEC. It strived to maximize the resources and authority at its disposal and was not content with blindly implementing the instructions of the Council.[23] The Treaty of Rome accorded the Commission a central role in managing the EEC's trade policy, for example granting the Commission authority to conduct the negotiations, although under the supervision of the Council. The very existence of trade negotiations with another country constituted a signifier of sovereignty and transformed the Commission into a body which ostensibly represented "Europe" externally. Thus, a close connection emerged tying the development of the common trade policy with the institutional power of the Commission. The Directorate-General for the External Relations in the Commission encouraged foreign diplomats to establish representations in Brussels to conduct relations with the EEC. The Commission also zealously guarded the Commission's authority to manage the negotiations and complained whenever Council representatives assumed an active role in the talks.

The Commission leadership was aware that they were walking a very fine line and therefore acted cautiously and usually with discretion; Israel similarly helped to maintain this necessary discretion. For this reason, the cooperation remained covert, was not organized and did not trickle down to the lower levels of the Commission. For the most part, the Commission sought to widen the authority granted to it by the Rome Treaty arguing that it was necessary to use legitimately the technical tools it had been given. The Council of Ministers understood that the Commission was trying to expand the boundaries of its authority and was concerned that the Commission would exploit the talks with Israel to strengthen the supra-national element and lead a line of foreign policy which would not be agreed upon by the states but would obligate them at the same time. On more than one occasion, the Commission found itself in conflict with the Council of Ministers regarding the Israeli question; for this reason the French requested that Council representatives participate in the negotiations with Israel, alongside the Commission delegation. Aware of the problematic situation, the Commission at times retreated, principally when it endangered its internal standing within the EEC. However, even these retreats were for the most part tactical and temporary; the Commission found new ways to advance cooperation with Israel as, for example, after Israel's submission of a formal request for association towards the end of 1960. Considering the opposition of the Council, the Commission officially divested itself of the idea of an association agreement, but in practice helped Israel to find an intermediate path in the form of a trade agreement, which Israel could view as a springboard to a comprehensive agreement in the future.

The trade agreement with Israel was of minor importance, and similarly to the member states, the Commission too recognized this fact. Therefore, it is important to examine the steps that the Commission took with Israel in the wider context of the attempt to boost the Commission's status, as well as the status of the EEC in foreign policy in general, and with regard to trade in particular. As a trading bloc which constituted an exception to the GATT trade system, the EEC was criticized for discrimination and undermining the system. For this reason, weaving trade links with other countries, even if their economic importance was doubtful, served the Europeans' interest. Therefore, the Commission endeavored to sign additional trade agreements, such as those with Greece (1961), Turkey (1963) and Lebanon (1965), and sought to developed links with former European colonies in Africa and Asia.[24] In the first stage, this legitimized the existence of the Common Market and downplayed trade diversion problems, and in the second stage, it reinforced the status of the EEC as a trade bloc in multilateral negotiations in the GATT, for example in the Dillon and Kennedy Rounds.

In theoretical terms, the Commission's deliberate attempts to strengthen its internal position within the EEC and the supra-national element of the EEC by using technical tools for political aims reveals that a technical spillover—as the neo-functionalist approach argues—is not necessarily a process whereby a certain need propels further integration, resulting in an unintentional intensification of integration. The neo-functionalist approach explains the process of integration as a gradual one, during which supra-national cooperation in areas which are largely technical or concerned with "low politics" eventually leads to cooperation in further domains, including "high politics." In this process, various players transfer their national loyalty to the supra-national framework. The focal point of integration revolves around the mechanism of spillover,[25] which can be technical or political. The source of technical spillover is the technical need to widen cooperation to encompass additional fields. These additional fields share interfaces and connections with the topic where cooperation exists, because the cooperation will neither be complete nor be effective otherwise. This is a functional process, in which the process is motivated by need or by non-governmental players who are widening cooperation as a source of potential gains. This technical spillover leads to political spillover: non-governmental groups and elites transfer their focus of activity and interest to the supra-national framework.[26] By contrast, the case study discussed herein reveals that in the process of integration through spillover, the causality can be inverted. In this case, the Commission's activities were guided by goals much wider than those necessitating trade and technical cooperation and were driven by the leaders of the Commission, agents who are not members of the non-governmental elites in the member states—with the aim of harnessing the technical tools to advance a political aim. In other words, the actions of the Commission leadership did not result first and foremost from a technical spillover according to which it was necessary to widen existing trade cooperation to improve its efficiency. Rather the opposite: the attempt to advance the supranational elements of foreign policy utilized the existing tools of trade cooperation to advance a different aim, one which was not necessarily connected.

This episode offers additional important insights concerning the COREPER and the relations between the representatives and their superiors at home. As was noted, the function of the Permanent Representatives was to serve as a link connecting between Brussels and each one of the member states.[27] These Permanent Representatives prepare and manage the agenda of the Council of Ministers, meet weekly, make or pass on decisions to the Council of Ministers, consolidate compromises and carry out every task which the Council of Ministers give them. The Representatives are faithful to the superiors who had appointed them—the ministers and heads of state—and are in fact ambassadors of the member states, expected to act in the interests of the country they represented and according to the instructions they receive from their home countries.[28] Unsurprisingly, from the first days of the EEC, experienced and senior diplomats were mainly appointed as Permanent Representatives.[29] Although the Permanent Representatives represent the interests of their countries, scholarly literature testifies that among the Permanent Representatives a process of socialization occurs; relations of deep trust, mutual responsiveness and discretion develop between them, enabling them to achieve compromises and strive to reach decisions by consensus.[30]

The story of the trade negotiations between Israel and the EEC undermines the distinction made by the literature, revealing that at least in this case a principal-agent problem existed between the countries and their representatives in the Council. The principal (the Foreign Ministry or Prime Minister in the home country) authorized the agent (the Permanent Representative) to act on his behalf; however, the agent had a motivation to act in his own interests, different to the demands of the principal. Throughout the negotiations with Israel, the Permanent Representatives halted the possibility of progress or posed difficulties. Apart from the case of Italy—where the behavior of the Italian Permanent Representative was consistent with instructions from the Foreign Ministry in Rome—the Permanent Representatives often acted in opposition to the directions they received from their capitals. While the senior leadership in the home country was ready to take significant steps towards meeting Israel's demands, this readiness was stopped by the Permanent Representatives. This absurd situation reached a pinnacle when the Belgian and Italian Foreign Ministers attended a meeting of the COREPER to ensure that their representatives would follow the instructions they had received. The tables had turned: rather than the COREPER acting for the ministers and enabling decision making on a lower level, the latter had to go themselves to the meeting of the Permanent Representatives.

One possible explanation for this situation, different from that which the literature outlines, may be consistent with the diagnosis of the socialization process affecting the Permanent Representatives, which brought them to view the interests of their countries as embedded in the interests of a wider Europe. However, in this case, the actions of the Permanent Representatives involved behavior in opposition to the instructions they had received—that same explicit national interest—due to a subjective understanding or their own re-interpretation of their national interest in the context of the EEC. Had this been a case of one action by one Permanent Representative, it would have been anecdotal; yet this behavioral pattern recurred repeatedly among the Permanent Representatives. This is an indication that the processes of building a European identity and transferring loyalty were at work in the EEC from a very early stage; the source of common identity and loyalty were not only a long-term process of social construction integrated with history and institutional inertia. A similar process can also be discerned among the Commissioners, although there, at least in institutional terms, the supra-national element acted as the guiding principle, in contrast to the character of the inter-governmental nature of the Permanent Representatives. The paradoxical result was that in the arena of the EEC, the representatives of the countries succeeded in isolating the political pressures which Israel exerted in the various capitals and which changed the approach therein. In this respect on the one hand, supra-national and informal motifs in European integration advanced the interests of each member state as a result of the community framework which succeeded in isolating the pressures which Israel exerted on national politics. On the other hand, the transformation of Brussels into a center of political activity reinforced in the long term the status of the European institutions. There is room to examine whether the episode described in this book is unique to the Israeli case study or perhaps is indicative of an additional level of complexity in the network of EEC relations and has occurred also in other instances.

*

The negotiations tale between Israel and the EEC reveals a further level, less well known, in the molding of the Community's foreign policy towards Israel and the Mediterranean countries. Indeed, we can discern the roots of this policy emerging from the first years of the EEC's existence, and not as part of the consolidation of the European Political Cooperation mechanism (EPC), as the literature argues.[31] This process was random rather than organized, yet the manner in which the EEC and the member states reacted, and the considerations behind the policy chosen, guided the way in which the relations with the Mediterranean countries and Israel were molded in later years. In theoretical terms, the negotiations between the EEC and Israel constitute an excellent example of a policy which consolidated due to a desire to solve current issues in the face of technical and political constraints. However, the response creates path dependency of great political significance in shaping future relations. Since the relations between the EEC and Mediterranean countries are broad and exceed the scope of this book, we will focus in the following on the shaping of European policy towards Israel and Mediterranean countries as far as these relations are related to Israel.

The EEC and its member states were concerned with the Israeli issue, in the context of their wider relations with the Mediterranean countries, since Israel contacted the Community seeking an association agreement and later a trade agreement. From the outset of the negotiations, the member states, the Commission and the COREPER were confronted by the question of how the Arab countries would respond to the signing of an agreement with Israel. Moreover, the very act of negotiating with Israel was likely to cloud European relations with the Arab states; this worried the EEC and influenced its decisions in this regard. The centrality of the Arab–Israeli conflict in shaping European foreign policy had a number of aspects. Firstly, in the background was the threat, made by the Arab states (including those outside the Mediterranean basin) that they would heighten the boycott; indeed, they indicated this to The Six at meetings, and in various letters and missives which were sent to the governments and international companies based in EEC member states. The Europeans tried to conceal the importance of the boycott in their considerations and therefore for the most part based their rejection of Israeli requests on legal, technical, or economic considerations. However, the Israelis were aware of their motives and occasionally these motives arose explicitly during the negotiations. Secondly, in principle there was no need for a special or specific policy towards the Mediterranean basin. However, the conflict forced the EEC to relate to the region differently. There was ostensibly no need for a special policy towards the Mediterranean countries because the EEC viewed the European Mediterranean countries (Greece and Spain) as a separate category of relations, while the relations with North African countries (apart from Egypt) and Lebanon could have been included in the frame of the EEC's development policy vis-à-vis former colonies. Moreover, the Rome Treaty did not mention the Mediterranean as an area which the EEC would view as an arena of activities. Indeed, article 327 of the Treaty mentions Algeria, but refers to it as an inseparable part of the Community, connected to France.[32] However, a need arose to relate to the countries in the region as one bloc because Israel was a Mediterranean country and the EEC's relations with it caused a reaction among the rest of the countries in the area. Therefore, the members of the EEC worked to create a kind of symmetry and reciprocity by balancing cooperation with Israel through similar cooperation with another Arab state such as Lebanon and Iran. Thirdly, it is evident that the Arab–Israeli conflict was of the utmost relevance and significance even before the events of 1967 (the Six Day War), 1973 (the Yom Kippur War) and the oil crisis of 1973. These events are considered formative in molding the European perception towards Israel and the EEC's need to consolidate a policy towards the conflict and the region.[33] However this book demonstrates that the conflict was of central significance even a decade earlier. Finally, it should be noted that European-Israeli relations in the context of the Israeli–Arab conflict at the end of the 1950s and the 1960s play down the Palestinian issue. The Palestinian question, which had existed since 1948—the division of the land of Israel, the creation of the refugee issue and the territorial conflict—was trivial during the first years of the EEC's existence, yet it became a central issue in European foreign policy towards the Mediterranean and Israel following the 1973 war, and officially only in the Venice Declaration of June 1980. In the latter, the EEC expressed the foundations of its perception regarding the solution to this problem, which accompany it to this day.[34]

The need to address the Israeli–Arab conflict—due to the negotiations with Israel concerning trade and association agreements—laid down the principles guiding the EEC's policy (and that of the European Union until today) in at least two respects: 1) the conflict and the attempt to solve it became basic elements of the Community's foreign policy towards the Mediterranean region; 2) an attempt to balance any cooperation with Israel by similar or joint cooperation with other states in the Mediterranean or vice versa.[35] These two characteristics are evident in all the foreign policy initiatives which the EEC formulated from 1970 to the present day, including the Euro-Arab Dialogue (1973–89),[36] Global Mediterranean Policy, Renewed Mediterranean Policy (1990–95), Euro-Mediterranean Partnership (1995), and finally the European Neighbourhood Policy (2004) and the Union for the Mediterranean (2008).[37] Leaders of the EEC and the political echelons in the member states similarly articulated these characteristics clearly. For example, in an interview with an Israeli journalist in 1965, Hallstein related how the member states proposed that after signing agreements with Israel, Iran and Lebanon, the EEC would develop a common policy for all the Mediterranean countries.[38] This also accorded with the article in the trade agreement with Israel stipulating that when concluding an arrangement with another orange-exporting country, the EEC would necessarily consult with Israel; in , this would lead to the creation of a unified policy towards all the Mediterranean countries.[39] Further evidence of this emerged at the ceremony to mark the signing of the association agreement between the EEC and Tunisia. At this event, held in Tunisia, Luxembourg's Foreign Minister Gaston Thorn emphasized that

> The EEC is interested in cooperation with all the countries on the shores of the Mediterranean, and he named explicitly Israel, Algeria and Libya . . . at the center of the [Common] Market in Brussels there are increasing sentiments, that it will be impossible to reach an agreement with Israel outside the frame of a regional cooperation agreement with all the nations of the Mediterranean basin.[40]

The characteristics of this policy were evident from the 1970s, particularly when the EEC sought to act bilaterally through trade and association agreements with specific countries: on the one hand the Community found itself unable to dismiss the need to maintain equilibrium regarding the level of agreement compared to that granted to Israel while on the other hand it constantly sought to bind the bilateral cooperation within a multilateral regional framework, as for example in the case of the European Neighborhood Policy. In hindsight, these characteristics did not necessarily give Europe any significant political or economic benefit because they restricted European foreign policy towards the Mediterranean region and prevented flexibility or opportunities for action with single states in the area.[41]

Notes

1 A number of studies mention the link between the bargaining position and the tendency to use arguments: Peter Kotzian, "Arguing and Bargaining in International Negotiations: On the Application of the Frame-Selection Model and Its Implications," *International Political Science Review* 28, no. 1 (2007); Nicole Deitelhoff, "The Discursive Process of Legalization: Charting Islands of Persuasion in the ICC Case," *International Organization* 63, no. 1 (2009).

2 According to Elster, one of the reasons that the stronger party employs normative arguments is to avoid humiliating the weaker side. See: Jon Elster, "Equal or Proportional? Arguing and Bargaining over the Senate at the Federal Convention," in *Explaining Social Institutions*, eds. Jack Knight and Itai Sened (Ann Arbor: University of Michigan Press, 1995).

3 Jeffrey Z. Rubin and Bert R. Brown, *The Social Psychology of Bargaining and Negotiation* (New York: Academic Press, 1975), 132.

4 Lee A. Borah Jr., "The Effects of Threat in Bargaining: Critical and Experimental Analysis," *Journal of Abnormal and Social Psychology* 66, no. 1 (1963).

5 Ole Elgström, "Norms, Culture, and Cognitive Patterns in Foreign Aid Negotiations," *Negotiation Journal* 6, no. 2 (1990); Jon Elster, "Wage Bargaining and Social Norms," *Acta Sociologica* 32, no. 2 (1989): 231; William Mark Habeeb, *Power and Tactics in International Negotiation: How Weak Nations Bargain with Strong Nations* (Baltimore: Johns Hopkins University Press, 1988); Fred Charles Iklé, "How Nations Negotiate," (New York: Harper & Row, 1987), 201–3.

6 Rubin and Brown, 32–3, 130–31; Roy J. Lewicki and Joseph A. Litterer, *Negotiation* (Homewood: Richard D. Irwin, 1985); Dean G. Pruitt, "Strategy in Negotiation," in *International Negotiation: Analysis, Approaches, Issues* (San Francisco: Bass Publishers, 1991).

7 James D. Fearon, "Signaling Foreign Policy Interests: Tying Hands Versus Sinking Costs," *Journal of Conflict Resolution* 41, no. 1 (1997).

8 Many studies have proved that the existence of an audience, especially one dependent on the negotiators, pushes the latter to insist on a more positive agreement from their perspective. See: Rubin and Brown, 44; Robert B. McKersie, Charles R. Perry and Richard E. Walton, "Intraorganizational Bargaining in Labor Negotiations," *Journal of Conflict Resolution* 9, no. 4 (1965).

9 Cornelia Ulbert and Thomas Risse, "Deliberately Changing the Discourse: What Does Make Arguing Effective?," *Acta Politica* 40, no. 3 (2005).

10 Ronald R. Krebs and Patrick Thaddeus Jackson, "Twisting Tongues and Twisting Arms: The Power of Political Rhetoric," *European Journal of International Relations* 13, no. 1 (2007); Frank Schimmelfennig, *The EU, Nato and the Integration of Europe: Rules and Rhetoric* (Cambridge: Cambridge University Press, 2003). The concept that argumentation is a triadic interaction, requiring an audience, is commonly found in academic literature. See, for example, Thomas Saretzki, "From Bargaining to Arguing, from Strategic to Communicative Action? Theoretical Distinctions and Methodological Problems in Empirical Studies of Deliberative Policy Processes," *Critical Policy Studies* 3, no. 2 (2009).

11 Ulbert and Risse; Nicole Deitelhoff and Harald Müller, "Theoretical Paradise— Empirically Lost? Arguing with Habermas," *Review of International Studies* 31, no. 1 (2005).

12 Harald Müller, "Arguing, Bargaining and All That: Communicative Action, Rationalist Theory and the Logic of Appropriateness in International Relations," *European Journal of International Relations* 10, no. 3 (2004).

13 Ibid.; Kotzian. Another alternative is that one party offers the first concession, hoping that the other side will reward this with a by reciprocating. See: I. William. Zartman, "The Structure of Negotiation," in *International Negotiation: Analysis, Approaches, Issues*, eds. I. William Zartman, Viktor Aleksandrovich Kremenyuk and Guy Faure (San Francisco: Bass Publishers, 1991).

14 James G. March and Johan P. Olsen, "The Institutional Dynamics of International Political Orders," *International Organization* 52, no. 4 (1998); see also Pruitt.

15 BDS refers to the Boycott, Divestment, and Sanction global movement against Israel.

16 A further qualification connected to this matter was the management of relations with former colonies through the EEC's development policy, rooted in the 1963 Yaoundé Convention. In this case too, the emphasis was mainly economic. See: Enzo R. Grilli, *The European Community and the Developing Countries* (Cambridge: Cambridge University Press, 1994); Marjorie Lister, *The European Union and the South: Relations with Developing Countries* (London: Routledge, 1997).

17 Brian R. Duchin, "The 'Agonizing Reappraisal': Eisenhower, Dulles, and the European Defense Community," *Diplomatic History* 16, no. 2 (1992); Edward Fursdon, *The European Defence Community: A History* (London: Macmillan, 1980).

18 Jeffrey Vanke, "An Impossible Union: Dutch Objections to the Fouchet Plan, 1959–62," *Cold War History* 2, no. 1 (2001).

19 Simon Hix, *The Political System of the European Union* (Houndmills: Palgrave Macmillan, 2005).

20 Vanke; Federiga Bindi, "European Union Foreign Policy: A Historical Overview," in *The Foreign Policy of the European Union: Assessing Europe's Role in the World*, ed. Federiga Bindi (Washington, DC: Brookings Institution Press, 2010).

21 Karl-Heinz Narjes, "Walter Hallstein and the Early Phase of the EEC," in *Walter Hallstein: The Forgotten European?*, eds. Wilfried Loth, William Wallace and Wolfgang Wessels (Springer, 1998): 124; Walter Hallstein, *United Europe: Challenge and Opportunity* (London: Oxford University Press, 1962): 67.

22 Note pour M. Seeliger, BAC 3/1978-323, December 18, 1962.

23 Antonis A. Ellinas and Ezra Suleiman, *The European Commission and Bureaucratic Autonomy: Europe's Custodians* (Cambridge: Cambridge University Press, 2012), 13.

24 Bindi.

25 Ben Rosamond, *Theories of European Integration* (London: Macmillan, 2000); Antje Wiener and Thomas Diez, *European Integration Theory* (Oxford: Oxford University Press, 2009).

26 Leon N. Lindberg, *The Political Dynamics of European Economic Integration* (Stanford: Stanford University Press, 1963); Leon N. Lindberg and Stuart A. Scheingold, *Europe's Would-Be Polity: Patterns of Change in the European Community* (Englewood Cliffs: Prentice-Hall, 1970).

27 Jaap W. de Zwaan, *The Permanent Representatives Committee: Its Role in European Union Decision-Making* (Amsterdam: Elsevier, 1995).

28 Fiona Hayes-Renshaw, Christian Lequesne and Pedro Mayor Lopez, "The Permanent Representations of the Member States to the European Communities," *JCMS: Journal of Common Market Studies* 28, no. 2 (1989).

29 Emile Noël, "The Committee of Permanent Representatives," *JCMS: Journal of Common Market Studies* 5, no. 3 (1967); David Bostock, "Coreper Revisited," *JCMS: Journal of Common Market Studies* 40, no. 2 (2002).

30 Noël; Jeffrey Lewis, "Is the 'Hard Bargaining' Image of the Council Misleading? The Committee of Permanent Representatives and the Local Elections Directive," *JCMS: Journal of Common Market Studies* 36, no. 4 (1998); "National Interests: Committee

of Permanent Representatives," in *The Institutions of the European Union*, eds. John Peterson and Michael Shackleton (Oxford: Oxford University Press, 2012).

31 It is a common view that the meeting of the EPC in Munich in 1970, at which the Middle Eastern issue was first on the agenda, was the turning point, at which the EEC began to mold a shared perspective and common policy towards the Middle East. Regarding the policy towards the Mediterranean states, see, for example, Lister; Bindi: 32–3; Kenneth Glarbo, "Wide-Awake Diplomacy: Reconstructing the Common Foreign and Security Policy of the European Union," *Journal of European Public Policy* 6, no. 4 (1999): 642–3; Alfred Tovias, *Foreign Economic Relations of the European Community: The Impact of Spain and Portugal* (Boulder: Lynne Rienner, 1990). For the Israeli perspective, see: Sharon Pardo and Joel Peters, *Uneasy Neighbors: Israel and the European Union* (Lanham: Lexington Books, 2009); Raffaella A. Del Sarto and Alfred Tovias, "Caught between Europe and the Orient: Israel and the EMP," *The International Spectator* 36, no. 4 (2001); Alfred Tovias, "Israeli Policy Perspectives on the Euro-Mediterranean Partnership in the Context of EU Enlargement," *Mediterranean Politics* 8, no. 2–3 (2003). Exceptional in that it concerns the year in which the Community was established is: Sharon Pardo, "The Year That Israel Considered Joining the European Economic Community," *JCMS: Journal of Common Market Studies* 51, no. 5 (2013).

32 Vittorio Ferraris, "The Mediterranean Basin as a Challenge and the European Response," in *Beyond Sovereignty: European Integration*, ed. Moshe Zimmermann and Werner Weidenfeld (Jerusalem: Academin, 1996).

33 Ilan Greilsammer claims in his book that the October 17, 1969 decision of the EEC council to open negotiations with Israel on a preferential agreement is also the origin of Europe's Mediterranean policy. See: Ilan Greilsammer, *Israël Et l'Europe: Une Histoire Des Relations Entre La Communauté Européenne Et l'État d'Israël* (Lausanne: Fondation Jean Monnet pour l'Europe, Centre de Recherches Européennes, 1981).

34 The Venice Declaration expresses the EEC's basic position towards the Israeli–Palestinian conflict, determining that the Palestinians have the right to an independent state and that the PLO should be involved in the peace process. The declaration was made one year after the peace agreement between Israel and Egypt and thirteen years before the Oslo process.

35 As was noted, this is not intended to blur the other important foundations of foreign policy which do not necessarily result from the Arab–Israeli conflict, such as economic interests, energy security, or the colonial heritage.

36 Haifaa Jawad, *The Euro-Arab Dialogue: A Study in Collective Diplomacy* (Reading: Ithaca Press, 1992); Bichara Khader, *The European Union and the Arab World: From the Rome Treaty to the Arab Spring* (Barcelona: IEMed, 2013); Paul James Cardwell, "Euromed, European Neighbourhood Policy and the Union for the Mediterranean: Overlapping Policy Frames in the EU's Governance of the Mediterranean," *JCMS: Journal of Common Market Studies* 49, no. 2 (2011); Federica Bicchi, "The Union for the Mediterranean, or the Changing Context of Euro-Mediterranean Relations," *Mediterranean Politics* 16, no. 1 (2011).

37 Cardwell.

38 David Lipkin, "Israel Is Not Entitled for an Associate Member State Status," *Davar*, March 24, 1965.

39 Victor Zigleman, "Israel's Position in Brussels," *Davar*, 1965.

40 Jacques Maurice, "Following the Denial of Israel's Request to the Common Market," *Davar*, 1969.

41 Lior Herman, "An Action Plan or a Plan for Action: Israel and the European Neighbourhood Policy," *Mediterranean Politics* 11, no. 3 (2006); Amichai Magen, "The Shadow of Enlargement: Can the European Neighbourhood Policy Achieve Compliance," *Columbia Journal of European Law* 12, no. 2 (2006); Magen, "Israel and the Many Pathways of Diffusion," *West European Politics* 35, no. 1 (2012).

References

Bicchi, Federica. "The Union for the Mediterranean, or the Changing Context of Euro-Mediterranean Relations." *Mediterranean Politics* 16, no. 1 (2011): 3–19.

Bindi, Federiga. "European Union Foreign Policy: A Historical Overview." Chap. 1 In *The Foreign Policy of the European Union: Assessing Europe's Role in the World*, edited by Federiga Bindi, 13–40. Washington, DC: Brookings Institution Press, 2010.

Borah Jr., Lee A. "The Effects of Threat in Bargaining: Critical and Experimental Analysis." *Journal of Abnormal and Social Psychology* 66, no. 1 (1963): 37.

Bostock, David. "Coreper Revisited." *JCMS: Journal of Common Market Studies* 40, no. 2 (2002): 215–34.

Cardwell, Paul James. "Euromed, European Neighbourhood Policy and the Union for the Mediterranean: Overlapping Policy Frames in the EU's Governance of the Mediterranean." *JCMS: Journal of Common Market Studies* 49, no. 2 (2011): 219–41.

De Zwaan, Jaap W. *The Permanent Representatives Committee: Its Role in European Union Decision-Making.* Amsterdam: Elsevier, 1995.

Deitelhoff, Nicole. "The Discursive Process of Legalization: Charting Islands of Persuasion in the ICC Case." *International Organization* 63, no. 1 (2009): 33–65.

———, and Harald Müller. "Theoretical Paradise—Empirically Lost? Arguing with Habermas." *Review of International Studies* 31, no. 1 (2005): 167–79.

Del Sarto, Raffaella A., and Alfred Tovias. "Caught between Europe and the Orient: Israel and the EMP." *The International Spectator* 36, no. 4 (2001): 61–75.

Duchin, Brian R. "The 'Agonizing Reappraisal': Eisenhower, Dulles, and the European Defense Community." *Diplomatic History* 16, no. 2 (1992): 201–21.

Elgström, Ole. "Norms, Culture, and Cognitive Patterns in Foreign Aid Negotiations." *Negotiation Journal* 6, no. 2 (1990): 147–59.

Ellinas, Antonis A., and Ezra Suleiman. *The European Commission and Bureaucratic Autonomy: Europe's Custodians.* Cambridge: Cambridge University Press, 2012.

Elster, Jon. "Equal or Proportional? Arguing and Bargaining over the Senate at the Federal Convention." In *Explaining Social Institutions*, edited by Jack Knight and Itai Sened. Ann Arbor: University of Michigan Press, 1995.

———. "Wage Bargaining and Social Norms." *Acta Sociologica* 32, no. 2 (1989): 113–36.

Fearon, James D. "Signaling Foreign Policy Interests: Tying Hands Versus Sinking Costs." *Journal of Conflict Resolution* 41, no. 1 (1997): 68–90.

Ferraris, Vittorio. "The Mediterranean Basin as a Challenge and the European Response." In *Beyond Sovereignty: European Integration*, edited by Moshe Zimmermann and Werner Weidenfeld, 192–206. Jerusalem: Academin, 1996.

Fursdon, Edward. *The European Defence Community: A History.* London: Macmillan, 1980.

Glarbo, Kenneth. "Wide-Awake Diplomacy: Reconstructing the Common Foreign and Security Policy of the European Union." *Journal of European Public Policy* 6, no. 4 (1999): 634–51.

Greilsammer, Ilan. *Israël et l'Europe: Une Histoire Des Relations Entre La Communauté Européenne Et l'État d'Israël.* Lausanne: Fondation Jean Monnet pour l'Europe, Centre de Recherches Européennes, 1981.

Grilli, Enzo R. *The European Community and the Developing Countries.* Cambridge: Cambridge University Press, 1994.

Habeeb, William Mark. *Power and Tactics in International Negotiation: How Weak Nations Bargain with Strong Nations.* Baltimore: Johns Hopkins University Press, 1988.

Hallstein, Walter. *United Europe: Challenge and Opportunity.* London: Oxford University Press, 1962.

Hayes-Renshaw, Fiona, Christian Lequesne and Pedro Mayor Lopez. "The Permanent Representations of the Member States to the European Communities." *JCMS: Journal of Common Market Studies* 28, no. 2 (1989): 119–37.

Herman, Lior. "An Action Plan or a Plan for Action: Israel and the European Neighbourhood Policy." *Mediterranean Politics* 11, no. 3 (2006): 371–94.

Hix, Simon. *The Political System of the European Union.* Houndmills: Palgrave Macmillan, 2005.

Iklé, Fred Charles. "How Nations Negotiate." New York: Harper & Row, 1987.

Jawad, Haifaa. *The Euro-Arab Dialogue: A Study in Collective Diplomacy.* Reading: Ithaca Press, 1992.

Khader, Bichara. *The European Union and the Arab World: From the Rome Treaty to the Arab Spring.* Barcelona: IEMed, 2013.

Kotzian, Peter. "Arguing and Bargaining in International Negotiations: On the Application of the Frame-Selection Model and Its Implications." *International Political Science Review* 28, no. 1 (2007): 79–99.

Krebs, Ronald R., and Patrick Thaddeus Jackson. "Twisting Tongues and Twisting Arms: The Power of Political Rhetoric." *European Journal of International Relations* 13, no. 1 (2007): 35–66.

Lewicki, Roy J., and Joseph A. Litterer. *Negotiation.* Homewood: Richard D. Irwin, 1985.

Lewis, Jeffrey. "Is the 'Hard Bargaining' Image of the Council Misleading? The Committee of Permanent Representatives and the Local Elections Directive." *JCMS: Journal of Common Market Studies* 36, no. 4 (1998): 479–504.

———. "National Interests: Committee of Permanent Representatives." Chap. 14 In *The Institutions of the European Union*, edited by John Peterson and Michael Shackleton, 315–37. Oxford: Oxford University Press, 2012.

Lindberg, Leon N. *The Political Dynamics of European Economic Integration.* Stanford: Stanford University Press, 1963.

———, and Stuart A. Scheingold. *Europe's Would-Be Polity: Patterns of Change in the European Community.* Englewood Cliffs: Prentice-Hall, 1970.

Lipkin, David. "Israel Is Not Entitled for an Associate Member State Status." *Davar*, March 24, 1965.

Lister, Marjorie. *The European Union and the South: Relations with Developing Countries.* London: Routledge, 1997.

Magen, Amichai. "Israel and the Many Pathways of Diffusion." *West European Politics* 35, no. 1 (2012): 98–116.

———. "The Shadow of Enlargement: Can the European Neighbourhood Policy Achieve Compliance." *Columbia Journal of European Law* 12, no. 2 (2006): 383–428.

March, James G., and Johan P. Olsen. "The Institutional Dynamics of International Political Orders." *International Organization* 52, no. 4 (1998): 943–69.

Maurice, Jacques. "Following the Denial of Israel's Request to the Common Market." *Davar*, 1969.

McKersie, Robert B., Charles R. Perry and Richard E. Walton. "Intraorganizational Bargaining in Labor Negotiations." *Journal of Conflict Resolution* 9, no. 4 (1965): 463–81.

Müller, Harald. "Arguing, Bargaining and All That: Communicative Action, Rationalist Theory and the Logic of Appropriateness in International Relations." *European Journal of International Relations* 10, no. 3 (2004): 395–435.

Narjes, Karl-Heinz. "Walter Hallstein and the Early Phase of the EEC." In *Walter Hallstein: The Forgotten European?*, edited by Wilfried Loth, William Wallace and Wolfgang Wessels, 109–30: Springer, 1998.

Noël, Emile. "The Committee of Permanent Representatives." *JCMS: Journal of Common Market Studies* 5, no. 3 (1967): 219–51.

Pardo, Sharon. "The Year That Israel Considered Joining the European Economic Community." *JCMS: Journal of Common Market Studies* 51, no. 5 (2013): 901–15.

Pardo, Sharon, and Joel Peters. *Uneasy Neighbors: Israel and the European Union*. Lanham: Lexington Books, 2009.

Pruitt, Dean G. "Strategy in Negotiation." In *International Negotiation: Analysis, Approaches, Issues*, 78–89. San Francisco: Bass Publishers, 1991.

Rosamond, Ben. *Theories of European Integration*. London: Macmillan, 2000.

Rubin, Jeffrey Z., and Bert R. Brown. *The Social Psychology of Bargaining and Negotiation*. New York: Academic Press, 1975.

Saretzki, Thomas. "From Bargaining to Arguing, from Strategic to Communicative Action? Theoretical Distinctions and Methodological Problems in Empirical Studies of Deliberative Policy Processes." *Critical Policy Studies* 3, no. 2 (2009): 153–83.

Schimmelfennig, Frank. *The EU, Nato and the Integration of Europe: Rules and Rhetoric*. Cambridge: Cambridge University Press, 2003.

Tovias, Alfred. *Foreign Economic Relations of the European Community: The Impact of Spain and Portugal*. Boulder: Lynne Rienner, 1990.

———. "Israeli Policy Perspectives on the Euro-Mediterranean Partnership in the Context of EU Enlargement." *Mediterranean Politics* 8, no. 2–3 (2003): 214–32.

Ulbert, Cornelia, and Thomas Risse. "Deliberately Changing the Discourse: What Does Make Arguing Effective?" *Acta Politica* 40, no. 3 (2005): 351–67.

Vanke, Jeffrey. "An Impossible Union: Dutch Objections to the Fouchet Plan, 1959–62." *Cold War History* 2, no. 1 (2001): 95–112.

Wiener, Antje, and Thomas Diez. *European Integration Theory*. Oxford: Oxford University Press, 2009.

Zartman, I. William. "The Structure of Negotiation." In *International Negotiation: Analysis, Approaches, Issues*, edited by I. William Zartman, Viktor Aleksandrovich Kremenyuk and Guy Faure, 65–77. San Francisco: Bass Publishers, 1991.

Zigleman, Victor. "Israel's Position in Brussels." *Davar*, 1965.

Appendix 1
List of archives and abbreviations

Archives Générales du Royaume Belgique—AGRB

    Fond Pierre Harmel—FH

Archives de Ministère des Affaires Étrangères (Français)—AMAE

    Communauté Européenne—CE
    Département économique—DE

Archives de Ministère des Affaires Étrangères et du Commerce Extèrieur Belgique—AMAECEB

Ben-Gurion Archives—BGA

    Ben-Gurion Diaries—BGD

Documents diplomatiques françaises—DDF

European Union Archive—EUA

    Commission—BAC
    Council of Ministers—CM2

Federal Foreign Office Political Archives—FFOPA

Israel State Archives—ISA

    Foreign Ministry files—FM
    Ministry of Agriculture files—MA
    Ministry of Finance files—MF
    Ministry of Industry and Trade files—MIT

Minutes of the meetings of the Knesset's Foreign and Defense Committee—KFDC

Prime Minister Office files—PM

National Archives of the Netherlands—NAN

Rapport général sur l'activité de la Communauté

Segreteria Generale-Archivio Storico—SGAS

Direzione Generale Affari Politici III

State of Israel's Foreign Policy Documents

Appendix 2

Illustrations

Table A.1 Israel's foreign trade, 1957–72, million USD, current prices

	Net exports	Net imports	Trade deficit	Diamonds (export)		Citrus fruit (export)		Tourism income
				$	%	$	%	
1957	140	433	−293	35.3	25%	48.4	35%	5.5
1958	139	421	−282	34.3	25%	48.4	35%	12
1959	176	427	−251	46.8	27%	45.9	26%	16.2
1960	211	496	−285	60.9	29%	46.6	22%	27
1961	239	584	−345	70.3	29%	40.5	17%	30.1
1962	271	626	−355	89.3	33%	49.2	18%	38.4
1963	338	662	−324	116	34%	74.7	22%	52.9
1964	352	816	−464	137.6	39%	52.8	15%	54.2
1965	406	815	−409	153.7	38%	71.2	18%	54.8
1966	477	817	−340	189.5	40%	74.7	16%	59.1
1967	517	757	−240	193	37%	85.3	16%	52
1968	602	1093	−491	229.3	38%	88.4	15%	97
1969	689	1304	−615	254.4	37%	91.5	13%	90
1970	734	1433	−699	245.8	33%	86.1	12%	105
1971	915	1812	−897	306.4	33%	113.8	12%	182
1972	1102	1958	−856	430.4	39%	109	10%	215

Source: Statistical Yearbooks of Israel 1959–70; Central Bureau of Statistics; Bank of Israel Annual Reports

Table A.2 Export of citrus fruit by country of destination (tons)

Country	1955	1958	1960	1961	1962	1963	1964	1965	1966	1967	1968	1969
Belgium	13628	16091	21240	14011	17157	26873	22843	30701	29683	33077	38972	31119
Germany (West)	12859	35574	60363	44210	64414	103367	79668	114884	119872	160347	188771	175374
Netherlands	11253	19401	35033	21582	20201	35884	30189	35818	33571	43671	50741	29792
France	12164	16338	10445	6698	13194	33495	23406	46827	44578	57075	63921	63898
EEC	—	87404	127081	86501	114966	199609	156514	229455	231015	297502	347324	306778
United Kingdom	115219	122246	183640	118456	131602	147408	147719	156676	152731	181203	191832	165339
World	257990	311851	400036	297280	383052	506926	450019	559258	569299	677812	737259	705520

Source: Statistical Yearbooks of Israel 1959–70, Central Bureau of Statistics

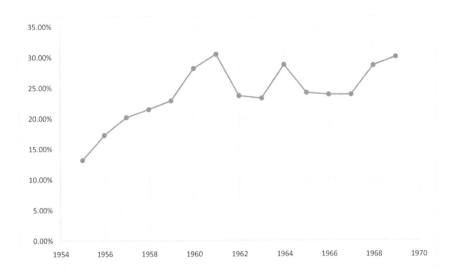

Figure A.1 Israel's exports to the EEC as a share of total exports, 1955–69
Source: Statistical Yearbooks of Israel 1959–70, Central Bureau of Statistics

Index

Adenauer, Konrad: EEC establishment 13, 14–15, 18; Israel negotiations 93, 147, 149, 246

Africa: aid and development 77–8, 192–3, 260; Israel's relationship 46, 59, 77–8, 89; north Africa *see individual countries*; Maghreb countries

agriculture: EEC formation challenges to Israel 42–3; Europe 21, 93–4; harmonization with EEC 223–4; Israel 35–7, *see also* citrus fruits

aid to developing countries in Africa and Asia 46, 59, 77–8, 192–3, 260

Algeria: France relationship 24, 42, 46, 88, 94, 138, 146, *see also* Maghreb countries

Arab League 138, 143, 228, 250

Arab states: Belgium 91; de-legitimization campaign against Israel 85; European negotiations and agreements 205, 250; Europe relationship 268–9; Europe reluctant to appear to support boycott 244; Europe seeking agreement 250; Europe's fear of worsening 45, 61, 80, 82, 86, 99, 108, 109–10, 138, 141, 143, 159, 243, 244, 262–3; Europe wanting balanced relations within Mediterranean countries 268; explicit threats to EEC 228–9; France 45, 46, 94, 138, 146, 149, 159, 242, 243; Israel conflict 44, 78, 80, 82; Israel cooperation 36, 220; Israel relationship, Boycott 53, 84–5, 95, 109, 138, 190, 220, 244, 251, 260, 262–3, 268; Italy 94–5; power balance 83–4, 92, 138, 143; Six Day War effects 243; threat to Israel influencing EEC negotiations 44, 53, 78, 83–5, 109, 251, 260, 268–9; West Germany 92, 133, 134, 174

armaments, France supplying weapons to Israel 83, 84, 88, 241–2

Asia, Israel's relationship 46, 59, 77–8, 89

association agreement with EEC: Council of Ministers 86, 88–9, 91; desired security benefits 44–5, 78, 83–4, 108–9; European Commission changing approach 86–7; European Commission in covert talks 87–8, 90–1; European Commission supporting 75–86; first attempt (October 1960) 98–102; formal request for new negotiations 227; Israeli policy decisions 75–7, 81–7, 89–90, 108–9, 110–11, 113–14; membership comparison 21, 44; negotiations towards first attempt 75–98; opposition 86, 92, 98–9, 102, 113; political motivation for Israel 78–9, 83–4, 108–9, 120–1; second attempt 220–5; step-by-step approach 137–41, 201

balance of powers: Arab–Israeli–EEC 83–4, 92, 138, 143, 242–3, 246; internal EEC relationships 67, 149–50; Six Day War effects 242

Ball, George 130

bargaining power, Israel over EEC 45–6

Bartur, Moshe: delegation to Council of Europe 58; discussions with EEC officials 80–1; establishing policy towards EEC 75–7, 89–90; maximum demands over pragmatic tactics 128–9, 163–4, 218; political aspects of EEC association 83–4; political characteristics 58; publishing in press 180n; supporting association with GAT 57; supporting association with OEEC

For Product Safety Concerns and Information please contact our EU
representative GPSR@taylorandfrancis.com Taylor & Francis Verlag GmbH,
Kaufingerstraße 24, 80331 München, Germany

Printed and bound by CPI Group (UK) Ltd, Croydon, CR0 4YY
01/05/2025
01858452-0005